Alex

Alex

The Life of Alexander Liberman

Dodie Kazanjian and Calvin Tomkins

Alfred A. Knopf New York 1993

This Is a Borzoi Book Published by Alfred A. Knopf, Inc.

Copyright © 1993 by Dodie Kazanjian and Calvin Tomkins
All rights reserved under International and Pan-American Copyright
Conventions. Published in the United States by Alfred A. Knopf, Inc.,
New York, and simultaneously in Canada by Random House of Canada
Limited, Toronto. Distributed by Random House, Inc., New York.

Library of Congress Cataloging-in-Publication Data
Kazanjian, Dodie, [date]
Alex : the life of Alexander Liberman / Dodie Kazanjian and Calvin Tomkins
p. cm.
Includes index.
ISBN 0-394-57964-X
1. Liberman, Alexander, 1912–   .   2. Artists—United States—
Biography.   3. Publishers and publishing—United States—Biography.
I. Tomkins, Calvin.   II. Title.
N6537.L48K39   1993
709'.2—dc20
[B]   93-3040   CIP

Manufactured in the United States of America

First Edition

For Louise

Contents

Acknowledgments

The perils and pleasures of writing the biography of a living person are well known. A lot of information that you might never be able to track down otherwise can be had for the asking; on the other hand, there is the problem of how to evaluate the accuracy of such information, and there is also the problem of becoming "too close" to the source. Can there be an objective, balanced view of a life that is still in progress? Probably not. But the joint expedition on which biographer and biographee embark, with all its wrong turns, contradictions, and unexpected discoveries, offers unique rewards.

On that late August Saturday in 1988 when we drove up from the city to Alex's country place in Warren, Connecticut, to work out the ground rules for this project, Alex himself was still uncertain about it. In fact, he had telephoned us that morning to say that he had decided against the whole idea. "But come anyway," he insisted, "and we'll talk." We came, we talked, and, in the end—won over not so much by any persuasive arguments of ours as by his own gambler's instinct for the fresh start and by his lifelong respect for the gods of chance—he said, "Okay, let's do it." Over the next five years, he kept up his end of the bargain—full disclosure, no control—without exception. There were arguments and disagreements along the way, to be sure, and even a minor tantrum or two, but the end result is our book, not his, and we are infinitely grateful to Alex for the honesty of his self-searching and the strength of his friendship.

Special thanks also go to Francine and Cleve Gray, who know Alex in more ways than anyone else, and whose deep affection for him informed and guided us at every turn.

Melinda Pechangco gave a new dimension to Alex's life, and also to this book, when she became Mrs. Alexander Liberman in December 1992. She has been unfailingly candid and openhearted.

André Emmerich, who has been Alex's dealer and his friend for more than twenty-five years, helped to make the book possible and provided many helpful insights along the way.

Crosby Coughlin, Alex's assistant at Condé Nast, was an indefatigable source of information. He can do anything, we learned, and do it with imagination and precision.

Irving Penn and Richard Avedon, the most influential photographers of their time, have been wonderfully generous. Their very different views of the Liberman phenomenon served to thicken the plot.

Barbara Rose's 1981 monograph, *Alexander Liberman*, has been an indispensable reference source, and so have Caroline Seebohm's biography of Condé Nast, *The Man Who Was Vogue*, and Martin Harrison's *Appearances: Fashion Photography Since 1945*.

We would also like to thank the many others who gave so much time and thought to answering our questions and ransacking their memories—a list that is necessarily incomplete:

Lawrence Alloway, Ruth Ansel, Peter A. Armour, Leon Azoulay, Daniel Berger, Rosamond Bernier, Nadine Bertin, Joseph Brodsky, Tina Brown, Joan Juliet Buck, Dr. William A. Cahan, Lorna Caine, Cynthia Cathcart, the Duchess de Caylus, Ethel de Croisset, Oscar de la Renta, Miki Denhof, Catherine di Montezemolo, Carrie Donovan, Gabé Doppelt, Susanna Doyle, Peter Duchin, Diana Etkins, Harold Evans, Simone Eyrard, Helen Frankenthaler, Tina Fredericks, Micheline Fried, Otto Fried, Henry Geldzahler, Gloria Gersh, Dr. Harvey Goldberg, Josef Gomez, Dolly Goulandris, Peter Gould, Donald Gratz, Luke Gray, Thaddeus Gray, Patricia Green, Alexis Gregory, Amy Gross, Louise Grunwald, Marcel Guillaume, Jane Gunther, Peter Homestead, Walter Hopps, Lance Houston, Robert Hughes, Edward Kasper, Ellsworth Kelly, Henry Kissinger, Bruce Knight, Hilton Kramer, William Layman, Dr. Jacques Le Beau, Leo Lerman, Bernard Leser, Beatrice Leval, Judge Pierre Leval, William Lehmann, Irène Lidova, William Lieberman, Kate Lloyd, Janet Malcolm, Frances

McLaughlin, Despina Messinesi, Grace Mirabella, Beatrice Monti della Corte, Edwin Morgan, Mabel Moses, S. I. Newhouse, Jr., Victoria Newhouse, Annalee Newman, Nancy Novogrod, Iva Sergei Voidato-Patcévitch, Alexandra Penney, Carol Phillips, Gladys Pohl, Susan Price, Robert Rauschenberg, William Raynor, Gregor von Rezzori, Linda Rice, Paul Richard, John Richardson, Phyllis Rifield, Barbara Rose, Joanna Rose, Dr. Isadore Rosenfeld, Nan Rosenthal, Alice Rostan, William S. Rubin, John Russell, Perry Ruston, Daniel Salem, Pierre Schneider, Gitta Sereny, Ludmila Shtern, Robert Silvers, Babs Simpson, Lucy Sisman, Sarah Slavin, Saul Steinberg, H. Peter Stern, Marti Stevens, Hilda Sturm, Geraldine Stutz, David Sylvester, Nathaniel Taft, Elena Tchernichova, Maura Thompson, Iuri Tiurin, Spencer Tomkins, Susan Train, Frederic Tuten, Rochelle Udell, Derek Ungless, Pamela Van Zandt, Diana Vreeland, Linda Wells, Anna Wintour, Marie Wynn.

Additional thanks to Andrew Wylie, whose support and encouragement has been unflagging, and to Shelley Wanger, our elegantly incisive editor, and Hellyn Sher, her more than able assistant.

The memory of Tatiana Iacovleva Liberman is a living presence. Without it, this book and this life would not have been what they are.

Alex

Alexander Liberman on his eightieth birthday.

A Luau

The day began with low clouds and the threat of rain, like so many other days in the cool, wet summer of 1992. There had been freak tornadoes in Westchester County the night before, but in Quogue, one of the few quiet, un-Hamptonized beach towns on the South Shore of Long Island, the sky gradually brightened throughout the morning. It was the Friday of Labor Day weekend, and traffic was already piling up on the Montauk Highway. In the corner bedroom of the fine old shingle-style beach house that he had rented for the summer, Alex put on white cotton pants and a white tennis sweater (from the Gap), ran a comb through his still-luxuriant silver hair, and headed downstairs for breakfast.

While he drank his weak, sweet tea (three quick dips of the English Breakfast tea bag in the pot, six packets of NutraSweet) and scanned *The New York Times*, the preparations that had been accelerating for several days in the house continued all around him. Hank, the caretaker, was raking the beach in front of the house to clear it of the seaweed that had washed up in last night's storm. Silvia, the cook, was poaching a huge salmon she had picked out the day before at Tully's Fish Market in Hampton Bays. Lance, the cheerful young butler, ran liaison between the kitchen and the outdoor rotisserie area near the garage, where a team of eight caterers had set up a six-foot-long charcoal grill to broil swordfish, chicken, beef, and vegetable dishes. In a short while, "Frenchie," Alex's Moroccan chauffeur, and his wife would arrive with the tureen of couscous that she had stayed up most of the night to make. The day's *pièces de résistance*, two roast suckling pigs, rested on platters in the pantry, gazing sightlessly with grape eyes, awaiting their final garnish.

Most of the other elements were already in place: the three-tier "fountain of champagne" on the terrace, the white canopy above the raised deck overlooking the ocean, the outdoor stereo system and wooden dance floor for the Filipino dancers, the rented cots set up for overflow visitors in the basement room that Alex had used all summer as a painting studio. Howard, Alex's major-domo, had nearly finished replanting the two dozen or so window boxes on the ocean side with fresh white chrysanthemums. And, yes, the clouds were definitely lifting. It was not going to rain on Alexander Liberman's eightieth-birthday party.

Francine du Plessix Gray, his stepdaughter, and her husband, Cleve, had had their breakfast an hour earlier. They had been for a long walk on the beach, and then Francine had gone into Westhampton to have her hair washed and set. Luke, the younger of their two grown sons, pulled in around ten o'clock, by taxi from the Quogue train station; Thaddeus, his brother, was expected around one, which was when the party officially started. "Alex invites [name of guest handwritten] to a Luau on Friday, September 4th, 1 to 7 p.m. on the beach," the blue invitation card had read, giving rise to some perplexity among the hundred and fifty recipients. A luau? There was no mention of it being his eightieth birthday, but somehow everybody knew that; the luau part, as only those who were closest to Alex could be expected to know, was Melinda's doing.

Melinda Pechangco, born and raised in the Philippine Islands, was the wonderfully competent and devoted nurse who had cared for Alex's wife, Tatiana, in her last years and who, since Tatiana's death the year before, had pulled Alex through his own near-fatal heart surgery. She was now his closest companion, his vigilant protectress, and perhaps (rumors had been flying for months) his future wife. Quite a few people were wondering whether the luau would turn out to be an engagement party. Alex had talked to Cleve the night before about marrying Melinda—had talked about it as something that might happen in a year or so, although Cleve and Francine both suspected that it might happen a lot sooner than that. But Alex told another confidant that he had not yet discussed marriage with the prospective bride, and in a later conversation he informed Cleve that the prospective bride had said she didn't want to get married, so the Grays, who wanted Alex to be happy but who had ambivalent feelings about the early remarriage, were somewhat confused.

Melinda had planned the luau. She had ordered the suckling pigs, located the champagne fountain, commissioned the chocolate-and-gold-colored birthday cake that served as the fountain's base, and even managed to line up a troupe of six dancers from the Philippine National Dance Company, which happened to be in New York at the time. Although her unfailing discretion kept her from acting like the hostess, the army of cooks, waiters, and other service people took their orders from her.

By two-thirty, most of the guests had arrived. They parked their cars on the other side of the bridge over the canal that separated Dune Road from the rest of Quogue, and were ferried to the door in one of three chauffeur-driven cars that had been laid on for the occasion. For a while, it seemed to be mainly people from the Condé Nast empire: Irving Penn, the legendary photographer, who thought of Alex as his closest friend and alter ego; Anna Wintour, the editor in chief of *Vogue*, with her husband, Dr. David Shaffer, and their two young children; Tina Brown, lately of *Vanity Fair*, since June the editor-elect of *The New Yorker*; Harold Evans, Tina's husband, editor in chief of Random House; Linda Wells and Lucy Sisman of *Allure*; Nancy Novogrod of *House & Garden*; Rosamond Bernier, lecturer and longtime contributor to *Vogue* and *House & Garden*; James Truman of *Details*; Tom Wallace of *Condé Nast Traveler*; Lorna Caine, Susan Price, and Maura Thompson, Alex's secretaries; and Crosby Coughlin, his special assistant. Donald Newhouse, who ran the newspaper, television, and radio divisions of the empire, was there with his wife, Sue, who brought purple-orchid leis for Alex and Francine. (They both had to bend way down so the diminutive Mrs. Newhouse could reach up to drape them around their necks.) But where was Si Newhouse, the other brother, the one whose power base encompassed the twelve Condé Nast magazines, and whose long and close relationship with Alex Liberman had been so vital to their continuing success? Si and Victoria Newhouse were in Florida. The day before, though, Alex had received a handwritten note from Si, on yellow legal paper, folded in half, stapled at both corners, and sealed in an envelope:

Dear Alex,

My thirty-year share of your eighty has been the most meaningful experience of my life. What wonderful times we've shared! And how you've shaped and changed me! Associate, friend, brother, father . . . there have been elements of all these in our relationship with none of the tensions there might have been.

I hope we continue forever—in a deep sense we will —and on this day, this special day, I send an expression of my special gratitude and love.

Si

To most of the Condé Nast editors present that day, the relevant phenomenon was Si Newhouse's continuing need for and dependence on Alex Liberman. After fifty-one years on the job, Alex was still the best in the business, the editorial director of all the Condé Nast magazines, the resident genius whom Si counted on to rejuvenate a flagging franchise or to conceive and develop a brand-new one. In the highly volatile world of big-time magazine publishing, where editors and art directors are as expendable as first wives, it was astonishing that anyone had managed to stay on top as long as Alex had. One possible explanation was that there had never been a clearly definable Liberman style—no signature look to the magazines he directed, nothing you could point to and decide was out-of-date. The Liberman style was protean and infinitely renewable. He had always pushed for journalistic variety at the expense of anything that smacked of an art director's concept of "good design." He responded so intuitively and so sensitively to changes of every kind—changes in social attitudes as well as changes in photography and art and visual communication—that he always seemed to be one or two jumps ahead of everyone else in his field, and because of this, the magazines he directed stayed fresh and innovative and very much alive. Amy Gross, who had worked closely with him for years as *Vogue*'s features editor, used to talk about the "split" in his editorial approach. "There's a part of him that goes for the deepest humanity and the deepest meaning, and there's a part that loves a cheap thrill—and loves it really cheap," she said. "It's the elitist point of view, where you either go high or low, but you don't muck around in the middle, because it's boring and banal. I think really the key to him is that he's not predictable."

Si Newhouse and others saw the key to Alex in his refusal to stand still or to take fixed positions. "Anything is possible with him," Si had said. "The only issue is how well it can be done." There were some less admirable aspects to this refusal, of course. He could be contrary and capricious, and even devious at times. His habit of hiring two people for the same job and letting them fight it out had been responsible for many of *Vogue*'s overstaffing problems through the years. You couldn't be sure where you stood with Alex, whose opinions were subject to instant revision, and whose ironic courtliness masked a relentlessly critical mind. He could seduce anyone with his world-class charm—could coax whatever he wanted from domestics and headwaiters as well as from editors and photographers—and he could also turn his back on people without a qualm. Alex became famous early on for rejecting layouts at the last possible moment before going to press and then getting everyone to work feverishly doing them over. Although the editors and art directors he worked with usually agreed that the effort had been worth it, and that the magazine had been—to use one of Alex's favorite words—"enriched," the process was costly in more ways than one. Madison Avenue is littered with art directors who learned too late that working with Alex Liberman basically meant doing what he suggested.

Nobody could really define the full extent of what Alex did at Condé Nast. The absolute authority of his eye, his taste, his critical judgment, and his creative energy reached throughout the empire, affecting everything from picture captions to corporate decisions. Newhouse was not alone in thinking him a magazine genius, someone ideally equipped by mind and temperament to orchestrate the monthly seduction of twelve million readers. "It's a process that's never finished," as Condé Nast executive Rochelle Udell put it, "a sort of dance that goes on between dresses and hairdos and makeup and paintings and rock-and-roll groups and how you picture them, and how they feed back into the culture." And if the process was like a dance, then Alex, who could move effortlessly from one image to another, one subject to another, one magazine to another without missing a beat, was the ballet master, the deft choreographer of a thousand daily decisions, the energizing collaborator whose sole commitment was to excellence and to something beyond excellence: an indefinable "nobility" that would infuse and redeem the whole enterprise.

There was, however, another explanation for his professional longevity. It could be said that he never grew stale because he never took his magazine work too seriously, believing that his true métier lay elsewhere.

For more than thirty years he had been an artist of recognized significance—recognized less in recent years than in the sixties, when his work had been ahead of its time, but still active, and still exhibiting regularly with one of the top New York galleries. His abstract paintings were in the Museum of Modern Art, the Metropolitan, the Guggenheim, and other important collections. His monumental welded-metal sculptures were prominently installed in public and private spaces throughout this country and abroad; during the seventies and eighties, in fact, he had become better known as a sculptor than as a painter. He also qualified as a photographer and a writer, most notably as the author of *The Artist in His Studio*, a famous book that provided remarkable insights, in pictures and text, into the working lives of all the major artists of the School of Paris; but because Alex considered photography a useful method of documentation and nothing more, he tended to look upon his own efforts in that area as a sideline. No, it was as an artist that he hoped to be remembered, and the fact that he wrote "editor" rather than "artist" on passport applications did not mean he had given up that hope.

There were those who believed that an upward re-evaluation of Liberman's work as an artist was sure to occur sooner or later. "Although long ago he earned the right to be ranked among the most original and genuinely creative talents of our time," Lawrence Campbell wrote in *Art News*, "many critics have been unable to forget or forgive the fact that part of Liberman's life is devoted to the world of high fashion." He was certainly a unique case. No one else in this century had combined a high-level career in publishing (or any other commercial enterprise, for that matter) with the serious, sustained practice of painting or sculpture, and it was certainly true that the uneasy association of art and fashion in Liberman's double career had worked against him. *Vogue*, the magazine he devoted most of his time to over the years, became under his guidance an important showcase and forum for modern art, and Liberman himself became an influential tastemaker—someone with the power to enhance reputations and further careers. At the same time, his close ties to the fashionable world of haute couture and jet-set living put him in the category of people who talk about art and sometimes even buy art but do not, as a rule, produce it. All this had made it easier for people to dismiss his own work.

Whether Alex Liberman could have been a better artist if he had decided to quit Condé Nast and devote his life to painting is a question that haunted him for years. It is a question that can never be answered, of course, and one that he stopped asking himself some time ago. At a certain point in his career he decided that life was more important than art, and by this he meant his life with Tatiana, the extraordinarily beautiful, extraordinarily demanding woman he was married to for fifty years. Pleasing Tatiana, keeping her comfortable, amused, and protected, providing the stage on which she could act out the drama of her larger-than-life personality, was always his central preoccupation. Alex poured more energy and imagination into that effort than he gave to his painting and sculpture or to his work at Condé Nast, and he did so without a trace of resentment or regret. Tatiana in a sense was his most complex work of art, his sacred monster, the idealized goal of his existence. He often said that she had made his own life and his career possible—that without her he would have achieved nothing. In spite of the unconfronted anger and tension in their long relationship, in spite of her narcissism and his willing servitude, the strange, simple truth was that they loved each other deeply. One day near the end of her life, their friend Oscar de la Renta asked Alex about her, and Alex, who rarely showed his emotions, alluded to her failing health and then said, in a wistful tone that de la Renta found inexplicably moving, "If I could just keep her that way." Even her diminished presence was enough to make him happy.

"I never felt that Tatiana dominated me, but I enjoyed leading her life," he said. The apparent contradiction here troubled him not at all. Although he believed that he owed her everything, she righted the balance by being totally dependent upon him. "Alex is Superman," she would say, in proud reference to his skill at making the great world bend to her needs. She never lost her own ability to surprise him (surprise being one of the keys to her own tantalizing and sometimes infuriating allure), and his playful, imaginative struggle to please and amuse her kept him young. Alex liked to quote Picasso's remark that it takes a long time to become young (*"Il faut du temps pour devenir jeune"*). He was younger than Tatiana—by six years, or perhaps by more than six—and as he aged, his aristocratic features became increasingly handsome. On his eightieth birthday, tanned and happy, he looked younger than many of the guests who had come to celebrate the event and pay homage to the man.

It was not all Condé Nast editors at the house in Quogue that day. The contingent of Russian friends included Mikhail Baryshnikov, with his wife and two young children, and Joseph Brodsky, who arrived after seven p.m. and promptly fell in love with the house—Brodsky said he wanted to come and stay there for a month the next summer. Both Baryshnikov and Brodsky spent the night, and so did Dr. Isadore Rosenfeld, the heart specialist who had ordered the triple bypass operation that made it possible for Alex to have an eightieth birthday. (Rosenfeld had recently started to write a monthly medical column for *Vogue*—another indication of Alex's continuing ability to call the shots there.) Representatives of the New York art world were relatively few in number. André Emmerich, Alex's dealer, was there, and Barbara Rose, the critic, who had written a major monograph on Alex's work in 1981, and Helen Frankenthaler, an old friend he hadn't seen for years, and Roy and Dorothy Lichtenstein, whom Alex met that day for the first time (they were friends of Cleve and Francine).

Some of the other guests had known Alex since his first years in America. Marcel Guillaume had been in the art department at *Vogue* when Alex started work there in 1941. Mabel Moses—the incomparable Mabel—had come to cook for Alex and Tatiana in 1943; she had run their New York household for forty-five years, and although retired now, she was still on Alex's personal payroll, one of the permanent beneficiaries of his extravagant Russian largesse. Carrie Donovan, a *Vogue* editor before she moved to the *Times*, arrived early and stayed late, as did eight members of the Layman family—Bill Layman and his sons had built almost every one of Alex's monumental sculptures, at their place in Connecticut. And then, of course, there was the Duchess, Tatiana's sister Lila, age eighty-four, wearing a dazzlingly white, alarmingly short-skirted piqué suit and an abundance of gold jewelry. The Duchess was most decidedly present, in a way that Tatiana, who could never stand her, would have taken steps to prevent if she had been alive. "Poor Tatiana," Alex said afterward. "She would have cried. Tatiana had such an extraordinary sense of shame. But, then, Tatiana would never have given a party like this one."

It was not really Alex's style, either, this Long Island luau, but he seemed to savor every moment of it. He was gratifyingly amazed when the single-engine plane circled over the house again and again, towing a sign that read "HAPPY BIRTHDAY ALEX." He and Melinda sat close together, hand in hand, while the tiny Filipino dancing girls performed their stylized movements and gestures, and Alex jumped to his feet to cheer the troupe at the end of the rousing last number, in which a male and female dancer hopped nimbly in and out of the danger zone between two long bamboo poles being clapped together with increasing rapidity.

Alex moved among his guests that day with grace and ease. He paid close attention to each and every one of them, and managed at the same time to appear slightly bemused by the homage that was being paid him. Originally he had decreed that there should be no presents, but experienced Liberman-watchers understood that a gift would not be taken amiss. The public celebration had all the elements of a new chapter in his life. "I've never had a party like this before," he said later. But then, Alex Liberman had already led several different lives in his lifetime, and what was to stop him from beginning another one now?

Three-year-old Alex, St. Petersburg.

Russia

In a memory of early childhood, he is in the sitting room of his family's St. Petersburg apartment, squeezing paint from a tube of artist's color. His mother, wearing a gold Fortuny gown, reclines on a leopard skin–covered divan. She is having her portrait painted, and she has told the artist to let the three-year-old boy help prepare his palette. "From the beginning, you see, she wanted me to be a painter."

Alexander Liberman often spoke of his mother with amazement and chagrin. For a man whose later career would have so much to do with the female image, she provided the reality of an overwhelming erotic presence. Henriette Pascar, who preferred not to be known by her husband's name, was exotic-looking rather than beautiful. She had a voluptuous figure that she kept well into her seventies, abundant dark hair parted in the middle, black eyes, and a theatrical way of moving and carrying herself. In those years before the Russian Revolution she lived the life of a pampered bourgeoise, denying herself little, receiving her lovers at home in the bedroom of her comfortable apartment. Alex didn't mind the lovers so much —not then, at any rate. What he did mind were the times when she would fix all her intermittent maternal passion on him. Later he sometimes wondered why he had never bothered to learn more about her life before she became his mother. He never read the two heavily fictionalized autobiographies that he encouraged her to write, in which she presented herself as a willful and seductive woman, a "nomad of love" who was adored and worshiped by many men, but whose deepest emotional commitment (as she never tired of reminding him) was to her son.

Henriette Pascar was born in Romania, the eldest of twenty children in a family of well-to-do Bessarabian timber merchants. Her mother's family was Jewish. Her father was a Gypsy, dazzlingly handsome in her memory, and not to be depended on; he had been accepted grudgingly into the family and the timber business. She remembered swimming nude with him in the river while her scandalized mother screamed at both of them from the bank. She remembered also the cruel streak that caused him periodically to drag his children into one of the sheds on their property for whippings; it seemed to her that he took sadistic pleasure in stripping them and applying the switch.

She ran away at seventeen (the year was 1903), and stayed for a while with some Gypsy cousins. When she came home, there was no controlling her. She left again soon afterward to find work and independence in the Ukrainian port city of Odessa, the nearest big town. But instead of independence she fell into a disastrous liaison with a handsome idler who got her pregnant, married her for her dowry, and then proceeded to gamble the money away in a few months. The baby was stillborn. The marriage was annulled, and Henriette returned to her parents' household in humiliation.

She recovered soon enough and left home once again, this time with a railroad ticket to Paris in her purse. For the next two years she lived a precarious existence in that city, taking courses in French literature at the Sorbonne and earning her living as a nurse. She spent one summer in Biarritz, working for a doctor who fell in love with her—although not sufficiently to consider leaving his wife. (Fourteen years later the same doctor became the Libermans' family physician and helped to get Alex into an exclusive private school.) There must have been other disappointments, because 1911 found her back in the Ukraine, living with a married sister in Kiev. She made friends there with a group of young people who believed in revolutionary social action, and it was through this group that she met Semeon Isayevich Liberman and was overcome, as she put it, with the desire to have a child by him.

Passion in this case was informed by good sense. Semeon Liberman, whose beginnings were much more humble than Henriette's, had raised himself from total obscurity to a position of considerable influence for someone his age, and he had done so in a remarkably short time. The son of a Jewish tenant farmer, he had grown up under oppressive conditions in a small village in the Ukraine. He ran away from home at sixteen, to the nearby town of Zhitomir, where he lived with a distant cousin, worked at odd jobs, and (here the parallel to Henriette's experiences breaks down) studied hard to prepare himself for a university education. He also joined a secret Jewish self-defense unit and was severely wounded by a Cossack's saber during one of the periodic pogroms which marked that era of Russian anti-Semitism. The wound, and subsequent police interrogations, helped to turn him into a Marxist. As he made clear in his autobiography, however, Liberman's revolutionary ardor was guided neither by orthodox Marxism nor by any other social theories, but by his own lofty ideals, in which there was always a strong undercurrent of Jewish mystical thought. "I had come out of that Jewish milieu where the old traditions of romantic mysticism were still alive, where the word 'miracle' was a true clarion call that woke men's hearts," he wrote. In Zhitomir he also came under the influence of the philosopher Nicholas Berdyaev, who had been exiled there from Moscow because of his Marxist teachings. Berdyaev had renounced Marxism, which he could not reconcile with his mystical belief in the Russian Orthodox church—a belief that did him no good after the 1917 revolution. Semeon Liberman helped to get him out of Russia in 1922, and they remained close friends until Liberman's death, more than twenty years later.

Semeon Liberman knew that without a university degree he could never break out of the oppressed underclass in Russia, but no Russian university would accept a poor Jewish student. To escape this vicious circle, he made his way to Vienna and enrolled in its famous university, which was then a hotbed of radical social and political thinking. The events of 1905, when strikes and revolutionary activities swept over Russia and came close to toppling the czarist regime, drew him back to his homeland. He joined the underground Social Democratic organization in Odessa, took part in illegal labor-union actions, and narrowly escaped arrest several times. The government's massive 1907 crackdown on all subversive activities destroyed the Odessa underground. Liberman took temporary refuge with his parents in the village where he was born; when the authorities pursued him there he fled to the large city of Kiev.

Cut off from his contacts in the Social Democratic movement, penniless, and without friends, he managed to get a minor clerical job in the office of a Kiev timber-exporting firm. Almost immediately, and to his own amazement, he found himself engrossed in the complex mathematical calculations and specialized knowledge that the lumber business required.

"Each oak called for a masterful analysis before it was chopped down and transformed into salable boards," he wrote years later in his autobiography. "The analysts, the calculators, the merchants, and the exporters dealing with Russia's wealth of forests had to be virtuosos." Within a few years Liberman had become a virtuoso himself—a recognized expert, the author of a table of timber calculations that eventually came into standard use throughout the industry. His rapidly escalating salary soon enabled him to attend Kiev University in his spare time. Several timber firms put him on their board of directors while he was still a student. The university sent him abroad to study the European markets for Russian timber, and the czar's Ministry of Agriculture made him a member of a special commission to improve timber sales to Germany. His meteoric rise in influence and earnings did nothing to alter his belief in the need for radical social change. He established contact with the revolutionary underground at Kiev University, and he attended clandestine meetings of the Social Democratic party, which at that time included both the Bolshevik and Menshevik branches of the Marxist movement. Liberman himself was a Menshevik. He believed in the broad-based ideal of the people's ability to govern themselves and felt a deep mistrust for the Bolsheviks' insistence that a small revolutionary elite must act on behalf of the masses.

How and when he met Henriette Pascar is not clear. In their autobiographies, both of them indicate that they had come into casual contact through the Socialist underground in Odessa, before Henriette went to live in Paris. According to Henriette, Semeon had been dreaming of her ever since. When they met again in Kiev, she found him greatly changed —"a well-groomed man with a marked European bearing" rather than the "carelessly dressed Nihilist" she had known before. Liberman was only two inches over five feet tall—shorter than she was—but there was a certain elegance about him, a distinguished look that would later be formalized by English tailors. Her desire for him this time was as compelling as his was for her. (Liberman's autobiography, called *Building Lenin's Russia*, is political rather than personal; he barely mentions their meeting and has very little to say about their relationship, then or later.) They were married shortly before the birth of their son, Alexander Semeonovitch Liberman, in Kiev, on September 4, 1912.

The old Russia that was to vanish forever five years after he was born left indelible traces in Alexander Liberman's memory. "I've always carried this deep awareness of Russian life and the Russian countryside and the Russian language," he said decades later. "It's something very basic in me. I had to marry a Russian woman." In St. Petersburg, where his parents moved soon after he was born, he spent the first five years of his life in a six-room apartment just off the Nevsky Prospekt, with a nurse to look after him and take him to play in the small park that adjoined the nearby cathedral. His nursery was a white oasis in the dark apartment— his mother had had the novel idea of having everything in it painted white; the only spot of color he remembered was his wooden rocking horse, the little hump-backed *koniok-gorbunok* of Russian fairy tales and legends. He also remembered a polka-dot dress that his nurse wore ("a brown dress with quite large white dots"), and he remembered a little girl in a green coat with a fur collar: "I met her outdoors, playing on a sled. I think she called me on the telephone later. I was madly in love."

He saw relatively little of his parents. After the move to St. Petersburg, Henriette Pascar had discovered a new spiritual home for herself in the theater. She took acting lessons and yearned to become a professional performer. "Lassia," the name she gives herself in her book *The Errant Heart*, says to her husband at one point, "I've never gotten on well with reality or with the world. In the theater I find myself. My feelings are most intense in the realm of fantasy." Semeon Liberman apparently had no objections to this new interest. He adored his wife, in spite of her infidelities and indiscretions, and rarely put obstacles in the path of her monumental self-indulgence. His own career in the timber business kept him away from home for weeks or months at a time. By 1914 Liberman was running three large timber firms, whose forest holdings stretched from Russia's western borders to Siberia. Some of the country's wealthiest landowners periodically engaged him to survey and calculate the market value of their vast forests. His clients included Grand Duke Michael, the czar's brother; Prince Oldenburg, the czar's uncle; and the fabulously wealthy Balashov family, which owned some 2.7 million acres of land throughout Russia. He spent a month traveling through the Balashov forests in the Urals, carrying huge loaves of bread and hard-boiled eggs, because he often went for three or four days without seeing any sign of human habitation. When he surveyed Prince Oldenburg's forests in the Caucasus, he was given the use of the prince's private railroad car. Alex accompanied his father on at least one of those train trips; he remembered the red damask curtains, the electric candlesticks with little shades in the dining car, and the wonderful, enveloping sense of luxury. For the rest of his life, he would associate luxury with a feeling of safety and protection.

All this ended abruptly in February 1917. To Semeon Liberman, the Russian Revolution came as a vindication of his deepest beliefs. He immediately wrote letters of resignation to all the companies he worked for

and offered his services to the provisional government in St. Petersburg
(soon to be renamed Petrograd). His services proved to be invaluable. The
timber industry, which had always been of major importance to Russia's
economy, became crucial to the country's survival in the early years of the
revolution. Cut off from its coal and oil supplies by civil war and foreign
intervention, the government was dependent on wood fuel for its industries
and its transport. Liberman, with his encyclopedic knowledge of Russian
forests and timber production, was made vice chairman of a committee to
organize the supply of wood fuel to the railroads. He threw himself into
this effort with great enthusiasm, working virtually night and day.

In October, when Alexander Kerensky's provisional government
fell and the victorious Bolsheviks consolidated their power, Liberman's
patriotic feelings took precedence over his anti-Bolshevik convictions. He
followed the new government to Moscow in the spring of 1918, met Lenin,
and became one of the most important of the non-Communist *spets*, or
specialists, in the new regime, working directly under a three-man "dictatorial triumvirate" that was in command of all the timber resources of
Soviet Russia.

His high position was no insurance against the terror that stalked
the country in those days. Young Alex (his parents called him "Shoura" or
"Shourik," affectionate diminutives of Alexander) remembered looking out
the window of their St. Petersburg apartment at dusk and seeing vast crowds
marching on the Nevsky Prospekt, chanting the "Internationale," waving
red flags, and burning a life-size oil portrait of Czar Nicholas II. A few
days later, he went to look for his mother at a neighbor's apartment and
found her being forcibly detained there, along with several other people,
by a Red Army soldier. "It was a trap," he said. "What was called a
lavoushka. If a family was suspected, a soldier would be stationed to catch
anybody who knew them. I think it was because I was so small—four or
five—that my mother and I were allowed to leave." Far more frightening
was the experience of seeing both his parents lying on the floor at home,
dead drunk. This happened soon after they moved to Moscow. As a government official, Liberman and his family had been assigned several rooms
in a private house on the outskirts of the city. (Alex remembered that his
mother had an affair with the house's former owner.) Although they were
relatively comfortable there, the turmoil and uncertainty of daily existence
generated tensions that often seemed unbearable. Now and then, Alex's
mother told him later, someone in the house would bring home a pail of
vodka and they would all drink until they passed out. "I can't even swear
if it was my parents I saw lying there," Alex said. "But to this day, when

Right: Alex and his mother on vacation in the Crimea.

Below: Age fifteen months, with his father.

Bottom: Alex in Moscow, 1919. This was the costume for the sailor's dance that he was too shy to perform.

Portrait of Henriette Pascar, Alex's mother, 1915. Three-year-old Alex helped
squeeze out the paints for it.

Henriette's production of *Tom Sawyer* at her state children's theater in
Moscow. Set and costumes by Ilya Fedotov.

I open a door sometimes I half expect to see some horrendous sight, a body on the floor."

Semeon Liberman's position in the new government was never a secure one. As a former Menshevik who refused to become a member of the new ruling party, he was looked on with suspicion by several highly placed Bolsheviks, including Felix Dzerzhinsky, the powerful head of the Cheka, or secret police. Liberman came under periodic attack over issues whose absurdity did not make them any less dangerous. Obliged one day to listen to a lengthy proposal for solving the fuel crisis by mobilizing children and old people throughout Russia to gather pine cones, he nodded gravely and told the author of the plan, a dentist whose main credential was his Bolshevik party membership, that he would refer the project to his scientific committee. He thought no more about this crackpot scheme, but then, five months later, on the day he returned to Moscow from a trip to England to negotiate timber sales, he was summoned before the Council of Labor and Defense for a special session to discuss the newly created Chief Pine Cone Administration. The session was held in Lenin's office. As Liberman came in, he could not help noticing the pile of pressed pine cones stacked beside the little iron stove in the corner; he also recognized the Bolshevik dentist, sitting at the table and regarding him with an expression of malice. What followed was a series of denunciations of Liberman, who was accused of ignoring or neglecting to act on the dentist's brilliant proposal. Lenin, who had the disconcerting habit of reading a book during meetings and still managing to hear everything that was said, finally raised his eyes from the page and said, "Comrade Liberman, how do you explain your carelessness and negligence?" Liberman proceeded to point out why the dentist's plan was unworkable. For one thing, he said, it would require more fuel to transport the pine cones from the forests in northern Russia and Siberia to the factories in the Ukraine than the pine cones themselves could possibly provide. His explanation seemed to impress no one except Lenin, whom Liberman had found to be "always receptive to common sense." With a hint of a smile, Lenin dictated a resolution for the minutes:

"Firstly, to reprimand Comrade Liberman for his negligent approach to a matter which deserved serious study and implementation.

"Secondly, to refer the entire matter to a special scientific board, which is also to be given all the arguments presented by Comrade Liberman."

Liberman left the meeting feeling humiliated and anxious. That evening, at home, he got a telephone call from the Kremlin. Lenin came on the line. "I noticed that the council's resolution made you sad," he said.

"Ah, but you are a soft-skinned intellectual! The government is always right. Go on with your work as before!"

The Chief Pine Cone Administration and the dentist's project were quietly shelved, but Liberman's problems with the Cheka and other factions continued. Without Lenin's personal support, he would undoubtedly have been purged, and probably executed. As it was, in 1921 he became one of the chief architects of the New Economic Policy, under which Lenin's government, faced with widespread famine, peasant uprisings, and the sailors' revolt at Kronstadt, temporarily abandoned "integral communism" to allow a partial re-establishment of free trade in small industries and made a series of concessions to the peasantry. Lenin needed Liberman's expertise and his organizational ability. This did not prevent Dzerzhinsky's Cheka from harassing him, spying on his movements, and using any pretext to build a case against him as an enemy of the state. One day when he was talking to Lenin about his difficulties with the Cheka, Lenin said, "Now you see for yourself that you wouldn't have had all these troubles if you were a member of our party."

"Vladimir Ilyich," Liberman replied, "Bolsheviks, like singers, are born, not made. I simply wasn't born to be a Bolshevik." Lenin did not argue the point.

While Liberman walked the tightrope of power, his wife found a way to put her own restless energy to work for the new state. Henriette Pascar used to say that she got the idea of a children's theater from watching her son play in his all-white nursery in St. Petersburg, but it was in Moscow, where the revolution had left hundreds of abandoned and homeless children to roam the streets, that the idea suddenly took on the validity of a social purpose, as a means to occupy the minds of hungry children. Pascar brought her proposal to Anatoly Lunacharsky, the commissar of education, and this imaginative bureaucrat (a former lover of Henriette's, according to Henriette) pulled strings and secured funds to set up the first state children's theater, in 1919. At the beginning, Pascar was one of several directors on the theater's advisory board, a group that also included Constantin Stanislavsky. By 1920, however, she was in full command, as director-producer and artistic decision-maker.

In later years, her son would say that this was the best thing she ever did—the only thing, perhaps, that made him feel unabashedly proud of her. During that brief period when the most advanced artistic ideas flourished in Moscow, before the Stalinist regime destroyed all initiative, Pascar drew from a remarkable reservoir of talent to create her children's theater of "fantasy, dreams, and tales." The Constructivist artist Ilya Fedotov designed the sets and costumes for her productions, which took their cue from the antinaturalism of Vsevolod Meyerhold and the Moscow Art Theater. (Fedotov naturally became her lover.) She used professional actors, who stayed after each performance to discuss the play with their youthful audience. The four-hundred-seat theater was always filled to capacity. Tickets were free, and sandwiches would be served afterward to the children, many of whom were half-starved.

An adaptation of Kipling's *Jungle Book*, called *Mowgli*, was the first production, in March 1920. The repertory soon grew to include eight more plays and spectacles, including *The Nightingale*, by Hans Christian Andersen; *The Bear and the Pasha*, by Eugène Scribe; and adaptations of *Tom Sawyer*, *Treasure Island*, and *The Nutcracker*. In Pascar's fictionalized memoir, her young son spent most of his time at the theater, helping to paint sets, watching every rehearsal and performance, serving sandwiches to the hungry children, and rushing backstage at frequent intervals to tell his mother how much he loved her. Alex did spend many hours at his mother's theater, but there were other times when both his parents were too busy to pay much attention to him—times when he felt as abandoned as the street kids with whom he often played.

The Libermans had moved from the private house on the outskirts of Moscow to an apartment building in town. There was a vacant, rubble-filled lot in back, where Alex used to join in the dangerous games of vagabond children. "Some were my age, some older," he said. "We had organized battles. We dug trenches and covered them with metal roofs. We threw stones and broken glass. I remember sometimes boys getting head wounds. The summit of victory was to defecate in the enemy's trenches."

A thin, nervous, undersized boy without much stamina, he seems to have made himself accepted by the street children through acts of generosity. He stole food from his parents' larder to give to his friends. Sometimes he brought Pavlik, the son of the building's janitor, up to their fourth-floor apartment and put fistfulls of thick white honey from a barrel into his pants pocket so he could have something sweet to suck on all day. Alone in the apartment, Alex would spend hours improvising sounds on a grand piano that had been left behind by previous tenants. His parents disagreed about his schooling. Henriette wanted him to be tutored at home. She believed in giving free play to a child's imagination; schools inhibited fantasy, she argued. Alex was enrolled, nevertheless, in a school that was on the other side of town. Each morning, he would give the sandwich that his mother made for his lunch to a truck driver, in exchange for a ride to school. (His distaste for walking never abated; throughout his life, he avoided going anywhere on foot if he could help it.)

His privileged backstage life at the children's theater did not keep him from being paralyzed by stage fright at school. "There was a school festival of some sort, in which everyone was expected to perform," he recalled. "My mother decided that I should do a sailor dance, and so, of course, I was taken to the Bolshoi Theater and tutored by one of the dancers. I went two or three times a week to learn that dance—you know, pull imaginary ropes, three steps right, three steps left, and do the jig with your arms crossed. The big day came, the piano started playing for my dance, the curtain opened. I went out and just froze. The curtain closed, the pianist started again. I couldn't do it. I ran off the stage crying. Ever since then I've avoided public appearances or public speaking of any kind. I just refuse to do it, cannot do it."

At school, his behavior became a serious problem. He fought with other children, pulled girls' hair, assaulted his teachers. The teachers eventually found him so unmanageable that he was taken out of school and tutored at home—as his mother had wanted him to be all along. Tutors came and went with great frequency. (One of them had taught English to the children of the last czar.) He locked them in closets, kicked and raged at them. He wet his bed at night and suffered the only beating his father ever gave him because of it. "My father picked up a big leather belt, folded it, and told me to lie down on the sofa. My mother was in the next room, screaming through the door for him to stop." Ordinarily, Alex's contacts with his father were quite distant. He remembered a telephone call from his father at the ministry, quizzing him on the multiplication tables: "If I learned them up to twelve-by-twelve, I could go to the Bolshoi Ballet that evening. I was dying to go, and I did." At a very early age, Alex sensed that his father resented him. Henriette's ardent attachment to her son, which caused Alex such intense discomfort, made his father jealous.

The Libermans now were reduced to living in three rooms. The apartment's other rooms had been assigned to two working-class families, who shared the common kitchen and whose drunken quarrels made life noisy and brutish. On holidays, however, the Liberman family could escape to a country house in the tiny village of Krukovo, where they had the use of a dacha on an estate whose former owners had been exiled or liquidated. "The walls were unpainted pine boards that smelled wonderful," Alex recalled, "with beautiful etchings of ancestors in gilt frames. And there was a pond, which we couldn't swim in because it was full of leeches, and a field of wildflowers, which I remember my mother's brother Naum riding through on a horse, bareback. He had come to see us one weekend. A charming little girl lived in a house nearby. She came to visit once, and there was a thunderstorm, and she couldn't go back. She was put to bed in my bed. I thought that was absolutely marvelous. She was a little older than I was, blond and very lovely. I remember that aureole of blondness."

Alex's "hysteria," as his fractious behavior was referred to in the family, became more and more troubling. Semeon Liberman consulted several doctors, who told him that his son was seriously disturbed; the only way to help him, they said, would be to get him out of the country. Liberman had already made one trip to England for the Soviet government. When a second trade mission to London was proposed, he decided to take Alex with him and applied for a passport. Lenin agreed to it, but Dzerzhinsky did not. The matter was taken up at the next meeting of the Politburo, where it was decided by a three-to-two vote: Lenin, Ryckov, and Kamenev in favor; Dzerzhinsky and Zinoviev opposed. In Henriette Pascar's melodramatic account of the departure in *The Errant Heart*, she learns only at the last moment that her husband is taking their son abroad, and the separation is so painful that she attempts suicide. In fact, she must have known about and agreed to the plan. She gave Alex a bible on the day he left, with the inscription, "September 1921—Mama." It was his last memory of Russia.

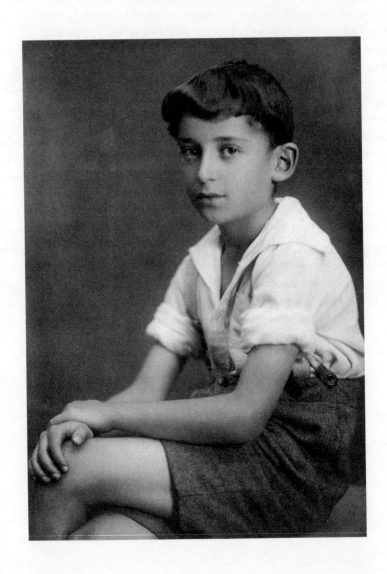

Alex at nine, in England.

England

Τ he strange, bitter taste of beer, which his father bought from a
station platform vendor in Riga, became his first memory of the
new life. Two days later, they were installed in the Hotel Esplanade
in Berlin, while Liberman held meetings with representatives of European
lumber firms. The hotel's wide corridors and large suites, its paneled elevators and splendid dining room made an indelible impression on the boy,
after the grim poverty of Moscow. "My father loved luxurious hotels and
luxurious living," according to Alex (who quickly acquired similar tastes).
The Cheka took note of this, of course, in its mounting dossier on Comrade
Liberman.

After a week in Berlin they went by train to London, arriving late
in the evening. The sight of red-uniformed Grenadier Guards in the fog
outside Buckingham Palace thrilled the tired boy; it was like something in
a fairy tale. The Royal Palace Hotel in Kensington was not nearly as grand
as the Esplanade. After a few days, though, they moved in with the large
and exceedingly lively Krassin family, whose impressive red-brick house in
Hampstead would be Alex's home for the next year. Leonid Krassin was
one of the leading figures in Lenin's government. A Bolshevik activist before
the abortive 1905 revolt and a close friend of Lenin's, he had gone on to

become (like Liberman) a highly successful businessman, working first as
an electrical engineer for the German company Siemens und Schuckert,
in Berlin, and eventually becoming director of that firm's factories in Russia.
After the revolution, Lenin put him in charge of supplies for the Red Army.
He became commissar for foreign trade in 1918, and led the first Soviet
trade mission to Europe in 1920—a mission that resulted in substantial
timber sales to England. (Semeon Liberman was his principal deputy on
that and subsequent trips abroad.) No Western European government recognized the Soviet regime at this point. Britain was willing, however, to
do business with capitalism's archenemy (Lloyd George, the prime minister,
had said, "After all, we deal with cannibals, too"). London was still the
great hub of world trade, and Krassin had stayed on there, after the successful 1920 mission, as the Soviets' unofficial envoy and primary trade
representative. His wife and children had joined him, and their well-staffed
Hampstead mansion, with its formal gardens, chauffeur-driven limousines,
and other nonproletarian luxuries had become a meeting place for Russian
exiles as well as for those who were interested in doing business with the
Communists.

The Krassins had six children, only three of whom were by Leonid.
(His wife had had two previous husbands.) The three youngest—all of
them high-spirited and very good-looking girls—would figure prominently
in Alex's life for years to come. Katia, the most beautiful and the most
willful, was fifteen when Alex came to stay with them; Ludmilla, quieter
and more responsible, was thirteen; Lubov (called Luba) was eleven, barely
two years older than Alex, and, in his vivid recollection, "madly seductive,
aggressive in a flirty yet boyish way." Alex became a kind of stepchild in
this exuberant Russian family, and also something of a pet for the girls.
They used to tie him up in his bedsheets, dress and undress quite casually
in front of him, and tease him about his uncouth manners. He enjoyed all
this tremendously.

Before Semeon Liberman went back to Moscow, he enrolled his
son as a boarder in a small private school for young boys that was not far
from the Krassins' house in Hampstead. It was the first of three English
schools he attended, and the teachers there, unlike their Russian coun-
terparts, seemed to have no difficulty taming his unruliness. "English education turned me inside out, like a glove," he often said. "They simply
beat you until you stopped crying." When questioned, Alex had to admit
that he himself had never really been subjected to the vigorous canings that
he saw inflicted on some of his schoolmates. It may have been that the
teachers were reluctant to beat a foreign student, for fear of diplomatic

incidents, or it may have been that Alex Liberman had already taken on, at age nine, the protective coloring of an exile and a survivor, the chameleonlike adaptiveness that would serve him throughout his mature life. At the Hampstead school he learned table manners and self-discipline, along with the English language, which would be such an indispensable asset to him later on.

He spent his weekends with the Krassins. They outfitted him with the right clothes from Rowe, the upper-class children's clothing store on Bond Street, and in no time at all he became a proper English boy, which is to say a snob. When his mother made a brief visit to London in 1922 and came to meet him at his school, he was mortified to see "this rather square, dumpy woman" in the courtyard. "She had changed a lot," he said. "She was fatter, and in my opinion she was badly dressed. She took me for the weekend to a hotel near Trafalgar Square—I think it was the Charing Cross Hotel. Time came for dinner. I had on my blue suit. I looked at her and I said, 'I can't have dinner with you looking like that.' It was partly that I was trying so hard to conform to British standards, but it was also that I didn't like my mother—didn't like her physically, then or later."

His next academy was the much stricter University School in Hastings, a seaside village near Brighton. There were military drills twice a week, and uniforms with brass buttons to be shined and puttees to be rolled and rifles to be shouldered, and weekly tub baths, with ten boys taking turns in the same water ("If you were number ten, the water was black"), and there was more-or-less constant hazing by the masters. Although Alex never got caned on the bottom, he had his palms rapped smartly with the sharp edge of a ruler on the slightest provocation, and there were other humiliations. "Don't gape, Liberman," one of his teachers would call out whenever he caught Alex daydreaming. One day, denied permission to leave class to go to the bathroom, he couldn't hold it in; he put an atlas under him to avoid soiling his chair, but the volume's red cover bled into his pants, betraying him. He still wet his bed occasionally. The most embarrassing moment of his young life occurred in a hotel room in Cornwall, where he had gone on vacation with the Krassins. There were not enough rooms for the family, and Alex, who was sharing a large bed with the three Krassin girls, woke up to find a mortifying dampness in the sheets. He thought—hoped—that the girls were not aware of it. ("I was on the outside, thank God.") He spent his vacations and many weekends with the Krassins, who threw themselves enthusiastically into English upper-class life. Horseback riding was unavoidable. Alex learned to ride during their holidays in Cornwall, and on weekends in London he would often ride with the Krassin girls in Hyde Park. He once suffered the exquisite humiliation of falling off his horse in a particularly crowded and muddy pitch on Rotten Row.

From time to time his father made a business trip to London, but he could never stay very long. Liberman was crucially involved in planning and carrying out the New Economic Policy, and after Lenin's death in 1924 he became increasingly burdened by the need to defend himself against his enemies in the Soviet bureaucracy. Henriette Pascar was completely absorbed in her own work there. The success of her state children's theater was having wide repercussions; the English stage designer and director Gordon Craig came to Moscow, saw several performances, and wrote about them enthusiastically. Alex, alone in the strangeness of English life, often felt that his parents had abandoned him. He wrote them heartbroken letters, which often went unanswered. "I cried very much yesterday, thinking of you," went one. "My darlings, why is it that you don't write me?" In later years, Alex was unmoved by his mother's ritual claim that she had sacrificed everything for him. "In England," he remembered, "I felt like an outcast."

The Russian Revolution, at this point, was beginning to devour its children. Henriette Pascar had been warned that her theater, whose great success had come from its adaptations of Western classics, was failing to teach proper Bolshevik values. She ignored the warnings. Then, during a late rehearsal of Robert Louis Stevenson's *Treasure Island*, right after the cast had shouted "Long live the king!" an unidentified male voice called out from the rear of the darkened theater, "Why not, 'Long live the Soviet Socialist Republic'?" The speaker never revealed himself; the rehearsal continued. *Treasure Island* opened on schedule, but after two performances it was shut down by order of the Soviet authorities, and Henriette Pascar was dismissed. Deprived of the work that had sustained her for six years, she requested permission to accompany her husband on his next business trip to London. She never went back.

With remarkable aplomb, Henriette set herself up in a large and comfortable house at 7 Albert Place, in South Kensington, near the Albert Hall. Alex was never quite sure where the money to buy this house came from. Semeon Liberman had established a personal relationship with Chatterton Sim, of Churchill and Sim, the leading English lumber importers; although he was still working for the Soviet state, he may have been able to get a loan from this firm, which he joined officially in 1926, after his own decision to go into exile. "My father had been helping Churchill and Sim to get Soviet government contracts," according to Alex. "Maybe they felt indebted to him." Alex was occasionally invited to spend the weekend at Georgian House, the Sims' country estate in Maidenhead. Far more

Right: Alex's first letter home to his mother. "My beloved little mother, I'm certain that you miss me....I have put on a lot of weight....Kissing you hard. Shoura."

Below: Alex and Henriette soon after she left Russia. "This is how my mother looked when she first came to see me in London—big and awkward."

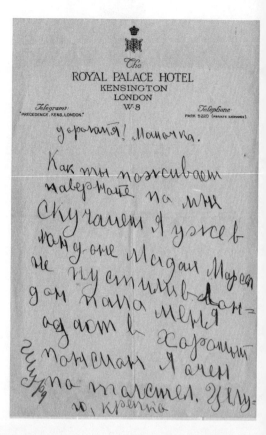

Дорогая! Мамочка.

Как ты поживаеш наверъмаете на мне Скучаеш Я ужев Лон у оне Мадам Мара не пустилив дан дом папа меня ад ает в хароший пансман Я очен шура маетел Целу, Крепка

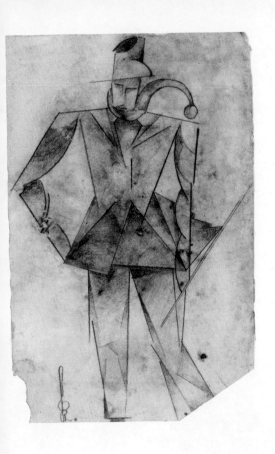

Left: "Constructivist" drawing by Alex, done soon after his visit to the 1925 Exposition des Arts Décoratifs.

Below: "A view from my bed at the rue Schoelcher apartment."

impressive than the Krassin household, it was a huge mansion on the Thames, with great rolling lawns, legions of maids and butlers, and baronial rooms full of Chippendale furniture—grand luxe in the English style.

Semeon Liberman himself never lived in the Albert Place house. His life and Henriette's veered further apart after she left Russia. She acquired a roster of English lovers, including a rich banker named Loeb who paid for her clothes and took her on a trip to Italy. She also made efforts to establish a children's theater in London, but the project never got off the ground, partly because Henriette became more interested in performing herself. On Liberman's trips to London he rented rooms in South Kensington, with a chauffeur and a butler to attend to his needs. It was here that the infallibility of English butlers was decisively disproved. Liberman brought out a large tin of caviar on one of his trips from Russia, and Cracknell, the butler, who had never seen caviar before, asked what it was. When told that it came from a fish, he did what the English always did to fish, which was to immerse it for a long time in boiling water.

The Albert Place house was beautifully furnished. It also came equipped with a two-story studio that Henriette planned to turn into a private theater for her own pantomime performances—the latest outlet for her theatrical ambitions. Alex remembered the place very well, although the time he spent there was limited to occasional weekends and holidays. (By then he was a boarder at St. Piran's in Maidenhead, his third English school.) His bedroom was on the top floor. There was one other bedroom up there, which the cook shared with Nellie, the very pretty young English maid whom his mother hired soon after her arrival. Alex had a crush on Nellie. He used to try to climb into bed with her when the cook wasn't there—a favor that she would sometimes grant but more often refuse. The three Krassin girls also visited the Albert Place house on weekends, and their teasing and free-and-easy ways kept Alex in a state of erotic confusion. "I remember seeing them all in the bathroom once, taking a bath," he said. "They didn't mind. They covered up a little, but not much."

Alex was entering puberty. After a bout with appendicitis when he was ten, he had suddenly grown several inches. At St. Piran's, full of manly pride in his new height and his newly learned ability to box, he slipped into the sort of cockiness that invited retaliation. Having agreed to a boxing match with a fellow student, he found himself confronted by about thirty of his critics, who pushed him around a bit without doing any real damage; when he protested this breach of sportsmanship, he was matched against a Siamese boy whose nose was too small to hit. Alex's nose, which was much larger, was soon bleeding profusely. He nearly got into much worse trouble when he warned a younger student not to drink from a mug that hung near the water tap—the matron, he said, used it to pee in. The student reported this to his parents, who notified the headmaster, who called Alex into his office and demanded to know whether he had said what he was reported to have said. Alex stoutly denied it, and kept on denying it under subsequent interrogations; the headmaster's failure to break him down gave him an exhilarating sense of having outwitted authority.

In none of his English schools was he persecuted for being Jewish, perhaps because nobody knew he *was* Jewish. Alex barely knew it himself. When he was a very young child in St. Petersburg, an older boy had yelled something incomprehensible at him on the street. Alex had come home in tears and asked his mother what the word "kike" meant (*Jid* in Russian). Although his parents never denied their own Jewish origins, neither of them was a practicing Jew. Semeon Liberman was opposed to all religions. Henriette Pascar tended to emphasize her Gypsy rather than her Jewish heritage. Going to English schools, young Alex attended Anglican chapel services and recited the Apostles' Creed without understanding it, just as his classmates did. His Russian origins seemed to shield him from prejudice as well as from canings.

He spent a lot of time in the school darkroom, developing and printing his own photographs. His interest in photography went back several years, to the time when his father, returning from a trip abroad, had brought back to Moscow a can of Spam and a vest-pocket Kodak camera for Alex. He took a lot of photographs at St. Piran's. At this stage he had no particular interest in art, in spite of all his mother's efforts to instill one. Since leaving Russia, she had made him go to museums with her at every opportunity. In the summer she took him to Italy, where visits to the major galleries filled the hours that she did not spend in the company of some new or prospective lover. Henriette Pascar had lost some weight and learned how to dress in the Parisian style, and her erotic life was taking on new dimensions. In Bergamo she picked up a count who invited her and Alex to his palazzo for lunch. They both sat paralyzed at the long table, unable to decide which of the six or seven forks to pick up first, until the count, seeing their dilemma, broke with protocol by taking the first bite. Henriette always insisted that Alex tell her which of her new gentlemen friends he preferred; that summer, he usually named the one they had met in Venice. He had found that it was easier to give an answer than to pretend indifference.

On their visits to European museums, Henriette bought copies of famous old-master paintings, which she hung in her two-story Albert Place studio. Ersatz Titians, Rubenses, and Rembrandts filled the whitewashed brick space above the eight-foot-high wood paneling, like icons in a Russian church. There was a flight of steps at the far end, which she curtained off as a stage for performances. But the performances never took place, because her husband sold the house out from under her to his business associate, Chatterton Sim. Sim's wife, who was known as Doffey, an auburn-haired English beauty with pale lavender eyes, had taken a great fancy to Henriette. (Not so Chatterton, who didn't like her at all.) Doffey was fascinated by this Russian savage who paid no attention to etiquette, said exactly what she thought, and took lovers whenever and wherever she felt like it. Doffey herself was subservient to her domineering husband, who liked her to be in bed waiting for him when he got home from the office every day. The admiration that Doffey felt for Henriette, however, was clouded by jealousy. At a certain moment, when a money crisis descended on the Libermans, Doffey announced to her husband that she wanted Henriette's house (which was much grander than the Sims' own London flat), and Chatterton Sim got it for her. It may have been that Sim had paid for the house in the first place, rather than lending Liberman the money to buy it. At any rate, Henriette was furious. "I think she never really forgave my father for that," Alex said. "She was practically in hysterics, screaming at him, saying she'd never speak to him again. Of course, she did speak to him. But she moved to Paris right after that, and he stayed in England."

Henriette Pascar in performance at the
Théâtre des Champs-Elysées in Paris, 1928.

"Vous Me Plaisez"

The Restaurant Prunier, on the rue Duphot, near the Madeleine, was one of the early gems of the Art Deco style. Its polished black floor and mirrored walls, with stylized fish etched into the glass, made it seem like the inside of a dark aquarium. At the *bar de dégustation* in the front room, barmen in blue aprons and fishermen's caps opened and served the freshest *coquillages*, which the customers often ate standing up, coming in at any time of the day in season for a platter of oysters with a glass of chilled white wine.

Sitting at Prunier's one day in 1924, not long after her arrival in Paris, Henriette Pascar could not take her eyes off the man at the other end of the bar. He had the head of a sculptured Greek deity, with classically refined features and a glossy, neatly trimmed beard. His dark English suit was faultlessly cut. (Henriette herself was wearing a dress by Poiret and a modish cloche hat from Reboux.) Never one to hesitate in these matters, she scribbled a note and told the barman to give it to the handsome gentleman. The note read, *"Vous me plaisez"*—three words whose implication in French is a good deal more provocative than the English "I like you." This was the beginning of her love affair with Alexandre Iacovleff—an affair that would have profound and far-reaching effects on Alex Liberman's future.

Alexandre Iacovleff was one of the not inconsequential number of upper-class Russians who, cast out by the revolution, had managed through enterprise and moderate talent to achieve an immoderate success in postwar Paris. He was an artist—an extraordinarily facile artist, whom John Singer Sargent called one of the greatest living draftsmen. His portrait drawings in *sanguine* (red chalk) of celebrities and rich Americans had brought him fame as well as a constant stream of new clients. His biggest client was Citroën, the automobile firm: Iacovleff was the official artist for the Citroën "Croisière Noire" to Africa in 1924—an early public-relations expedition that captivated the French popular imagination. (There was a "Croisière Jaune" in 1931, to Asia.) His sketches of native chieftains and natural wonders took the place of photographs in those days before hand-held cameras and color film; they were exhibited in Paris on the expedition's return, and reproductions of them were published in special albums that enjoyed a wide sale. At this point in his life Iacovleff was a favorite of the Paris beau monde. He knew a great many influential people, most of whom looked upon him as a major artist—not to be confused with clumsy char-latans like Picasso or Matisse.* He exercised daily to keep in trim, spoke perfect French, and was known for his glamorous mistresses (his affair with the legendary Anna Pavlova had ended a year or so before he met Henriette Pascar). He never married, nor did he ever share a household with anyone. It would appear, however, that Iacovleff was sincerely in love with Henriette. Their affair continued for at least three years, and their friendship lasted much longer.

Iacovleff probably helped Henriette to find her studio apartment at 11 bis, rue Schoelcher, overlooking the Montparnasse cemetery. The build-ing was one of several that had been put up in this quarter to accommodate the city's growing population of artists—Picasso had a studio there at one time, and so did Iacovleff. Henriette's apartment consisted of a large two-story room with a staircase at one end that led up to her bedroom and bath; underneath her bedroom was a little alcove where Alex slept when he came home from school. Alex was now a boarder at L'Ecole des Roches, an exclusive private school in the Normandy countryside, about sixty miles west of Paris. Leaving England had been a wrench for him—another blow to his shaky equilibrium, another language to master in haste. He remem-

---

* Iacovleff's work is currently being re-evaluated both in Russia and in New York, where his work now sells for high prices.

bered coming to Paris with his father at the end of the school term in 1925. They stayed at the Hotel Bedford and, looking for a nearby restaurant on their first evening, found a table at a very lively place called Le Boeuf sur le Toit, which neither of them had ever heard of; they liked the piano music, but if Jean Cocteau or any of the other regular patrons had been there that night, they would not have known it. Semeon Liberman went back to London a few days later, leaving Henriette to investigate French schools. She and Alex visited several exceptionally dreary-looking Paris *lycées*, but Henriette, who did not especially want to have her adored son living with her, had heard from an old friend of hers about L'Ecole des Roches, and, against all odds, she decided that Alex must go there.

L'Ecole des Roches was, and still is, the French equivalent of Eton or Harrow—a school for the sons (now also the daughters) of the governing elite. It was expensive, academically rigorous, and, unless you came from the right background, virtually impossible to get into. The old friend who had told Henriette about it was Dr. Rollin, the Biarritz physician who had fallen in love with her years earlier, when she was a young girl living in France. She had met him again in Paris, and he had put her in touch with his brother, who was a deputy in the French parliament. Armed with a letter from the deputy, Henriette presented herself and her son to the headmaster of Les Roches, who was sufficiently impressed. Alex entered the school as a boarder in March 1926. He was thirteen years old, tall for his age, shy, apprehensive, and not yet fluent in French. He was also the first Jewish student ever admitted to the school.

Les Roches was organized like an English school, with much emphasis on athletics, cold baths, and moral purity in thought and deed. In Alex's application papers, on the line listing religion, his mother had put down "Protestant." She had even suggested to Alex that he should use the name Pascar instead of Liberman, but she did not insist on this. (In France, their name was usually spelled "Lieberman," and pronounced *Li-eberman*; Semeon eventually had the spelling changed officially to "Liberman," so it would be pronounced the way it had been in Russia. He also changed the spelling of his own first name, from Semeon to Simon.) Alex went to Protestant chapel services and became rather deeply attached to the school's Protestant pastor, a Swiss named Jean Cellerier. "He was very delicate and tactful," Alex remembered. "Through him I had my first real contact with spiritual life. I don't know how he managed it, but I was baptized in his church so I could take my first communion. Everyone receives a present at their first communion, and I still have the little Gospel he gave me—still keep it by my bed, in fact. He wrote in it, 'You are the salt of the

earth.' I never wanted to deny my Jewishness, you know, or to pretend
that I'm not what I am. But the truth is that my life, my culture is based
very much on Protestant, Calvinist ethics."

Although it was like an English school in certain respects, Les
Roches was thoroughly French in its intellectual severity. "Well-Armed
for Life," the school's motto, referred primarily to mental armor, and the
rewards and punishments reflected this. Instead of being caned, refractory
students were made to memorize and recite two thousand lines of Corneille
or Racine. Alex found this rigorous mental climate far more congenial than
the old-boy rituals at St. Piran's. A quick learner with intense motivation,
he soon established himself as one of the top students, and profited accordingly. He became popular with classmates as well as teachers. Invited
to spend weekends at the houses of his new friends, he observed the manners
and customs of the French upper class and assimilated their forms of
snobbery, which were quite different from the English. His best friend,
François Latham, went home to a seventeenth-century chateau not far from
the school, near the town of Broglie. Latham's stepfather was the novelist
Jean de La Varende. He espoused violently right-wing views on most questions, as did the parents of Alex's other close friend, Jean-Pierre Fourneau,
who lived in a picturesque villa in Ascain, in the Basque country, near the
Spanish border. Provincial landowners in France, Alex learned, often talked
as though the French Revolution had been a grave but temporary error.

Summer vacations were a problem. His mother would either farm
him out with friends during the long holidays or, more rarely, take him
along on her travels with Iacovleff. When Alex was still going to school in
England, he and his mother had spent part of the summer at Salsomaggiore,
an Italian spa where Henriette received treatments for "female problems"
of an unspecified nature. They had stayed at the luxurious Grand Hôtel
des Bains and been invited to the nearby castle of the Duchesse de Gramont,
née Ruspoli, who took a fancy to good-looking young Alex. (Iacovleff
and Anna Pavlova had stayed with her the summer before, when their
three-year affair was nearing its end; Iacovleff had painted frescoes in the
private theater of the gloomy old medieval fortress.) Also staying at the
Grand Hôtel was the marquis de Cuevas, a heavily made-up grandee who
had not yet secured his future by marrying the Rockefeller heiress Margaret
Strong. He took a fancy to Alex, too, inviting him for rides in his horse-
drawn fiacre and giving him silver pencils as mementoes; but nothing
improper took place. The next summer, Alex was packed off to the Atlantic-
coast beach resort of St.-Jean-de-Luz in the care of Ludmilla Krassin, the
responsible daughter, on whom he naturally developed a crush. To his

embarrassment, though, he could never afterward recall the times he was taken to the beach at nearby Hendaye later that summer by a striking blond Russian girl named Tatiana Iacovleva, whom he would eventually marry. Tatiana was Alexandre Iacovleff's nineteen-year-old niece, whom Iacovleff had recently managed, through his Citroën contacts, to get out of Russia; she was visiting Hendaye with her aunt Sandra, Iacovleff's sister. Tatiana remembered taking the gangly thirteen-year-old boy swimming and then to a *pâtisserie*, but she did not like to dwell on the recollection; it opened up the question of the difference in their ages.

The biology teacher at Les Roches was a White Russian refugee named Monsieur Imchenetsky. Alex, who had left Russia before he learned to write, was already starting to forget his native tongue. He relearned it from Imchenetsky, who was engaged to tutor him in Russian during the summers of 1926 and 1927; they spent the first summer in a *pension* at La Baule, on the Brittany coast, and the second in a small hotel in Cannes, with Imchenetsky acting *in loco parentis* on both occasions. By now thoroughly at home in both English and French, Alex touched something deep in himself through reading Russian literature and poetry with this bookish, deeply religious scholar, who also tried unsuccessfully to convert him to the Russian Orthodox faith. Sixty years later, Soviet writers and artists on a visit to New York would fall silent and listen in rapt attention to Alex's Russian; most of them had never heard the language spoken so beautifully, in the cadences of an older time.

On the infrequent weekends and vacations that he spent at the rue Schoelcher, the erotic atmosphere made literature seem superfluous. Henriette liked to have pretty young women around her; she may have felt that they accentuated her own seductive appeal. Luba Krassin, a great favorite of Henriette's, often came to visit. (Leonid Krassin had been named Soviet ambassador to Paris in 1923, and Luba, the youngest of his three daughters, was working as a fashion model for Vionnet.) Alex was fascinated by Luba: when he came home on vacation he would sometimes call on her, bringing along a bottle of what he hoped was a well-chosen wine, a baguette, and a ripe Camembert. But his teenage lust just then was focused mainly on Nellie, the English maid, whom his mother had brought with her from London. He embarked on a campaign to persuade Nellie to let him photograph her nude, or at least partially nude. "This went on for months," he said, "right up to the time my mother left the rue Schoelcher. Finally, Nellie allowed me to take one picture of her nude to the waist, which seemed to me a tremendous achievement."

He was also trying very hard to learn how to draw and paint like

Iacovleff, who gave him a few lessons. Alex had gone to the 1925 Exposition des Arts Décoratifs in Paris, which more than any other single event brought modernism in the arts to the attention of a wide public in France. He was particularly struck, as were many others, by the graphic arts in the Soviet Pavilion, where the Constructivist experiments in architecture, typography, and poster design were prominently featured. Aside from this brief exposure, though, he had very little knowledge of modern art. What he aspired to then was Iacovleff's facile realism in portraits and figure studies. At Les Roches, Alex took drawing classes twice a week, working mainly in pastel. "There were about four or five others in the class. One was a Turkish boy who had enormous facility—he drew beautifully, and his drawings were exhibited at the school. I was always awkward and clumsy, but Mademoiselle Vignetey, the teacher, seemed to think I had something. She encouraged me." The boys could also take optional afternoon classes in the so-called practical arts. There Alex learned how to bend and shape metal, and he experimented with sculpture, modeling a mother and child in Plasticine. The class he enjoyed the most, though, was the one in mechanical drawing, where he learned to use a compass and other instruments to depict engine parts, cylinders, screws, and geometrical shapes. Although he knew nothing about abstract art, the precision and purity of the designs he could make with mechanical aids appealed to his own longing for order, logic, and proportion—a longing that went back to the chaos and violence of his childhood.

Alex rarely saw his father in those years. Liberman had been summoned home from London in October 1925 to answer a host of grave new charges brought against him by the Cheka. Russian friends in England warned him not to go; a number of non-Communist government *spets* had been liquidated since Lenin's death, and Liberman, his friends said, would be arrested the minute he stepped off the train. After several sleepless nights, though, he decided that "it was my duty to my family, to my son, to go back to the Soviet Union and defend myself against slander."

Although he was not arrested, Liberman nearly broke under the strain of daily interrogations during the next two months. Often he would be called in the middle of the night to the offices of the secret police, where he would be grilled for hours about the cost of his son's school or his wife's apartment in Paris. The unrelenting war of nerves led him to consider suicide. He kept a razor under his pillow at night, to be used when the secret police came to arrest him. And then, on the second day of January, 1926, he was suddenly informed that "Comrade Dzerzhinsky instructs you to leave the Soviet Union within twenty-four hours." A Swedish timber

Right: A drawing of Alex by Iacovleff. "I sat for it in his Montmartre studio. There was an extraordinary art library, all bound in leather and the volumes stamped with his initials in gold."

Below: Alexandre Iacovleff in Capri. "People said he looked like a Greek god, and that's why he cultivated that little beard—to make him look more like a Greek sculpture."

Alex and his tutor, Monsieur Imchenetsky, on the beach
at La Baule in Brittany. The more substantial of the two
ladies—both of whom happened to be staying at the same
pension—was the cabaret singer whose nude picture Alex
had recently discovered in his father's trunk.

On the soccer field at Les Roches: Alex, François Latham,
and a friend.

syndicate wanted to negotiate an important new contract with the Soviet government. The Swedes had insisted that Liberman be a member of the Soviet delegation to Copenhagen, where the negotiations were to be held, and Dzerzhinsky, who was now the chief of the Supreme Council of Economy, had decreed that he would go.

He traveled first to Berlin. A few days after his arrival there, Liberman received a telegram from Moscow. All the charges against him had been dismissed; the government expressed complete confidence in Comrade Liberman and requested his continued services. Feeling dazed by this miraculous reversal, he moved on to Copenhagen. The complex negotiations with the Swedish syndicate were highly successful. From Copenhagen he went to visit his wife and son in Paris, and it was then that he decided not to go back to Russia. The decision precipitated a nervous breakdown, which he spent six weeks recovering from in a Swiss sanitarium.

His health restored, Liberman negotiated his own conversion from communism to capitalism. He formed a business connection with Chatterton Sim's firm, Churchill and Sim, in London, and, toward the end of 1926, established himself as a private consultant to the European timber market, based in Paris. His resources must already have been more than adequate, for he took a large apartment in a brand-new building on the avenue Frédéric-Le-Play, a fashionable Left Bank street near the Ecole Militaire. Henriette gave up her rue Schoelcher studio and moved in with him; the apartment was spacious enough to provide a separate bedroom suite for her and a room for Alex. It was the first time they had all lived together since 1921. Normal family life, however, did not ensue. Henriette received Iacovleff and other intimate friends in her bedroom at the back of the apartment, while Liberman worked in his office in the front. (One of the gentlemen visitors Alex recalls seeing in those days was Jean Monnet, the future architect of the European Community.) When Alex was in town, Iacovleff often stopped by his room, which opened off the long corridor, to see his latest drawings and comment on them. ("Go deeper!" was his frequent admonition.) Liberman made no objection to Iacovleff's visits, and Henriette accepted her husband's much more discreet liaisons—he seems to have had a particular fondness for opera singers. Looking through the drawers of his father's empty steamer trunk one day in the basement of the Frédéric-Le-Play apartment, Alex found a photograph of a nude woman, whom he recognized, to his amazement, as a featured singer with the Chauve-Souris cabaret troupe.

Although they could accept each other's love affairs, his parents now had violent quarrels over money. "My father would complain about the huge bills from the couture houses," Alex recalled, "and she would go into hysterics. She'd say the most awful things about him to me. She'd say she was leaving him forever, and she would drag me off to Versailles, where we would spend two or three nights in a hotel. I remember scenes in the apartment when she would tear her clothes and threaten to throw herself off the balcony—we lived on the sixth floor. Once, I came home from school and found her crying. I must have been thirteen or fourteen. I just stood there, and she slapped my face. I smiled and said, 'Do you feel better?' That was my English schooling, never to show emotion. She slapped my face again and again, in absolute hysteria. I didn't cry, I didn't move. This, of course, drove her mad. Finally she dropped onto a couch in terrible tears. I was sorry for her, but I'd seen her cry like that too often.

"Almost always the scenes were about money. She was so involved with expensive clothes, jewelry, lingerie, perfume—I think her dream was to be a great courtesan. She used to take me with her to the fashion houses for fittings. I remember going to Lanvin and Poiret, which were her favorites. 'Do you like this one better?' she would ask me. I was bored but at the same time flattered that she consulted me. Her affair with Iacovleff really broke up when she went into Vuitton and ordered a very expensive set of luggage and had them send the bill to him. I think he refused to pay for it. There was something so pathetic about all this. When things got to be too much for her, she used to go and see Nicholas Berdyaev. My father had somehow arranged to get him out of Russia, had paid for him to come. He lived in Clamart, just outside Paris, with his wife and his wife's sister, who was madly in love with him. Berdyaev was a religious philosopher and a mystic, and in a way my mother was for him some kind of possessed being. He loved her, wanted to help her. She would go there and just sit with him while I waited out in the garden, and he would calm her. My mother could well have been possessed by the devil—she was so wild, so consumed by the idea of erotic love."

Alex always felt that his father had the intelligence in their family. Once, standing in the corridor outside a train compartment in which his parents were riding (they were on their way back from the Polish resort of Zakopane, where his father had gone on business, taking Henriette and Alex along for once), he heard his father say, in Russian, "Pity the boy's not intelligent." It was one of those remarks that can never be forgotten. Alex did not have deep conversations with his father. "I thought he was jealous of my mother's passion for me," he said. "When he would reprimand me for something, he'd say, 'I'm not your mother, I won't spoil you.' " The emotional distance between them made Alex all the more vulnerable to his mother's enveloping influence.

Henriette's theatrical ambitions had in no way diminished. The large, sparsely furnished salon in the avenue Frédéric-Le-Play apartment, with its murals by the Russian-French painter Léon Zack, was the scene of frequent performances, before small groups of invited guests, of the choreographed movements and gestures that she derived partly from the French mime tradition and partly from Isadora Duncan and her followers. Unlike her son at the time, Henriette felt a real affinity for the modern movement in the arts. She bought Cubist-inspired furniture and had her bedroom painted by a disciple of Le Corbusier, with each wall a different color. Many of her friends were artists—Russian artists, for the most part, although her circle also included Fernand Léger and Jean Cocteau. Natalia Goncharova, Mikhail Larionov, and Marc Chagall, fellow victims of Stalinist repression, came to her soirées and introduced her into the circle around Diaghilev and the Ballets Russes. She formed a close attachment to Bronislava Nijinska, the dancer-choreographer sister of Nijinsky, who helped to choreograph Henriette's own performances. Inevitably, Henriette's creative obsession demanded a larger public and a wider stage. Solo performances à la Duncan were not uncommon in Paris then, and Simon Liberman, whose deep affection for his wife withstood all the strains that both of them put on the marriage, agreed in 1929 to finance a Pascar evening at the ultrafashionable Théâtre des Champs-Elysées. For Alex, the event precipitated an emotional and physical crisis that had been building up for a long time.

Alex had been doing extremely well at Les Roches. In addition to being one of the top students, he had driven himself to become an athlete of sorts, training hard every summer to improve his speed in the hundred-meter dash and other track and field events. (He once overheard a boy from a visiting school's track team say to a teammate, as they walked by him, "I didn't know they had Jews at Les Roches.") In his senior year he was made prefect (head boy) of his house at school. Foreign students, whose tuition was twice that of the French boys, were not eligible for the school's top prize, a trip to Indochina that was awarded annually to outstanding achievers. Alex received glowing reports from all his teachers, however, and in his senior year he worked hard to prepare himself for the most difficult of the all-important *baccalauréat* examinations. He had decided to take not only the regular examination but the special exams in mathematics and philosophy as well. Since his intelligence stopped short of genius (something his mother naturally refused to admit), this effort required many extra hours of study, and as a result, he lost a lot of sleep that spring.

There were other pressures on him as well. François Latham, his best friend, on a weekend visit to the avenue Frédéric-Le-Play apartment, had gone to bed with Henriette. Latham was sexually precocious; thumbing his nose at the school's obsession with moral and physical purity, he had even managed to bed one of the housekeepers at Les Roches. Alex always claimed that his mother's dalliance with his best friend didn't bother him in the least; this sounds disingenuous. In any case, Alex had a new sexual obsession of his own at this point. He was in a swoon of love for Louise, the young French girl who had replaced Nellie as his mother's personal maid.

"My mother hired her just when that film came out with Jeanette MacDonald and Maurice Chevalier—I think it was called *The Love Parade*—and Louise looked a lot like Jeanette MacDonald," he said. "She was very, very pretty, with extraordinary green eyes and long dark hair. She was from a little town near Bordeaux. I remember telling Latham that there was this marvelous young woman, and that somehow I had to break down the barrier between us. I would go and sit in the room where she was sewing and chat and flirt with her, but she was very proper. She was a virgin. I wrote her a letter from school, a very passionate letter. After that, when I came to Paris we would go for walks. It was very difficult, because there was always the damn concierge watching everyone, and to have the young master go out with the maid was—well, she had to use the back entrance, and I'd go out the front, and we'd meet. She kept saying she was too old for me—she was six or seven years older. But I had this theory that somehow men can arrive at their ends by persistence, by overwhelming pursuit; that if you really want something, however difficult, it's possible. It took a long time with Louise. She was really a lovely human being. Then, one day, what was supposed to happen happened, and it was a complete disaster. We were both totally innocent and incapable. After that, we became great friends."

Alex was in the throes of his unconsummated love for Louise in May 1929, when he came up from school to watch his mother perform at the Théâtre des Champs-Elysées. The performance was in the small, two-hundred-seat Comédie des Champs-Elysées theater, above the main hall, and in his memory it was well attended. Alex himself had helped Alexandre Iacovleff design the poster, which had been plastered on kiosks and billboards for weeks in advance. Marc Chagall had done the sets and designed Henriette's tight, body-revealing costumes. The music was by Darius Milhaud, and the choreography was by Nijinska. "Unfortunately, my mother had broken her knee the year before, in a bobsled accident she had when we all went to the ski resort of Zakopane, in Poland. She had insisted on being taken in a bobsled, and it had turned over. The knee was operated on by the best bone specialist in Italy, but the accident left her with a slight limp, and so the choreography had to accommodate that. She walked around the stage striking attitudes and making slow gestures, this rather stocky, middle-aged woman. I must tell you, I cringed. It was the most embarrassing thing I had ever seen."

Alex went back to school the next day. That afternoon, he vomited blood. For several weeks he had been having black stools, an indication of internal bleeding, but he had been afraid to tell anyone. This time, he went to the infirmary. "The male nurse there said, 'Nonsense, nobody vomits blood.' He thought I'd eaten too much red currant jam or something. But I felt awful, so I made the decision to go back to Paris, two hours away on the train. I sort of staggered into the apartment, and Dr. Rollin, who was our family doctor, was called. He came, he examined me, and he said it was nothing. 'Just don't eat any game,' he said. My parents went out to a dinner party. And during the evening I had the most appalling hemorrhage, blood just pouring from both ends. I didn't have the strength to call out, but I managed to throw my shoe against the ceiling. Louise's bedroom was directly above mine, and she heard it and came down. She cleaned up the blood and stayed with me. When my parents got home, my father went out in person to get Dr. Rollin—maybe because he didn't answer the phone —but his wife came to the door and said he had left town. Finally, my father found a local doctor who turned out to be very good."

There was no anodyne in those days for bleeding ulcers, which is what Alex had. He was put to bed in the darkened living room, where he remained for more than a month, looked after by his beloved Louise. He had lost so much blood that the doctor thought at first he might not live. In retrospect, Alex always said that the multiple tensions he had been under at school—the pressures to excel in every way and the anxiety about passing his double *baccalauréat*, not to mention his unacknowledged Jewishness—must have been responsible for the ulcers. He also blamed the school food and the Normandy cider that they all drank in such large quantities. But what triggered the attack, he felt sure, was seeing his mother perform on stage.

Hilda Sturm, in Megève, photographed by Alex.

Hilda

I t took him most of the summer to get well. After a month in bed at home, he went with his mother to Evian-les-Bains, where he drank the waters and studied for the *baccalauréat* exam he had missed by being sick. He took the first part of his *bac* in late July, at the Sorbonne, in Paris, and passed with an honorable mention. In the fall he went back to Les Roches to prepare for the second part. He decided to skip the mathematics exam, but he studied hard for the philosophical section, which he passed —once again with the coveted *mention bien.* His excellent showing on these all-important exams qualified him to enter one of the advanced institutes in Paris, whose graduates are automatically in line for careers in government, industry, or the professions. This would have pleased his father, but not his mother, who had never stopped wanting him to be an artist. As Alex often said, he really had no choice.

By the time he took the final *baccalauréat* exam he had already enrolled in the private atelier of André Lhote, a minor Cubist painter who was thought to be the best teacher of advanced modern art in Paris. It was his first sustained encounter with modernism, and it did not take. Lhote expected students to copy his method of painting, which was a superficial, mannered Cubism. Passing by Alex's easel one morning, the teacher flew into a rage over the variety of colors on the canvas. "He picked up a brush and began scrubbing away at the wet pigment, which blended together to make a sort of dull gray, and then he drew some Cubist outlines in the gray area, of a bowl with black apples." Deeply offended, Alex began to think about other careers. Architecture, for example. Auguste Perret, a highly regarded modernist architect who had pioneered the use of reinforced-concrete construction, was teaching then at the Ecole Spéciale d'Architecture, on the boulevard Raspail, in Montparnasse. Alex eventually quit Lhote to enter Perret's school, where he received high marks and frequent praise from Perret himself.

After six months, though, discouragement set in again. He was depressed by the amount of mathematical and scientific knowledge that modern architecture seemed to require. Perret's school, moreover, did not offer the official diploma that was required to become a practicing architect in France; only the Ecole des Beaux-Arts did that. Although he wasn't at all sure that he wanted to be an architect, Alex decided to take the very demanding entrance examination for the Beaux-Arts school of architecture. He passed it and was admitted to the Atelier Defrasse, the oldest and most academic division of the Ecole des Beaux-Arts. His ability to work very hard while keeping a low profile served him well here; he escaped the rough and sometimes dangerous hazing usually meted out to new students, or *cochons*, as they were called, and he achieved in his first term the somewhat dubious distinction of being named *chef cochon*. Almost before he had settled into the Beaux-Arts routine, though, a chance meeting deflected his career plan in an entirely different direction.

In the garden of a modest seaside *pension* near Hyères, on the French Riviera, where Alex and his mother were taking a summer holiday in 1932, Henriette struck up a conversation with a good-looking man sitting alone at the next table. He turned out to be the graphic artist Cassandre, whose arresting, boldly stylized posters for wines, magazines, steamships, and railways were transforming advertising design as radically as Picasso and Braque had transformed the art of painting. A Russian exile whose real name was Adolphe Mouron, Cassandre responded gallantly to Henriette's overture. The conversation continued after lunch, and Alex, to pass the time, took out his pad and pencil and sketched a portrait of their new friend. Cassandre was impressed by it—so impressed, in fact (whether by the portrait or by the mother is uncertain), that he asked Alex to come and work for him. Alex was already doing some free-lance design work by this time—redesigning a publication that was something like a French version of *Consumer Reports*, working up a prototype for a magazine called *Pour*

Vous. To earn pocket money, he also sold sketches for book bindings to a small, luxury bookbinder in Paris, for fifty francs apiece. He had been looking around for other jobs, and Cassandre's offer proved irresistible. Alex began going out to Cassandre's studio in Versailles every afternoon, while continuing to attend the Ecole des Beaux-Arts in the morning. "There was one other assistant," he said. "Cassandre would sketch out his design, and we would execute it. At the time, he was working on that famous Dubonnet poster—'Dubo, Dubon, Dubonnet'—and I remember tracing things, and scrubbing down failed efforts in the courtyard, and using the airbrush. But after about two months he called me in and said, 'Look, I don't think you're the kind I need. I need a *nègre*, a slave.' He said I had too much talent, which was a polite way of firing me."

Alex was rehired almost immediately by Lucien Vogel, his mother's newest lover. Vogel (pronounced Vo-*zhel*) was a well-known publisher in Paris, the founder of two elegant fashion journals and, more recently, of a photographic news weekly called *Vu.* His wide circle of friends included both Cassandre and Alexandre Iacovleff; Vogel had published the drawings of Chinese and Japanese theater sets that Iacovleff had made during his roundabout migration from Russia via the Far East, and he also printed the special editions of Iacovleff's sketches for the Citroën expeditions. Alex met him for the first time in the hallway of the avenue Frédéric-Le-Play apartment, where he had recently become a privileged visitor. He looked just like Mr. Pickwick, Alex thought—a ruddy, round-faced man with blond hair and blue eyes, dressed in a parody of British style: brown-and-white-checked tweed suit, pale yellow waistcoat, and a high, starched collar with a bow tie. Vogel questioned Alex about his interests and his schooling, and then said, in his categorical way, "A young man who has worked for Cassandre belongs in my art department at *Vu.*" It was as simple as that. Without further struggle or uncertainty, Alex fell into the journalistic career that had been waiting for him all along.

Vogel's first publishing venture had been *La Gazette du Bon Ton,* an exquisitely printed little magazine in which the latest Parisian dress designs were interpreted, on hand-colored plates, by a group of stylish young artists. When *La Gazette du Bon Ton* was forced to shut down during the First World War, it was bought by Condé Nast, the publisher of *Vogue,* who was interested mainly in keeping Vogel's artists from working for the rival Hearst organization. After the war, Vogel and his talented wife, Cosette de Brunhoff, edited another fashion journal called *Jardin des Modes,* which appeared as a supplement to the magazine *L'Illustration*; Condé Nast bought that, too, in 1921, and kept the Vogels on as editors. Vogel was really more interested in politics than in fashion, however, and he had become intrigued by the largely untapped possibilities of photography as a means of documenting current events. In 1928 (eight years before the advent of Henry Luce's *Life*), he started one of the first photographic news magazines. Like Stefan Lorant's *Münchener Illustrierte Presse* in Germany, the slightly earlier pioneer in the field of photojournalism, Vogel's *Vu* was an erratic (and sometimes chaotic) mix of politics, spot news, sports, cultural reporting, Paris fashions, and miscellaneous features; it occasionally carried illustrated excerpts from the adventures of Babar the Elephant, by Cosette's brother, Jean de Brunhoff. Typographically it was way ahead of its time. The magazine's bold logo, designed by Cassandre, stood out like a beacon in the magazine racks of Paris newsstands. Vogel was getting advice from Cassandre and from Charles Peignot, a typographic genius who had bought Balzac's former printing press and was using it to develop new fonts and typefaces. He could not afford to hire experienced design people, though, and one of the incentives for making nineteen-year-old Alex Liberman the assistant art editor in 1933 was that he could get him for fifty francs (then about ten dollars) a week.

Alex quit architecture school to work for Vogel. It was the end of his formal education, but he had no regrets about that. Although the hours were long and the salary was tiny, from the start he loved the excitement and the quick decision-making involved in putting out a weekly magazine. His arrival doubled the staff of the art department, which was the province of a dynamic, dark-haired young Russian émigré named Irène Lidova. Alex learned the basic elements of magazine layout from Lidova. She taught him how to size the photographs, using a slide rule to figure out the correct proportions. Everything had to be done by hand. They would sketch proposed layouts with a pencil, and then try to approximate them mechanically, never seeing the finished page until the magazine was printed. The darkroom was right next to the art department; Alex spent a lot of his time there, projecting pictures on layout paper, cropping and juxtaposing images, learning the techniques of photomontage. He sometimes worked until four in the morning and occasionally slept in the office, on a narrow cot.

Although Lidova was in charge of layout, Alex soon took over responsibility for the magazine's covers. Vogel would make suggestions or do a rough sketch, and Alex would work it out in the darkroom, juxtaposing images and text in bold patterns that often took their cue from the Constructivist designs he had seen at the 1925 Exposition des Arts Décoratifs. His efforts delighted Vogel, who was starting to encourage a much bolder approach to the photo layouts. An enthusiastic photographer himself, Vogel

Right: Irène Lidova, art director of *Vu*. In later life she became a ballet impresario and discovered Roland Petit.

Below: Alex's cover for *Vu*'s special 1934 issue on colonization. Photograph by Hoyningen-Huene, photomontage by "Alexandre."

Right: Lucien Vogel.

Below: La Faisanderie, Lucien Vogel's country house in St. Germain-en-Laye, outside Paris. The Sunday lunches there attracted writers, painters, journalists, photographers, and many others.

had a keen sense of how to use photographs to tell a story. His willingness to blow up a photograph and run it across two pages made a huge impression on Alex. "He taught me a great deal," Alex said years later, "the use of typography, how to give sequence to a story, how to be cinematic. It's funny, his other publishing ventures were all sort of classical, luxurious, and noble—all except *Vu*, which was modern. He was very conscious of making the first really modern illustrated magazine." Vogel set the magazine's political tone, which was left-of-center. The rise of fascism in Italy and Germany was documented in special issues, and the bloody 1934 riots in Paris by the French ultra-rightist groups Action Française and Croix de Feu were covered in detail. The year before Alex came to work there, *Vu* did a special issue on Soviet Russia. Subsequent special numbers examined dictators past and present, and the atrocities of the Great War, on both sides. The magazine was nothing if not eclectic, however; there were also annual supplements on tourism, the automobile, and Paris fashions.

The editors got the bulk of their photographic material from the photo agencies of that era, such as Wide World and Keystone. But *Vu* also published pictures by Henri Cartier-Bresson, Brassaï, André Kertész, Maurice Tabard, Robert Capa, Eric Solomon (who invented the concealed camera), and other pioneers of the documentary approach that had been gathering momentum since the 35-millimeter Leica camera was introduced in 1924. Their work was looked upon by Alex and the magazine's other editors as raw material; in the early years of *Vu* the photographer was not always identified or credited. Alex never even met Cartier-Bresson at *Vu*. He did work closely with Brassaï, who became the magazine's specialist on Paris-after-dark; penniless and often hungry, he developed his prints in a bidet and was overjoyed by every sale. It was Alex who brought Kertész to Vogel's attention—this was after he had supplanted Lidova as art director—but, as he later put it, "the idea that a photograph might be art was unheard of, so far as we were concerned." Vogel sent Robert Capa to cover the Spanish Civil War in 1936. Capa's famous photo of the Loyalist soldier who had just been shot turned up on Alex's desk a month or so later; he took it right in to Vogel's office, and it appeared for the first time in the September 23 issue of *Vu*.

Alex's photomontage covers for *Vu*, signed "Alexandre," brought him extra money—an arrangement that Vogel seems to have agreed to in lieu of giving him a raise. Alex was chronically short of cash. He supplemented his low salary by taking free-lance jobs outside the magazine—he did window displays for Galeries Lafayette, and designed catalogues for Bon Marché. Once, he tried his hand at an advertisement for Peugeot. The result—a two-page spread in the Christmas issue of *Vu*, showing Santa's sleigh being pulled by six Peugeot sedans—was a great embarrassment to Alex: never again would he step over the line (a very thin one today) that separates advertising from editorial content. Eventually he started writing movie reviews for *Vu*, under the pseudonym "Jean Orbay." He loved American films, especially the light and corny Hollywood comedies of the Depression era. Their unabashed entertainment value appealed to him enormously and made him yearn to go to the United States.

His father did go there in 1937, and he moved to New York permanently the following year. Simon Liberman's consulting business, which had been hit hard by the Depression, was recovering nicely by this time. He had developed some important timber interests in Canada, but his move to New York was motivated primarily by the political situation in Europe. The rise of Mussolini and Hitler shocked him deeply, and so did the bitter conflicts between right and left in France, and the anti-Semitism that was becoming more and more virulent there. When Alex and his father went together to get their passports renewed in 1936, the uniformed official looked at the papers, looked at them, and said, "You're just a couple of kikes [*youpins*], aren't you?" His father said nothing, and the hint of obsequiousness in his manner humiliated Alex more than the official's remark. "I began to realize that I would always be classified a Jew," he said, "even though being Jewish didn't really exist for me. I began to feel like an outcast in France. My parents became French citizens, but if you were my age the only way you could do that was to serve in the army, and my ulcers ruled that out. For years, as a Russian refugee, I had a Nansen passport. But there had been a ruling in France that stateless persons had to take the nationality of the country that issued your original entry visa, so I was listed as a Soviet citizen, and Soviet citizens in France were not welcome. That, and being Jewish, gave me a real sense of not belonging."

Although Alex continued to live in his parents' apartment until 1936, he shared with his school chum François Latham a *garçonnière* around the corner from the avenue Frédéric-Le-Play, a studio flat that they used mainly as a love nest. Latham got more use out of it than Alex, who was still struggling with the vows of chastity that Les Roches had imposed on him. When he was thirteen, and still begging his mother's maid, Nellie, to let him photograph her nude, he had dated a twenty-three-year-old model named Odile, whom he met when he visited his father in the sanitarium near Lausanne—she had been a patient there, on the verge of being released. "It was very funny," he recalled. "She was looking to be a kept woman, and I didn't even know how to order at the restaurant we went to." A few years later, in the midst of his passion for Louise, he managed to persuade the attractive woman who lived on the ground floor of his parents' apartment building to let him take her dancing once in Montmartre. ("Her husband was away, and so was my mother.")

Apart from Louise, though, his first serious love affair was with his *Vu* colleague Irène Lidova. Like the others, she was several years older than he was. She was also Russian, and married (to a photographer), "a very strange woman," according to Alex. "She had a lot of emotional and physical problems, and she was terrified of getting pregnant." Their affair, such as it was, continued for at least three years, complicated by the fact that he was gradually supplanting her as the art director. He took her to the little *garçonnière*, where their separate anxieties and inhibitions ruled out anything more than heavy petting. Alex introduced Lidova to his mother, who disliked her intensely. His mother often said how much she wished he would fall in love with someone like Tatiana Iacovleva, Iacovleff's niece, who sometimes came to parties at the avenue Frédéric-Le-Play. Now, there was a Russian girl worthy of her only son.

It is difficult not to suspect that the main obstacle in the young man's relationships with women was Henriette Pascar. Ever since he could remember, she had paraded her lovers in front of him, drawing him into an erotic complicity that naturally excluded her husband. She had gone to bed with his schoolmate and with his boss. Henriette assumed that her only son would have the same powerful sexual appetites that she had, and this apparently made her very anxious. She would occasionally fling open the door to his room at five in the morning, expecting to catch him with a girl in his bed. She never did. Although he had been falling in love with pretty girls since he was four years old, Alex, not surprisingly, was far more inhibited than most of his friends. His youthful imagination had embraced the romantic ideals of chivalry during his school years in England, when he had become an avid reader of the King Arthur legends and the novels of Sir Walter Scott. Part of him would always tend to see the women he was attracted to as shining creatures, spiritualized nymphs whose inner light precluded the kind of gross sensuality that embarrassed him so much in his mother. At Les Roches, Alex had made the French schoolboy's obligatory visit to a brothel. "It was a point of honor," he recalled. "You went to the Sphinx, which was then the most famous house in Paris, and you danced with the girls. One of them said to me, 'Do you want to go upstairs?' I said no. It was enough to tell my friends, afterward, that I had been there."

Although he had long ago developed a protective shell of indifference toward his mother's amours, Alex was increasingly dismayed by her physical presence. Her stocky but still voluptuous figure, excessive makeup, and ultrafeminine taste in clothes embarrassed him as much as her provocative behavior; for the rest of his life, he detested lacy underwear and any sort of "feminine frills." He didn't even like the way she spoke. Back in 1923, in London, her lower lip had been badly cut in a taxi accident. Many stitches were required, and afterward her expression and her way of speaking were different—"pinched, and mannered somehow." Henriette's determined battle against the aging process would eventually make nearly everything about her seem mannered and artificial to Alex, and yet, like his father, he was bound to her by deep and complex emotions. Father and son sat loyally in the mezzanine of the Olympia music hall in Paris for the opening performance of Henriette's weeklong appearance there in 1933, three years after the Théâtre des Champs-Elysées debacle. Somehow she had persuaded the Olympia's manager to book her act at this famous landmark on the boulevard des Capucines, where Edith Piaf and Maurice Chevalier and countless other stars had triumphed; but when she came out to perform her suite of stylized movements and gestures, there was almost no one in the audience. The only people to applaud were her husband and son, who then had to keep up their frenzied clapping while a stagehand carried in the five dozen red roses that Simon Liberman had provided for the occasion.

Her belief in a "creative" destiny never flagged. She threw herself into the effort to re-establish her children's theater in Paris,* and actually managed to put on a production of Les Enfantines, with music by Mussorgsky, and L'Ours et le Pacha, by Scribe. The sets and costumes for the latter were by her son, identified in the program as "Alexandre." It was not a success, and her Scaramouche theater, as she called it, foundered for lack of funds. Several years later, on a visit to the United States with her husband, she managed to gain an audience with Eleanor Roosevelt, who wrote favorably in her newspaper column, "My Day," about Henriette's ideas for a children's theater. Henriette, noticing that the First Lady had brown spots on the backs of her hands, advised her to wear gloves. In New York she saw Clifford Odets's play Golden Boy and was seized by the desire to bring it to Paris. Liberman bought the foreign rights for her, and Henriette actually managed to get the piece translated, cast (with Jean-Pierre Aumont in the lead), and produced at the Théâtre Wagram, where

---

* Henriette's book Mon Théâtre à Moscou, published in 1930, had been rather well received in Paris.

Henriette Pascar making an entrance at the Marquis de Cuevas's masked ball.

Simon Liberman at the house in Chatou. "He always paid great attention to his clothes."

it closed after one performance. According to Alex, the French critics found the notion of a prizefighter who wanted to be a violinist completely incomprehensible.

That his mother was sleeping with his employer was not the least of Alex's embarrassments. She constantly pressed to get herself invited to La Faisanderie, the Vogels' weekend house in St. Germain-en-Laye, where Sunday lunch was always a lively get-together of writers, artists, journalists, entertainers, and celebrities of all kinds. Vogel's other mistresses were usually present on these occasions (along with his wife, Cosette, and her current *ami*), but Henriette seldom got invited. Although Vogel acted like a pasha, the ladies really ran the show there, and the ladies—spearheaded by three Armenian ex-mistresses for whom Vogel had found positions on *Jardin des Modes*—couldn't stand Henriette. "It was the custom at La Faisanderie for everyone to promenade around the lawn and the grounds," Alex recalled, "but when my mother was there the ladies refused to come out of the house. They thought she was ridiculous, trying to be what she was not—and frankly, so did I."

Alex himself was always welcome at La Faisanderie. Slim and tall, his dark hair slicked back in thirties' fashion, his pencil-line mustache trimmed to perfection, he looks, in photographs of the period, like a later era's image of a gigolo; but at the time, he was the epitome of French masculine style. He had the extra advantage of being able to speak perfect English. Vogel, Charles Peignot, and the rest of their set had a mania for everything English in those days. The men appeared at La Faisanderie in plus fours, smoked pipes, and talked endlessly of golf and horse racing. Alex fitted in so well that Vogel began to think of him as a potential son-in-law—he had two very attractive unmarried daughters, Marie-Claude and Nadine. Alex did fall seriously in love with Marie-Claude Vogel, the elder of the two, in 1935. "She had blue, blue eyes and reddish-blond hair, and she was passionately attached to leftist ideas," he said. "Later she married Paul Vaillant-Couturier, who became the head of the French Communist Party, and during the war she was one of the great heroines of the Resistance. Marie-Claude was caught and sent to the Ravensbrück concentration camp, but miraculously she survived." Alex once said that if Marie-Claude's political ideas had not grated so harshly against his own leanings, which were somewhat to the right of center then, he might very well have married her. His friend Latham had recently married a stunning girl—and had insisted that Alex come with them on their honeymoon. "The French love threesomes," as Alex explained. "Something like *Jules et Jim*, but different in this case. We drove down to the Riviera and went to a wonderful small hotel in Port Cros. It was all very friendly and lots of fun."

Alex and Marie-Claude went skiing together that winter in the French Alps, at a new resort called Alpe d'Huez, where they spent long days climbing up the mountain on sealskins—there were no lifts as yet. Although chaperoned by her uncle Jean de Brunhoff, the creator of Babar, they also spent a considerable amount of time in Alex's bed at the hotel, kissing and hugging. But Marie-Claude's moral code was even stricter than Alex's; she returned from the Alps with her virginity intact.

Sports generally bored him, but Alex had discovered that skiing was an excellent way to meet girls. In February 1936, on a ski slope at Megève, he met the most beautiful girl he had ever seen. Her name was Hildegarde Sturm. A first-class skier, she was also a model, and when Alex first saw her she was being filmed for a winter sports movie. "I saw this blond goddess on top of a mountain, with the sky and the snow, and it just blinded me," he said. "I had to meet her. I did meet her, and I fell madly, overwhelmingly in love."

The daughter of a schoolteacher in Bonn, Hilda was living in Paris at the time. Alex called her as soon as she got back from Megève and started taking her out. Lidova and Marie-Claude Vogel were forgotten, extinguished by Hilda's "aureole of blondness." She was twenty-five, two years older than he was. When they had been seeing each other for three months, Alex proposed marriage. "I am not the sort one marries," Hilda replied, in her disarmingly frank way. She had made no secret of her previous liaisons. For a year or more she had been the mistress of a wealthy man-about-town named Bunau-Varila, the owner of the powerful Paris daily *Le Matin*, and when she met Alex she was also involved with an American sports promoter named Charles Michaelis. For Alex, however, the prospect of rescuing this slightly tarnished goddess was an aphrodisiac; he had recently read Tolstoy's *Resurrection*, and he was ready to abandon everything for a great love. Hilda, as it turned out, was available for rescue. Perhaps she longed secretly to become respectable. Alex's mother violently opposed the marriage, of course. His father did, too (although Simon Liberman rather liked Hilda personally), and so did Lucien Vogel, who still hoped Alex would marry his daughter. All the more reason to defy them, then—to seize life by the throat and escape at long last (or so he fancied) from his mother's suffocating control. Alex and Hilda were married on August 25, 1936, in a civil service in Paris. The magistrate went on and on, irritatingly, about the significance of joining in matrimony a German and a Soviet citizen, whose respective countries were so antipathetic toward each other. Neither of his parents attended the ceremony.

The marriage got off to a predictably bad start. They went to the mountains at Annecy for a two-week wedding trip, in a secondhand Peugeot roadster that Alex had been able to acquire through the good offices of Bunau-Varila, Hilda's former lover; in addition to *Le Matin*, Bunau-Varila owned a garage on the rue Marbeuf. They swam, boated, fished, dined out every night, and went dancing at the Casino. Alex took many nude photographs of Hilda in a variety of esthetic and athletic poses. The trip, however, did nothing to resolve the sexual problems between them. Alex felt that Hilda was used to a high level of performance in her sexual partners—a level that he himself, with his ulcers and his limited experience, could not match. On their honeymoon, he felt humiliated by her attempts to advance his sexual education. Before they made love, he said, Hilda would strip the bed, turning it into "a sports arena." He tried hard—probably too hard—but he never quite overcame his own sense of inadequacy. He also suspected that Hilda was still in love with the sports promoter.

Back in Paris, they moved into a two-room flat that Alex had rented on the rue Boileau, in an out-of-the-way corner of the sixteenth arrondissement. Bunau-Varila and his new wife came to dinner there. (The wife later married Hervé Alphand, one of France's most distinguished diplomats; when Mme. Alphand and Alex met again at a Washington, D.C., dinner party in the fifties, they reminisced about how awkward that evening at the rue Boileau apartment had been for both of them.) One day Alex came home to find Hilda playing with a white poodle. It was a gift from Michaelis, the sports promoter—a sort of live-in reminder.

The troubles in the marriage were exacerbated by the troubles at *Vu*. The magazine's left-wing slant was alienating more and more of its advertisers. Social unrest had nearly paralyzed Léon Blum's Popular Front government at this point; strikes and riots occurred nearly every day in Paris, and many people feared that class conflicts in France were getting out of control. Unable to keep the magazine afloat, Vogel sold out in the fall of 1936 to a right-wing businessman who was a close friend of Pierre Laval, the future collaborationist premier under the Nazis. The new owner persuaded Alex to stay on and made him the managing editor. Alex redesigned the magazine, streamlining layouts and getting rid of some features that he considered old-fashioned. He also continued to design covers under the name "Alexandre" and to write movie reviews under the name "Jean Orbay." To appease his mother, who constantly pestered him for publicity, he even did a tongue-in-cheek review of the Scaramouche children's theater, singling out for special mention the "beautiful sets and ravishing costumes

Alex and Hilda on the slopes at Megève, 1936.

One of Alex's nude pictures of Hilda taken on their
wedding trip to Annecy.

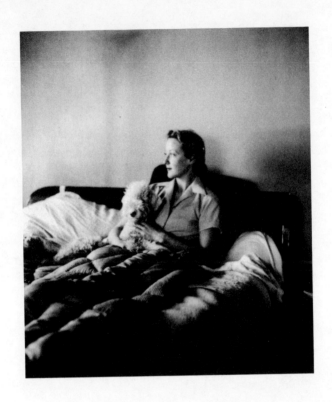

Hilda and the poodle at Villa Scaramouche.
Photographed and painted by Alex.

by Alexandre." By the end of the year, though, he was ready to quit. The magazine's political orientation was moving too far to the right, even for someone of Alex's conservative views, and his ulcers were getting steadily worse.

At Christmas he took Hilda skiing at Kitzbühel, hoping to recapture some echo of their glorious first meeting in the snow. This time, though, Hilda was forever surrounded by bronzed ski instructors and photographers—a picture of her in ski clothes would appear on the cover of the December 1937 American *Vogue*. Alex didn't know quite what to do with himself when they got back to Paris. He had left *Vu*, and there was no other job in sight. He rather resented the fact that his increasingly affluent father would not do more for him financially. Simon Liberman had established a trust fund in Alex's name ten years earlier, but the amount was fairly modest—ten thousand English pounds—and there were all sorts of restrictions on its use. Alex felt that huge amounts of money were being spent to gratify his mother's whims, and that his father could easily have afforded to arrange for his only son's financial independence. "He didn't want to do that," according to Alex. "He wanted me to be dependent on him." Liberman did invest at this time in a film project, as a means of giving his son something to do. The film, directed by Alex with the assistance of the Louvre museum staff, was a survey of female portraits over three centuries—one of the first films to be shot in color, it was called *La Femme Française dans l'Art*—and it occupied him for most of the next year.

Alex and Hilda spent a lot of time fixing up their new apartment, a larger and more attractive place in a block of detached houses called Villa Montmorency, on the avenue des Tilleuls. Hilda's mother came from Germany to stay with them there. She spoke neither French nor English, and Alex spoke no German, so communication was laborious; he compensated by painting her portrait. After she left, the couple took to spending weekends at Alex's parents' recently acquired country house in the Paris suburb of Chatou, the town where Renoir had painted his *Luncheon of the Boating Party*; a far-from-modest villa with a beautiful garden, it had been remodeled, to Henriette's specifications, by one of the leading modernist architects of the period. Their visits gave Alex's mother new opportunities to undermine the marriage. Henriette hired detectives to follow Hilda. "Do you know where your wife went today?" she would ask her son, nodding significantly. During the weekends at Chatou, Hilda sometimes announced that she was going in to Paris to buy some special ham for Alex—ham was supposed to be good for his ulcers. Alex's suspicions that she was going to

see the poodle man were not infrequently confirmed by his mother's detectives.

Simon and Henriette went to New York for several months in 1937,
and Alex and Hilda had the Chatou house to themselves that summer. It
didn't help. Alex knew that Hilda was secretly meeting Michaelis. He felt
sick a good deal of the time, and he read the news with mounting anxiety:
riots, violent anti-Semitism, the Spanish war. In late September, he reacted
to the accumulating strains in his marriage and in the world at large by
having an ulcer attack and a nervous breakdown.

When Europeans of Alexander Liberman's class and generation got
sick enough, they went to a sanitarium. In many ways this was far more
satisfactory than modern antibiotics; imagine the relief of simply leaving a
disintegrating marriage and going off to spend three months in the care of
the immaculate and tactful Swiss. Alex's haven was a small clinic on Lake
Geneva called La Lignière, where he did little but read and sleep. He read
Tolstoy and Balzac and *Gone with the Wind*. His ulcers calmed down. At
the end of December, Hilda came from Paris to join him, and they went
off together to a new life in the south of France.

In addition to the house in Chatou and the apartment in Paris,
Simon Liberman had acquired a villa in Ste. Maxime, on the Côte d'Azur,
which he offered to let Alex and Hilda use. The offer also included a modest
allowance on which they could live while Alex, who was still weak from
the ulcer attack, devoted himself full-time to becoming an artist. He had
decided at the sanitarium that this was what he wanted to do—a decision
that was fervently ratified by his mother. "It was a dream moment in my
life," he remembered. "I was free, I could paint, I could live like the
Impressionists." He had hardly painted at all since going to work for *Vu*
five years before, and he wasn't quite sure now what sort of artist he wanted
to be. The ferment of the modern movement in Paris had barely touched
him. He was dimly aware of Picasso, but the new work of Matisse, Braque,
and the Surrealists was as foreign to him as it was to most of the readers
of *Vu*, whose otherwise up-to-the-minute pages ignored the world of modern
art. Alex's esthetic gods were Leonardo and David. He longed to have
Iacovleff's facility in drawing, and despaired of acquiring it; the only post-
Impressionist artist he truly admired was Cézanne, whose clumsy drafts-
manship gave him hope. Now, at least, he could try to follow Cézanne's
example. He took his palette and easel outdoors and did some *plein air*
landscapes of the countryside near St. Tropez.

After a week of that, he attempted a portrait of Hilda, but it did
not go well. The painting was stiff and lifeless—nothing like the blond

goddess of the mountain whose beauty had blinded him the year before. Poor Hilda was bored to tears. Alex wrote to Brentano's bookstore in Paris for the largest jigsaw puzzle they had—something like a thousand pieces. Hilda worked at it every day while Alex painted. Then, one day, she was gone. She got up very early in the morning, before Alex was awake, and drove off in the Peugeot, and that was that. No note, no explanation, and no demands of any kind, then or later. "She never asked for a thing," Alex said. In many ways, her departure was a great relief.

After divorcing Alex, Hilda married the sports promoter. They had a son and were happy together. More than fifty years later, when she was a cheerful eighty-year-old widow living not far from the rue Boileau in Paris, she was amazed to hear about Alex's career as editorial director of a vast publishing empire. "That doesn't seem like him at all," she marveled. "Alex was always dreaming. He did everything to be nice and to make me comfortable. There was finally something missing, though, and I think it was that he was an artist, and I was not an artist. But he could have called me sometime."

Tatiana in Ste. Maxime, just before she and Alex met again.

Like a Blinding Flash

The end of his first marriage left no lasting scars. Alex never spoke against Hilda afterward. He often said, in fact, that he had learned a lot from her about how a man of the world conducts himself in public as well as in private situations—lessons that she herself had picked up from Bunau-Varila and the poodle man. (She even taught him that a man's undershirt should be worn outside the drawers, rather than tucked in.) Taking advantage of his new freedom, he went to bed with one of his father's former secretaries, a young Russian woman whom he met by chance in Ste. Maxime and persuaded to come home with him for the night.

That spring he put his architectural-school training to work by supervising the renovation of the gardener's cottage that went with the villa in Ste. Maxime, turning it into a small house and studio for himself. He also found an ideal bachelor's nest in Paris—a large, one-room studio with attached garden in the same block of villas where he and Hilda had had their second apartment. There was still work to be done on the Louvre film. He also started to make a film on English art—a project that was never completed—and this took him to London, where he looked up his old friend and childhood nemesis, Luba Krassin. The youngest and wildest of the Krassin girls had recently divorced her first husband, Gaston Bergery, a left-wing deputy in the French parliament who (according to Alex) had hoped to win Communist votes and influence by marrying a daughter of the well-known Soviet ambassador to France. She was working now as a fashion model for Schiaparelli in London, where she lived with her widowed mother (Leonid Krassin died in 1936) and her eight-year-old son, Lalo.

Alex had had a crush on Luba since he was Lalo's age. In the days when she used to boss him around and tie him up in his bedsheets he would often say, "You just wait until I grow up," and over the years this had developed into a provocative game between them. "She always treated me like a kid," he said, "even though she was only two years older. She called me 'Shourik,' which was the youngest diminutive of 'Shoura,' my childhood name. Every time I'd see her, I would try to make her take me seriously." He had seen quite a lot of her when she and her family were living in Paris, before she married Bergery. "She wasn't really beautiful," he said, "but she had a wonderful animal grace and extraordinary lavender eyes and a sexy, put-together quality that the French call *chien*. She was also very promiscuous."

In London, the game between them became more provocative than ever. They started living together, without becoming lovers. Alex still felt paralyzed with her, unable to take the initiative sexually, but when it was time for him to leave he invited Luba to come to the south of France. They stopped off for a few days in Paris, where they took pains to conceal their liaison; she stayed in a hotel near the Etoile, he slept in his own apartment. He bought her an expensive pair of silk pyjamas. That same evening, when he came to her hotel room, he noticed a round hole burned in the pyjama top. "She explained, without the least embarrassment, that a friend had come to the house, and that he had seemed so depressed. . . . Clearly, she had taken off the pyjamas and draped them over the lamp while they made love. I found that rather appalling." Alex and Luba went down to Ste. Maxime, nevertheless, where life got increasingly complicated.

The Ste. Maxime villa was poorly furnished. Alex did what he could to upgrade the decor, and one day, in an antique shop, he saw a pair of armchairs that looked just right. The proprietor said he couldn't sell them, though, because they were reserved for Comtesse du Plessix. "That's Tata," Luba suddenly announced. "Where is she?" Tata was Tatiana, Iacovleff's blond niece, the girl Alex could not quite remember having gone to the beach with at Hendaye in 1925. She had been married in 1929 to Bertrand du Plessix, the scion of an ancient and aristocratic French family,

Luba Krassin, 1937, in the south of France.

but, as Luba explained to Alex, the marriage had ceased to function some years earlier, when Tatiana had come home from a trip and surprised her husband in bed with the notoriously promiscuous Katia Krassin, Luba's older sister. (One of Katia's more exalted bedmates, according to Alex, was Averell Harriman.) Alex and Luba found out that Tatiana was staying near Ste. Maxime, in the company of a Russian-born naturalized-American plastic surgeon named Eugene de Sawitch. "We must call her," said Luba, who was never deterred by emotional complexities. Call her she did, and Tatiana and Dr. de Sawitch came to dinner with Alex and Luba the next evening.

Alex may not have remembered Tatiana at Hendaye, but he certainly remembered having seen her more recently at his mother's cocktail parties in the avenue Frédéric-Le-Play apartment, "She usually came with Prince Meschersky, a tall, handsome Russian aristocrat who was one of her admirers then. She dressed with great style, mostly in black, and with her long legs and blond hair she looked absolutely glorious. I always saw Tatiana then as being in movement—extraordinary movement, active and dynamic, like the *Victory of Samothrace*. If the *Victory of Samothrace* had a head, it would look like Tatiana's, I thought." One of her other admirers, the French brain surgeon Jacques Le Beau, would never forget his first sight of Tatiana, walking on top of the tables in a crowded nightclub, "like a Valkyrie," to get to where her friends were sitting.

When Alex and Tatiana met again that summer of 1938, her striking looks and imperious manner were just as he had remembered, but there was also a fragility, a vulnerable quality that was new. She had been in a terrible automobile accident two years earlier, in August 1936. (Alex learned later that the accident had occurred on the same day he had married Hilda Sturm.) As she rode in a friend's open convertible, on her way to a luncheon party at Aldous Huxley's house in Sanary, the car swerved and overturned, and she was pinned underneath it. What kept her from being killed instantly was the driver's wooden leg; the man was thrown clear, but his artificial limb, torn off and lodged near her neck, was just thick and stout enough to prevent her from being fatally crushed. When help arrived, the one-legged man had to beg them to attend to Tatiana—the police were sure that the unconscious, black-faced woman under the car was dead. Unable to detect a pulse when they finally did extricate her, they took her to the morgue at Hyères, the nearest town, which is where her husband found her many hours later. She was alive, but just barely.

Her injuries included a damaged larynx, multiple fractures, and severe burns from the battery acid that had dripped on her hand and back while she lay under the car. After two weeks in the Toulon hospital, du Plessix got her moved to the American Hospital in Paris, where Dr. de Sawitch rebuilt her burned right hand, arm, and back with 360 skin grafts, falling in love with her in the process. "He operated on me twenty-two times," Tatiana said once, "and between the anesthetics he tried to persuade me to divorce du Plessix and marry him." She came out of the ordeal with a partially crippled right hand and a hoarse speaking voice, but with her enormous vitality intact.

She was delighted to see Luba and Alex, and they both liked Dr. de Sawitch, who had given up hope of marrying Tatiana although he was still very obviously in love with her. The four of them saw each other frequently during the next two weeks. They went to the beach together, tried out new restaurants, and went dancing at night. Alex found himself increasingly attracted to this statuesque woman—she was five feet, nine and a half inches, half an inch shorter than he was—whose bold and sometimes overbearing manner did not quite hide her inner hurts and anxieties. (She kept her damaged right hand wrapped in a silk scarf at all times.) Tatiana was clearly attracted to Alex, who had two of the three assets that she always looked for in a man: upper-class manners and a well-kept, aristocratic-looking body. (He lacked the third asset, which was a title.) One day on the beach, he felt an odd sensation. "She was sitting down; I was standing. I turned around and saw her looking at me in a curious way, and I just felt that something was happening. Another time, we were driving home from a restaurant; Tatiana and I were in the back seat, and I touched her arm and said, 'You have wonderful skin.' There was also an evening when Tatiana and I escaped from the others and went dancing at some place in Ste. Maxime. At a certain point I said I had to get back to Luba. And it's strange, it was very strange—the minute I began to feel emotionally involved with Tatiana, I was able to treat Luba as a real mistress. That hadn't happened before."

For two days during this period, Tatiana left them to go on an overnight cruise to Corsica with a very rich French banker named Wormser, to whom she seemed to have some mysterious obligation. She arranged for Alex to paint de Sawitch's portrait while she was on Wormser's yacht—a project that was carried out with considerable glumness on both sides of the easel. Alex never did understand Tatiana's relationship with Wormser. Although he wanted to marry her, she said, she refused to let him touch her. She caused Alex intense pain a year later, though, by spending a week with Wormser in St. Moritz.

When Luba had to go back to London and her job at Schiaparelli, Alex went with her and rented a house for them in Kensington. To occupy his time, he painted a portrait of her son, Lalo, who was becoming quite attached to Alex by this time. Luba seems to have decided that she and Alex would get married, but her mother, who was a great friend of Alex's father, undertook to protect Simon Liberman's son from her unpredictable daughter. "Just go, Shoura," she warned him. "Leave. This is not for you. You're going to be hurt." Alex knew she was right, but what gave him the strength to act was a letter he received from Tatiana in Paris. She wrote to ask whether he would be interested in buying her uncle's library. Alexandre Iacovleff had gone to the United States in 1934. He had been invited to teach at the School of the Museum of Fine Arts in Boston, and he had had considerable success there as a society painter, but his seemingly charmed life had been cut short, at the age of forty-eight, by cancer. As the executor of his will, Tatiana was responsible for disposing of an estate that consisted for the most part of a few pieces of good furniture, hundreds of relatively worthless sketches, and a library of art and general reference books in several languages. Did she really think of Alex as a potential buyer, or was she sending him a signal? It hardly mattered. He left for Paris immediately, saying nothing to Luba or Lalo. "I did what her mother had been telling me to do," he said. "I abandoned them, to my shame. I left her the way Hilda had left me."

Alex bought Iacovleff's books—the art histories, the Russian classics, J. H. Fabre's ten-volume *Souvenirs entomologiques*. They followed him to America and occupied his own library shelves, mostly unread, for the next half century. The real prize, though, was Tatiana, and he pursued it obsessively. She and Bertrand du Plessix still shared an apartment on the rue de Longchamp, although they led separate lives inside and outside it; they were keeping up appearances for the sake of their daughter, Francine, who was eight years old in 1938. Alex came to dinner there one night. He and Tatiana were lovers by then, and it was an excruciating embarrassment for him to sit at the table with her and her suave, polished husband and her flirtatious younger sister, Lila, making polite conversation while Tatiana directed unsettling and even provocative remarks to him. "She was completely self-assured and quite wild," he recalled. "Twice during that evening she pulled me into another room, closed the door, and covered my face with kisses."

They saw each other every day, sometimes more than once. Tatiana brought Francine to his studio at the Villa Montmorency so he could paint her portrait; Francine remembered thinking he was the nicest man she had ever met. When du Plessix went to visit his family in Brittany, Alex took Tatiana and Francine skiing at Megève. Tatiana loved to ski, although she was no better at it than Alex. "Her legs were too long, and she was not that well coordinated," he said. "She tore some ligaments on that trip, so we had to go back early. She was tomboyish and aggressive, a bundle of uncivilized energy in many ways, but glorious. She would take the most incredible risks, and she moved with such flamboyance and daring. Everything about her was big and exciting. Her clothes were from Piguet, one of the best dressmakers in Paris then—Dior used to work for him. Piguet admired her style so much that he gave her things for practically nothing. It was good publicity for him."

The night they became lovers, they had dinner at a Montmartre bistro with Dr. de Sawitch and one of Tatiana's older woman friends. When the two ladies went to the powder room, de Sawitch told Alex that there was "absolutely nothing between Tatiana and me." The words seemed like a signal. Later, Alex and Tatiana slipped off by themselves to the Villa Montmorency studio. "I was both afraid and triumphant," Alex said. "Fear and trembling. She was wearing—I don't know. Am I betraying her by speaking of it? She would be appalled if she knew. She had such *pudeur*—

a word that doesn't really translate into English—such purity of mind and body. I think she was wearing a black or green satin gown, and she had a jacket with that curly black fur, and a Cossack hat on her blond hair. And the extraordinary thing was this absolute commitment to love. I must have been yearning for that all along. It was like a blinding flash, like a revelation, the most extraordinary experience of my life. After we slept together for the first time, I knew that my life had changed forever."

Tatiana at Va-et-Vient in 1939—"the greatest moment of our life."

Tatiana

Tatiana's daughter, Francine, who became the writer Francine du Plessix Gray, has distilled from family tales this description of her mother's 1925 arrival from Russia at the Gare de l'Est in Paris, where she was met by her "Baboushka" (grandmother) and her aunt Sandra: "The tempestuous teenager who steps off the train—gorgeous, unwashed, dressed in rags, as untutored and unmannered as any other Communist youth—spends the next hour vociferating her extravagant desires, her high expectations of Parisian life. Where can one buy the cheapest furs? What do diamonds look like? Which are the best parties, where does one meet the most glamorous, well-born Frenchmen? As the three women get into the cab to go home, Baboushka whispers to . . . Sandra: 'All the Communist garbage we'd expected, and on top of it she wants to be a countess.' "

That she achieved this goal within four years came as no particular surprise to her relatives. Tatiana's high expectations went back to her earliest childhood in St. Petersburg, where she was the pampered favorite in a well-to-do, upper-class, intellectually distinguished family. (Tatiana's younger sister Lila, "the Duchess," always maintained that they belonged to the aristocracy.) Her mother's father had been a high-ranking government official. Her father's family, the Iacovleffs, had achieved eminence in diplomacy, the navy, and the sciences—Tatiana's paternal grandfather is said to have invented the principle of the diesel engine and sold it to the German firm Mercedes-Benz. Alexander Herzen, the nineteenth-century revolutionary leader and writer, was a distant relative, and so was Constantin Stanislavsky. Tatiana's parents spoke French to one another, in the manner of czarist aristocrats, and dressed their two daughters in Paquin frocks imported from Paris. Lila (Ludmilla), two years younger than Tatiana, was chronically jealous of the attention that her older sister demanded and received.

Alexis Iacovleff, their father, was a government-employed architect who specialized in designing theaters. Just before the First World War, when Tatiana was seven, he won a competition to build the new opera house in Penza, a good-sized provincial town about four hundred miles southeast of Moscow. The family moved there with him, bringing along a bevy of servants—cook, coachman, German governess, maids—and continued for another year or so to enjoy their privileged and somewhat eccentric life. Iacovleff, who loved tinkering with engines, managed to buy a used airplane—he named it "Mademoiselle"—which he taught himself to fly, frightening the cows and amazing the peasants, who used to run up to the house after one of his bumpy landings and say, "The master has fallen down!" When war seemed imminent, he volunteered his services and was made a commander of the first motorized unit in the czarist army. In 1917 he was sent to Japan on a military procurement mission. The revolution broke out while he was there, and either because he could not return to Russia or because he simply decided not to risk it, Alexis Iacovleff made his way to the United States and an entirely new life. He changed his name to Jackson, acquired a Russian-émigré wife (by then Tatiana's mother had divorced him and remarried), and lived out the rest of his days working as a mechanical engineer, first in San Francisco, then in Rochester, New York, and eventually in New York City.

His abandoned family had a very hard time of it, in those desperate years immediately following the revolution. Penza was in one of the worst famine areas. "In that region," Tatiana remembered, "there were cases of parents eating their children." Gradually reduced to living in one room of their boarded-up house, the three women made soup from nettles and cabbage stems, and burned books from their extensive library to keep from freezing in the winter. Fourteen-year-old Tatiana sometimes brought home potatoes that she had earned by reciting poetry to soldiers. Although she had received only one year of formal schooling, her childhood tutors had awakened in her a passionate love of Russian poetry and literature. She knew by heart the works of Pushkin, Lermontov, Blok, Essenin, and others, and her street-corner recitations often brought tears to the eyes of her awed and home-sick listeners. The years of privation took their toll, however; she became gaunt and hollow-eyed, and in 1925 she developed the first symptoms of tuberculosis. It was at this point that her uncle Alexandre Iacovleff stepped in like a deus ex machina, inducing the auto magnate André-Gustave Citroën to use his contacts with the Soviet government to spirit Tatiana out of Russia in the sleeping compartment of the French ambassador to Moscow.

The grandmother and the aunt who met Tatiana at the Gare de l'Est were formidable personalities. Grandmother Iacovleff had been the first woman to graduate from the University of St. Petersburg, receiving a degree in mathematics there in 1890. Aunt Sandra was a dramatic soprano. She had been one of the stars of the St. Petersburg opera, and she continued to perform in public after leaving Russia, often teaming with her former colleague Boris Chaliapin. The two women had been in Paris since 1923, living in a five-room apartment in Montmartre, supported to a large extent by the earnings of Alexandre Iacovleff, Sandra's artist brother, who had his own duplex studio-apartment a few blocks away. Tatiana showed great respect for her new guardians, who were, after all, extremely proper Old World White Russians. She did what they told her to do, for the most part, and went to great lengths to avoid causing them undue distress. Henriette Pascar used to tell people that Iacovleff had brought his niece around to her apartment a day or so after she arrived from Russia and told her to "dress this savage"—a story that Tatiana indignantly denied. According to Tatiana, her uncle himself took her to his great friend Gabrielle Chanel, who dressed her from head to toe. Tatiana's aunt Sandra, the opera singer, took her off that summer to Hendaye, where she was cured of the spot on her lungs. Tatiana remembered meeting Henriette's son, Alex, there and taking him to the beach. She found him extremely polite.

In a long interview with Gennady Smakov, a Soviet émigré who once planned to write Tatiana's biography but who gave up the idea because he felt she was withholding vital information, Tatiana described her early life in Paris as an unbroken series of triumphs. Refusing to accept support from Uncle Sacha (Alexandre), she gives up her early ambition to become a concert pianist and enters the Ecole de Couture. Her grandmother's friend Fatma Hanoum (a Turkish woman "from a very noble *Caucasian* family," as Tatiana puts it) teaches her about millinery, and soon she is earning good money as a designer of ladies' hats. She does some modeling for Christmas cards and stocking advertisements ("I had extremely beautiful legs"), meets and charms all the amusing people, and discovers that she has "extraordinary sex appeal." Men fall in love with her right and left, beginning with her uncle Yura Kuzmin (one of her mother's brothers), who writes her a love letter that is found by her grandmother, creating a scandal. Uncle Yura, banished from the household, gives way to a thoroughly respectable cousin named I. I. Mechnikov, a real Russian aristocrat, who becomes her official fiancé. He takes her to museums, where she acquires a lifelong appreciation for the art of previous centuries. On a weekend visit to Amsterdam with Mechnikov, she "discovers" Vermeer—"the greatest artist in the world, whom no one knows." (A lot of teasing from her relatives over that.)

She plays Brahms piano duets with Sergei Prokofiev, who had gone to school in St. Petersburg with Uncle Sacha. ("He was a sweet, timid person, and he played in a very funny manner, like a rabbit, throwing his hands on the keyboard in short movements.") Her musical talent draws her into the orbit of her uncle's great friend Zizi de Svirsky, a pianist who was unable to give public concerts because the sight of an audience caused him to faint. Svirsky falls in love with her and invites her to evenings of piano music at his house, where she meets *le tout Paris*—André Gide, Jean Cocteau, Louis Aragon, Elsa Triolet, Marie-Laure de Noailles, Jean-Paul Fargue, Christian (Bébé) Bérard, Boris Kochno, the Prince de Bourbon-Parme, and so on. "I was a great success at his parties. My uncle Sacha was frightened by my unbelievable success—he was afraid I would become a courtesan. I understood my power over men only in Paris."

Then comes the meeting that links her to history. It is late October, 1928. On her way to a doctor's office, where she is going for treatment of severe bronchitis, she sees Elsa Triolet, a Russian-born poet living in Paris. (She later married the French poet Louis Aragon.) Tatiana recognizes Triolet from Svirsky's parties, but not the tall, elegant-looking man with her. He could be English, in his stylish suit, but the crew cut and the flow of Russian words belie this first impression. He is Vladimir Mayakovsky, the leading literary figure of postrevolutionary Russia. "I was astonished by Mayakovsky's manners," she remembered. "They were simple and exquisite." Mayakovsky insists on taking her to the doctor's office himself, in a taxi, and on the way, while she tries to avoid coughing in his face, he declares his infatuation for her. "He fell on his knees in the taxi and proposed to me," according to Tatiana. "Elsa called me the next day and invited me for dinner. I told my grandmother that I was going to Svirsky's. If she had known I was going to dinner with a Bolshevist poet, she would have had a heart attack."

Elsa Triolet had invited Tatiana to dinner because she was at a loss for ways to entertain Mayakovsky, who spoke no French. She also thought it would be amusing to pair Mayakovsky with a Russian girl who was nearly as tall as he was. The great love of Mayakovsky's life had been Lili Brik, Elsa's sister. Lili, her husband, Osip Brik, and Mayakovsky kept a sort of ménage à trois in Moscow that reflected the new style of "open" relationships among Communist intellectuals; Mayakovsky had always felt free to have affairs with other women, and Elsa was not overly disturbed by his sudden passion for Tatiana Iacovleva. Not the least of Tatiana's attractions was that she knew a great many Russian poems by heart—she told him about reciting them to Red Army soldiers in exchange for potatoes. He was clearly enraptured by what he called her "absolute ear" for Russian poetry, which he compared to a musician's perfect pitch. "Tatiana was young and pretty," according to Triolet. "It was a short-lived beauty, but in the period of its flowering she made a great impression. She was very tall, had long legs and arms . . . Mayakovsky fell in love with her on the spot."

They saw each other every day for the rest of the time he was in Paris, meeting at the Coupole, in Montparnasse, not far from the Hotel Istria, where Mayakovsky was staying. "I was sure I wouldn't see my grandmother there," Tatiana recalled. "My aunt was away from Paris, performing with Chaliapin, and my uncle was also on a trip." She and Mayakovsky went to the theater together, and she attended all his public recitals; before long, the recitals included two poems inspired by his new love. Mayakovsky's "Letter from Paris to Comrade Kostrov on the Essence of Love" opens with these lines:

> Picture this:
>
> a beauty
>
> all inset in furs
> and beads,
>
> enters a drawing room.
> I
> seized
> this beauty
> and said:
> . . . Comrade,
> I come from
> Russia;
> I am famous in my land . . .

His urgent proposals to marry her and take her back to Russia with him, and her hesitation, are reflected in the last lines of the "Letter to Tatiana Iacovleva":

> You don't want to come?
> > Stay there and hibernate.
> This insult
> > I will string onto a thread with many others.
> I will
> > conquer you
> > > one day—
> Alone
> > or along with Paris.

"I understood perfectly well that everything in Mayakovsky's life changed when he saw me," Tatiana told Gennady Smakov. "From the beginning of our relationship I felt such tenderness and concern toward me. . . . When did I fall in love with him? I think by the end of his first stay in Paris. He was the first man I loved seriously."

The poet returned to Moscow in December. Lili Brik "broke everything in the house" when he told her about Tatiana (according to Tatiana); other accounts indicate that while Lili was upset by the "Letter to Tatiana Iacovleva," she assumed the affair was no more serious than the many others. Later on, she burned Tatiana's letters to him. Mayakovsky wrote to Tatiana that he was working "twenty hours a day" on his new play, *The Bedbug*. "I work like a bull, lowering my muzzle with its red eyes over the desk. . . . When I am altogether tired, I say to myself, 'Tatiana,' and again, animal-like, bite into the paper. . . . I do not write to you much (professional hatred of writing), but if all my conversations with myself concerning you were put together, all those unwritten letters, unsaid affectionate things, then my collected works would be three times as fat with sheer lyrical stuff."

He returned to Paris the following February and redoubled his efforts to take her back to Russia with him. Her reluctance was understandable. She felt no nostalgia for the country where she had nearly starved to death and where, because of her father, she was considered an enemy of the state. On the other hand, she had fallen deeply in love with the poet. Her family knew about the affair by this time and naturally disapproved of it. (Mayakovsky had instructed Lili Brik to send some money to Tatiana's mother in Penza.) Tatiana and Mayakovsky were remarkably alike in temperament—voluble, impulsive, emotionally reckless. Tatiana had a strict sense of propriety, however, and she refused to go to bed with him. "Her upbringing prevented it," according to Iuri Tiourin, the confidant of her last years. "Besides, Mayakovsky had made a formal proposal, and she saw no reason to rush things." Tatiana appears to have been somewhat less committed than he was, though, for she managed to keep several other suitors on the string at the same time. Mayakovsky caught a glimpse of her kissing one of them in the dark entranceway of her apartment building after he had dropped her off there one night. He told Elsa Triolet about it, saying, "It's finished. A broken cup can be glued, but it's still broken." He and Tatiana continued to see each other afterward, though, and when Mayakovsky went back to Russia in April, Tatiana told close friends that he would return for her in the fall and that she was going to marry him. Before leaving, Mayakovsky gave a large sum of money to a Paris florist, with orders to deliver flowers to Tatiana every Sunday.

Back in Moscow, he managed to procure an exit visa for Tatiana's younger sister Lila to come to Paris. This was probably unwise. Mayakovsky's scathing attitude toward the new Soviet bureaucracy, powerfully expressed in his poems and plays, had made him many enemies, and this effort in behalf of a White Russian family gave them extra ammunition. By a cruel irony, the authorities revoked his own passport in September, just as he was preparing to go back to Paris. There is speculation that Lili Brik may have gone to the secret police to keep him from leaving. She knew by then that Mayakovsky was desperately in love with Tatiana, and that even though he was currently pursuing a new love affair with a young actress, he fully intended to marry Tatiana. On October 11, Lili received a letter from her sister in Paris, Elsa Triolet. She opened it in Mayakovsky's presence and read it aloud. Two sentences stunned them both: Tatiana Iacovleva was going to marry a *vicomte*, Elsa wrote; a church wedding was planned for December. Mayakovsky said nothing. Six months later, profoundly depressed by a mountain of political and personal woes (including the imminent breakup of his affair with the young actress), the poet shot himself through the heart. "I knew I loved him," Tatiana told Smakov. "I would have left if he had come for the third time."

The man she married instead of Mayakovsky was an aristocrat, if not quite a *vicomte*. He was Bertrand du Plessix, a handsome, polished young Frenchman from a very old but rather impoverished family, whose ancestral seat was in the Vendée. His father held the title, but never used it; the family was scornful of such affectations. Bertrand, who was not even eligible for the title (he had four older brothers), nevertheless began using it after he married Tatiana, no doubt at her insistence—titles mattered to

Tatiana all her life—and the young couple had the family crest embossed
on their linens and calling cards. A brilliant scholar who was fluent in four
languages, Bertrand had recently passed the examination for the French
diplomatic service. When he took his bride to Warsaw, his first diplomatic
posting, she was pleased to be known as Madame La Vicomtesse du Plessix.

Life in Polish diplomatic circles was very grand then. The couple
were entertained at vast estates where feudal customs still prevailed, and
chambermaids were corrected by slaps in the face. The wife of the French
ambassador, Pauline La Roche, took it upon herself to instruct Tatiana in
the intricacies of official etiquette: how to seat the guests at dinner according
to rank, how to plan menus for state occasions, and so forth. Tatiana never
forgot these useful lessons; she applied them to her own social gatherings
for the rest of her life, and she was contemptuous of anyone who picked
up the wrong fork at dinner. Before long, though, she began to feel intensely
homesick for Paris. This may have had something to do with the birth of
their daughter, Francine, in September 1930.* She began to miss the
comforts and amenities of her adopted city, and to feel an increasing an-
tipathy toward the arrogance and anti-Semitism of the Polish upper class.
(Tatiana's best friend in Warsaw was a wealthy young Jewish woman named
Irene Baruch.)

There are conflicting explanations for their abrupt departure from
Warsaw. According to one, Tatiana put such pressure on Bertrand to buy
her expensive clothes, furs, and jewelry that he became involved in selling
diplomatic favors to shady commercial interests, got caught, and was forced
to resign from the foreign service. In another version, Tatiana, at a formal
dinner party, was heard to say in a very loud voice, *"Je déteste les polonais!"*
Late in 1930, at any rate, the young couple and their infant daughter
returned, in something resembling disgrace, to Paris, where Bertrand, no
longer in the diplomatic corps, tried his hand first at journalism, then at
various business ventures.

They settled into a pleasant apartment in the sixteenth arrondissement and began to lead an active and glittering social life. Tatiana and
Bertrand won prizes for waltz contests at the most exclusive society balls.
Tatiana's earlier friendships with musicians and writers gave them access
to the lively cultural scene; Bertrand's brief diplomatic career provided them

---

* A number of Soviet literary enthusiasts have suggested that Francine was Mayakovsky's daughter. Since the poet left Paris for the last time in May 1929, their
enthusiasm cannot be shared.

with a different set of friends, which included a number of Americans—among them William C. Bullitt, George Kennan, and Walter Duranty—who would later prove helpful to Tatiana in the United States. Tatiana and Bertrand were an exceptionally handsome couple, especially at white-tie evenings, where Tatiana's regal figure was set off by her Piguet ball gowns. Tatiana and her friend Lee Miller, the American photographer, were said to be the two most beautiful women in Paris. The worm in the apple was that Bertrand found quite a few other women more appealing. He took a series of mistresses, the first of whom was Katia Krassin, Luba's older sister, whom he must have met through Tatiana.* When she found them in bed together, the marriage sustained a fatal blow. Tatiana, in her extreme and implacable pride, could not accommodate infidelity. She and Bertrand moved into separate bedrooms and assumed separate lives.

Tatiana's automobile accident in 1936 did not bring them any closer together. After spending months in the hospital, Tatiana went to convalesce in Antwerp with her American friends John and Irene Wiley—Irene Baruch, Tatiana's friend in Warsaw, had married John Cooper Wiley, a foreign-service officer who was serving then in the U.S. embassy in Belgium. Her complete recovery took two years. Although she and Bertrand moved to a new apartment in the fashionable rue de Longchamp in 1938, they were further apart than ever. "Your mother is an intelligent but misled woman who does not love us," Francine remembers her father saying to her. Du Plessix was a great charmer, a highly intelligent man who excelled at sports (he became a crack airplane pilot) and who was well liked among the upper-class international set in Paris; he was also a snob, a fervent right-winger, and an anti-Semite. Francine remembers being terribly ashamed when she heard him refer to Alex Liberman as a "dirty little Jew." By this time, eight-year-old Francine was totally won over by Alex, and the remark was like "a slap in my own face." Du Plessix was obviously aware that Tatiana and Alex were having an affair.

In Alex's mind (and in Tatiana's) it was much more than an affair. His passion for her encompassed all the chivalrous ideals of his lonely, bookish childhood: she was the fair lady of medieval romance for whom no sacrifice could ever be too great. She was also his soulmate in eros; with her, the fears of sexual inadequacy that had haunted all his previous re-

---

* The Russian-exile colony in Paris was incestuously intertwined. Simon Liberman, who adored opera singers, apparently had an affair at one time with Tatiana's aunt Sandra.

Tatiana soon after her arrival in Paris.
She is modeling jewelry for French *Vogue*.

Right: Tatiana Iacovleva and
her *karmilitsa* (wet nurse),
St. Petersburg. The baby clothes
were imported from Paris.

Below: Vladimir Mayakovsky, whose
poems to Tatiana have become
Russian classics.

Bottom: Bertrand and Tatiana du
Plessix, at a "White Ball" in Warsaw,
1930.

lationships with women simply disappeared. "The extraordinary thing with Tatiana was this absolute abandon to me and for me," he said. "She would go beyond what I thought was possible."

"You know how to love me as no woman has ever loved," he wrote to her in 1939, "and through your thoughts, a man was born."

In Paris, he organized his life around the times they could be together. Tatiana had a workshop in the back room of her apartment, where she designed hats for a number of wealthy society women. (One of her customers was Henriette Pascar.) Alex helped deliver the finished creations, driving Tatiana around Paris in the new silver-gray Citroën convertible that his father had bought for him. When she was unavailable, he spent most of his time working in his studio, "trying to paint like Vermeer, to please Tatiana." Bertrand reacted to the situation by becoming more and more possessive of Francine, who until then had been brought up mainly by a fanatically overprotective Russian governess. When he took Francine off on a trip with him at the beginning of 1939, Alex and Tatiana were able to spend eight days together in Ste. Maxime. She came there straight from St. Moritz, where she had been invited by her banker friend, Wormser—an anguished week for Alex, but one that probably made her seem even more desirable to him. Their reunion in Ste. Maxime was "the greatest moment of our life," Alex said. "The feeling was indescribably strong. I knew, and I'm sure Tatiana knew, that this was for life."

The storm that was gathering over Europe then gave an extra urgency to personal events. Tatiana had been visiting her friends the Wileys in Vienna, their new diplomatic post, when the *Anschluss* took place, in March 1938. She saw Hitler's triumphal entry and was appalled by the wild enthusiasm of the Austrian street crowds. The Czechoslovakian crisis that September coincided with the start of her affair with Alex. When Germany invaded Poland a year later, Bertrand du Plessix was called up immediately. An officer in the French air corps who spoke Polish, he was sent as a member of the French mission to Poland, where the German blitzkrieg obliterated all resistance in a few days. Du Plessix escaped with a remnant of the defeated army through Romania and managed eventually, after several months, to make his way back to France by way of Egypt.

When war was declared in September, Francine was sent with her governess to Arcachon, near the Atlantic coast, where Tatiana's uncle Yura Kuzmin had a small house. Alex persuaded Tatiana at this point to come and live with him at his parents' villa in Chatou, outside Paris. His mother was there, too, and not at all pleased to have a live-in rival. Although she had once praised Tatiana to Alex as a woman who might be worthy of him,

Henriette had clearly revised her opinion. "Tania is everything to me," Alex explained in a letter to his father, in New York. Although he added, hopefully, that "even Mama is beginning to see her qualities," he conceded in a subsequent letter that "Mama is . . . as jealous as ever." Tatiana had joined a civil defense unit in Paris, whose job was to help people in the event of poison gas attacks. (The fear of gas attacks had been the main reason for sending Francine away from Paris.) She was trained to identify the different chemical agents by smell and outfitted with a cumbersome protective uniform and a small Fiat ambulance to drive to the target areas.

Alex himself expected to be called up for military service, in spite of his ulcers. The patriotic fervor of the moment and Tatiana's civil defense work were making him feel like a slacker. "I'm ashamed of doing nothing when all my friends have been drafted," he wrote in a letter to his father. He divided his time between painting a portrait of Charles Vildrac, a well-known novelist and playwright, and working on his film about English art. He was able to get gas for his car during this period of rationing because he could claim to be the director of a film company—his own, which his father had set up for him. Hoping to do something for the war effort, he besieged the Ministry of Education with ideas for propaganda films.

The Chatou ménage broke up in the early spring, when Tatiana and Francine moved back to their apartment on the rue de Longchamp. Bertrand du Plessix, repatriated at last, was in the Val-de-Grâce military hospital in Paris with a severe case of jaundice. Tatiana brought him lunch every day; Alex drove her there in his car and waited outside during the visit. Tatiana was merely doing what she felt to be her duty. The marriage was over, she had told Alex, and nothing could interfere with her commitment to him. Alex's father kept urging his wife and son to leave Paris and join him in New York, but both of them had reasons for wanting to stay, and like many Parisians during this period of what was being called the "phony war," they had great faith in the Maginot Line defenses. Alex was hurt that his father's letters never mentioned Tatiana. "I believe that neither Mama nor you has understood how lucky I was to meet her," he complained, "and the two of you don't grasp the depth of my feelings."

The German blitzkrieg that May took everyone by surprise. One hundred thirty-six German divisions overran Belgium and the Netherlands, then wheeled south into France. Alex received orders to report to a military unit in Paris—at this point everyone was being called up—but when he presented himself he found that the unit had already been sent to Royan, on the Atlantic coast, north of Bordeaux, and Alex was told to catch up with it there. After a hurried, painful parting from Tatiana, who apparently did not seem as upset as he thought she should, he loaded his little Citroën two-seater with extra cannisters of gasoline, picked up his mother at the house in Chatou, and joined the frantic exodus. It was June 10. The roads were clogged with refugees and retreating French troops. Strafing raids by German planes spread terror and confusion, and kept French reinforcements from moving up. "At one point," Alex said, "a French officer put a revolver to my head and said, 'Get off the road, the army has to come through.' And somehow, I did manage to get off the main road and continue on byroads. I had maps, and I knew the roads pretty well. I thought that maybe in small villages there would still be some gasoline left, and in one or two instances there was. After many detours we got to Royan, where I was supposed to find my army unit, but by then the fighting was more or less finished. In Royan we heard Marshal Pétain's voice on the radio announcing France's capitulation, and little white posters went up on all the walls saying that it was forbidden to move, that the roads must be kept free, that the friendly German forces were going to occupy the town, and that everyone should remain calm."

Tatiana had told Alex that she was taking Francine to a friend's chateau near Tours. He wrote to her there, begging her to join him in Royan. "I cannot live without you," she replied. "You are absolutely indispensable to me." But there was no time for a reunion. Being Jewish, Alex knew that he and his mother had to go south, away from the Germans, before it was too late. "My life, my everything!" he wrote, "I left Royan with a breaking heart and kept thinking every second, what if you arrive several minutes after I've gone? My soul hurts for our country, I feel so helpless! Everything is happening on such a universal scale that personal pains, sufferings and emotions seem ridiculous, but at the same time the sum of these emotions create the events. Whatever happens, thanks to you I was so happy. . . . Since we parted, your image has always remained before my eyes, and at every turn of the road it seems to me that maybe I will find you there!—and I believe I will."

Alex and Henriette had left Royan early in the morning on June 12, two days before the Germans entered Paris. "As it happened," Alex recalled, "I had a pink slip of paper that was called a *permis de circuler*, a permission to travel. I had managed to get it the year before, from a man named Alfred Mallet, who was the main business representative of the new, right-wing owner of *Vu*. He had political connections. I had asked Mallet if he could get me a permit so I could go to our house in the south of France (there were travel restrictions even then), and he had asked what I could do for him in return—everything was corruption and bribery. He said, 'You know, I need a car.' And so I borrowed money from my father in New York and bought a secondhand Fiat and gave it to Mallet, and he got me this pink paper from the War Office. When I drove out of Royan with my mother there were gendarmes on the road, and we were stopped. The gendarme said nobody was allowed to move. I showed him the pink slip. He said, 'No, no, the orders are that nobody moves. You have to go back.' I turned the car around and drove about two hundred yards, and then I decided this was too stupid. I went back to the same gendarme and said, 'How can you stop me? Look at this paper. It says, "Allowed to circulate in the war zone." And he said, 'Well, go ahead then.' What I learned in that moment was never to take no for an answer."

They drove all the way south, to the country house of his old school chum Jean-Pierre Fourneau in Ascain, in the hills above St.-Jean-de-Luz, keeping to back roads and miraculously finding gas when they were just about to run out of it. "And all the way my mother was practically hysterical and saying horrible things about Tatiana. 'I'm glad that's finished,' she'd say. 'Forget it. She is back with her husband, of course. She would never have married you. She'll never let go of her title,' and so forth. And at that time I was wild with anxiety over Tatiana, not knowing what had happened to her and not being able to find out. We stayed for several days with the Fourneau family. By that time it had been announced that there was to be an unoccupied zone in the south of France, where the French would retain sovereignty, and so I decided that we should go to our house in Ste. Maxime. It took four days, traveling by back roads and looking for small villages where we could buy gas."

Three days before the Germans took Paris, Tatiana and Francine had left the city in the little Fiat ambulance, heading west toward Tours. They had lost contact with Alex and with Bertrand; out of the hospital since May, Bertrand was with a French air force unit in Bordeaux when the exodus began. Francine, who had spent relatively little time with her mother up to this point, was amazed by her boldness and her resourceful energy. For the next two months they lived in the Château de Villandry near Tours, helping to care for refugee children. The chateau, with its famous gardens designed in the seventeenth century by Le Nôtre, belonged to Tatiana's friend Isabelle de La Bouillerie. She had turned it into a hospice for children who had been separated from their parents (or whose parents had been killed) during the exodus. At one point they were feeding 122 children, along with quite a few adults who were hiding there from the fighting around Tours. A sixteen-year-old Hungarian girl named Gitta Sereny, whom Tatiana had met at the refugee center in Paris where both of them had been

doing volunteer work, also turned up at the chateau. She remembers Tatiana scrubbing floors with great energy, although "suffering humanity
really wasn't her speed." During a bombing attack one night, some local people sought shelter in the cellars of the estate. Tatiana took it upon herself to
keep them from striking matches and setting fire to the dry hay stored there;
she strode through the cellars at night like a Polish *seigneur*, delivering furious tongue-lashings and slaps to anyone she caught smoking.

When the fighting in the area ended, Tatiana drove her ambulance
into Tours to see about getting a permit to go to the south of France. She
took Francine with her, because she was afraid to leave her alone. In Tours,
which had suffered heavy damage, their Fiat was rammed head-on by a
German staff car going the wrong way on a one-way street. Tatiana described what happened: "My car was overturned. The Germans in the
Mercedes pulled me out and pulled out Froska [Francine], whose forehead
was cut and bleeding, and told me that I had attacked a German officer. I
said that it would be very stupid for me to attack such a huge car in my
little one, and that if I had been going to do that I would hardly have
brought my daughter along. I also told them I was on my way to see the
German commander in Tours. I showed them my papers and said, 'Take
me to the *Kommandant*.' They took me to the *Kommandant*'s office, and he
received me after seeing my visiting card. I entered his office with Froska,
who was holding a handkerchief to her bleeding forehead. He asked what
he could do for me. I requested a bandage for Froska's forehead. A German
woman in uniform came and dressed the cut. Meanwhile, the *Kommandant*
had been looking at my card. Suddenly he said, in beautiful French, 'Madame du Plessix, are you a descendant of the Duc du Plessis de Richelieu?'
I answered defiantly, 'No, I am a descendant of la Dame aux Camélias.'
He started laughing when he understood the joke. [In Dumas's play, the
heroine's name is Duplessis.] It turned out that he had been a professor
of French literature. After that he was very cooperative and gallant—he
wasn't a Nazi. He opened a drawer in his desk and took out a cigar box,
which he offered to Francine and then to me. They were chocolate cigars."

A few days later, the same Mercedes staff car pulled up at the door
of the Château de Villandry with a message for Tatiana. She was to come
to the *Kommandant*'s office right away. When she got there, the *Kommandant*
told her that she must pick up her car (which was being repaired at a
garage in Tours) and drive directly to Vichy, the seat of the collaborationist
Pétain government, where she would receive news about her husband. She
had to go alone—her daughter would stay behind as a hostage—and she
must be back within forty-eight hours. Tatiana didn't see a single civilian

car on the road to Vichy. When she got there in the late afternoon, she went straight to a hairdresser she had known in Paris, to get rid of the head lice that afflicted everyone at the Château de Villandry. He treated her free of charge and gave her a bottle of medicated lotion for Francine. The next morning she found out that her husband was missing in action and presumed dead.

Lieutenant Bertrand du Plessix had flown his plane to North Africa in response to General de Gaulle's appeal, issued on June 18 by radio from London, for volunteers to join him and defy the capitulation. (Du Plessix's quick response would lead to his being cited posthumously as one of the first four heroes of the Resistance.) In Casablanca he joined a squadron of ace pilots, whose plan was to fly to Gibraltar; the British navy would take them the rest of the way to England, where they would join de Gaulle's forces. Approaching Gibraltar on June 30, though, the squadron came under attack by the Spanish antiaircraft batteries on the surrounding hills, and du Plessix's plane was shot down. The French authorities told Tatiana that her husband was listed as missing in action, and warned her to leave the occupied zone as quickly as she could, because those who had gone over to de Gaulle were considered traitors, and their families could expect no mercy.

Back in Tours, the gallant *Kommandant* also advised her to leave. He arranged everything for her—travel documents, permits, gas coupons. It was the middle of August by then. Alex, in Ste. Maxime, had been able finally to get through to her on the telephone. "I was trembling when I waited for your voice on the phone," she wrote him, "and, of course, was a little disappointed because you did not yell like a red Indian but asked me, in a European way, how I was." Tatiana set off with Francine for the south of France in late August. She did not tell Francine about her father; perhaps she still hoped the information might turn out to be false. They had a frightful trip. Their car kept stalling and breaking down, and Tatiana kept getting out to telephone Alex. There was a terminal breakdown at Montélimar, close enough for Alex to send a car and chauffeur to rescue them. Francine remembers their arriving at the Ste. Maxime house near midnight, "driving into this sort of green enclave, and Alex leaping out of the bushes into the headlights to greet us, and the enormous excitement after these long days of worry."

In spite of their joy at being together after a three-month separation (Alex and Tatiana would never again be apart for more than a few days at a time), life in Ste. Maxime was far from idyllic. There was very little to eat, for one thing. With the shortage of gas, trucks could not make deliveries to the markets, and strict rationing was in effect. Alex knew one store in town that catered to English visitors; it stocked corn flakes and catsup, items that no self-respecting French citizen would touch but which became the staple of many meals *chez* Liberman. They played a game to dampen their appetites—sitting around the table and making up the most disgusting food combinations they could think of. The winner was Francine's sardines with hot chocolate sauce. Now and then Alex managed to catch a fish. Because children were allotted milk quotas, Francine could buy milk and sometimes eggs from neighboring farms—Francine detested milk, but Alex needed to drink it for his ulcers. Francine came to think of Alex as the provider, "just like a god with a hundred arms taking care of everybody." He provided a bicycle for her birthday in September and taught her how to ride it; he also taught her to swim. Since they couldn't drive, Alex built a three-wheeled cart that he could attach to his own bicycle for trips to St. Tropez; Tatiana rode in the cart while Alex pedaled.

This life of improvisation was exciting for ten-year-old Francine, but less so for Tatiana, who had to deal with the unrelenting hostility of Alex's mother. Alex, Tatiana, and Francine slept in the cottage that Alex had remodeled. They had christened it "Va-et-Vient" ("Come and Go") when the two of them had their romantic idyll there in 1939, and for them the name always had sexual overtones. Henriette lived in the villa up the hill ("Villa Scaramouche," she called it), where she lost no opportunity to denigrate the woman whom she was obliged to see as a much more serious threat to her domination over Alex than Hilda had ever been.* Tatiana wisely refrained from joining the fray; she never hit back and behaved, as Alex said, "like a saint" toward his mother. In fact, she swallowed her anger, and suffered splitting headaches and attacks of vomiting as a result. Several years later, Alex wrote a three-character play based on this domestic triangle. Entitled *Two Plus One*, it was full of lines such as (the mother speaking): "You are weak. She will use you, use you. You are defenseless, putty in her scheming hands." The manuscript, which makes it abundantly clear that Alex was not cut out to be a playwright, may at least have helped him to exorcise a lot of guilt.

Irène Lidova and her husband, Serge, who had also fled Paris, were staying at Va-et-Vient when Tatiana and Francine arrived. Having his former *Vu* colleague (and lover) on the premises was awkward for Alex; it

* Henriette had traveled back to Vichy a week or so earlier, by train, to get her visa in order, and while she was there she had sought out Tatiana and told her not to come to Ste. Maxime. Alex, she had said, was having an affair with a woman who lived next door to them.

became a good deal more awkward when Lidova, in response to some now-forgotten remark, slapped Francine's face. Francine remembers her mother explaining to her afterward that because of wartime tensions people were not acting normally. Tatiana was not acting too rationally herself. She still had not told Francine about her father. (His death was confirmed by an official letter in December 1940.) Like Alex, she could act decisively in a crisis, but she shrank from emotional confrontations. Her failure to deal with this one would cause bitter feelings later on.

The worst tensions had to do with exit visas. Simon Liberman, in New York, was doing all he could to procure the necessary documents for them to come to the United States. He was able to get money to them, but Alex had to keep asking him for more as the weeks dragged on. He promised to pay it all back when they got to New York, saying that he intended to work there "as a portrait artist, or for the newspapers or in films," and citing the "sizable amounts of money" that Tatiana would receive "after all the legal formalities have been cleared up." (Tatiana had instituted a lawsuit to recover insurance costs relating to her car accident; the claim was settled after the war, but by then the devaluation of the French franc had reduced the amount she received to an insignificant sum.) Alex refused to leave without Tatiana, "the woman I love and for whom I am responsible." Several people were working on Tatiana's visa, including her own father, who was living then in Rochester, New York; her diplomat friend John Cooper Wiley, who had returned to Washington, D.C.; the U.S. ambassador to France, William C. Bullitt; and John Vail, the head of the Emergency Rescue Committee, which was helping European artists, intellectuals, and political enemies of fascism to escape from France. The visa requirements kept changing, though, and the process was maddeningly slow. Henriette left before them, alone, furious because Alex was staying with Tatiana; she had passage on a boat from Lisbon. When Alex and Tatiana went to inspect the villa up the hill, they found that she had locked up all the sheets and linens and taken the keys.

Tatiana went to Paris for a week in November. She lied to Alex, telling him she was simply taking the train to Vichy to settle Bertrand's estate—trains were running then between Nice and Vichy. From Vichy she made a clandestine and very hazardous trip to Paris, at night, hidden under some mattresses in the back of a truck. (Travel in and out of Paris was strictly controlled; the underground group that took her charged one thousand francs each way.) Why did she go? "I had to see du Plessix's relatives," she said. "They didn't know that he had been killed. I also wanted to pick up some personal belongings."

Walking toward the Champs-Elysées on the avenue Kléber the next morning, in what struck her as a dead and deserted city, she realized she was being followed by someone in a gray car. The car stopped, and a very tall, slender man in the uniform of a German officer got out to greet her. She recognized him immediately. It was Hans Gunther von Dincklage, known by all his friends as "Spatz" ("sparrow"), a clever and engaging member of her social set in Paris, where he had been living for half a dozen years. Dincklage had endeared himself to his many French friends by refusing to divorce his Jewish wife (whom he did not live with); what could be better proof of his anti-Nazi sympathies? In fact, he was a German spy. He had done his work so well and so charmingly that none of his friends had suspected a thing—none, that is, except Simon Liberman, who after meeting him at Va-et-Vient in 1939, on his last visit from New York, had said, "Who is this spy?"

Spatz had prevailed on Tatiana some years earlier to introduce him to her close friend Hélène Desoffy, a wealthy countess who had a house in the south of France near Toulon, and who often invited to her dinner parties there high-ranking officers from the Toulon naval base. He had become Hélène's lover (Spatz was a notorious seducer), and her letters to him, intercepted by French intelligence agents, had landed her in jail. When Spatz stopped Tatiana on the avenue Kléber, he warned her not to stay long in Paris and said he had something very important to ask of her. They arranged to meet that evening at a restaurant. Spatz knew everything, it seemed; he even knew that she was living in the south of France. What he wanted was for her to deliver a message to Count Desoffy, Hélène's husband, in Toulon. If the count could get word to Hélène in prison telling her to say that she had collaborated knowingly with Spatz, he could get her released. Tatiana did give the message to Desoffy, but his wife refused to perjure herself. After the war, she was tried and acquitted of the charge of collaboration. Spatz himself spent the war years comfortably ensconced at the Ritz in Paris with his new lady love, Coco Chanel, whose later career suffered from but survived the liaison.

Before leaving Paris, Tatiana went to Alex's studio and rolled up as many of Alex's paintings as she could carry. She also brought the print of his Louvre film. She drew out all her own remaining cash and securities from the Westminster Bank (they turned out to be of little value after the war), and she rescued some of Alex's mother's belongings from the avenue Frédéric-Le-Play apartment, including Henriette's mink coat. Then she made her way back to Vichy, and from there by train to the Midi. Her foolhardy errand made Alex all the more anxious to get her out of France.

"I know she would have joined the Resistance if we hadn't left," he said, "and she would certainly have got herself killed."

The necessary papers for Tatiana and Francine finally came through in December. The three of them boarded a train that took them to the Spanish border, where they took another train to Madrid. They had tickets to Lisbon, the neutral embarcation point for most refugees in those desperate days, but when they got to the Madrid railroad station they found a scene out of Dante's *Inferno*. "People were hanging from the windows," Francine remembered, "and fighting and shoving and clawing at each other to get on the train." Tatiana's nerve failed her. Afflicted with severe claustrophobia ever since her automobile accident, she said it was impossible— she could not go. Once again Alex refused to take no for an answer. Having found out that there was not another train for a week, he literally pushed Tatiana and Francine onto the packed car. He found a place for them in the lavatory, where they rode for the entire trip, standing up when passengers came in to use the facilities. Alex kept guard over them in the corridor. Even so, Francine's coat was stolen during the trip. They bundled her up in Henriette's mink until they got to Lisbon, where Alex bought her a stylish new camel-hair polo coat that she wore with great pride that winter and the next.

Lisbon seemed like a paradise. There was plenty of food, no rationing, and relief from the terrible tension and uncertainty of the last months in France. They left at the end of December, on the *Carvalho Araujo*, a tiny steamer that usually plied between Lisbon and the Azores —it had never crossed the Atlantic before. They traveled first-class, in separate cabins; Alex shared his with a concert flutist named Réné Le Roy. Tatiana and Francine were seasick for most of the rough voyage. Alex, walking the decks on the stormiest days, felt "an extraordinary sense of deliverance and anticipation." He was twenty-eight years old, fluent in English, confident that he could make his way in America. "I'll live by doing my portraits above all else," he had written to his father. "Because through all the tragic events, I am sensing with increasing certainty and sureness that painting is my path, and that I must banish everything that separates me from it." He was deeply proud that he had been able to lead Tatiana out of danger. He bought her a late Christmas present on the ship, a Portuguese gold filigreed pin from a display cabinet in the lounge. "I was so obsessed with Tatiana," he remembered, "that nothing else really mattered."

Tatiana and Alex, summer 1942, on Long Island.

New York

The *Carvalho Araujo* was too small to dock at the Hudson River piers on Manhattan's West Side. It tied up in Brooklyn, on the cold, clear morning of January 8, 1941. Francine, primed for skyscrapers, was disappointed by the flat, industrial landscape of the Brooklyn docks, but she was awed by the immensely tall man who had come to meet them—it was Alexis Iacovleff, Tatiana's father, who now called himself Alexis Jackson. The emotional undercurrents of this meeting between a father and a daughter who had not seen one another for twenty-four years were kept under strict control; Tatiana, who never understood why her father had abandoned the family, treated him with respectful formality. Alex shepherded his party through customs inspection at pierside. When the inspector handed back his stamped passport and Alex said, "Thank you," he was amazed and touched to hear the man say, "You're welcome"; having learned his English in England, he was not aware that Americans used this phrase as a matter of course, and he thought the inspector was welcoming him to America.

Tatiana's father hailed a taxi for the ride across the Brooklyn Bridge to Manhattan. They stopped first at the Windsor Hotel at Sixth Avenue and Fifty-eighth Street, where Alex's father had booked separate rooms for them—a double for Tatiana and Francine, a nonadjoining single for Alex. After checking in, Alex, Tatiana, and Francine went immediately to Simon Liberman's penthouse apartment at 4 East Sixty-fourth Street. Alex's mother was not there to greet them. Postponing the joy of a reunion with her son, she used this opportunity to reaffirm her animosity toward Tatiana. Ten-year-old Francine found Alex's father the reverse image of Tatiana's —short, plump, and warmly welcoming. (She apparently brought out a side of his nature that Alex rarely saw.) "He had the first battery-operated radio I'd ever seen," she recalled, "and he let me use it. A radio without wires—this was magic. I kept cradling it like a talisman."

The main outlines of Alex and Tatiana's new life fell into place with amazing rapidity in the weeks that followed, but the transition period was not an easy one. There were times when Alex felt overwhelmed by the responsibility of having to provide for Tatiana and Francine, neither of whom spoke a word of English. Tatiana, for all her social daring, had a puritanical streak, and being in a strange country accentuated this. She was the one who had insisted on their having separate rooms on the boat and at the hotel. Within a day or two of their arrival, in part because her sense of propriety balked at the thought of their living in the same hotel, she arranged for Francine to go and stay with her grandfather Jackson and his second wife, Zina, who lived upstate in Rochester. (Francine found an unexpected ally in Zina, a Russian-American woman whose motherly sweetness helped to lessen the pain of separation.) Tatiana did not wish people to know that she was living with a man to whom she was not married. The New York *World-Telegram* had carried a front-page picture of Tatiana and Francine the day after their arrival under a headline saying "French Countess Arrives with Child"—titled refugees were still news in those days. There was no mention of her traveling companion.

The Suydam Cuttings, wealthy Americans who had once met Tatiana's uncle Sacha (Alexandre Iacovleff) on a trip to Tibet, where he had painted their portrait, saw the *World-Telegram* story, recognized the du Plessix connection, got in touch, and invited Tatiana and Alex to their house near Bernardsville, New Jersey. It was their first country weekend in America—the first of many that they would spend at houses of the well-to-do. The Cuttings, who knew all sorts of people, had also invited Ray Bolger; Alex used his father's home-movie camera, which he had borrowed for the occasion, to film the dancer doing an improvised comic turn on the Cuttings' front porch.

Within three days of their arrival, Tatiana was designing hats for Henri Bendel. Her father opened that door to her, in a roundabout way.

Arriving in New York, 1941. Francine is wearing the
camel-hair coat Alex bought her in Lisbon.

The 1941 *Vogue* cover by Alex that made Frank
Crowninshield decide there was "a genius in the
art department." Horst took the photograph.

First summer in America, at a Sands Point, Long Island, beach cottage. It was here that Francine learned of her father's death.

Although Alexis Jackson lived in Rochester, New York, where he worked as an engineer for Eastman Kodak, he had gone into business on the side with another Russian émigré named Vadim Makaroff, the son of a famous Russian naval hero; they were partners in a small firm that had developed an improved hydraulic lift for automobile service stations. Makaroff, who lived in New York, was married to a New York society woman with good connections. Her close friend Hélène Hoguet, the wife of a prominent New York surgeon who had lost an arm in an accident and was therefore unable to practice, worked on commission to steer wealthy clients to the fashion salon at Bendel's, and Madame Hoguet, who knew her customers, was more than pleased to find a place at that elegant store, at seventy-five dollars a week, for Countess du Plessix. (Tatiana's transition from *vicomtesse* to countess was as effortless as her assumption of the title in the first place.)

Alex's father had offered to give Alex two hundred dollars a month in America so that he could pursue his chosen "path" of becoming an artist. The offer precipitated a conflict in Alex's mind between the rival demands of art and life that would never really be resolved, although his response this time set the pattern for future decisions. Two hundred dollars (five hundred, counting Tatiana's salary) was a fairly significant amount of money in those days, but Alex felt that he had to succeed on his own in America—and not just as an artist—in order to provide the degree of comfort and security that Tatiana required; he suspected, moreover, that the offer was part of a calculated effort by his mother to pry him loose from Tatiana. Alex wanted to pry himself loose from any further dependence on his father, who had paid for their passage from Lisbon and who was paying for their rooms at the Hotel Windsor. He felt, perhaps unfairly, that there was a message in his father's choice of a less-than-first-rate hotel to put them up in, a subtle reminder that the son did not merit the same degree of luxury that Simon Liberman invariably lavished on himself; when he first came to New York, he had lived at the Plaza. Alex was not aware that his father's investments in the Canadian timber industry were running into difficulties. The elder Liberman, who would lose the better part of his fortune to unscrupulous partners during the next few years, never ceased to indulge his own, post-Bolshevik penchant for fine clothes and expensive living arrangements, and he tried his best to satisfy Henriette's uninhibited demands. Alex longed to be free of the obligations that financial dependency required; but, more important, he had decided that Tatiana's and Francine's needs took precedence over his ambition to be an artist. He was determined to get a job.

The obvious profession for a former managing editor of *Vu* was magazine journalism. Irène Lidova had provided him with a letter of introduction to Alexey Brodovitch, the art director of *Harper's Bazaar*; she had worked for him in Paris some years earlier, when he had been the head designer for the Trois Quartiers department store. Alex went to see Brodovitch the first week he was in New York and was enormously impressed by him. A fellow Russian who had been a cavalry officer in the White Army, Brodovitch had become the recognized leader of a design revolution that was affecting the look of magazines, books, advertisements, and commercial photography in this country; he was also a teacher whose students would spread that revolution in many other areas of graphic design. Brodovitch told Alex to design a sample page of ideas for women's shoes; one of the perennial problems for fashion magazines, then and now, is to present shoes in attractive new ways. Alex came up with a design that he described, years later, as "perfectly awful," in which the shoes traced the outline of a face. Brodovitch rejected it, and that was that.

By then, however, Alex had discovered that Lucien Vogel was in town. His former boss, who had escaped from occupied France only two months earlier, was now a consultant to Condé Nast, the publisher of *Vogue, House & Garden*, and *Glamour*, as well as *Jardin des Modes*, the French fashion magazine started by Vogel and his wife. Vogel invited Alex and Tatiana to his apartment on Sutton Place South, and there Alex renewed his acquaintance with Iva Sergei Voidato-Patcévitch, yet another dazzling Russian émigré, whom he had known earlier as the business manager of Condé Nast's Paris operations. The Condé Nast photo studio was located just across the hall from the *Vu* offices at 65, avenue des Champs-Elysées, and Vogel and Patcévitch used to lunch together regularly. Patcévitch was now Condé Nast's main financial adviser, the number-two man in the organization and Nast's chosen successor; he would become president of the company when Nast died, a year later. He readily agreed with Vogel that Alex should come to work for Condé Nast. (Vogel, who spoke little English, had insisted that he needed Liberman.) Patcévitch said he would speak to Nast about it.

A few days later, Alex came in to the *Vogue* offices to meet Mehemed Fehmy Agha, the art director of all three American Condé Nast magazines. Dr. Agha, as he liked to be called, was known around the *Vogue* office as the Terrible Turk. He had a cynical, sarcastic wit that intimidated nearly everyone, but he was greatly respected throughout the magazine world for the way he had modernized the look of Nast's magazines. Born in Russia of Turkish parents, Agha had learned the principles of Bauhaus design at first hand in Germany, where his early graphic layouts for the German edition of *Vogue* had caught Condé Nast's eye. Nast brought him to New York in 1929, and since then Agha had steadily extended his empire. In a tongue-in-cheek tribute celebrating Agha's tenth anniversary with the company, Frank Crowninshield, the former editor of *Vanity Fair*, described him as having "spread out so rapidly that an additional floor had to be engaged in the Graybar Building in order to prevent his bulging out of the windows, growing through the roof, or occupying the elevator shafts and ladies' rooms." The portly, monocled Dr. Agha (whose doctorate was in political science) received Alex Liberman with barely veiled disdain and told him to report for work in the art department the following Monday. When Alex appeared that morning, he was given the job of designing a double-page spread of drawings by the *Vogue* fashion illustrator Jean Pagès. He spent most of the week on this rather mundane assignment. On Friday, he was called into Agha's office. The Terrible Turk pointed to a number of what he called "holes" in Alex's layout and said, "I'm sorry, you're not right for *Vogue*."

Alex picked up his paycheck and went back to the Windsor Hotel. He felt crushed and desperate; maybe he wouldn't be able to find a job after all. The telephone rang. It was Mary Campbell, Condé Nast's personal secretary, telling him that he had an appointment with Mr. Nast, whom he had not met, on the following Monday morning.

Nast's office was much bigger than Agha's. "You had to walk the length of this huge room," Alex remembered, "and there was Condé, at a banker's desk, wearing his little pince-nez. Basically, publishers are all accountants at heart. Nast was an accountant, Patcévitch was an accountant, Si Newhouse is an accountant. Anyway, it became clear very quickly that Nast did not know that Agha had already hired and fired me. We talked about various things—*Vu*, and French publishing, and Vogel—and I showed him a certificate I had brought along, for a prize I had won at the Universal Exposition in Paris in 1937. It was for a photomontage display on how magazines are created, and it had won a gold medal. There was this certificate with my name on it, although to tell the truth I don't really remember doing the montage. The minute Nast saw it, he said, 'Well, a man like you must be on *Vogue*.' And he pressed a buzzer, called Mary Campbell, and said, 'Please send in Dr. Agha.' Agha came in while I was sitting there. Nast said, 'Dr. Agha, this is Mr. Liberman. I would like him to be in the *Vogue* art department.' And Agha said, 'Yes, Mr. Nast.' Agha never said another word about it, I never said a word, and that's how I started on *Vogue*."

Irving Penn's 1947 portrait of Francine, Alex, and Tatiana.

The Authentic Journal
of Society

One of Condé Nast's more level-headed mistresses, the writer Helen Lawrenson, described him as looking in his sixties like a sedate, impeccably mannered banker. "He was about five foot nine," Lawrenson wrote, "bald with a fringe of thinning grey hair at back and sides, small eyes behind rimless pince-nez glasses, a thin-lipped mouth turned down at the corners." At the famous parties that he threw several times a month in his Park Avenue penthouse, where writers, artists, and celebrities rubbed elbows with the ultrarich and the socially elite, his shyness was legendary. No matter how much he drank (again, according to Lawrenson), "he consistently displayed the vivacity of a stuffed moosehead." In spite of these self-effacing qualities, Condé Nast's publishing ideas were more astute and, in the end, more influential than those of his competitor William Randolph Hearst, whose ego never slept.

Nast had started out in publishing in 1897, when he accepted his college classmate Robert J. Collier's offer of a job as advertising manager of *Collier's Weekly*, a family-owned fact-and-fiction magazine with a circulation of 19,159. In his ten years there, the circulation zoomed to 568,073, and its annual advertising revenue—a feeble $5,600 when he arrived—reached a million dollars. At some point during this apprentice decade, it dawned on Nast that success in magazine publishing did not necessarily require huge circulation figures. In a direct challenge to the philosophy of Cyrus H. K. Curtis and other mass-market publishers, Nast formulated his theory of "class" publications, directed to specialized groups of readers. By deliberately eliminating the mass public, he reasoned, you could offer advertisers a select audience whose tastes and interests were relatively well known, thereby reducing the element of chance. Since it was becoming clear that the real money in magazine publishing lay not in paid subscriptions but in ad revenues, this strategy cut both ways: a better return for the advertising dollar and a greater margin of profit for the magazine. If all this seems obvious today, it was much less so at the time.

When Nast bought *Vogue* magazine in 1909, he acquired what seemed to him the ideal class publication. *Vogue* had always been a magazine for the rich. Established in 1892, with the backing of Cornelius Vanderbilt and a number of New York's other first families, it was designed to be "the authentic journal of society, fashion and the ceremonial side of life," and in its early years its appeal was directed as much to men as to women. Nast knew he could convince advertisers that *Vogue's* readers were an elite group of stylish, well-to-do customers—the kind whom every purveyor of luxury merchandise yearned to reach—and within a year he had proved himself right. In 1910, although its circulation was a mere 30,000, *Vogue* carried 44 percent more advertising than *Ladies' Home Journal* (circulation 1,305,030); 78 percent more than *Woman's Home Companion* (circulation 698,568); and 292 percent more than *Harper's Bazar*, its considerably older rival publication.*

Throughout his publishing career, Nast picked first-rate editors. Edna Woolman Chase, whom he installed as the editor of *Vogue* in 1914, was a fine example of his spot-on perceptiveness. Born in Asbury Park, New Jersey, where she was brought up by her Quaker grandparents, Edna Chase was far enough removed from the social hierarchy to become an avid student of its traditions and mores. She had started work in the circulation department at *Vogue* in 1895, when she was eighteen. By the time she took over the editor's chair she was already a formidable personage, a small, delicate woman whose ladylike manner masked an iron determination and an absolute assurance about the kind of material that belonged (or did not belong) in the pages of *Vogue*. Working in complete harmony with Condé Nast, Chase steadily broadened the magazine's agenda without diluting its

---

* Established in 1867, *Harper's Bazar* did not acquire the extra *a* in its title until 1929.

elitist appeal. Pages of society news—births, deaths, marriages, debuts—shared space with the latest fashion news from Paris, presented in sprightly drawings by the top fashion artists. There were feature articles on society leaders and their various amusements, and until the 1940s there was a regular department devoted to their dogs and cats. Mrs. Chase's authority in these matters extended even to life at *Vogue*, where the top editors (many of whom were society women, working for minuscule wages) were required to wear hats and white gloves in the office, and who were never, ever seen in open-toed shoes. When a despondent editor tried unsuccessfully to commit suicide by throwing herself under a subway train, Mrs. Chase was deeply chagrined. "My dear," she said when the woman returned to work, "we at *Vogue* don't throw ourselves under subway trains. If we must, we take sleeping pills."

The year before Edna Chase became the chief editor of *Vogue*, Condé Nast had installed Frank Crowninshield as the editor of a new magazine called *Dress & Vanity Fair*, an amalgam of two moribund journals he had bought for practically nothing. Crowninshield shortened the title to *Vanity Fair* and made the magazine over in his own image, as great editors do; it was soon the most sophisticated magazine of its time, an effervescent and irreverent potpourri of articles and pictures with emphasis on the latest developments in art, theater, music, and current events. Condé Nast, meanwhile, kept right on expanding. In 1915, he bought *House & Garden*, an architectural journal that he turned into a magazine of interior decoration, and that same year, as we have seen, he also assumed control of Lucien Vogel's *Gazette du Bon Ton*. The beautifully printed French fashion journal was about to shut down because of the war; Nast bought it mainly to secure the services of its talented fashion artists for *Vogue*. There were good reasons for Nast to publish in France; Paris remained the unchallenged arbiter of couture, and most of *Vogue*'s fashion pages were made up there. *Vogue* had started publishing a French edition in 1920; it was edited first by Vogel's wife and later on by her brother, Michel de Brunhoff. Then, in 1921, Nast bought the Vogels' fashion journal *Jardin des Modes* and thus went into competition with himself. Almost everything he tried seemed to turn out well, however; *Jardin des Modes* became a great success, and a reservoir of editorial and pictorial talent for French and American *Vogues*.

Photography did not become a significant part of *Vogue* until 1914, the year Condé Nast signed Baron Adolphe de Meyer to an exclusive contract with *Vogue* and *Vanity Fair*. Nast himself had a keen interest in photography and saw it as the wave of the future. Although hand-drawn covers and fashion illustrations by Carl Erickson ("Eric"), René Bouët-

Willaumez, Christian Bérard, and other artists continued to appear prominently in *Vogue*, de Meyer's misty, backlit portraits of society doyennes and well-known actresses, swathed in the latest Paris modes and posed against exotic backgrounds, marked the beginning of a new era. It became a badge of status to have one's portrait done by the exquisite, charmingly louche baron, the photographer of English royalty—his title had been awarded by the Prince of Wales, so that the de Meyers could attend his coronation as members of the peerage. De Meyer's work for Condé Nast established fashion photography as a respected profession, and great was the anguish at *Vogue* when he became the first of many staffers to be lured away by *Harper's Bazar*. The rival fashion journal, which had been bought in 1913 by William Randolph Hearst, was making a well-financed assault on *Vogue*'s entrenched position. Offered a much higher salary and the chance to live in Paris, de Meyer defected in 1922, after eight years at *Vogue*.

Although Edna Chase never forgave him, his leaving turned out to be another stroke of luck for Condé Nast. The man whom Nast hired to replace him was Edward Steichen, whose portraits and fashion studies in *Vogue* and *Vanity Fair* almost immediately made de Meyer's work look out-of-date. Steichen was already well known by then as a master photographer, one of the pioneering band whose leader, Alfred Stieglitz, had worked tirelessly since the early years of the century to establish photography as a legitimate form of art. He brought to the Condé Nast magazines this group's belief in "straight" photography, untrammeled by soft-focus, chiaroscuro, or other tricks whose main purpose was to make photographs look like paintings. Steichen's clean-cut pictorial realism not only provided marvelously detailed views of the clothes being modeled; it also presented the models in a new way, as real women. Years later, Alexander Liberman would point out to young photographers Steichen's 1927 picture of Marion Morehouse, one of the first professional fashion models (she quit the profession soon afterward to marry the poet E. E. Cummings), and tell them that it was "the key to modern fashion photography." The picture shows a superbly confident, sophisticated young beauty in a glittering Chéruit dress, hands on her hips, smiling, fully alive in the present tense rather than in some ethereal studio never-land. "The fashion showed very clearly," Liberman said, but the picture offered something far more important: "an image of a woman at her most attractive moment."

By the time Steichen left Condé Nast in 1938, photography had largely replaced hand-drawn sketches in the fashion press. This was due in part to technical improvements that made halftone reproductions cheaper and more accurate, and also to the development of faster film and the 35-

millimeter Leica camera. It had become possible for fashion photographers to move out of the studio and to work with natural light. Toni Frissell, a society girl–turned–photographer who loved outdoor sports, began to develop a breezy new approach to the medium at *Vogue*, using hand-held cameras to show models on the beach, the golf course, or the ski slopes at St. Moritz. The work of some other leading *Vogue* photographers of the 1920s and 1930s—notably the Russian-born George Hoyningen-Huene, the German Horst P. Horst, and Britain's Cecil Beaton—tended to ignore these advances; by and large, they continued to present women as haughty, aloof creatures in fanciful studio settings. The changeover from hand-drawn to photographic illustration had subtly undermined the whole concept of *Vogue* as "the authentic journal of society," however; photographs—even elaborately posed studio fantasies—carried the modernist virus of change, the sense of passing moments that would not recur, and they made the old format of *Vogue* begin to seem increasingly obsolete.

Drastic changes took place in the early 1930s under the guidance of Carmel Snow, who had been named *Vogue's* New York editor in 1929, and Mehemed Fehmy Agha, the acidulous new art director. Several years before Alexey Brodovitch started his transformation of *Harper's Bazaar*, Agha was overseeing many of the same innovations at *Vogue*. He got rid of the frames around pictures and text blocks, and threw out italic typefaces and much of the hand-drawn script in favor of bold sans-serif letters. Sometimes he tilted columns of type at a slight angle to the vertical, and combined words and pictures to carry the message in visually exciting ways. The first "bleed" page ever used in an American magazine—the photo extending to the edge of the page, with no white border—ran in the September 1932 issue of *Vogue; Harper's Bazaar* followed suit two months later. (Alex had been struck by Vogel's use of bleed pages that same year, when he started at *Vu*.) Agha's most imaginative work was done at *Vanity Fair*, where Frank Crowninshield gave him a lot more leeway than the tradition-minded Edna Chase did; nevertheless, he tried hard to undermine the antiquated "album" concept of *Vogue*, and his work there might have received more credit than it did if he had not offended so many of his colleagues. Hoyningen-Huene quit *Vogue* in a fury in 1934 after an argument with Agha and went over to *Harper's Bazaar*. Edna Chase, jealous of her art director's increasing power and influence, found his sarcastic wit a constant trial. Agha's cynicism extended even to his own profession. "Personally," he once wrote, in a letter opposing some suggested changes in *Vogue's* approach, "I might be inclined to [the view] that a fashion magazine's conception of beauty, elegance and taste might be insipid and nauseating, but I firmly believe that a fashion magazine is not the place to display our dislike for these things."

The *Vogue* conception of beauty, elegance, and taste was changing rather rapidly at this point, and so was the magazine's audience. Having started out as an elegant mirror of the social life of New York's impregnable Four Hundred, it was becoming a guide for all those who yearned to join those exalted ranks—or, at least, to look as though they had. Circulation was climbing rapidly, and feature articles, which in earlier times had dealt primarily with the living arrangements of Vanderbilts, Astors, Van Rensselaers, and other tiaraed heads, now reflected a wider range of interests. Carmel Snow, the dynamic young Irishwoman who had been promoted from fashion editor to New York editor in 1929, and who was supposedly being groomed for the top post when Edna Chase retired, opened the pages of *Vogue* more and more to the cultural scene that Nast and Chase had been content until then to consider *Vanity Fair*'s territory. Both Nast and Chase were stunned when Snow quit and went to *Harper's Bazaar* in 1932. There had obviously been some friction between Edna Chase and her protégée—Snow later claimed that Chase had been planning to demote her to society editor—but the defection came as a complete surprise at *Vogue*, and it signaled a major turning point in the rivalry between the leading fashion magazines. For the next two decades, the brilliant collaboration of Carmel Snow and Alexey Brodovitch (whom she brought to *Bazaar* in 1934) made *Harper's Bazaar* one of the most fervently admired magazines in America. Its coverage of fashion, the arts, and the contemporary scene was consistently more lively and more imaginative than *Vogue*'s; its graphic design and layouts were more elegant; and its reputation for hiring the best photographers and giving them a relatively free rein was a frequent embarrassment to the rival publication. The incorporation of the failing *Vanity Fair* into *Vogue* in 1936, which brought Frank Crowninshield and some of his more talented contributors under the *Vogue* imprint, helped right the balance to some extent, but until the 1960s *Bazaar* remained, by general consent, the top fashion magazine in every area except circulation and advertising revenue. Although *Harper's Bazaar* drew even with *Vogue* in these areas in the mid-forties, when both magazines were printing about 200,000 copies per issue, it could never quite manage to translate its acknowledged creative superiority into commercial terms.

Condé Nast had only a little more than a year to live when he hired Alex Liberman in 1941. His health was failing, but he didn't want anyone to know it. Nast never showed any outward signs of the stress he was under. He had lost all his money in the 1929 crash, and he had almost lost the magazines as well. What had saved them was the generous intervention of Lord Camrose, the British press lord, who bought up the stock, gave Nast a working interest and a big infusion of cash, and let him continue to run the magazines as he saw fit. (Camrose was motivated in large part by personal gratitude; Nast had been very kind to the Texas-born Edwina Pru, a former *Vogue* staffer who had become Camrose's wife.) In spite of a serious heart condition that sapped his energy, Nast remained very much the man in charge. He worked long hours and issued endless memos; one 1941 critique of *Vogue* was sixty-five pages long. It struck Alex that Nast was trying to make *Vogue* more and more like a news magazine. "I always thought that was why he seemed interested in me," Alex said, "because of my journalistic background at *Vu*. He sent out memos calling for captions on the pictures and titles at the top of the page. He wanted labels on the cover to let people know what was inside; that was really the beginning of cover lines. He wanted a much clearer presentation, and, as it turned out, I worked very closely with him on that."

From the beginning of his career at *Vogue*, Liberman seemed to enjoy a special relationship with Nast. Sitting at his desk in the layout department on the nineteenth floor—there were six other desks and six other layout artists, all senior to him—Alex would receive a summons to Nast's office, where he would be asked to give his opinion of a particular spread. Not infrequently, Nast would stick his head out the door of the little viewing room next to the art department, waggle his finger at Alex, and say, "Mr. Liberman, would you come in here, please?" Alex would go in and find Nast, Edna Chase, Dr. Agha, and several of the top editors looking at eight-by-ten color photographs of possible covers under a special light. "Which of these do you like?" Nast would ask him. When Alex picked out one, Nast would hand it to Agha and say, "That's the one I like, too. Let's use it."

Alex himself worked mainly on *Vogue* covers. One day during his first month on the job, he was playing around at his desk with a Horst photograph of a girl in a bathing suit. The model was lying on her back with both legs in the air, balancing a red beach ball on her feet; Alex, doodling with the image, made the ball substitute for the *O* in "Vogue." (The magazine had no fixed logo in those days, and the title looked different with each issue.) Frank Crowninshield, since *Vanity Fair*'s demise the "Fine Arts Consultant Editor" of *Vogue*, happened to be walking through the art department just then; he stopped to look at Alex's design, which impressed him enormously. "There's a genius in the art department," he told Nast. The beach-ball picture became the May 15, 1941, cover of *Vogue*, and

Alex's stock went up several more notches. Crowninshield took the young genius under his wing after that, inviting him to lunch at the Knickerbocker Club, introducing him to actors and writers, and generally making him feel at home in the broader cultural context of New York. He was a wonderfully urbane friend who seemed to know everyone worth knowing, and Alex, alert as always, learned a great deal from him.

Crowninshield, known to his friends as Crowny, appeared to be everything that Condé Nast was not. He was infinitely gregarious, witty, unpredictable, soft-hearted, improvident, and addicted to practical jokes, such as sending fake telegrams to vacationing Condé Nast secretaries, signed "Rudolph Valentino" or "Ramon Novarro." The breezy irreverence that he encouraged in the contributors to *Vanity Fair* sometimes got the magazine into trouble: a 1935 cartoon of Emperor Hirohito of Japan carting the Nobel Peace Prize in a wheelbarrow, drawn so that the scroll looks like a cannon, drew an angry protest from the Japanese ambassador in Washington and required a letter of apology. Nast was very fond of Crowny, though, and never tried to rein him in; he knew how much *Vanity Fair* and, after 1936, *Vogue* benefited from his inventive editing and his illustrious circle of friends. Although Crowninshield got along with everybody, he was, in fact, a tremendous snob—"the greatest snob I've ever known," according to Alex Liberman. "His god was Mrs. Cornelius Vanderbilt. One of the first *Vogue* covers I ever worked on was for a special issue on the Vanderbilts. Mrs. Vanderbilt was photographed in color by Beaton, sitting in her mansion and wearing a tiara, and there was a double-page spread of a dinner for forty-six people. Crowninshield had arranged that for us, and it was considered the coup of coups."

In spite of all the design changes at *Vogue*, and the pressure from Condé Nast to make his magazines more journalistic and more service-oriented, *Vogue* still clung to its elitist origins. "Condé Nast kept the *Social Register* on his desk," Alex said, "and it was the arbiter of who got into the magazine." Many of the *Vogue* editors were in the *Social Register* themselves. Lucien Vogel took Alex aside soon after his arrival and pointed out that he and Allene Talmey, the features editor, were the only "Israelites" on the staff. This was a touchy subject. Cecil Beaton had been banished from *Vogue* in 1938 after the discovery that a drawing of his in the magazine had some tiny, almost subliminal references to "kikes" written in the margins; somebody alerted Walter Winchell, who reported on it in his column, and Nast felt obliged to fire Beaton as a result. (He also had to reprint the entire issue.) During the war, though, *Vogue* published Beaton's photographs of London under the blitz, and by 1945 he was completely reinstated.

Printed anti-Semitism might be taboo, but anti-Semitic jokes and anti-Semitic attitudes were still part of the fabric of New York upper-class society in those days, as Alex was frequently reminded. Real estate agents informed him that certain apartment buildings were "restricted"—meaning that he need not apply. His mother, under the name Pascar, rented a house in a restricted beach community on the Connecticut shore one summer, but Alex was too embarrassed to use it. "It was a tremendous blow to me and Tatiana, who had tried to belong to upper-class life in Paris, to escape from the Nazis and then find so much anti-Semitism in America," he recalled. Alex occasionally overheard Tatiana telling people that he was a Protestant. He had also grown used to their being introduced at parties as "the Countess du Plessix—and dear Alex." He himself never denied being a Jew. "I felt it was shameful to hide it," he said. "But, in fact, I *was* a Protestant. I had been baptized at Les Roches, and I was deeply influenced by my Calvinist teachings there." On his Condé Nast employment form, he had identified his religious affiliation as Protestant.

Alex adapted easily enough to the magazine's vestigial snobbism, but he never lost the underlying sense of insecurity and doubt that came from being a refugee and a Jew in a country whose feelings about refugees and Jews were often as ambiguous and unresolved as his own.

On the beach at Menemsha, Alex and Francine in batik bathing suits
from Nassau. "This was the nudist beach," Alex said,
"but none of us dared undress."

Marriage

To many of the wartime refugees from Europe, New York City seemed a delightful haven. Theaters, movie houses, and restaurants were plentiful and not too expensive, decent apartments could be found without much trouble, and in 1941 the war still seemed far away. Alex and Tatiana soon felt at home in the city, and enjoyed seeking out its particular charms. They visited the Metropolitan Museum and the Frick Collection with Alex's father, who knew New York well by this time and who took them for Sunday brunch afterward at the Plaza. Their favorite places to eat were Hamburger Heaven and the Automat on Fifty-seventh Street—"a magical place," Alex said. "You put a nickel in a slot, turned a knob, and a piece of apple pie came out. I loved the simplification of life in America and the speed and clarity of things."

In April they left the Hotel Windsor and moved into two small apartments (on separate floors) in a building at 230 Central Park South. Tatiana painted the rooms and everything in them white, and she went to Macy's and bought metal garden furniture with white seat cushions; the whole set cost thirty-four dollars. They went out nearly every night. Frank Crowninshield often got them opening-night tickets to the theater. Tatiana had no winter coat for evening wear—they hadn't been able to save enough money to buy her one—and on cold nights Alex would have to fight for a taxi and bring it around to where Tatiana was huddling inside the theater lobby in her thin silk evening wrap.

They went to the gatherings of the White Russian colony in New York, into which they were introduced by Iva Patcévitch and Vadim Makaroff, Tatiana's father's business partner. "Suddenly one became an intimate friend of Prince Obolensky," said Alex, "and all those ex–cavalry officers and former czarist court officials. It was like something out of Tolstoy. Obolensky, who had married an Astor, was running the St. Regis Hotel. Vava [Vladimir] Adlerberg, whose father had been Czar Nicholas II's chief marshal, was an adviser to Harry Winston, the jeweler. Alexander Tarsaidze was in public relations, and then, of course, there was Igor Cassini, who had become the gossip columnist Cholly Knickerbocker. All aristocrats, using their titles to impress the American WASP society.

"Valentina, the dress designer, gave Russian Easter parties at her house on East Seventy-eighth Street, where you ate all the traditional Russian dishes, and Russian New Year's parties, where you threw pieces of molten lead into a basin of water to learn your fortune and wrote down wishes on little slips of paper that you then had to swallow. Valentina was very funny and outrageous. In a restaurant she would send the food back ten times, and she would protest about the roughness of towels in hotels. Greta Garbo used to come to her parties. Valentina's husband, George Schlee, was Garbo's financial adviser, and her lover, too; it was also said that Garbo and Valentina had been lovers. Garbo would appear in a sweater and slacks, and she had a hearty laugh that was so different from what you expected. I found her much more attractive in person than in her films."

Tatiana left Bendel's in the spring of 1942, when Saks Fifth Avenue offered her $125 a week to run her own hat salon there. Hats by Tatiana of Saks—large, colorful, and rather flamboyant hats, freighted with artificial flowers and fruit (one *Vogue* editor said privately that they felt "like cement")—were becoming a status symbol among women of a certain age and social standing. (Adam Gimbel, the president of Saks, was so enchanted by the cachet of a Russian-French countess that he told her not to learn any more English.) Tatiana's workshop was an airless room under a staircase at Saks; it was stifling in the summer, when she and her assistants had to make fur hats for the winter collection, and badly ventilated at all times, but for two years she was earning more money than Alex. Their joint income did not provide many luxuries. Like so many displaced Russians, though, they had a tendency toward extravagance in everyday matters— they took taxis to work, never buses, and Alex overtipped in restaurants.

They also led an ambitious social life, and they sent Francine to an exclusive Manhattan private school. Francine entered the Spence School in April 1941, on the recommendation of two alumni: Hélène Hoguet, the Makaroffs' socially prominent friend, and Pat Green, the wife of Justin Green, a child psychiatrist whom Tatiana had come to know some years earlier, when he was living in Paris. Justin Green and his new young wife had come to see Tatiana and Alex at the Windsor Hotel on the day of their arrival in New York. "I was still somewhat of a bride then, and rather shy," Pat Green recalled, "and when we walked into Tatiana's room at the Windsor I was just speechless. It was a modest room, not large, but there was a beautiful fur coverlet on the bed, and on the dressing table there was a silver brush-and-comb set, and red roses on another table, and a smell of good perfume. Tatiana was very glamorous—I remember being a little terrified by her—but Alex was so sweet and kind that I got over it pretty quickly." The Greens had a house on Eleventh Street, in Greenwich Village, and when Francine came back to New York after two months with her grandfather in Rochester, she lived there for a while, in the Greens' guest bedroom. Just before she started at Spence, Alex and Tatiana took their separate apartments at 230 Central Park South, and Francine moved in with her mother.

A good deal of emotional tension was bottled up in this ravishingly pretty, high-strung child. Francine could hardly help feeling excluded when she was sent away, a day or so after their arrival in America, to live with strangers. Tatiana, who had not paid much attention to her daughter when she was small, now had to deal with a backlog of resentment as she tried to atone for it. She did not really know how to talk to a ten-year-old, and most of the time, rather than make the effort, she simply avoided difficult subjects. Tatiana still had not told Francine that her father was dead. In Francine's young mind, Bertrand du Plessix had joined the French Resistance and was fighting somewhere in the underground, unable to get messages out to them. One of the ways in which Francine dealt with her own subconscious fears and resentments was to become a brilliant student. She learned English so quickly that she won the lower-school spelling bee in her second semester at Spence, prompting another girl's mother to accuse Tatiana of being a fraud. "You said she didn't speak a word of English when she arrived," the indignant parent complained.

Wary of her mother's timid attempts at intimacy, Francine turned increasingly to Alex for guidance and reassurance. "He assumed both maternal and paternal roles," she wrote years later, "rehearsing my memorizations of Milton or Blake, dealing with report cards, dentists, teachers, imposing curfew hours and taboos on lipsticks, instructing me about the period, the dangers of early sex, the mysteries of birth control." Francine remembers Alex telling her once that it was important for a woman not to give herself too readily or too often to a man—any man, even her husband; he said that was the great secret of her mother's allure. She trusted Alex completely and tended to take his side in arguments. Several times a year he brought her in to visit the Condé Nast offices. She wore her best dress, with white gloves, and Alex introduced her to Edna Chase and the other editors, making her feel important and valued "in a way my mother never did."

Francine had also developed a great affection for Alex's father. The elder Libermans had moved to a large and luxurious apartment at 1133 Fifth Avenue, near Ninety-fifth Street. Francine, whose school was only three blocks away, used to walk over every Thursday after school—Thursday was the night she and her parents had dinner at the Libermans'—and spend several hours alone with Simon Liberman. He was writing his autobiography, *Building Lenin's Russia*, and the process had reactivated the mystical idealism of his gentle, scholarly nature. (It may also have caused him to pay less attention than he should have to his business affairs.) He introduced Francine to the writings of Kierkegaard and Berdyaev, listened sympathetically to her own soul-searchings, and helped to instill in her quick mind a lifelong belief in nonviolence and in Christian pacifism—a belief that would eventually sustain some of her best writing and lead her to go to jail briefly in protest against the Vietnam war.

Henriette "was very sweet to me, but distant at the same time, and completely caught up in herself," Francine recalled. "She was too much a narcissist to be able to give much to a child. I remember her coming through the room now and then and blowing me a kiss, and then going back to her masks." Henriette's current form of performance involved masks. She had bought dozens of them and had others made for her— Oriental and African, ancient and contemporary, tragic and comic—which she wore while performing heavily stylized pantomimes. She performed on a raised platform at one end of her large Fifth Avenue living room, accompanied by a pianist, before motley audiences of European refugee artists (Léger, Chagall, the diminutive Frederick Kiesler), critics, and downtown bohemians who came for the food and drink. Henriette loved to mix the cocktails herself, with wild and extravagant flourishes. Leo Lerman, a young writer for *Vogue, Harper's Bazaar*, and other magazines who seemed to know everybody in New York, was a frequent guest at what he called this "center of hospitality and hostility"; he recalls suppressing the giggles when a hush settled over the room and Henriette began to "cavort about between great draperies." Lerman thought she was wonderful, "an elderly woman who was girlish," but he also saw how painful her performances were for Alex. "Thank God she wasn't my mother," he remembers thinking.

Alex made dutiful, pained appearances at these events, but Tatiana did not. Although Henriette had bowed to the inevitable sufficiently to carry on a conversation with Tatiana at the Thursday-evening family dinners, the two women still couldn't stand each other. Henriette continued to talk against Tatiana to Alex. She accused her of "stealing" her mink coat—the one Tatiana had carried from Paris to the south of France in 1940; it had been stolen in Lisbon, just before they embarked on the *Carvalho Araujo*. Caught in the middle, as always, Alex could never avoid feeling guilty toward one or the other.

To escape the heat of their first summer in New York, Alex rented a cottage for the month of August in Sands Point, on the North Shore of Long Island. They shared it with Lucien and Cosette Vogel, who paid half the $550 rental. There was only one bathroom, but they had a black woman, Sally Robinson, to do the cooking and housekeeping, and they invited friends out from the city on weekends. Wartime food rationing was in effect, so the guests were expected to bring something for the table—a chicken, or a leg of lamb. One midsummer evening, Tatiana's strong-minded young friend Gitta Sereny, who had been with her at the Château de Villandry in 1940, told Francine the truth about her father.

Gitta Sereny had arrived from Europe a month earlier, after walking over the Pyrenees to escape from occupied France. She was appalled to find that Francine, whom she had come to adore at the Château de Villandry, still thought her beloved father was alive. "I said to Tatiana, 'You can't do this, you must tell her,' and Tatiana said, 'I can't. I cannot hurt her that way.'"

"But you're hurting her far more," Gitta remembers telling her. "Somewhere inside she knows he's dead, but she's fighting to keep him alive."

Tatiana kept on repeating that she simply could not do it, and finally she said to Gitta, "You tell her." After an hour or so of futile argument, Gitta reluctantly agreed. Tatiana didn't want to be there when it happened. She and Alex went to spend the night with their friends the Levals, who had rented a summer house nearby. Alone with Francine, Gitta told her the truth, "as gently as I possibly could, but very directly." Francine's reaction, as Gitta recalls it, was much less violent than they had anticipated. "She cried, but not uncontrollably. I think she really knew, and I think it was an enormous relief for her to hear it. I stayed with her all that night, sitting in a chair by her bed, and she slept peacefully. We were having breakfast outside the next morning when Tatiana and Alex appeared. Francine jumped up and flew into her mother's arms, and Tatiana held her and said, 'Ma chérie, ma chérie,' and they went off for a long walk together, and Alex sat down and had coffee with me."

Francine herself has no clear memory of these events, aside from her sobbing, "Why didn't you tell me?" and her mother saying, "I'm sorry, I'm sorry, I didn't know how." According to Alex, trying half a century later to remember this painful episode, both he and Tatiana were "quite surprised and quite annoyed" that Gitta had taken it upon herself to break the news to Francine—a version that Francine herself more or less espoused when she wrote about it in her first novel, but one that does not have the ring of truth. Neither Tatiana nor Alex had ever been able to confront difficult emotional situations; their feelings of guilt over this one may have led them to blame the messenger.

Although learning the truth that night in Sands Point seemed to bring Francine and Tatiana closer together at the time, the fact that they could not talk about it afterward left a residue of distrust that they never overcame.

A subtle shift was taking place in the relationship between Alex and Lucien Vogel. They had worked together in the spring on a project to redesign *Glamour*, the magazine that Condé Nast had started in 1939. (It had originally been called *Glamour of Hollywood*.) Nast wanted to change its editorial focus, cutting back on the features showing movie stars at home and turning it into a fashion magazine for young American career girls—a rival to Street and Smith's *Mademoiselle*. Nast had rejected the maquette that Alex and Vogel came up with, though, and after that, Alex had started to work more and more closely with Nast on *Vogue*. Vogel had said that he needed Liberman to work with him at Condé Nast, but as Alex's cover designs for *Vogue* continued to find favor with Nast, Crowninshield, and Patcévitch, it became clearer and clearer that Alex did not need Vogel. "I was more or less taken over by Mr. Nast," as he explained it. "Probably at some moment I got too busy, and I had less time for Vogel. He had a tiny little office. His English was rudimentary, and people treated him with respect but with a trace of condescension." Alex thought that Vogel's ideas were out-of-date. Although he had been ahead of his time with *Vu*, Vogel now seemed tied to the old concept of fashion magazines as elegant albums for the rich—a concept that Nast himself was in the process of dismantling.

There was, in addition, the social problem. Vogel didn't really fit in at *Vogue*. His Parisian bonhomie, his English tweeds, and his somewhat rumpled style seemed out of place next to the sleek, polished good manners of Iva Patcévitch and socially prominent editors like Barbara (Babe) Cushing, Mary Jean Kempner, and Millicent Fenwick. Alex, who fitted in very well, would never have said or done anything to undercut his friend, but the time was coming when he would be obliged, as he later described it, to "cast him off." For a refugee and a survivor, such divestitures were sometimes unavoidable. Everyone felt relieved when the Vogels moved back to Paris in 1946 and devoted their attention once again to *Jardin des Modes*.

The work at *Vogue* was amusing, as the society beauties on the staff liked to say, and not very taxing. Although the magazine came out twice a month then, most of the work was done by a handful of well-paid professionals (besides Edna Chase and Dr. Agha, this group included the managing editor, Jessica Daves; the features editor, Allene Talmey, whom Frank Crowninshield had brought over from *Vanity Fair*; and the fashion editor, Bettina Ballard); the society beauties and lower-echelon staff members had a lot of free time on their hands. They played darts on slow days in the art department. There was a weekly "French" lunch at Le Bistro on Lexington at Forty-fifth Street (no English speaking allowed), and there were convivial lunch hours on other days at Jansen's, the German restaurant on the ground floor of the Graybar Building, at 420 Lexington Avenue, where the Condé Nast offices were located. Condé Nast himself would often be at Jansen's, having what he called a "quick-and-dirty" lunch with Edna Chase or Iva Patcévitch; on a few occasions he invited Alex to join him. One or two afternoons a week, Alex would take an hour off to go swimming with Tatiana and Hélène Bonnet, the future French ambassador's wife, at the Shelton Hotel pool nearby. Tatiana's airless workroom at Saks was not nearly as agreeable as the *Vogue* art department, and the exercise helped to renew her formidable energy.

Bettina Ballard and her husband took Alex and Tatiana to Yankee Stadium one night to see their first baseball game. Alex was tremendously struck by the visual impact of walking through a dark tunnel and suddenly seeing the brilliant green of the illuminated field—"a much stronger experience than the bullfight," he said. Bettina Ballard, sophisticated and impeccably chic, had been the Paris editor of *Vogue* until 1941, and at one time she had had an affair with Bertrand du Plessix. Alex never quite knew whether or not Tatiana was aware of this; it was one of those subjects that they did not discuss. Tatiana liked Bettina, although she failed to see the point of baseball. She said that it was really just *lapta*, an old game played

by Russian children. At another Yankee game, which they went to with
the photographer Irving Penn, Joe DiMaggio hit a home run in the first
inning; when he hit another in the fifth, Tatiana got up to leave. "This is
where we came in," she said. Alex became a fan, nevertheless. At World
Series time, he would invite a group of *Vogue* colleagues to the house and
serve them hot dogs and potato chips while they watched the game on
television.

The Libermans rented an even smaller summer house in 1942,
farther out on the North Shore, in the village of Miller Place, near Port
Jefferson. It had no proper bathroom—you washed in the kitchen sink—
but once again they engaged Sally Robinson to cook and keep house, and
this time their co-renters were Iva and Nada Patcévitch. Nada, Patcévitch's
English-born wife, had become Tatiana's closest friend. They enjoyed each
other's company immensely; Nada's lean greyhound looks and witty conversation made an interesting counterpoint to Tatiana's imposing figure and
brusque, Russian-accented pronouncements. The bond between Alex and
Patcévitch was even stronger. For Alex, the silver-haired, strikingly handsome Patcévitch embodied the old Russian aristocracy. The son of a high
official in the czarist government, he had been a cadet at the St. Petersburg
naval academy when the revolution broke out. He escaped to Constantinople
aboard a British warship and eventually made his way to the United States,
where he got a job as a runner for a Wall Street securities firm. His head
for figures and his charming manners sent him quickly up the corporate
ladder at Hemphill Noyes, which he left in 1929 to become the chief
financial officer at Condé Nast. (Nast's daughter, Natica, who had met
Patcévitch socially, was the one who brought him to her father's attention.)
If Nast had taken Patcévitch's advice in 1929 and sold some of the stocks
he was holding, he would not have lost most of his money in the crash. As
it was, Patcévitch played an important part in holding the company together
during the Depression, and Nast, who in 1942 had a serious heart condition
that he didn't want anyone to know about, had dictated a confidential letter
to Mary Campbell, his secretary, naming Patcévitch to succeed him as
president in the event of his death. Alex and Tatiana and the Patcévitches
were at Miller Place in September when Condé Nast died. Sally Robinson
came hurrying down the long flight of wooden steps to the beach to say
there was an important telephone call for Patcévitch. He went back to New
York on the next train and was shown the letter that Nast had dictated
four months earlier.

The special relationship that Alex had enjoyed with Nast quickly
evolved into an even more special one with Patcévitch. He was promoted

Alex and Tatiana's dining room. The metal table and chairs from Macy's cost thirty-four dollars.

in the fall, becoming one of two art editors on the *Vogue* masthead (the other was Arthur Weiser, the top layout man in the art department). The slight increase in salary that went with the promotion was mainly symbolic—an indication of larger rewards in the near future.

Alex and Tatiana were living on the Upper East Side by this time. They had rented a floor-through apartment at 125 East Seventy-third Street, which Tatiana painted all white and furnished with the garden chairs from Macy's. Tatiana's sense of style was unerring. The people who came to their parties found the decor as original and striking as the hostess, whose halting, heavily accented English never interfered with her social bravado. They had started to give cocktail parties for new friends and friends-of-friends and, whenever possible, a celebrity or so to season the mix. Patcévitch had taken them to one of Condé Nast's parties, and that sort of wide-ranging social mélange became the model for their own, more modest gatherings. (If parties were the most direct route to social success, they were also good for business; Tatiana found some of her best customers that

Tatiana, photographed by Irving Penn.

Tatiana in her workroom at Saks.

Costume party at the Levals': Alex (as Napoleon III), Beatrice Leval,
Fernand Leval, Tatiana.

The Libermans at home, with Sally Robinson, their maid from Long Island.

way, and Alex often made useful contacts.) They also gave musical soirées. Zizi de Svirsky, Tatiana's old friend from Paris, played Bach and Prokofiev and Chopin on a rented upright piano, and sometimes accompanied René Le Roy, the concert flutist who had shared Alex's cabin on the boat from Lisbon. There were also less formal evenings, when Yul Brynner, a Russian-born apprentice actor, brought his guitar and sang Gypsy songs. Tatiana's friends John and Irene Wiley, whom they visited once or twice a month in Washington, D.C., had introduced them to some of the more agreeable members of the diplomatic colony. Henri Bonnet, the Free French Ambassador, came with his beautiful wife, Hélène, who turned out to have something in common with Tatiana: she, too, was making and selling hats.

"Tatiana was an absolute volcano" at her parties, according to Rosamond Bernier, a *Vogue* editor whose name then was Peggy Riley and who was welcome at Alex and Tatiana's because, besides being lively and charming, she spoke perfect French. "Tatiana had this colossal vitality and energy. She was very gruff, interrupting people all the time, but with great good nature. Alex was more in the background; he treated her with tender amusement and indulgence." Another frequent guest said that Alex and Tatiana "were, of necessity, a couple on the make. The people at their parties in those days were often second- and third-rate countesses, rather tawdry café-society types, women with very red lips and long red finger-nails—not really top-drawer. Then, gradually, as his star rose at *Vogue*, the names got brighter."

At Seventy-third Street, Alex and Tatiana preserved the fiction of separate living quarters by having Alex sleep in the small back bedroom suite behind the kitchen. Their friends the Levals urged them to put an end to this sort of nonsense by getting married. It was obvious how much they adored one another, so why wait? One reason involved Francine. The previous February, they had taken Francine to Rumpelmayer's for hot chocolate on a Sunday afternoon and asked her how she would feel if they were to get married. Francine's reaction had been a shock to all three of them: uncontrollable sobs, more bitter than the tears she had shed six months earlier when she learned of her father's death. She wept all the harder because she did not know why she was weeping. Understanding did not come until years later: "The wedding news attempted to confirm a death which I was decades away from totally accepting." There was no more talk of marriage after that—at least, not in Francine's presence.

Beatrice and Fernand Leval kept after them about it, though, in their concerned and proprietary way. Alex and Tatiana had met the Levals in 1941, at a dinner party in Greenwich Village. Driving uptown afterward in a taxi with them, Alex had offended the well-to-do, Swiss-born Fernand, the president of Louis-Dreyfus and Company, by complaining about how much things cost in New York—things like taxis, and having one's breakfast sent up to the apartment from the corner restaurant. "I can save you some money right there," snapped Leval, who did not quite see why a refugee who was making fifty dollars a week should be obliged to have his breakfast sent in. "You go to a hardware store and buy an orange-juice squeezer and a coffeepot, and you go to a grocery store and buy oranges and coffee." Their next meeting took place, quite unexpectedly, at one of Toscanini's farewell concerts at Carnegie Hall. Finding themselves sandwiched between Alex and Tatiana on one side and Alex's rather talkative mother on the other, the Levals switched seats with Henriette. For a while afterward the Levals wanted no part of those "awful" Libermans, but that summer they took a house in Manhasset, Long Island, which was close to Alex and Tatiana's house in Sands Point, and Beatrice was reintroduced to Tatiana at a lunch given by a mutual friend. After lunch she gave Tatiana a lift home in her car, stayed for tea, and was won over by her directness and warmth and her "wonderful, disconnected way of speaking." The friendship blossomed from that moment.

When Alex and Tatiana finally did decide to get married, in the fall of 1942, it was the Levals who made all the arrangements. They persuaded their friend Judge Benjamin Schreiber to perform the ceremony during his lunch hour, which was the only time the bride and groom said they could get away from work, and they brought their car to pick up Tatiana at Saks. "Ferdie let me off at the Fiftieth Street entrance," Beatrice remembers, "and I took the elevator upstairs to the millinery department. And there I saw Alex, looking absolutely green. I said, 'Where's Tatiana?' He said, 'She's over there, waiting on somebody important. *You* go get her.' I went over to where she was showing hats to this man—I found out later he was somebody from Hollywood who wanted a lot of hats for a picture he was making; it was a big deal—and I said to her, in French, 'I'm terribly sorry, Tatiana, but you just have to come.' Tatiana turned back to the man and apologized, said she had to leave, but that it would only be for an hour, and could he please come back after lunch? I grabbed her arm and we ran to the elevator, picking up Alex on the way, and down to the street, where my husband was going round and round the block in the car. We drove downtown to the Supreme Court building, and they got married in the judge's chambers, with us as their witnesses. And afterward Tatiana went back to work."

The Levals gave a dinner party for the newlyweds at their East

End Avenue apartment. The guests included Iva and Nada Patcévitch, Justin and Pat Green, and a rather glittering assembly of New York literary and theater people. Alex had wanted Beatrice to invite his parents, but she had refused. "I said, 'Alex, please don't ask me that.' I don't know how I did it, but I did. His mother was the kind of person who would take off her clothes while she was dancing. I thought that was so horrible, and I was so embarrassed for my friend Alex to have his mother do that in front of his friends, that I didn't want to be part of it. And he suffered terribly because of that, I'm afraid."

Francine was not invited, either—to the dinner party or to the wedding. She came home from school that afternoon and found a lot of telegrams congratulating Alex and Tatiana. That was how she learned they were married.

Alex shortly after he became art director of *Vogue*. The decor is still
Dr. Mehemed Fehmy Agha's. "I'm wearing my uniform—
a gray flannel suit, navy knit tie."

No Visions of
Loveliness

Mehemed Fehmy Agha, his monacle firmly in place, walked into Iva Patcévitch's office at *Vogue* and issued an ultimatum. "Either Liberman goes," he said, "or I go."

Agha had resented the rising young star of the art department ever since his decision to get rid of him, after one week on the job, had backfired so ignominiously. He had managed to keep his feelings to himself while Condé Nast was alive, partly because he thought that Liberman, like most of the other young men on the staff, would soon be drafted for military service. But when Alex went for his Selective Service physical exam toward the end of 1942 and was classified 4-F because of chronic duodenal ulcers, Agha's cup of bitterness overflowed. Unfortunately for Dr. Agha, his own authority had been undermined over the years by his cynical and often scornful attitude toward everyone else. "I was not in the habit of accepting ultimatums from employees," Patcévitch explained many years later. "Besides, I liked Alex very much, he was very talented, and he was Russian." Another factor in the decision may well have been Agha's $40,000 annual salary, which had become something of a burden. At any rate, Patcévitch's decision was not long in coming. He announced Agha's resignation from Condé Nast in February 1943, and a month later Alexander

Liberman's name appeared on the masthead as the new art director of
Vogue.

Although Alex was only thirty years old and had been with Condé
Nast for a scant two years, his appointment was a popular one. He had
demonstrated great ability without stepping on other people's toes, and his
personal charm—which his stepdaughter once described as a "gift for persuasion that had to do with thoughtfulness, attentiveness, and phenomenal
memory"—seemed the perfect antidote to Agha's intellectual bullying. In
addition, he had what Leo Lerman called "star quality"—a quiet presence
that made others respect and defer to him. The responsibilities of the job
did not seem to daunt him at all. Having been art director and then managing
editor of *Vu*, he felt confident of his ability to make the multiple daily
decisions and judgments that his new post called for. His increased
salary—$12,000 a year—gave a sizable boost to his confidence; it meant
that he would be earning more money than Tatiana.

Within a few months of his accession, the magazine looked different. He got rid of most of the whimsical hand-lettering that still littered
some of the fashion pages, and he changed the magazine's dominant typeface
to Franklin Gothic, a bold, no-nonsense, sans-serif letter favored by the
Daily News and other tabloids. Titles, captions, and text blocks became
clearer and more informative, and the pages became more crowded. All
this was very much in line with the late Condé Nast's wish to move away
from the "album" concept and to turn *Vogue* into something more like a
news magazine. "The album-type layout was static and out-of-date," Alex
said. "It didn't have the cinematic flow that I was interested in. I also
thought it would be provocative and exciting to use practically the same
type as a tabloid newspaper in this very different context. It brought vitality
to the page."

Alex's increased use of photographs, at the expense of drawings by
René Bouët-Willaumez, Carl Erickson ("Eric"), René Bouché, and the
other fashion artists, also reflected Nast's thinking, and so did the informal,
girl-next-door look of some of the photographers' models. The all-American
girl was replacing the haughty, European-style mannequin, largely because
the war had shut down Paris as the international center of haute couture.
The war was giving a great boost to American-based designers such as
Mainbocher, Valentina, and Charles James, who responded ingeniously to
the problems of wartime price controls and the strict rationing of silk and
other fabrics, and who were being featured in the pages of *Vogue* and
Harper's Bazaar as never before. Moreover, the sporty, informal clothes of
Claire McCardell and other young designers seemed to call for a new sort

of model and a new photographic approach—one that emphasized spontaneity and movement over aristocratic hauteur. Models had not been able to move naturally in the past; the dresses they showed were often fitted on the model in back with clothespins, and besides, ladies were not supposed to be active. The new freedom and informality of American fashion coincided with Alex's own ideas about the real purpose of *Vogue*. "I wanted to involve women in the life of the moment," he said, "and the war furthered this by destroying fantasy. Clothes had to be practical for women who worked. No more Ophelias dancing through the Plaza at dawn." *Vogue* had its first all-American fashion issue in February 1942, called "U.S.A. Fashion on Its Own." The magazine ran regular features on women in uniform or in other war-related activities, and it published Cecil Beaton's pictures of bombed-out sites in London. Lee Miller, a beautiful former model who had learned photography from Man Ray—with whom she lived for several years in Paris—was assigned by British *Vogue* to cover the war in Europe. She was one of the first war correspondents to photograph the horror of the concentration camps. After much soul-searching, and considerable pressure from Alex, Edna Chase made the courageous decision to publish her pictures of Dachau in American *Vogue*.

Changing attitudes required new photographers. While *Vogue* and *Harper's Bazaar* continued to give plenty of work to their established (and mostly European) master photographers—George Hoyningen-Huene and Louise Dahl-Wolfe at *Bazaar*, Horst P. Horst and Cecil Beaton at *Vogue* (Edward Steichen, who had left in 1938, spent the war making films for the U.S. Navy)—both magazines also took on younger photographers, whose best work seemed to emerge when they shot outdoors, in natural light. *Harper's Bazaar* was the leader, of course. Martin Munkacsi, the Hungarian-born photographer whom Carmel Snow had hired in the late thirties, was the first to specialize in dynamic action photographs of models in motion. Toni Frissell at *Vogue* had been shooting outdoors for years, of course, but Alex was not a great fan of her work—he thought she "treated the outdoors like a studio," setting up carefully posed shots with little feeling of spontaneity—and he was not distressed when she defected to *Harper's Bazaar* after the war. John Rawlings and Frances McLaughlin, whom Alex hired and helped to train, provided the kind of straightforward, unencumbered fashion reportage that he was looking for. In Alex's opinion, their work was considerably more imaginative and refined than Frissell's.

He also took an interest in an Albanian-born photographer named Gjon Mili, who was one of the first to explore the possibilities of strobe light for stopping action. Mili worked mostly for *Life*. He had never done fashion work before, but Alex got him to photograph models pushing shopping carts in a supermarket and ran a Mili cover shot of a girl tossing her wet hair in an arc of droplets. He gave a lot of assignments to Serge Balkin and Constantin Joffé, two highly talented Russian refugees (there were times when you heard as much Russian as English spoken in the *Vogue* offices, according to some staffers), and he had a particular fondness for Erwin Blumenfeld, another European refugee, who had a genius for solarizations and other technical manipulations of the medium. "I loved Blumenfeld," he recalled. "He was the most graphic of all the photographers, and the one who was most deeply rooted in the fine arts. He was always terribly proud of his work. He would bring it in to the office and say, in his terrible German accent, 'Put it in the mid'—meaning in the middle of the book, the most important spot."

André Kertész presented a different kind of problem. Alex, who had worked with him on *Vu*, signed Kertész to an exclusive contract with Condé Nast in 1946, but it immediately became apparent that he would never be a fashion photographer. The solution that Alex found was to make him the star photographer for *House & Garden*; by this time Alex was art director of all three Condé Nast magazines. He felt slightly guilty about Kertész. "It was the first time in history," he once said, "that a great artist had been asked to photograph interiors." But he did not really think that Kertész was a great artist, or even a great photographer. According to Alex, he was "sentimental"—an unforgivable failing. Later, when *House & Garden* decided that he was too difficult to work with any more and let him go, Kertész told an interviewer that Alex Liberman had ruined his career.

The two young Americans who would revolutionize and dominate the field of fashion photography in the postwar era were spotted very early by Alex Liberman. He missed getting Richard Avedon, who had his heart set on working for Alexey Brodovitch at *Harper's Bazaar*. When Alex tried to recruit him for *Vogue*, Avedon said he had just accepted an offer from *Bazaar*, which was hardly the case—although he had been pushing for months to get an appointment with Brodovitch, at this point he hadn't even met him. With Irving Penn, though, Alex established the closest and the most fruitful working relationship of his professional life—a relationship that Penn has always been quick to acknowledge. "Some of the best work for *Vogue*, though it may bear my signature, is in fact ours, the result of a special and close collaboration," Penn wrote in *Passage*, the 1991 book of his photographs.

Irving Penn had wanted to be a painter. As a student at the Philadelphia Museum School in the mid-1930s, though, he had fallen under the spell of Brodovitch, who taught a course in design there. "Brodovitch was the first person to show me the mystical quality in photographs," Penn said. For two summers Penn had worked as Brodovitch's assistant at *Harper's Bazaar*, and some of his first photographs—of street scenes and shop windows—had been published in that magazine. Saks Fifth Avenue made Brodovitch its consultant art director in 1940, and Penn came along as his assistant. He inherited the job when Brodovitch left, a year later, but the work bored him. Penn still wanted to be a painter. He decided to go to Mexico and spend a year painting, and it was at this point, looking for someone to replace him at Saks, that he first met Alex Liberman. Brodovitch had suggested that Penn discuss the job with Liberman, so Penn called him and arranged a meeting. Penn took an immediate liking to Alex, and was secretly pleased that Alex had no interest in the job. Penn went off to Mexico, where a year's effort convinced him that he was not going to be a painter. He returned to New York early in 1943, and Alex, who had become art director of *Vogue* in the meanwhile, and who had been very impressed by Penn at their first meeting, promptly hired him as his personal assistant.

Penn was installed in a tiny cubicle next to Alex's office, and his first assignment was to think up ideas for *Vogue* covers. "I gave my ideas to Horst, Blumenfeld, Beaton, and Rawlings," Penn said, "and they just gave me the back of the hand." With the unrelenting self-doubt that has always been one of his distinguishing traits, Penn told Alex that he had "failed" his assignment. "Why don't you take the picture yourself?" Alex suggested. Penn said that he wouldn't know how to go about it, but Alex, who must have sensed the intensity of the vision behind all that self-doubt, kept pushing and nudging him. He gave him a space in which to work in the magnificently equipped photo studio that *Vogue* maintained for its photographers in a nearby office building, and he provided Penn with an assistant to help him master the complexities of the eight-by-ten studio camera. (Most of Penn's previous photographs had been taken with a Rolleiflex.) The experiment succeeded in ways that neither Penn nor Liberman could have foreseen. The failed painter rediscovered himself as an artist —one of the most original and powerful photographers of his time.

Penn began as a still-life photographer, and his initial efforts appeared on the cover of *House & Garden*. His first *Vogue* cover, for the October 1, 1943, issue, was a still life of "New Accessories"—belt, gloves, handbag, scarf—arranged on a wooden table, against a wall on which hung an engraving in color of oranges and lemons. The carefully thought-out composition, the solidity and weight of the ensemble made it seem almost too austere for a fashion cover, and this may have been why it troubled the redoubtable Edna Chase. "If you're going to do such a radical thing as a still-life cover," she asked Alex, "why don't you get the best still-life photographer?" Alex knew why, but he could not explain it to Mrs. Chase. There was a quality to Penn's photograph—a clarity of vision and an absence of extraneous detail—that made it unflinchingly modern. This quality became more evident in subsequent Penn still lifes, which made up a large part of his early work for *Vogue*. The photographs of salad ingredients, or of playing cards, dice, chessmen, and other "after-dinner games," with their meticulously arranged elements and rigid compositional structure, might appear to have the solidity of old-master paintings, but there was always a jarring or discordant note somewhere—cigarette ashes, insects, a half-burned match—that made them a little disturbing. His pictures were "ascetic," as Alex put it. "Penn liked apples that were rotting, or flowers that were shedding their blooms. There was a sort of grittiness that kept them from being merely charming. And seeing them that way, in the context of an elegant fashion magazine, was a shock."

Penn volunteered for the American Field Service in 1944. He served in Italy and in India, driving an ambulance and photographing soldiers in action and in repose. In letters to Alex, he spoke nostalgically of the bond of understanding that they shared. Penn was hurt that Alex did not answer any of his letters (to this day Alex rarely answers letters). After the war, although they lunched together frequently and talked every day, their friendship remained more professional than personal. They didn't call each other by their first names—it was always "Mr. Penn" and "Mr. Liberman," spoken in a tone of affectionate irony.

When Penn came back to work at *Vogue* in 1946, Alex encouraged him to embark on the series of black-and-white portraits that established his mature reputation. Penn photographed just about everyone of importance in the arts at that time. He devised an oddly confining setting for these studio portraits: a corner formed by two converging walls, with a worn and shabby piece of carpet to lend the proper Penn-style grittiness to the scene. Sometimes he threw the carpet over a crate to make a mound-like table, on which his subjects—many of the pictures were group portraits—could rest their elbows. For writers, actors, artists, dancers, intellectuals, and eventually government leaders in Washington, D.C., being the subject of one of Penn's somber, penetrating portraits became a mark of success.

Penn stubbornly resisted taking fashion pictures. Although he had photographed the twelve top fashion models of the forties, in a 1947 group portrait that was one of the era's icons, he insisted that he knew little about fashion and couldn't possibly do it. (Persuading Penn to take a photograph at all was a considerable undertaking.) In 1948, though, Alex managed to send him off with a model on a fashion assignment to Lima, Peru. The model, a very pretty girl named Jean Patchett, soon found out that working with Penn was not like working with anyone else. Each morning she would appear on time, carefully made up and dressed, and Penn would spend the next eight or nine hours deciding that whatever setting they elected to try was not possible. After several days during which he did not take a single photograph, Patchett was feeling frustrated and depressed. They went into a café. "I sat down and said to hell with it, and picked up my pearls," she recalled. "My feet were hurting, so I kicked off my shoes. He said, 'Stop!' " This picture, which has been reproduced in many anthologies of fashion photography, shows the girl in profile, elbow on the table, holding the pearl necklace to her lips while she stares moodily past the man whose half-profile is just visible at the extreme left. It is different from any other fashion photograph taken up to that time, and it had a profound influence on a great many photographers. "Instead of an artificial pose, here was a woman caught in an everyday moment," Alex Liberman said later. "It's the imperfection of actual life."

That imperfection was the essence of what Liberman was looking for—the breakthrough from fantasy and artifice into the here-and-now. It was the antidote to the "visions of loveliness" that Mrs. Chase and generations of *Vogue* readers cherished—visions that Alex wanted to banish forever from the pages of *Vogue*, in part because he felt that they were demeaning to women. *Vogue* was not really about fashion, he always said; it was about women. To photograph women as divine, ethereal creatures posing alongside Greek columns or in elaborately concocted studio imitations of royal boudoirs seemed to him to mock their dignity as human beings; it was a male-imposed vision that Alex, a proto-feminist, found silly and offensive. The fact that Penn shared this point of view became one of the key aspects of their developing collaboration. "Alex and I were interested in women," Penn said. "We were always searching for some delectable and seductive quality." Another early Penn image that became famous showed a girl delicately removing a shred of tobacco from her tongue. "The real gesture of a real person," as Penn put it. "That's what Alex found in looking at the contact sheets, and what he taught me. The image was an accident."

Penn stayed on in Peru after the fashion assignment was done. In Cuzco, he rented a local photographer's studio during Christmas week and made a series of portraits of peasants, egg sellers, and Indian families that became the first of his celebrated studies of Third World peoples, which he published in *Vogue* and in a 1974 book called *Worlds in a Small Room*. The direct, unadorned, unsentimental clarity of these images might appear to have little in common with fashion photography, but this was in fact the same quality that Penn brought to the fashion work that he did for *Vogue* during the next few years.

Alex sent Penn to Paris in 1949 to observe the collections—not to photograph them, but to see how the fashion world looked and worked. (Paris couture had regained its former pre-eminence two years before, with the unveiling of Christian Dior's "New Look.") In 1950, Penn went back to Paris to photograph the fall collections. Working virtually around the clock, in a studio that the models had to climb five flights of stairs to reach, he produced a series of photographs that were as stark—and as compelling—as his portraits of Peruvian peasants. He posed his models against a gray nineteenth-century theater curtain and photographed them head-on, characteristically looking straight into the lens. The details of the couture were brilliantly revealed, without tricks or distractions, but the photographs went deeper than most fashion photographs. "Penn's 1950 pictures provide no references to plot or circumstance, no suggestion of old chateaux, or perfect picnics, or delicious flirtations in Edwardian drawing rooms, or footlights, or *avant* Freudian dream worlds," John Szarkowski, the Museum of Modern Art's director of photography, wrote in his catalogue text for the 1984 exhibition of Penn's work at MOMA. "They are not stories, but simply pictures." Later, Penn himself would draw a distinction between his portraits and his fashion work. He said that in fashion photography, the true personality of the model should never intrude, whereas in his portraits he was looking for something "more profound . . . the person." Penn has also said, however, that he falls in love with the models he photographs. (He married Lisa Fonssagrives, the top model of the 1940s, who was one of the models he photographed in Paris in 1950.) The indelible *presence* that causes so many Penn photographs to linger in the memory is the record of an intense interaction between the photographer and his subject, and in these early years at *Vogue*, the presence was often as strong in the fashion photographs as it was in the formal portraits.

Ironically, Penn's work had none of the fluid, spontaneous qualities that Alex and others admired so much in the pages of *Harper's Bazaar*. The team of Carmel Snow and Alexey Brodovitch continued to keep *Bazaar* well out in front of *Vogue* in its creative use of photography. Brodovitch had moved away from his highly structured, Surrealist-inspired layouts of the previous decade and was using sparer graphics and more white space on the page. From 1945 on, he and Snow gave increasing emphasis to the photographs of Richard Avedon, who was rapidly becoming the most imitated photographer of his generation. Avedon's action shots of models jumping off curbs or turning cartwheels or mingling with carnival performers on Paris streets had a dash and an excitement that *Vogue*'s pages conspicuously lacked. He became a master of the expressive blur—blurred backgrounds, blurred movement—a device that Brodovitch himself had used when he photographed ballet dancers in motion for his 1945 book *Ballet*. Nothing could better exemplify the diminishing role of needle-sharp "straight" photography and the birth of new techniques that enlisted the viewer's active participation. In the process, fashion itself became progressively less important; the new subject—in *Bazaar*, at any rate—was not the clothes so much as the life style of the people who wore them. Edna Chase and her loyal editors could not see the point of this. "Avedon would go to Paris, and there would be elephants," Alex said (referring to the famous photo of Dovima in a ball gown standing between two elephants at the Cirque d'Hiver), "but with Mrs. Chase every button counted." *Bazaar* published portfolios of nonfashion work by Brassaï, Cartier-Bresson, Bill Brandt, Robert Frank, and Lisette Model. It ran short stories by Truman Capote, Carson McCullers, and other young writers, and provocative nonfiction on a wide variety of subjects. Although it never surpassed *Vogue* in circulation or in advertising revenue, *Bazaar* consistently showed more snap and dazzle in its editing and its graphic layout, and Alex often pointed this out in discussions with Patcévitch and Edna Chase, arguing that it made *Vogue* look stodgy and pedestrian by comparison.

At a deeper level, though, Alex did not want to imitate what Brodovitch and Carmel Snow were doing. Much as he admired the cinematic elegance of the layouts in *Bazaar*, he felt that Brodovitch and Snow were still adhering to the concept of fashion magazines as luxury products for an upper-class audience. "Elegance was Brodovitch's strong point," he said. "The page looked very attractive. But in a way, it seemed to me that Brodovitch was serving the same purpose that Agha had served, which was to make the magazine attractive to women—not interesting to women, attractive to women. What I wanted—and what Condé had been trying to do—was to make it something more than lovely and attractive. I thought there was more merit in being able to put twenty pictures on two pages than in making two elegant pages. The one clear idea that I brought was the idea of anti-design. What is design? It's making the use of the material—the way it's used—more important than the material itself. In

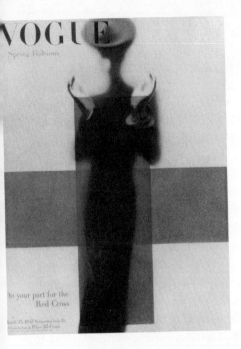

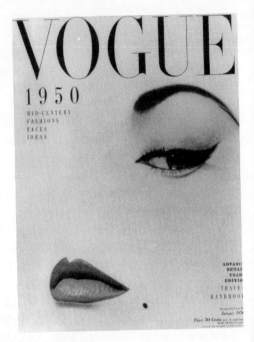

Vogue covers, clockwise from top left:
Erwin Blumenfeld, March 1945;
Erwin Blumenfeld, January 1950;
Irving Penn, April 1950;
Irving Penn, October 1951 (the
Franklin Gothic type that Alex chose
for this cover did not go over well).

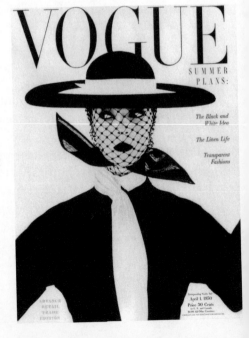

Reception committee for Francine's return from
Colorado. From left, Iva Patcévitch, Nada Patcévitch,
Tatiana, Bettina Ballard, Elena Schouvaloff, Francine.

On the *Queen Mary*, 1947. From left, Ilka Chase, Edna
Woolman Chase, Patcévitch, Nada, Francine, Tatiana,
Richard Newton (Chase's husband).

my experience with *Vu*, design didn't count. I never designed a layout at
Vu. I'd look at the material and say, this is a wonderful picture, let's make
it big, don't let's have the title damage it. Or, conversely, I might allow
the journalistic content of the title to dominate the image. I came to believe
in the unexpected, in chance, in doing things that hadn't been done before
and didn't conform to any established design principles. At *Vogue*, I wanted
to break the design obsession, so I defended a more journalistic approach
—rougher lettering, no white space, crowded pages, messier layouts."

He was tilting at windmills, of course. Edna Chase, who had been
editor in chief of *Vogue* since Alex was two years old, was not interested
in messy layouts. She warned Jessica Daves, her eventual but necessarily
patient successor, that the art department must never be allowed to "take
over" the magazine, and from time to time she would call Alex into her
office (Mrs. Chase never went to the art-department offices, at the other
end of the long hall) and ask him to explain to her why he had chosen to
use a photograph that struck her as singularly inelegant. As often as not,
the photograph was by Penn, and Alex could find no words to explain its
strength or importance. Once she summoned him to a meeting at Patcévitch's house to complain about the tabloid-style lettering that kept appearing in *Vogue*. She said it was causing people to cancel their subscriptions. Alex didn't argue the point, and from then on, until Mrs. Chase
retired, there was less of the offensive Franklin Gothic type in the
magazine.

Alex and Mrs. Chase liked and respected one another, but good
manners kept him from telling her what he really thought. He was developing a useful contempt for what he did at *Vogue*—a contempt that was
as thoroughgoing in its way as Agha's had been, although, unlike Agha,
Alex was much too clever to let it show. He knew perfectly well that he
could never really break down the *Vogue* traditions of class and elegance,
and his efforts to do so became a kind of amusing game, whose victories
and defeats need not be taken too seriously. Alex felt, for example, that
the title "art director" was a joke. The material that he dealt with in the
art department every day was not art. The facile drawings of Eric or
Willaumez were not art, and in Alex's mind photographs—even Penn's
photographs—could never be works of art, either. Photographs to him were
documents—momentary glimpses of something that could be printed in ink
on a magazine page and eventually discarded. That was their function and
their fate. Although he had scarcely painted since he left Europe, Alex
thought he knew what it meant to be an artist, and that knowledge, held
in reserve in the back of his mind as something to which he could always

return, made the absurdities and the frustrations of fashion journalism more bearable. "In a curious way I felt myself superior to everybody I was dealing with and to everything that I was doing," he said, "because I felt that I was an artist. I knew what real art was, or thought I knew, and this gave me a great deal of self-confidence—the kind of unquestioning self-confidence you need to be a good editor or a good art director. I felt that if I chose something, a picture or a layout, it must be right and it must be good. It was right because I chose it."

Iva S. V.-Patcévitch, president of Condé Nast, and Alex, mid-1940s.

Circles

"S uccess?" said Tatiana Liberman to her daughter. "There is really nothing else in life." Tatiana had slight tolerance for those on whom fortune had not yet smiled. Francine, grown tall and modishly slender, remembered passing canapés several times a month "to the likes of Salvador Dali, Christian Dior, Ray Bolger, Charles Addams, John Gunther, Adrian of Hollywood, Jacques Fath, Hubert de Givenchy, Elsa Maxwell, Irving Penn, Marlene Dietrich, Claudette Colbert," and other bright stars of the moment. The Libermans had moved into a four-story town house at 173 East Seventieth Street, which they got for a relatively low rent ($200 a month) because it was so close to the Third Avenue elevated subway tracks, and because nobody wanted a town house during the war, when domestic help was so hard to find. To help pay the rent, they leased the top floor of the house to Elena Schouvaloff, a Russian countess whose husband was with the 82nd Airborne Division in Europe. The Schouvaloffs had belonged to the highest level of the Russian aristocracy before the revolution, and so had Elena's own family, the Tatischeffs. (Her cousin, the screen actor Jacques Tati, became famous for his films about Monsieur Hulot.) Elena was without resources, though, and Tatiana had managed to find her a job in the millinery department at Saks.

Alex and Tatiana had already learned to live like the rich without being rich. It was a trick they picked up early and improved on year by year. One of the basic elements was having good servants, and they had found the requisite jewel in Mabel Moses, an indefatigable black woman who, with some initial help from her husband, Matthew, took care of all their domestic needs. Mabel and Matthew had worked previously for Julia Ansbury, a society woman who had once bought hats from Tatiana in Paris. The Libermans and the Patcévitches rented the Ansbury house in Greenwich, Connecticut, during the summer of 1943 and fell in love with Mabel and her cooking—especially her fried chicken with cucumbers and sour cream. When Julia Ansbury moved to Washington, D.C., in the fall, Alex persuaded Mabel, Matthew, and their young son to come to them. "Mr. Liberman said, 'If you stay with me, you'll never have to worry for the rest of your life,' " Mabel remembered, "and that's exactly how it turned out."

Mabel stayed for forty years, sharing the benefits of an increasingly extravagant standard of living. Matthew, the butler, a light-skinned man who looked a lot like Harry Belafonte, had a briefer tenure. He remained long enough to father another child with Mabel—they named her Tatiana—and to take painting lessons from Alex, but then he had an affair with one of the women in Tatiana's weekly canasta group. The marriage to Mabel broke up as a result, and Matthew followed his new love to California, where he died a few years later in an industrial accident. Mabel largely took over the job of raising Francine. ("She didn't get much mothering, so I thought maybe I better do that.") She provided practical information about the menstrual period and other facts of life (Alex's explanations were more theoretical) and kept a sharp eye on the boys whom Francine occasionally brought home from school. "My parents were hardly ever home in the evening," Francine recalls, "so I spent a lot of wonderful time with Mabel."

Tatiana was a scintillating hostess. Still beautiful, with her strikingly tall figure and white-blond hair, she dressed in a highly individual style (black tunic and slacks, worn with a lot of big costume jewelry) and displayed more aggressive vitality than anyone in the room. She bullied and taunted her guests in a growling, Russian-accented voice, making up nicknames for them (a self-important Russian became "the Inspector General"; a man she found trivial was "Dirka," the Russian word for "hole"), showering affection and ridicule in equal measure, issuing proclamations that would get repeated around midtown lunch tables the next day: "Snobs are always right"; "If you never lie, you are rude"; "One doesn't argue with winners." A shy young school friend of Francine's who appeared at the house in one of the clear plastic raincoats that were in style that year was observed from the top of the stairs by Tatiana, who called down, "You look like a contraceptive!" When Pat Green showed up at a Liberman cocktail party in a new dress and said she had bought it at Bloomingdale's, Tatiana drew herself up to an impossible height. "Bloomingdale's," she rasped, "is for sheets!"

Everyone thought Tatiana and Alex were perfect together. Alex's suave, rather formal good manners offset Tatiana's larger-than-life exuberance, in much the same way that his articulate conversation in English or French made people appreciate all the more her colorful manglings of both languages. He obviously adored her. They called each other "Boubous" in private, and sometimes in public (it was a meaningless term of endearment whose origins even they had forgotten), and friends often noticed them holding hands. Alex was proud of the way Tatiana reigned over their social gatherings. Although he did not have as good a time at cocktail parties as she did, he agreed with her that it was a way of fostering one's career. To be part of what was then referred to as "café society" counted for more on the social scale than making hats or producing eye-catching covers for *Vogue*, and it gave them access to people who could be useful to them. Besides, "If we gave a party for a designer, or for somebody whose book was just coming out, Condé Nast would pay for it," Alex said. (A generous expense account was one of the secrets of living like the rich without being rich.) They also gave a great many card parties. Elsa Maxwell, the era's most famous social organizer, had popularized this form of entertaining during the war; she would get up six or eight tables for bridge every Sunday at the Waldorf-Astoria, where she lived rent-free in those days. Tatiana and Alex invited Elsa to their Saturday lunches at East Seventieth Street, after which the guests would repair to card tables and play bridge all afternoon. Alex, who loved to gamble, always played for the highest possible stakes and frequently ended up losing money. Tatiana, who preferred to play for five cents a point, usually won.

The Libermans had a standing invitation to Gregor and Lydia Gregory's house in East Hampton. Lydia Gregory's father had been a famous lawyer in Russia before the Revolution; Lydia herself, an ardent admirer of Mayakovsky, knew about Tatiana's love affair with the poet and developed a sort of schoolgirl crush on her as a result. Alex and Tatiana continued to see a great deal of Iva and Nada Patcévitch, whose rich friends became theirs as well. "I owe everything—my whole life in this country—to Pat," Alex once said, with untypical exaggeration. "He had a great sense of luxury, for one thing, and maybe that coincided with my yearnings or

Tatiana's yearnings. Making money never really interested me, but luxury has always been very important, I guess because it gives me a feeling of security. Pat took us to parties, to the best restaurants, to the best of everything." Patcévitch, with his silver-gray hair, youthful good looks, and superb physique, was an extraordinarily successful womanizer. According to a fashion editor who started working at *Vogue* in the 1940s, "When it was known that he was going to Paris, the ladies would start calling the office to book him way in advance. His girl friends would occasionally be foisted off on us afterward as hat editors." Nada Patcévitch took the mistresses in stride, until his affair with Marlene Dietrich got out of hand and destroyed their marriage.

The Libermans and the Patcévitches were inseparable, going to the same dinner parties, sitting next to each other at theater openings and at concerts, sharing summer rentals. After the 1943 summer in Greenwich, they reverted to Long Island's North Shore, where for the next three summers the Libermans and the Patcévitches played host to successive waves of house guests in the Devereaux Emmetts' large, white-columned colonial house in St. James, overlooking Long Island Sound. (Emmett was a patrician and an early designer of golf courses; his fortune had dwindled, however, and he was obliged to rent the property. Tatiana knew Emmett's daughter, Patricia, who had been a great friend of Zizi de Svirsky in Paris.) "It had beautiful old tacky bedrooms," Alex said, "like a Russian dacha."

Alex's father died in January 1946, after a yearlong struggle with inoperable cancer. Alex was with him at the end; Henriette had called him in the middle of the night, and he had come to their Fifth Avenue apartment. "My father is the only person I've literally seen die," he said. "I think he recognized my presence, although he didn't speak." Alex felt that his father had gradually come to approve of him ("He told people I'd made a great career in publishing"), but they had never managed to become close, and Simon Liberman had not told his son about his own mounting business problems. By the time he died, his Canadian partner had siphoned off most of the profits from their timber interests. Although Simon managed to keep on paying the rent for their large Fifth Avenue apartment, he was unable or unwilling to buy Henriette the fur coat that she unceasingly demanded (to replace the one she claimed that Tatiana had "stolen"), and he left her very little in his will. For the rest of her life (she lived until 1974), Henriette depended on Alex for financial support, but, to Alex's and Tatiana's great relief, she decided in 1947 to return to Paris. She had never really liked New York or felt at home there; when Tatiana relented and let her come to one of their parties, she spent her time chatting with the bartender, whom she said was the only interesting person there. In a letter to Alex soon after her husband's death, she sounded the note of reproach and disapproval that would echo through all her voluminous subsequent correspondence with him:

> Do you understand, my love, that you have become a slave to a certain "milieu." In my view, there is nothing live, original, or human in it. Conventions, clichés, formulas from the *Annals de Politesse*, etc. etc. All your milieu, without one single exception, consists of salon snobs or of people who strive to become snobs. . . . Do you realize how many interesting, remarkable people have been at the house of your mother; in how many countries I have been received by extremely interesting people (London, Russia, Italy, France). I did not create my own "genre," I have just been myself. When I like somebody, I can say a tender word; if I do not like them—I tell them to go to hell!
>
> No, my darling, I will not become a dried-out society lady who for hours can sit and play cards. I prefer solitude to such a milieu—until now I have not seen at your house one single *live* person. For me you are a living human being who "mummifies" himself among the dead.
>
> If you do not like this letter—tear it up!
> *But I love you.*

When his mother left New York for good in 1947, Alex and Tatiana strained their resources to buy her a waist-length leopardskin jacket, hoping perhaps to atone for the protracted fur-coat dispute. She sent it back to them with a furious note: only housemaids, she said, would wear such a cut-rate item.

Neither Alex nor Tatiana ever seriously considered the idea of moving back to Europe. The patriotic fervor that had seized Alex in France during those early months of the war was totally forgotten, swallowed up in his and Tatiana's all-consuming drive to make a place for themselves in the exciting, fast-moving social and professional worlds of New York. Alex, who had filed for United States citizenship within two months of his arrival in 1941, received his naturalization papers on May 27, 1946. It took Tatiana until 1951 to get hers, mainly because of her difficulties with the language.

About the time he became a U.S. citizen, Alex also became a

property owner. The house on Seventieth Street had been put up for sale. Some prospective purchasers walked in on Tatiana while she was in the bathtub one day—an invasion of privacy so traumatic that Alex felt obliged to put aside his own money worries and buy the house himself. Iva Patcévitch arranged for Condé Nast to lend Alex $20,000—half the purchase price—and he got a bank mortgage for the rest. Tatiana was overjoyed. She had already converted the place into a series of pristine white rooms —rooms as white as Alex's childhood bedroom in St. Petersburg—furnished with the garden chairs from Macy's, a few antiques picked up at auction for almost nothing (most of them got painted white, too), and some odd pieces given to them by friends: the living-room sofa, designed by the ineffable Zizi de Svirsky, had been passed on to them by Irene Wiley, who didn't like it; the baby grand piano in the library came from the Patcévitches.

Tatiana decorated the white rooms with fresh flowers, mirrors, and framed sketches by Salvador Dali, René Bouché, and other artists Alex worked with at *Vogue*. Marcel Vertès gave them one of his wittily painted screens, which Tatiana adored. She was utterly confident in matters of taste. She felt no need for showy furniture or Baccarat crystal when she entertained, and her guests thought it was frightfully chic of her to have furnished the house so inexpensively. Tatiana owned one good piece of jewelry—a huge ring whose cluster of garnets (once thought to be rubies) had come from an old bracelet of her grandmother's; Johnny Schlumberger, Tiffany's top jewelry man, had helped Tatiana design the setting, and she wore it all the time. Like Alex, she owned relatively few clothes—most of them came from Christian Dior or his successor, Yves Saint Laurent, who was so grateful for her allegiance that he gave her clothes from time to time—and they hung in her closet on wire hangers from the dry cleaner's. Fancy lingerie had no allure for Tatiana, either; she saw no need, in fact, to wear any underclothing at all. Of the two of them, Alex was by far the more extravagant spender. He was earning more money each year—his salary rose from $15,000 in 1944, the year he was named art director of all three Condé Nast magazines, to $30,000 a year in 1946—but it was never enough to pay for the life they led, and he was always going to the bank or to Patcévitch for loans or advances. Extravagance, for Alex, was a necessity of life.

Alex was starting to paint again. As long as the war lasted, he had felt that painting was impossible for him; except for an academic oil portrait of his father, he had scarcely touched a brush since coming to America. During the summer of 1946, though, while he and Tatiana were visiting Beatrice and Fernand Leval at their house on Martha's Vineyard, Alex

Alex with Priscilla Peck (center) in the *Vogue* art department, mid-1940s.

The *Vogue* studio photographers in 1947, by Penn.
From left, Serge Balkin, Cecil Beaton, George Platt Lynes,
Constantin Joffé, Dorian Leigh (the model as muse), Horst,
John Rawlings, Alex, Erwin Blumenfeld.

Léger drawings in the library on Seventieth Street (*above*), and the living room (*below*), with works by Villon, Kupka, Picasso, and others. Vertès screen at left.

became so enchanted by the "American quality" of the boats and the houses and the landscape that he wanted to paint it. He did some small, realistic views of the town of Menemsha and the bay, and in August, when the Libermans and the Patcévitches returned to the Emmett house on Long Island, he painted a number of landscapes in a freer, more painterly style. "Little by little they became rather fauve," he said. "I would pile on the paint in thick impastos—very garish."

He did little painting that winter, immersed as he was in the demands of *Vogue* and New York social life. The following summer, Alex and Tatiana went back to Europe, for the first time in seven years. The art director of *Vogue* could hardly remain aloof from Paris, which had regained its hegemony over the world of high fashion earlier that spring with Dior's "New Look." The Libermans spent two weeks in Paris (their first-class boat passage and hotel suite at the Crillon paid for by Condé Nast), after which they went off on a six-week vacation in the brand-new Buick they had brought over from New York on the boat with them.* They drove to Venice, stopping first in Geneva to see Albert Skira, the art-book publisher, and then in Padua to see the Giotto frescoes in the Arena Chapel. Their room at the Gritti Palace Hotel in Venice, which had only just reopened, looked out on the Church of Santa Maria della Salute, and Alex spent a good part of his time there painting its Baroque dome and voluted arches. He made a large number of gouache drawings, getting the forms established in his mind, sketching them at sunrise and sunset and other times of the day as the watery light of Venice worked its changing magic. When he attacked the subject with oils, he built up the surface with heavier and heavier impastos, laying down paint in short, loaded brush strokes or with his fingers, filling up the sky around the dome with swirling rivers of color that looked, he feared, too much like Van Gogh's. (A year later, he showed some of these canvases to the French dealer Aimé Maeght, saying apologetically that they were probably too close to Van Gogh. " 'My God, they're nothing like Van Gogh,' Maeght said. This opened my eyes to the possibility that they were quite horrible.")

They left Venice early in August, driving over the Alps to Genoa and from there through the south of France to Ste. Maxime. The larger house on their property there had been sold two years earlier. Acting on Simon Liberman's instructions, Alex's school chum François Latham, now

---

* Simon Liberman had given them a car before he died. Alex traded that in for a black Buick convertible with green leather upholstery—a stylish model that "caused a sensation in Paris."

a wine grower, had sold both the Villa Scaramouche and the house in Chatou, near Paris, for sums that already seemed absurdly low. The smaller house in Ste. Maxime, the one that Alex and Tatiana called Va-et-Vient, had been occupied by the Germans after Alex and Tatiana left in 1940, but it was in relatively good condition, and there was enough land left around it to give them a sense of privacy. The gardener who had worked for Alex's parents had a daughter, Maria Coppo, who became their *femme de ménage* and the best cook they ever employed. She excelled at all the tasty Provençal dishes—bouillabaisse, ratatouille, grilled sardines. Every morning she went to the market and came back with the freshest fish and local produce in the basket of her ancient bicycle. (Eventually Alex bought her a little Citroën 2CV.) They enjoyed their brief stay there so much that they would return every summer for the next sixteen years.

By the time they got back to New York, Alex was too deeply involved with painting to put it aside. He turned the second-floor library of their house into his studio, covering the floor and the piano with drop cloths (removable for parties, of course) and setting up his easel by the window. During the next two years, he used whatever time he could reserve for himself on weekends to catch up with modern art, working through his "admirations" for Cézanne, Monet, Van Gogh, and Seurat, and experimenting with Cubism, Expressionism, Fauvism, and more recent developments. He painted a portrait of Francine whose distortions suggested Soutine, a brooding self-portrait straight out of Edvard Munch, and several lively, Dufy-like studies of Artur Rubinstein and other musicians whose recitals he and Tatiana regularly went to hear at Carnegie Hall.

A return visit to Venice the following summer led to more paintings of the Salute, in thicker impastos and more intense, "barbaric" colors. In the back of his mind then was some half-remembered yearning for what he called "the blinding of light, the brilliance that can be communicated through light or through paint, something Oriental or Byzantine." Sitting on the Lido beach with Tatiana, he tried to capture, in gouache, the shimmering effect of light on the sea, squeezing out little dots of white from the tube and applying them directly to the paper. He was working more and more abstractly, as his friend René Bouché had been urging him to do for some time. Bouché, whose career Alex had helped to secure by making him one of *Vogue*'s top fashion artists, was also a talented painter with aspirations beyond fashion. "In his personal work he had moved toward abstraction," Alex recalled, "and, as a friend, he wanted me to be abstract, too. He and Ilsa Getz, the very interesting woman he lived with, who was also an artist, became close friends of ours. They stayed with us several times during the summers, and he did portraits of Tatiana and Francine. I used him a lot on *Vogue*. He was a dark, wiry little man, quite ugly, a Jewish refugee from Austria or Germany who had probably changed his name, and he was something of a satyr. Nearly every time we sent some girl to pose for him, he'd try to rape her."

Alex was aware that revolutionary developments were taking place around this time in New York's small and hermetic art community. A number of New York painters, reacting in their individual ways to the wartime presence of Max Ernst, Fernand Léger, Marc Chagall, Piet Mondrian, André Masson, Roberto Matta Echaurren, Kurt Seligmann, Yves Tanguy, and other European refugee artists, had started to find new paths that would alter the course of modern art. Although Alex knew Léger and Chagall from Paris, where they had been friends of his mother (Henriette at one point had to help Léger pay his New York rent bill), he had little or no personal contact with the Surrealists in exile. Virtually the only one of them he got to know was Salvador Dali, whose courtship of *Harper's Bazaar, Vogue,* and other journalistic showcases helped to get him excommunicated from the Surrealist movement by André Breton, the movement's charismatic and dictatorial poet-leader. Alex went to see the Surrealist exhibitions at Peggy Guggenheim's Art of This Century Gallery. Almost by accident, he had acquired a painting by Jackson Pollock, a year or so before Pollock's first one-man show at Peggy Guggenheim's, in November 1943. He had gone to a charity auction at the Knoedler Gallery, for the benefit of Bundles for Britain. There had been no bids at all for a small Pollock drawing called *She-Wolf,* a semiabstract study that set off titters of laughter among the black-tie audience, and Alex, more out of annoyance at the laughter than admiration for the work, had raised his hand and acquired the lot for $150. He had never heard of Jackson Pollock until then. Two years later, the art historian James Johnson Sweeney included Pollock in his *Harper's Bazaar* article "Five American Painters," and a small number of art-world insiders, influenced by the writings of the critic Clement Greenberg, began to argue that he was the most important American artist of his generation. Pollock's post-1947 drip paintings were looked upon by right-thinking people then as bad jokes or abominations, however, and Edna Chase would not hear of featuring them in *Vogue*. Not until 1951 did Alex find a way to show Pollock's work in the magazine—as a backdrop for some Cecil Beaton photographs of fashion models wearing "The New Soft Look." The models were posed in front of Pollock's mural-sized *Lavender Mist* and *Autumn Rhythm*, which were on view then at the Betty Parsons Gallery.

Edna Chase saw no virtue whatsoever in contemporary art. Although Frank Crowninshield had introduced the readers of *Vanity Fair* to Matisse, Picasso, and other modern masters, *Vogue* remained a bastion of what Alex referred to as "Park Avenue taste" in art, the sort of "rich, uneducated taste" that considered Christian Bérard a great artist and thought the watered-down modernism of Segonzac superior to the real thing in Picasso and Braque. In what must have been a seizure of naive enthusiasm, Alex had set out to challenge the prevailing orthodoxy as early as 1942, when he commissioned Marcel Duchamp to design a cover for the second annual "Americana" issue of *Vogue*.

The artist whose *Nude Descending a Staircase* had been the *succès de scandale* of the 1913 Armory Show, Duchamp kept himself somewhat aloof from the New York art scene, but he was enormously respected by the Surrealists, whose leader, Breton, tried to claim him as a presiding deity. Duchamp had been the idea man behind the sensational "First Papers of Surrealism" exhibition in the fall of 1942, at which the "difficulty" of looking at modern art was heightened by the installation: the pictures were sequestered in a maze formed by two miles of knotted and crisscrossed string. Alex, who saw the show, got in touch with Duchamp soon afterward. Deferring to the legendary artist's reputation, he gave him only the vaguest of guidelines; the cover, which was for the February 15, 1943, issue, should convey some sense of Americana, he said, but Duchamp could interpret that any way he liked.

Duchamp's submission, which he brought in by hand to Alex's nineteenth-floor office a few weeks later, was a portrait of George Washington. The unmistakable profile, cut out in blue cardboard, was filled in with a collage of surgical gauze, pinned down by thirteen gold-colored stars and liberally stained with a reddish-brown tint that distinctly resembled dried blood. Turned on its side, the portrait's outline traced the map of the United States, but Alex, in his acute embarrassment, never realized that. What he realized all too clearly in the first moment of looking at it was that he could not even show this unnerving little bombshell to Edna Woolman Chase. (Among the many later interpretations of the piece, some contended that it seemed to be made out of used sanitary napkins.) Alex told Duchamp he loved it, and Duchamp left the work with him. Not until two months later, when Duchamp telephoned to ask what had happened to it, did Alex find the courage to tell him it was "not right for *Vogue*." The offending artwork, returned to the artist with a check for fifty dollars for "expenses," was then purchased by André Breton, who published a reproduction of it on the cover of the Surrealist magazine VVV. Now owned by the Musée National d'Art Moderne in Paris, it is a well-known artifact in the Duchampian oeuvre, its fame forever tinged by a sulphurous whiff of contempt for the marriage of art and fashion.

No doubt about it, though: art and fashion were discovering one another. Dali applied his fecund and tireless imagination to fashion drawings for both *Harper's Bazaar* and *Vogue*—drawings in which his "paranoiac-critical" distortions did not quite obscure the real clothes and accessories being depicted. Dress designers had not yet begun to derive inspiration from Mondrian's colored grids or Pollock's weblike skeins of dripped paint, but that day was not far off, nor was the era when Richard Avedon and other photographers would come to look on their fashion work as part of a total artistic oeuvre worthy of being shown in art galleries and museums. In fact, some of the most interesting photographic work of this period— the most innovative, technically advanced, and imaginative uses of the medium—was appearing not in the picture magazines *Life* and *Look* but in *Vogue* and *Harper's Bazaar*. While Alex did not believe in photography as an art form, he had an unerring eye for photographs that were on the cutting edge of innovation. He also maintained, despite the Duchamp fiasco, a lively interest in undermining the foundations of Park Avenue taste in art, and so did at least two of his *Vogue* colleagues.

Allene Talmey had been the last managing editor of *Vanity Fair*. When that much-admired magazine was folded into *Vogue* in 1936, she became features editor of the combined publication. A fine editor who also happened to be a skillful writer, Talmey was primarily interested in the cultural scene. She loved the theater, the opera, and the ballet, and she had a keen sense of what was interesting and important in new fiction and poetry. (*Vogue*'s "People Are Talking About" feature was Talmey's invention.) She brought to *Vogue* a lot of the cultural excitement that had made *Vanity Fair* so appealing to the sort of people who came to Alex and Tatiana's cocktail parties; thanks largely to her efforts, the magazine became much more competitive with *Harper's Bazaar* as a showcase for high as well as popular culture. The person who really opened Alex's eyes to contemporary art, however, was Priscilla Peck—"an extraordinary woman who was very, very influential in my life."

He found Priscilla Peck by acting on an impulse. For several months, Alex had been intrigued by a cartoon feature appearing in the magazine *Town and Country*, about the adventures of an academic character called Professor Tarragon. The drawings, signed "P.P.," were witty and stylish, and Alex decided that he had to meet the artist. He made inquiries, as a result of which "a very interesting young woman named Priscilla Peck appeared in my office. She was neat and dark-haired, very chic in an American way, very sophisticated, very intelligent, a chain smoker. She showed me more of her drawings, and I just thought, with her personal style and dash and ability to draw, let's bring her in. Arthur Weiser, the art editor, had recently left, and I thought she would be a marvelous art editor for Vogue. She had no training, but I was against design training, with all those silly rules, and I felt instinctively that a woman like Priscilla—not a design person but someone of culture and wit, an enlightened amateur—might handle typography and illustration in unexpected and unpredictable ways. It was a gamble that paid off."*

Priscilla Peck was in charge of layout at Vogue, under Alex's supervision, for the next twenty-eight years. What Alex called her "devil-may-care attitude" did away with much of the stodginess that had overtaken Edna Chase's magazine, and until she turned against him in the 1960s, she and Alex saw eye to eye on almost everything. Even more important, though, from Alex's point of view, was the way she stimulated his thinking. Lunching together once or twice a week at Jansen's—Priscilla always ordered steak tartare—they would have long, deep, philosophical discussions. "She had read enormously—Ouspensky, Gurdjieff, and all that mystical business, and also Kandinsky's Concerning the Spiritual in Art and László Moholy-Nagy's Vision in Motion, books that had influenced modern artists. I was very impressed by her absolute dismissal of things that I revered. I remember telling her that Cézanne was one of my gods, and her saying, 'My dear, Cézanne is not that great.' She had tremendous self-assurance and self-confidence." An artist herself, Priscilla was a close friend of Betty Parsons, whose gallery had inherited Jackson Pollock, Mark Rothko, Clyfford Still, and most of the other first-generation Abstract Expressionists in 1947, when Peggy Guggenheim closed up shop and went back to Europe. She introduced Alex to Betty and to the avant-garde milieu—in those days a tiny and embattled band that included, along with the artists, a handful of dealers, two or three collectors, and the critics Clement Greenberg, Harold Rosenberg, and Thomas B. Hess. Without Priscilla Peck to stimulate and encourage Alex's thinking, it might have taken him a lot longer to make his own breakthrough as an abstract artist.

One after another in the late 1940s, the artists of the New York School had fought clear of past influences and laid claim to the unique,

---

* Peck was not as untrained as Alex assumed. By an odd coincidence, she had taken the job that Irving Penn had once offered Alex, as advertising director of Saks Fifth Avenue.

signature styles that made them famous. Pollock's first drip paintings and Clyfford Still's jagged-edged fields of color appeared in 1947; Willem de Kooning's interlocking, black-and-white abstractions and Barnett Newman's vertical-stripe paintings in 1948; Mark Rothko's floating chromatic rectangles and Franz Kline's broad-brush, girderlike verticals and diagonals in 1950. Discovering the new work of these artists at Betty Parsons's and Charles Egan's galleries, Alex realized that something momentous was taking place in American art. The painters of Pollock's generation had broken free of Cubism, the compositional method on which most previous attempts to make abstract art had been based. Cubism was an art of relationships; each line, shape, and color had a direct relation to its neighbors and to the unified composition, which also existed in relation to (and was complete within) the framing edges of the picture. The Abstract Expressionists moved away from relational art. They did so in "allover" paintings which had no single center of interest—paintings that looked as though they could be fragments of much larger pictorial wholes. Irving Sandler, one of the first historians of the movement, described the new "mass image" succinctly: "In contrast to the Synthetic Cubist image, whose distinct planes seem deliberately pieced together, balanced and contained within the picture limits, the mass image, composed of open and mobile painterly marks, appears to be impulsive and dynamic, and to expand beyond the framing edges." Liberman felt a tremendous admiration for what these artists were doing. Later on, he would come to see that in his own way, without being aware of it, he, too, had been struggling to escape from relational painting. At the time, though, he did not recognize an affinity between his own work and that of the Abstract Expressionists. It seemed to him that he was moving in a different direction.

The Venice paintings that he did in the summer of 1949 had been more abstract than those of the year before. The pointillist dots and daubs of pigment took on a life of their own, nearly obliterating the nominal subject in an allover pattern of horizontal and vertical marks that somewhat resembled Mondrian's "plus-and-minus" compositions of the 1930s. Confronting one of these canvases a few months later in his New York studio, Alex began to wonder how it would look if he could enlarge a small section of it, the way you enlarged a photographic negative. He took some sheets of white paper and isolated several areas, and then, after studying them for some time, repainted those areas, greatly enlarged, on new canvases. (This was several months before Franz Kline put one of his own figurative drawings in a Bell-Opticon projector and made a new style out of the magnified detail that it threw on the wall.) The experiments led to more paintings, in which the enlarged daubs of color grew into multicolored oval shapes, and then, in a further simplification, into large painted circles that suggested planets, or suns, floating in a kind of interstellar space. Alex had found his abstract image, but he was not satisfied with it. The breakthrough was incomplete.

After the fact, he would offer various explanations for what became a thirteen-year focus on circles. Sometimes he said it was the result of applying dots of white gouache straight from the tube to catch the shimmering effect of light on water at the Lido beach, or from putting black dots on a white background in a 1949 flower painting. Sometimes he thought it might have come from the Benday dot screen that printers use to reproduce photographs in ink on magazine pages. What made Alex's circles unique, though—different, for example, from the French artists Robert and Sonia Delaunay's prewar "*formes circulaires*" and from Adolph Gottlieb's later "burst" images—was their nondecorative directness, and the fact that, late in 1949, he started to make some of them on Masonite or aluminum panels instead of on canvas, using high-gloss enamel paint from the hardware store.

This sudden turn to industrial materials was motivated by a professional disaster. "Practically all the paintings I had done since the war were starting to peel and crack," he said. "I don't know if the paints I used were bad, or if I didn't use them right—put in too much drier because I had so little time to paint, or something—but in any case I just got disgusted with oil paint. I decided to find materials that would last forever, and I had total faith in the mass-produced products of American industry." But it was more than just new materials that he was after. His faith in American industry also led him to think that there could be an American art that was as direct, as anonymous, and as "brand-new" as a refrigerator or a Buick. Much as he admired the paintings of Pollock and de Kooning, he felt that they were still wedded to the European tradition of "painterly" expression—a tradition that Alex, as a newly minted American, was beginning to consider outmoded. Why should art have to express the individual and often inflated ego of the artist, after all? Like Duchamp, Alex was skeptical about artists' egos. He liked to quote Pascal's statement, "*Le moi est haïssable*" ("The self is hateful")—although not in the company of Abstract Expressionists. They would have considered it bizarre, to say the least, and Alex's notion of an anonymous art made of common, mass-produced materials in simple forms that could be reproduced exactly if the originals faded or became damaged would have struck them as an insult. The fact that Alex not only entertained such an odd notion but acted on it, and continued to do so for thirteen years with very little encouragement from anyone, indicates a stubborn strength of will that few of his friends ever saw. He was ahead of his time, and sufficiently confident to remain there.

The 1949 painting that he considered his first really original work of art, his breakthrough, was a finely drawn white circle centered on a four-foot black square. Now owned by the Museum of Modern Art, it predates Minimal Art by a decade. Its title is *Minimum*.

Alex with his Leica: documenting the creative process.
Photographed by Irving Penn.

Artists in Their Studios

Alex sometimes felt as though he had invented the circle. And what a discovery it was: a closed form that was open to a thousand interpretations. He could speak of its "eternal cosmic significance" and make reference to Tibetan mandalas. He could also refer to Cézanne's famous injunction to "treat nature in terms of the cylinder, the sphere, the cone"—something the Cubists, Cézanne's self-proclaimed heirs, had incidentally failed to do. Sometimes he thought of his circle paintings as a mode of visual research linked to the science of optics: "It is no accident that our eyes see through the round iris," he wrote. The circle, moreover, had erotic connotations that transcended its geometric precision. The formal and symbolic possibilities of the motif seemed limitless.

He was not, of course, the first modern artist to exploit the circle as a motif for abstract paintings. Vassily Kandinsky had used circles in his abstract compositions in the 1920s; Kasimir Malevich and the Russian Suprematists had done so even earlier, starting about 1914. Was Alex aware of this? Apparently not. He can remember seeing posters and agitprop materials by the Constructivist artists in the streets of revolutionary Russia, and some of his own childhood drawings, for posters and stage sets for his mother's theater projects in Paris, were obviously influenced by the same

Constructivist designs that impressed him at the 1925 Exposition des Arts Décoratifs. Barbara Rose, in her 1981 monograph *Alexander Liberman*, suggests that Alex saw paintings by Malevich when he was living in Paris, but that seems unlikely; there were no Malevich paintings on public view in Paris at that time.* He does recall seeing and being struck by Malevich's *Suprematist Composition: White on White* at the Museum of Modern Art in the 1940s, to be sure, and it may be that the austere, stripped-down purity of this famous white square against a white background played an indirect part in his own esthetic thinking. When questioned in later years about such precedents, however, Alex said he was unaware that Malevich or Kandinsky had painted circles, and that he "did not know what Suprematism was." His own breakthrough had come from within, and he prized it all the more highly for that reason.

He painted circles within circles, circles placed symmetrically and asymmetrically, and circles linked by Fibonacci curves. He did long, horizontal paintings in which the permutations of circular forms suggested musical notation or the passage of time. Some works had change and movement built into them: *Sixteen Ways* (1951) consisted of four panels whose order could be changed at will; *Untitled* (1950) was itself a cut-out plywood circle on which he had painted a blue circle within a larger black circle; you could roll it across the floor and watch the blue circle describe an internal trajectory. He combined primary and complementary colors to produce afterimages that resonated in the mind's eye, and he experimented with chance methods, tossing poker chips on a long canvas, marking their positions, and then filling in the circles with black pigment—he called the result *Six Hundred and Thirty-Nine*. His circles never overlapped. Each one was a complete unit, perfect and inviolable. "The circle is the common property of the two infinites from the immense sun to the infinitesimal atom," he wrote in a somewhat heavy-handed 1960 statement called "Circlism." "But above all the circle is the purest symbol because it is visible in its totality instantly."

His earliest circles had been drawn freehand. He soon began using a compass, though, rediscovering in the process the excitement of his mechanical drawing class at Les Roches. Absolute precision and absolute clarity were his goals. He wanted his paintings to have the visual impact of road signs or posters (Cassandre's Dubonnet poster, for example), but he also wanted them to go beyond visual sensation and to register in the

* Two Malevich paintings appeared in a small group show at the Galerie Charpentier in 1939, but Alex did not see them.

mind as pure ideas. "The black circle opposed to the white circle permits an uninterrupted flow of visual sensation," as he said in his "Circlism" statement. "Thus the mind can pass freely from the opposites of light and dark to the idea of opposite itself."

In 1950 he began using an assistant to prepare the Masonite or aluminum panels he painted on. Edward Kasper, a recent Yale graduate who wanted to be an artist, and who had sold some of his drawings and photographs to *Vogue*, was recommended to Alex as someone who could spray-paint with skill and precision. Alex "had done a number of circle paintings in oil paint on canvas," Kasper recalled, "but he wanted to go larger, and spray-paint them in lacquer on aluminum, so they'd be nice and glossy like an automobile finish. I started that for him. I went around and talked to people and found out how to make paint stick to aluminum, by sanding it first, and I chased all over looking for the particular colors he wanted." Kasper turned out to be an ideal collaborator. At Yale he had studied with Josef Albers, whose courses on the interaction of color influenced several generations of artists, and whose endless variations on the square as a motif for paintings set a precedent for Liberman's variations on the circle. Before long, Kasper was not only preparing the panels but executing the paintings. "Mr. Liberman would give me a drawing on tracing paper, with color swatches. At that point he was using mostly the primary colors, plus black and white, so there was no interpretation on my part," he said. "All the dimensions were figured out beforehand, and everything had to be perfect. His theory was that these paintings could be reproduced exactly, just like casts of sculpture or music from a score." Kasper also fabricated some small sculptures from Alex's designs: metal and Plexiglas cutouts of circular forms mounted on wire supports—tabletop pieces that carried his ideas into the third dimension.

Alex had decided that the key to permanence was repeatability. He wanted his work to look impersonal, anonymous. In his view, even Mondrian was too "painterly"; if you looked closely enough at Mondrian's geometrical grids, you could see the brush marks and other evidence of the artist's hand. By delegating so much of the handwork to an assistant, he was "testing the limits of what a painting could be," as he put it. He was also turning out a lot more work than he could have done on his own. Although Kasper continually marveled at his energy and enthusiasm, Alex tired easily. His ulcers continued to plague him—severe attacks of bleeding put him in bed for several weeks in 1943 and again in 1949—and in 1947 he found out that he was diabetic. On the weekends when Eddie Kasper slept over at the Seventieth Street house, though, he would always find

Alex up ahead of him in the morning. "He would be at the breakfast table, reading the paper. He'd ask what I wanted, and he'd get up and make it for me. And then he would take a tray up to his wife, who was still in bed." (Alex made breakfast for Tatiana every morning: black coffee, white toast, freshly squeezed orange juice.)

Tatiana did not think much of the circle paintings. Tatiana, who still thought Alex should try to paint like Vermeer, had no interest in modern art and little tolerance for modern artists; the only ones who came to her parties were those with close links to the fashion world—Marcel Vertès, René Bouché, and Salvador Dali. (Later on, she became very fond of Andy Warhol.) Alex, who gave his days to Condé Nast, his evenings to Tatiana, and his weekends to painting, had very little contact during the 1950s with the advanced artists of his own generation, the generation that was making New York the vital center of contemporary art. He saw their shows at the handful of galleries that exhibited advanced work—Betty Parsons, Sidney Janis, Charles Egan, Samuel Kootz—and he tried to let *Vogue* readers in on the first American school of art to achieve international influence, even if that meant using Jackson Pollock's paintings as a background for fashion photographs.

In October 1951, *Vogue* ran an article by Aline B. Louchheim (the future Aline Saarinen) on Betty Parsons and her artists. Alex admired Betty Parsons enormously. He had met her through Priscilla Peck, who was a close friend of the dealer—they were both charter members of the lesbian underground in New York—and to celebrate the *Vogue* article, which he had commissioned, he gave a lunch party for Parsons and her artists at Chambord, the most elegant and expensive French restaurant in New York. Betty sat at one end of the long table and Alex sat at the other end, flanked by Jackson Pollock on his right and Mark Rothko on his left. Clyfford Still was there, and Barnett Newman, and Ad Reinhardt. (This was before their quarrels split the New York School into warring factions.) In Alex's recollection the lunch was a quiet and mannerly affair. Newman and Rothko talked about the large-scale paintings they wanted to do—"Give us billboards," Alex remembers one of them saying. (It was right after this that Alex painted his first big picture, the 50-by-123-inch *Sixteen Ways*.) Pollock, who had come into the city from eastern Long Island for the occasion, stayed relatively sober. The party and the *Vogue* article "helped put over the gallery," according to Betty Parsons, who was still having a very hard time selling the work of the Abstract Expressionists at that point. "It helped me get the word to people. It helped the artists."

Betty Parsons came to Alex's studio one day in 1953. She brought

Barnett Newman, her closest confidant among the New York artists, and Clement Greenberg, the critic who had been the first to champion Jackson Pollock. "They stayed for a long time and seemed very interested," Alex recalled, "but nothing happened. I also got Sidney Janis to come, somewhat later. He looked at my circles, and he said, 'You ought to do ballet decor.' " Alex was dying to show his work. Although he worried that Parsons and Janis had merely humored him because he was the art director of Condé Nast, he tried hard to get other dealers to visit his studio. The problem was that his paintings did not fit into any recognizable context. Other artists were painting hard-edge, geometrical pictures, but nobody was painting circles in a purely symbolic, nondecorative way, and nobody was doing them (or having an assistant do them) with industrial lacquer on aluminum panels. The impersonal precision of Alex's work seemed to place it somewhere outside the recognized limits of art.

A breakthrough appeared imminent in 1954, when James Johnson Sweeney chose one of Alex's paintings for a group show of "Younger American Painters" at the Guggenheim Museum. Sweeney, the Guggenheim's director, was a powerful and respected figure in the New York art world. He had been told about Alex's work by Leo Lerman, who was then responsible for arts and culture for *Mademoiselle,* and knew everybody. (Lerman had even become, somewhat disconcertingly, a close friend of Alex's parents.) According to Alex, "Sweeney came to my studio and chose a painting called *Two Circles,* which I had done in 1950. It was two black circles side by side on a white ground—a picture that I happened to have executed myself. At least, I had painted the circles with black enamel, on a white background prepared by Eddie Kasper. I had used Du Pont's Duco enamel paint, thinking it would last forever—that was when I had total faith in the products of American technology; I knew nothing about built-in obsolescence—and the white background had turned to ivory in the three years since it had been painted. I asked Sweeney how soon he needed the picture. He said he needed it by the middle of next week, and I said, 'Good, I'll make a new one for you.' Sweeney nearly fainted. 'No, no, no, no,' he said, 'I want that one.' So I didn't repaint it, although it would have been much better if I had. My whole theory was that these pictures were repeatable and renewable."

Sweeney hung *Two Circles* in the last gallery of the show, giving it a wall to itself. Emily Genauer of the New York *Herald Tribune* wondered disdainfully how long such an image would "bear looking at," while the anonymous reviewer in *Time* dismissed it as "a pristine nothing . . . by the art director for Condé Nast magazines . . . as chic as two black eyes have

Minimum, 1949, enamel on composition board, 48" x 48".
Alex's breakthrough painting. Collection, The Museum of
Modern Art, New York. Gift of the Samuel I. Newhouse
Foundation.

Two Circles, 1950, enamel on Masonite, 40" x 40". James
Johnson Sweeney picked this painting for his Guggenheim
show in 1954. Collection of the artist.

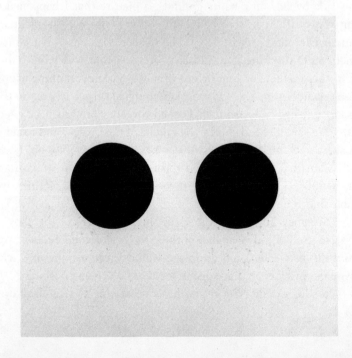

Alex's studio on the fourth floor of 173 East Seventieth Street, 1953.

become in café society." Jasper Johns and Robert Rauschenberg, two young artists who were trying to work their way out from under the already oppressive domination of Abstract Expressionism, found it one of the most interesting works in the show; Rauschenberg drew some circles, folded them in different ways, and mailed them to Alex, who was perplexed by the gift. (Francine had made friends with Rauschenberg at Black Mountain College in 1951, but Alex did not know him at the time.) Very few other people noticed Alex's circle painting, however, and no dealers came calling. *Two Circles*, in fact, was the only Liberman to be shown publicly until 1960.

While the anonymous and impersonal art that he pursued so rigorously for a dozen years set him apart from his own generation of artists, the project that he embarked on during the summer of 1948, when he photographed Georges Braque in his Normandy studio, put him in touch with an earlier generation. Aimé Maeght, Braque's Paris dealer, had come to see Alex in New York the previous winter; like other farsighted professionals, he sensed that *Vogue* was helping to expand the audience for modern art. Alex repaid the call when he and Tatiana came to Paris in June, and he made arrangements with the dealer to visit Braque at his country house in Varengeville, not far from Dieppe, on the Normandy coast. He had no particular reason for doing this. Although he proposed to take pictures, photography was just a convenient excuse—a pretext for meeting the artist. Alex felt increasingly regretful over having missed out on the School of Paris during the years when he was living there, and it occurred to him that now, as art director of *Vogue*, he had a fine chance to catch up with modern art.

Braque and his wife received the Libermans with reserved cordiality; warm biscuits and Muscadet were served under a tent on the lawn, in lieu of lunch. The visit left a deep impression on Alex nonetheless. He was struck by the studio—an immense, high-ceilinged room whose carefully diffused light made it seem like "a luminous womb." The order and efficiency of the working space, the bouquets of clean paintbrushes in jars, the pencils and pens laid out on strips of corrugated cardboard, the profusion of small stones, bits of wood, bleached bones, starfish, and other natural objects picked up and preserved—all these details fascinated him. "I want my paintings to be as hard as flint," Braque told Alex, "so that when struck by eye and light, sparks fly." The seventy-eight-year-old artist, who lived with his wife in an atmosphere of serene contemplation and "restrained luxury," seemed to him a "*grand seigneur* in art," one who had "solved the material problems of creation."

When he came to Paris the next summer, Alex visited and photographed four more artists—Henri Matisse, Maurice Utrillo, Marie Laurencin, and František Kupka. The idea of a series of photo-essays was taking shape in his mind. To some extent his inspiration came from the photographs of Matisse that Henri Cartier-Bresson had published in *Verve*—the indomitable artist defying age and illness, working in bed on his cut-paper masterpieces—and also by Brassaï's photographs of Picasso that had appeared recently in *Cahiers d'Art*. What Alex had in mind, though, was not a series of artist portraits. He thought it might be interesting to focus instead on the visual information that was left out of most art books—information about artists' studios, methods, and materials. "I thought that would be meaningful to a young painter," he said, "all that practical side of art. As I went further, I also felt that the twentieth century had been an extraordinary moment in French art, and that all that flowering of creativity was on the verge of dying out. I wanted to try to preserve some evidence of how these artists had lived and worked. And there was something else. I had taken a full-time job; I was involved in publishing; but maybe, subconsciously, I wanted to see what my life would have been like if I had devoted it completely to painting."

Alex and Tatiana spent two weeks in Paris that summer, three weeks in Venice, and a month at Va-et-Vient. The Patcévitches came to stay with them in Ste. Maxime. So did Alex's mother, whose behavior upset Tatiana as much as ever. Tatiana's word for Henriette was *"insortable,"* meaning unsuitable, the kind of person you couldn't introduce in public. She sunbathed nude on the upstairs veranda, used the intimate *tu* and *toi* with relative strangers, was rude to the Libermans' friends, and contributed a flow of irritating remarks. ("Tania, were there any generals in your family?" she asked when Tatiana was issuing her exuberant orders for the day's activities.) Mainly to get her out of the house, Alex took his mother off alone on an overnight trip to Aix-en-Provence. The idea of seeing Cézanne's studio had been on his mind ever since his visit with Braque; Cézanne, after all, was the artist he admired most. He made inquiries around Aix and found the house, a modest two-story building on the outskirts of the town, which he was able to get into and photograph. (This was some years before it became a national tourist site.) "By an accident of fate," as he would later write, "it was bought by a Provençal poet who lived in the lower rooms and did not touch the studio," which occupied the whole second floor. "Cézanne's beret, his cape, his paint boxes, his rosary, his skulls, his palettes and bottles of turpentine, all the objects that surrounded him during his work are there as he left them, untouched, unmoved throughout the years." Alex noted the contrast between the huge, luminous studio and the dark, cramped little rooms on the ground floor, where the artist lived. "This was the studio of Cézanne's old age," Alex said, "the room in which he painted *Les Grandes Baigneuses* and other late works. *Les Grandes Baigneuses* was so big that he couldn't get it out the door, so he cut a narrow slit in one wall. That's what sticks in my memory, that narrow opening at one end of the room."

Photographing the studios of the masters of modern art—some of them dead but the majority still living—took the place of painting for Alex during his summers in Europe. Curiously enough, he never thought of himself as a photographer. Irving Penn saw his prints of the Cézanne studio at the office one day and urged him to publish them in *Vogue*, which he did in 1952. After that, his documentation of artists in their studios became a *Vogue* project, but Alex continued to think of himself as an amateur, a record keeper who "sometimes got lucky." Patcévitch arranged to pay him $250 apiece for his photo-essays, the texts for which he wrote himself, with some editorial assistance from Francine, who had won the creative-writing award at Barnard and was working as a reporter for United Press. These payments took the place of the raise he kept asking for at Condé Nast, where his salary languished at a temporary plateau of $30,000 a year.

By and large, the artists were happy to cooperate with his project. Many of them felt overlooked and ignored by art history, and several were living in extreme poverty. Kupka, the Czech immigrant who had worked in obscurity for decades, spoke wistfully of watching dealers and collectors pass by the windows of his tiny house in the Paris suburb of Puteaux, on their way to the studio of his neighbor Jacques Villon, Marcel Duchamp's older brother, who had only just started to sell his own paintings after a lifetime of hard work. Georges Rouault, a modernist who hated modern art and never mentioned any contemporary artist except Matisse, nevertheless showed "flashes of extraordinary grandeur in his speech that contradicted the pettiness of what he said." Constantin Brancusi, ill and frail, but still powerful enough to move his heavy sculptures around without help, refused to be photographed. He was as superstitious as a primitive tribesman, convinced that if anyone took his picture, he would die. Brancusi let Alex take pictures of his cluttered studio in the Impasse Ronsin in Paris, though, and then flew into a towering rage when he saw the prints because Alex had cropped out the carved wooden bases that Brancusi considered an integral part of each sculpture. Alex sent him flowers and reshot everything. "I saw him every day for two weeks," he recalled. "I even emptied his urinal for him. He would get up and walk right in front of my camera sometimes; it would have been so easy for me to snap the shutter without his knowing, but I didn't do it."

Alex approached them all with respect and professional interest, and most of them responded in kind. One of his great assets, as Francine said, was the ability to give his total attention to other people—to make them feel he was the captive of their charm. He listened intelligently while recording many conversations on a wire recorder, which preceded the advent of audiotape. He worked quietly and unobtrusively, photographing with his Leica in whatever light happened to be available—no flashbulbs or flood-lights, and no assistant, either. (The one time he took along an assistant was when he photographed Matisse in his Paris studio. The assistant failed to screw the camera lens in properly, and Alex had to go back and do the sitting over a week later.) Anxious about overstaying his welcome, he kept his visits brief, and returned later if he needed more material. Some artists he went to see summer after summer—five visits in Braque's case; four each for Giacometti, Villon, and Chagall. Occasionally he took Tatiana along, although she did not really like artists or feel comfortable with them. "Tatiana was always shocked by the way the artists treated their wives," he said. Annette Giacometti, Madame Kupka, and others had sacrificed their own lives to art. They lived in tiny, dark rooms and devoted all their energy and ingenuity to supporting the work being done in the well-lit studios that were all too clearly the center of their own existence, as well as that of the artist-husband. To Alex, their sacrifice was moving but sad; to Tatiana, it was absurd. Of all the artists he photographed, only three were women: Sonia Delaunay, Natalia Goncharova, and Marie Laurencin.

Sometimes Alex asked the artist if he could buy a drawing. In those days you could buy a Picasso oil for five thousand dollars, and a painting by Jacques Villon for much less, but Alex couldn't afford that sort of outlay. He wanted a "souvenir," a watercolor or a pencil sketch, and several artists were happy to oblige. Giacometti gave him a number of drawings, and Léger, who had known Alex since he was a boy, let him buy as many as he wanted for ten thousand old francs (then about twenty dollars) apiece. He picked out a dozen, plus a gouache that was the final preparatory sketch for *La Grande Parade*, for which he paid five hundred dollars; but he offended Léger by declining to buy one of the small oil paintings that he had set out for "Liberman the collector."

The souvenir hunt led to some embarrassing moments. When Alex asked Lydia Delectorskaya, the woman who looked after Matisse in his

Alex and Picasso on the beach at Golfe-Juan, 1949.

Alex's photograph of Picasso in the back seat of the old Hispano-Suiza sedan,
from *The Artist in His Studio*.

The hands of Marcel Duchamp, from *The Artist in His Studio*.

later years, whether he might buy a drawing, she went to consult the master and came back with a brush-and-ink drawing of a nude. To his eternal shame, Alex asked whether he could not buy instead one of the more richly brushed ink drawings that he had seen recently in the Paris home of his friend Ethel de Croisset, a wealthy American who was married to the head of Condé Nast's French office. He left Matisse's studio empty-handed as a result, and his mortification was compounded when Alfred Barr published the drawing that he had rejected in his definitive book on Matisse. Embarrassment of a different sort marked his purchase of a drawing by Braque. "I picked out a charcoal drawing and asked how much it cost. He said, 'Five.' But five what? I didn't dare ask him. I was already committed to buying it. The five turned out to be five hundred thousand old francs, or about a thousand dollars, which was a terrible shock. I had to borrow the money from the Condé Nast office in Paris, because he wanted it in cash. I brought it to his apartment, which was near the Parc Montsouris, and he took the bills and put them under the mattress of the couch he was sitting on. It was a very amusing image of Braque—that old peasant tradition of hiding money under the mattress."

After he had published several of the photo-essays in Vogue, Alex began to think he might eventually make a book out of them. Rosamond and Georges Bernier, who had founded the lively French art journal L'Oeil, and who also published books on art, were interested in the project. As the European features editor of Vogue right after the war, Rosamond Bernier (then Peggy Riley) had visited Picasso and Matisse and arranged for photographs of their recent work to appear in Vogue before they appeared anywhere else. She had also introduced Alex to Albert Skira, the Swiss art-book publisher, and when Georges Bernier lost interest in Alex's book idea (he simply stopped taking or returning calls from Alex), Skira picked it up. The main problem at that point was that Alex had not been able to get to Picasso. He and Tatiana had actually met the great man in the summer of 1949, when Gjon Mili invited them to come along to a photo session he had scheduled with Picasso on the beach at Golfe-Juan. (The photographs were for Life, not Vogue.) Picasso had been in an affable mood, mugging for the camera and posing for several shots with the Libermans; he had greatly admired Tatiana's huge garnet ring, which he insisted on wearing for a while. Afterward, though, whenever Alex tried to arrange a studio visit, Jacqueline Rocque, the young woman who had replaced Françoise Gilot as Picasso's mistress and keeper of the gate, would say that Picasso was out of town. Skira, who had known Picasso for years, finally broke the impasse. He took Alex to Picasso's house in Vallauris, in the hills

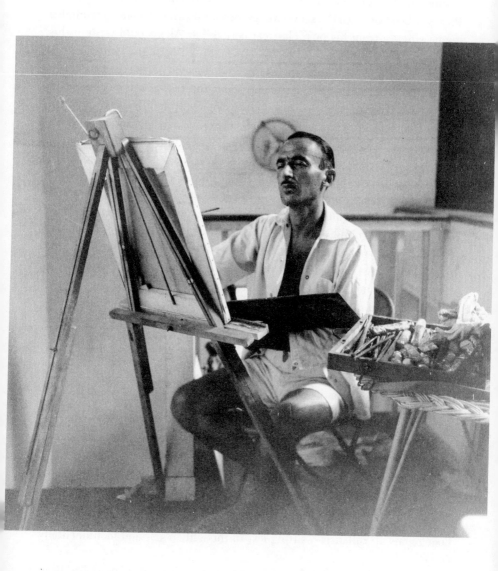

Alex painting on a squash court at their rented house
in St. James, Long Island.

above Cannes, early one morning in the summer of 1953. They walked around to the back of the house, where two servants directed them to Picasso's bedroom. "In the semidarkness of that shuttered room he reminded me of a figure from his own classical period," as Alex would write in his book, "a virile god of mythology, his torso covered with gray-white hair."

Acting more like a king than a god, Picasso got up, put on baggy shorts and a blue polka-dot shirt, and spent the rest of the morning conferring with his courtiers—a bull-fight promoter from Nîmes, the wife of a Spanish sculptor, and various other hangers-on. He appropriated Skira's Tyrolean hat and wore it until lunchtime. Over lunch, at a café on the beach at Golfe-Juan, Picasso signed autographs for tourists and laughed a little too uproariously at the antics of his grownup son, Paolo; Alex "felt as though he forced himself to laugh louder and stronger than the others because deep in him he was extremely sad." Afterward he turned to Alex and said, "I am going up to Montmartre"—a slip of the tongue; he meant Vallauris, but what came out was that other hill where he had lived during his earliest years in Paris. For three hours he showed Alex around the various studios in his great, cavernous "creative factory"—talking quietly, pointing out pictures, sculptures, and found objects in the incredibly cluttered rooms where nothing was ever thrown out or moved—and again Alex felt a deep sadness underneath the bantering talk. "He seemed not to live in that place, or any place," he recalled. "There was really no furniture." At one point Alex found himself telling Picasso about his own painting, drawing a circle on the floor of one of the studios with white chalk. "Leave it," Picasso said when he started to erase the chalk. "It is now part of my life."

Later, after many photographs had been taken, Picasso said, "Why don't you stay and work with me? Stay a few months, and we'll just go on working." His loneliness was evident, and clearly incurable. Alex captured it, memorably, in the photograph he took of Picasso sitting in the back seat of an enormous old Hispano-Suiza sedan that he kept in one of the ground-floor rooms at Vallauris—sitting lost in thought, regal, and monumentally alone.

That day was a milestone in Alex's life. Although Matisse had been "the most awesome" of the artists he photographed, Picasso had impressed him more profoundly. "I liked him in many ways," Alex said, "and I admired him enormously. I think he is really the seminal artist of this century, the only one who has really captured the tragedy of this time. There are things in *Guernica* and in the portrait of Dora Maar weeping that no one else has come close to touching." But the enormous cost at which great art was achieved—that was a lesson you could also learn from a day with Picasso. Alex had observed it over and over, in the bitterness of other artists' words and the meanness of their lives. Of all the artists he visited, Braque was the only *grand seigneur*, the only one who seemed to have "solved the material problems of creation." The others were more or less unhappy, more or less unfulfilled, more or less alone. As Fernand Léger used to say bluntly, "Either a good life and lousy work, or good work and a lousy life."

Alex and Tatiana at Va-et-Vient in the 1950s, when Ste. Maxime
was still a quiet retreat.

Alex Is Superman

The wives of the artists rarely appear in Alex's photographs. They are invariably mentioned, though, with a sort of fascinated admiration, in the essays that he wrote about each artist, and it is not hard to see why. If these infinitely selfless, nurturing women had one thing in common, it was their lack of any conceivable resemblance to Tatiana Liberman. We might even surmise that Alex responded to them so sympathetically because in his own marriage he was the one who did most of the protecting and nurturing. That he did it so gaily and wholeheartedly, and with such evident success, was a continuing source of wonder to his colleagues at Vogue.

Alex and Tatiana's marriage seemed impervious to the usual attritions. Surrounded at the office by attractive and intelligent women, Alex was quite aware of his own considerable sex appeal; he flirted with most of them, but only once in fifty years did he seem momentarily to lose his equilibrium. He "got a little bit enchanted," as he put it, with a British-born beauty named Brigitte Tichenor, who became accessories editor of Vogue in 1949. "It was a real organized attack on her part," he said. "She was very striking, with wonderful big eyes, and she made it seem as though we were having an affair. She would wait for me after work and ask if I'd give her a lift home, and I would. She was married; once I went up to her apartment and met her husband. We'd have long lunches at Chambord or Chateaubriand. She was very cultured, she knew a lot of people in the art and museum worlds, and I must say I enjoyed it. The whole thing was like a vacation, to have a beautiful woman pursue me that way." Alex apparently felt that there was no harm in the relationship because "I never touched her," but people talked, and one day, soon after Mrs. Tichenor had managed to travel to Europe on the same boat with Alex and Tatiana, Philippe de Croisset, the president of Condé Nast in France, took Tatiana aside in Paris and said, "My poor dear, I'm so sorry; I hear Alex is leaving you," and that was the end of that. Alex told Brigitte Tichenor that he had no intention of leaving Tatiana, and the lady cantered off in pursuit of Iva Patcévitch, who might well have responded more gallantly if he had not been in love with Marlene Dietrich at the time.

Nada Patcévitch got little support from Tatiana or Alex when Marlene came into the picture. Tatiana had met Marlene at Cap d'Antibes before the war, and they had taken to one another instantly. When Patcévitch reintroduced them in New York in the late 1940s, the intense friendship that sprang up between the two women proved more enduring than Marlene's love affair with Patcévitch. "It was the great friendship of Tatiana's life," according to Alex, "and possibly of Marlene's, too. They were like sisters." (Tatiana and Nada had been "like sisters," too, during their many summers together, but their bond had apparently been more ephemeral; Alex and Tatiana never made any great effort to see Nada after she and Pat separated.) Marlene and Pat and Tatiana and Alex were now the inseparable foursome, spending country weekends and vacations and Christmases together.

Marlene fascinated both Alex and Tatiana because two entirely different people seemed to coexist in her lovely skin—a professional seductress and a contented *hausfrau*. She loved to cook. She made chicken soup for sick friends and spent hours in the kitchen preparing simple bourgeois dishes. Francine never forgot her first sight of Marlene, making lunch in the kitchen of a rented beach house on Long Island. "She had on a man's shirt with nothing showing underneath. I assumed she was wearing a bathing suit, but when she bent over I saw the string of a Tampax peeping out from under the shirt." When Marlene danced, Alex was struck by "the extraordinary feline grace of her body. She was incredibly seductive. She was also such a perfectionist—in cooking, in acting, in dressing. She knew precisely the angle her face should be turned for the light to fall on it correctly. Life with Marlene was quite artificial in some ways, but at the

Top: Alex and
Valentina.

Center: Alex and
Christian Dior, Paris,
early 1950s. "He adored
Tatiana, and Tatiana
adored him. She
arranged card parties
for him in New York—
that was his favorite
pastime. He was a
great gourmet, as his
bulk shows, and his
house in Passy was
the most glamorous
in Paris."

Bottom: Alex and
Brigitte Tichenor, 1951.

Francine's wedding, 1957. Iva Patcévitch, Francine,
Cleve Gray, Marlene Dietrich.

Backstage in Boston, 1961. Marlene asked Tatiana and Alex to help her
get ready. Tatiana and Alex are visible in the mirror.

same time it was very homey. She was demanding but generous." Alex took many photographs of Marlene over the years, seventy of which appeared in his "personal memoir" of the actress, published soon after her death in 1992.

Patcévitch went through a lot of pain when Dietrich ditched him for Michael Wilding, her co-star in the Alfred Hitchcock film *Stage Fright*. He could hardly have been surprised; Marlene, one of the most promiscuous creatures of all time, had flaming affairs with Yul Brynner and several other men while she was supposedly "with" Patcévitch. But Pat was devastated by their breakup. He had loved many women, including such prominent *Vogue* beauties as Millicent Fenwick and Barbara ("Babe") Cushing Mortimer, the future Mrs. William Paley, but with Marlene he lost his aura of suave command. For the first time in his life he had felt more love than he inspired, and his distress at losing her was so acute that he would call Alex into his office at Condé Nast just to talk about it. Alex got him to take up painting as a distraction. Patcévitch would come over to Alex's studio on weekends and labor away at a Grandma Moses–type landscape while Alex executed another of the austere, abstract circle paintings that Tatiana, Patcévitch, and Marlene all thought were ridiculous, awful, and "not art." After Marlene, Patcévitch became increasingly dependent on the Libermans—even though Tatiana and Marlene continued to see each other whenever her career brought her to New York. He wanted to live nearer to them, and eventually he did, moving from his apartment on Sutton Place to a town house that Alex found for him a few doors west of theirs on East Seventieth Street. The solidity of Alex and Tatiana's marriage had become an important prop to his own well-being.

Alex and Tatiana, Tatiana and Alex—their friends saw them as a unit and marveled at how well the disparate elements dovetailed. They looked wonderful together, tall and handsome, aristocratic, perfectly dressed—Tatiana in loose-fitting stylish clothes by Dior, Alex in his New York uniform of an English-tailored gray suit, light-blue shirt, and navy-blue knit tie. He was losing his sleek, European-gigolo look, although no one would ever have mistaken him for a native-born American. A lot of people thought he resembled the actor David Niven. Tatiana, with her plucked and dramatically arched eyebrows, her wide mouth, and her frequently boisterous manners, seemed somehow to take up more room than Alex. The people who loved her (and there were quite a few of them) took delight in her larger-than-life qualities, which included tremendous warmth and a sort of childlike naughtiness that could be very funny if it was not directed at you. Of course, there were people who couldn't stand her. The

Libermans were invited to lunch once—and once only—by the William S. Paleys. Wondering why they had been dropped so summarily (Babe Paley, after all, had worked with Alex for a number of years at *Vogue*), he questioned the Paleys' decorator, whom he knew, and was told that Bill Paley found Tatiana "a bit too much." Alex himself once admitted that there were times when Tatiana's rudeness and her boisterous sallies made him cringe, but he never showed it, and he never tried to change her. His public attitude was that she could do no wrong.

Tatiana terrified younger men with her startling questions and pronouncements. Leo Lerman said that the first time he met her, at a dinner party, "she scared the wits out of me. She was one of the rudest women I'd ever met. She expounded. She didn't say much, but what she said was dramatic, and there was no arguing. Alex seemed deeply devoted to her, and she accepted that as her just due. Later, I realized that she was equally devoted to him."

Her grasp of English remained limited. She much preferred French, which she also spoke with a heavy Russian accent and frequent inaccuracies. At the movies one night during the 1940s, when Tatiana had taken to wearing her hair piled on top of her head, a lady sitting behind her leaned forward and asked her quietly to remove her hat.

"Vhat?" Tatiana shot back, in a very loud voice.

"Would you please remove your hat, madam?" the woman repeated, in a slightly louder whisper.

"Ees not hat!" Tatiana thundered, in a voice heard throughout the theater. "Ees my *hair*!" The audience was convulsed, the movie momentarily forgotten.

Alex always maintained that her brusque manner was a form of shyness, and that she fell back on provocative or aggressive remarks as a defense. She was atrociously impatient, and, like Alex, she never answered letters or wrote thank-you notes. Even the Patcévitches, when they gave Alex and Tatiana a baby grand piano for Christmas, received nothing more in acknowledgment than a telegram reading "Tra-la-la." Alex found nothing to criticize in this. Tatiana was clearly impossible to live with at times, and Alex coped with that superbly. Francine remembered her mother throwing across the room a yellow topaz brooch that Alex had given her for her birthday and yelling, "You sent your secretary to buy this. When you used to love me, you would send flowers!" The flowers, which had been ordered earlier, arrived shortly afterward, as they had on every one of her birthdays—twenty-four red roses. Alex returned the brooch to the store. "Flowers meant emotion and involvement," he said. "I was amused, not angry." His equanimity was an act of will, of course, but the amazing thing was that the anger and resentment that he must have felt at times did not manage to find other outlets. He never sulked, or snapped at her in public, or gave any evidence that their marriage, like other people's, might have its down side. Her bad manners and demands, her constant need for special treatment and attention seemed only to spur his admiration. "Every desire of Tatiana's became a challenge that I had to fulfill," he said. "It was like a sport, to constantly impress her with my agility. Crossing on the *Queen Elizabeth*, for example, instead of waiting in line for customs inspection, we were always the first off the ship. You had to tip certain people and arrange to have someone there to meet you. Tatiana wanted to have the best table in a restaurant or the best seats at the theater. It was a challenge that I enjoyed. 'Alex is Superman,' she would say, because I could perform these tricks."

The truth was that Alex liked and needed this sort of special treatment as much as Tatiana did. The sense of security that life's luxuries always gave him was nourished by the attentiveness of waiters and maitre d's, and Alex could never have enough of it. He set great store by getting the right table at La Grenouille or The Four Seasons, the Manhattan restaurants favored by the fashion and publishing power elite. Although he liked to say that he had no power, the cachet that came from his increasingly influential position in the fashion world meant a great deal to him, and it also worked to deflect any thoughts he might have of quitting his job and devoting himself full-time to being an artist. The life he provided for Tatiana was not for her benefit alone.

Tatiana worked hard at her hat making, and her income made it possible for them to indulge in their extravagances. At home, though, she took on the role of the helpless pampered female. It was Alex who engaged the caterers for their parties, called plumbers or electricians when needed, and, with the levelheaded assistance of Mabel Moses, their all-purpose cook and housekeeper, attended to the necessities of daily life. It may be that Tatiana's seeming helplessness was a game between them—one of many that they both enjoyed playing—but she had always been lazy and disdainful toward anything that bored her. "She was often like a child with me," he said a few months after her death in 1991. "She would make a certain face, put out her tongue, and I would roar with laughter in a way I never did with anyone else. It was a playful, enchanting relationship for fifty years. And you know, in all those years we never had a really serious talk. In the beginning, I would occasionally want to discuss this or that, and she would say, 'Are you going to start one of your Jewish conversations?' And of course

I would stop immediately. She thought it was bad to talk about personal things. I never did learn much about her past, because she didn't want to talk about it. Love can be talked to death, life can be talked to death—that was her attitude. Maybe that was our secret: if you want happiness, shut up. We had a deep respect for each other, and we didn't have to tell each other things. 'Why should I tell you?' she'd say. 'You are me.' And that's how I felt, absolutely." Physical passion lay at the heart of their relationship, he said—a deep erotic understanding that had existed from that moment in 1938, on the Côte d'Azur, when he had touched her arm and said, "You have wonderful skin." The sexual bond between them was not apparent to others. In the predominantly gay ambiance of the fashion world, it was sometimes said that Tatiana had saved Alex from becoming a homosexual; one person even claimed to have heard Tatiana say so herself, in conversation with two women. There was not the slightest evidence that Alex had ever leaned in that direction, however, and after Brigitte Tichenor, there was never a rumor of his being involved with any other woman.

Alex's mother kept asking why they didn't have a child. According to Alex, they never practiced birth control. (But Tatiana might have done so without telling him.) In his later years, he would say that it was probably his fault—that all the x-rays taken of his ulcers might have made him sterile. But he also said that neither he nor Tatiana had really wanted a child. "Tatiana felt that our affection should go undividedly to Francine," he said, "maybe because she had a guilty feeling about not bringing her up properly." As for Alex, the alternately adored and neglected son of an affirmed sensualist, he felt somewhere deep inside him that a child "takes away" from the parents' love. But did he really not want one? Gitta Sereny, the young friend who had told Francine about her father's death, remembers Alex saying to her in the early 1940s that he longed to have a child with Tatiana. When she asked him if Tatiana knew that, he said of course not, they could never discuss such things. Gitta, who lived with the Libermans for weeks at a time during this period, and who was quite fearless about speaking the unspoken (she went on to become a prominent journalist and a Third Reich scholar), broached the subject to Tatiana herself. "I said, 'Tatiana, you're so young and beautiful, and you love Alex, and it's not terribly good for Francine to be the center of both your lives—why don't you have a child?' And do you know what she said? She said, 'What? To put another Jew into the world?' My God in heaven, that was when she lost me forever." Gitta might have taken her too literally; since Tatiana was no anti-Semite, the remark was probably an example of her tendency to be outrageous.

Francine often felt that she was very far from being the center of their lives. The family portrait that Irving Penn took of the three of them in 1947 was "telling," she wrote many years later: "Mother and stepfather huddled together in a love mighty and impenetrable; stepfather leaning slightly towards the daughter, a bridge between the two women; sulking girl setting herself apart, feeling ostracized by the power of the parents' love." Francine continued to feel closer to Alex than she did to her mother. "To me, my mother is silence," she said once, "silence and narcissism. I can see her sitting in front of the mirror, designing those hats on herself, completely mirror-centered. I never had a real conversation with her, even after I found out that my father was dead. . . . My mother remained forever unable to discuss any problem under the sun." In retrospect, Francine marveled at the piano, ballet, horseback riding, and swimming lessons that Alex and Tatiana had managed to provide for her out of their limited income, in addition to her very expensive education. They always found the means to live like their much wealthier friends. One summer when she was fourteen, the Patcévitches paid to send Francine to a riding camp in Colorado. Going over a jump in muddy terrain, her horse fell on her, and she ended up spending three weeks in a Denver hospital undergoing surgery three times for a badly shattered collarbone. One of her vivid memories of those three weeks is that nobody came to see her.

Instead of rebellion, Francine chose distance. From the time she entered Bryn Mawr in the fall of 1948, Francine tried to live as much as possible outside her mother's social orbit. She got engaged at eighteen to a boy named Peter Burgard and spent most of her vacations with his relaxed, generous family (his stepfather was the opera singer Lawrence Tibbett). Two years later, the engagement broken off, she transferred to Barnard, where she lived in a dingy room off-campus. In the summer of her junior year, while her parents were in Europe, Francine was at Black Mountain College in North Carolina, absorbing the anarchic, antiestablishment thinking of John Cage, Robert Rauschenberg, Charles Olson, and other gurus of the emerging counterculture. She went back to Black Mountain the next summer, but before that she traveled to New Orleans with a jazz clarinetist and had to be rescued from "a haze of hashish" by Mabel Moses, who came down from New York for that purpose. Mabel had seen Francine through her troubled adolescence, sitting with her all those evenings when Alex and Tatiana were out, putting her to bed when she got too high at a cocktail party. Acting as chaperone this time, Mabel accompanied Francine and Jonathan Williams, a Black Mountain student (and future poet) who was in love with her, on a car trip through the bayou country en route from

New Orleans to North Carolina; segregation was still in force, so Mabel and Francine slept in a black motel (it was called the White House, to their amusement) and Williams in a white one.

Her first job after college was on the overnight shift at United Press, writing "World-in-Brief" vignettes on the Army-McCarthy hearings and other breaking news. She lived in a basement room in Greenwich Village and shunned the uptown world of what she had taken to calling "the fashion rabble." Then, in a complete reversal, she allowed Alex to get her a job with *Elle*, the leading postwar French fashion magazine, and moved to Paris, eager "to engage in a new life that would emulate my mother's and recapture her love. It was one last, desperate attempt to gain her attention by moving into her world, and it didn't work because I was totally unfit for it." She wrote about the collections, arranged fashion sittings, dined with the Rothschilds and the Aga Khan, had an affair with a French prince who worked for Eastman Kodak. Her letters home to Alex are like a fever chart of increasing desperation.

> Thank you darling for your letter—I know how little time you have to write. But believe me, each word from you clarifies my life and calms my spirit.

> One page a month from you packs in more affection than ten letters a month from any other father.

> God how I need a letter from you. You can't imagine what a state of crisis I'm in. I hate my life, I hate myself. . . . I'm ready to do almost anything to quit the job I have. . . . I have come to some kind of breaking point which is very hard to live through sanely, and I need your voice.

Francine developed a severe case of mononucleosis in the spring of 1956 and spent two months convalescing in the Swiss Alps. She came home that fall, in a state of emotional near-collapse. Alex, who did not believe in psychoanalysis, arranged nevertheless for her to go to Priscilla Peck's psychiatrist, and within six months she was in much better shape. "I had to find a very separate world," Francine said, "a scholarly, austere, contemplative world, and I found it through Cleve Gray."

She had met Cleve Gray the first weekend after her return from Paris. A painter, and a man of great refinement and deep culture, Cleve offered the emotional security and acceptance that Francine craved, and he also met, surprisingly enough, with Tatiana's instant approval—in part because he was a Princeton graduate and because he spoke fluent French. Cleve was older than Francine by twelve years—he was only six years younger than Alex. He was also Jewish, and steady enough not to be intimidated by Tatiana, who charmed him as completely as he charmed her. He moved Alex almost to tears when he came to the house and formally asked for Francine's hand in marriage. "I think," Alex said huskily, "that this is really a marriage made in heaven."

Cleve loved to tell the story of Tatiana's reaction the first time he came to the house on Seventieth Street. Descending the stairs from the third floor, she scrutinized him, turned back up the stairs, and could be heard calling out, "*Boubous*, okay, *il n'est pas pédéraste.*"

Out of the geometric straitjacket: as the art world welcomed Pop and Minimal Art, Alex Liberman moved in a different direction.

Carefully Calibrated Doses
of Modern Art

Edna Chase turned seventy-five in 1952. She had been at *Vogue* for fifty-seven years, the last thirty-eight of them as its editor in chief; now, in a graceful transition that future *Vogue* editors might well envy, she gathered her skirts and ascended to the ceremonial post of chairman of the editorial board. Her successor as editor in chief was Jessica Daves, a plump, rather dowdy, and decidedly prudish woman who had come to *Vogue* in 1933 from the advertising department at Saks Fifth Avenue, and who had been gradually assuming more and more of Mrs. Chase's editorial responsibilities. "Jessica certainly didn't have the look of a *Vogue* editor," according to Alex, "but she grew into a strong character." Her strength was directed mainly at preserving the status quo and making the magazine more practical and service-oriented; designers' names and store credits now appeared on the same page with the fashions, so readers would know where to buy them. Under her direction *Vogue* continued, through the 1950s, to be consistently less lively and innovative (although no less successful) than *Harper's Bazaar*.

Alex got along perfectly well with Jessica Daves, who depended heavily on his competence and his taste. (To the secret amusement of the other editors, she would put on lipstick before speaking to Alex or Patcévitch on the telephone; there was also a famous faux pas at one of Alex and Tatiana's cocktail parties, when she forgot to remove her veil before trying to eat a deviled egg.) Jessica Daves was married to the writer and art critic Robert Allerton Parker, and she approved of Alex's attempts to bring serious art to the pages of *Vogue*. There were limits to what he could accomplish in this area, of course. The fiasco of the Duchamp cover had taught him that commissioning artists to do things for *Vogue* was risky; *Vogue* was not *Verve* or *Minotaure*, after all, and the boundaries of art could not be stretched too far. Joseph Cornell, whose Surrealist-inspired boxes and collages Alex had seen at the Julien Levy Gallery, used to come in to the office every two weeks or so bringing fragile treasures—engravings from old French books, cut-out figures from antique games. Wanting to help this excruciatingly shy, inarticulate young man, Alex would arrange for *Vogue* to pay him two hundred dollars each time for what was billed as "research material." Although he got Cornell to design a Christmas cover for *House & Garden* in 1948, Alex managed only once to get his work into *Vogue*—an engraving of a French chateau, with a bottle of perfume showing in each window. "Cornell was mysterious, like a Florentine monk," Alex said. "I liked him very much. He gave me several boxes, which I eventually had to sell—for not much money, unfortunately."

In the mid-1950s, Alex commissioned Robert Rauschenberg and Jasper Johns, two young artists who were supporting themselves at the time by designing show windows for Bonwit Teller and Tiffany, to conjure up some ideas to use as backgrounds for photographs; but nothing came of this, because, as Rauschenberg said later, "I couldn't work with, 'Do anything you want.' I did some lousy work, and he spotted it." Rauschenberg also brought in some pictures he had made by placing a nude model, leaves, and other objects on long strips of blueprint paper and "painting" around them with a floodlight, but Alex could see no way to use them in *Vogue*. (*Life* did a "Speaking of Pictures" feature on them soon afterward, in 1951.)

Alex gave his readers an occasional glimpse of the old masters or the Impressionists, to enrich a Christmas issue or to coincide with an exhibition at the Metropolitan, and in the 1950s he spoon-fed them carefully calibrated, gradually increasing doses of modern art as well. In 1951, *Vogue* carried features on Giacometti and Utrillo (the latter photographed by Alex Liberman), and the December issue gave six pages to the Matisse chapel in Vence, photographed for the first time, by Alex, with a text by Father Couturier, the Dominican priest who had been instrumental in getting the Church to commission this great work. Alex's photos of Cézanne's studio ran in the April 15, 1952 *Vogue*; that November, the magazine published the first article on Kupka in any American magazine, with photographs by Alexander Liberman. His photo-essay on Braque appeared in 1954, and from then on his series on artists in their studios, written as well as photographed by Alex, became a recurring feature in the magazine. Alex wrote the texts in longhand, using a soft pencil, filling pages and pages with his oversize, upward-slanting script. His rather formless first drafts needed skillful editing to bring out the sharpness of his observations. They got it first from Francine, whose literary gifts were already becoming apparent, but the person who really helped to shape them into publishable form was Allene Talmey, the features editor at *Vogue*. The magazine gave great prominence to the series, whose installments were described as "part of a forthcoming book, to be published by Skira."

Painting on weekends, writing a book, and going out to parties or cultural events nearly every night of the week did not seem to cut into the prodigious energy that Alex brought to his job at Condé Nast. As the art director of *Vogue, Glamour*, and *House & Garden*, he made decisions quickly and without visible strain. He assigned the photographers, chose the covers, and laid out every page of *Vogue*, and roughed out the layouts of the other two. He also became known for scrapping layouts at the last moment, in order to "enrich" them (one of his favorite words) in new ways. Initially he had paid close attention to the technical problems of typography and paper and inks, to the shape and size of printed letters on the page; but as time went on, and the magazines lost the remaining vestiges of their genteel "album" style, he left more and more of the detailed layout work to Priscilla Peck and the other art editors. His focus was on each issue as a whole— the cinematic flow, the way the parts came together. A magazine should be made up of different textures, he felt, and they had to play off each other in interesting ways. An arresting still life by Irving Penn, for example, might be followed by one of Horst's dramatically posed fashion spreads; a Cecil Beaton fantasy by a double-page blowup of ready-to-wear spring coats. Alex had learned from Lucien Vogel that a mediocre photo blown up to fill the page often turned into a good one.

Alex had settled into his own style as art director—a style that was authoritative but not autocratic. He worked in a bare white cube of an office, behind a black Parsons table swept clear of everything but a pad of white paper and one sharpened pencil; there were no mementos or photographs in sight (he kept a picture of Tatiana in the desk drawer), and no decor of any kind. (In later years, he hung a couple of photographic blowups of his public sculptures on the wall.) Although he was never seen at the office without a jacket and tie, his office manner was informal,

Alex

friendly, and good-humored. He flirted with the ladies in nonthreatening ways, commenting on hairdos and new dresses, making them feel good about themselves. He was intensely curious. He listened carefully to other opinions and welcomed a good idea whether it came from a top editor or a mailroom clerk. He rarely criticized other people's work directly. His usual method, when confronted with a proposed layout, was to praise it; ten minutes later, though, he would be on the phone to the editor with a few suggestions. "Dear friend, don't you think it might be better this way?" he would ask. "Think about it." After three or four such calls, the editor would start to realize that the whole layout was being redone. Alex never wrote memos (unlike Condé Nast) and never seemed to give orders or to act like a boss; but if his suggestions were ignored, there would be repercussions—critical remarks, a chill in the air. "If you question him at all, he gives you that basilisk look of icy coldness," a longtime *House & Garden* editor once remarked. "He shuts you out with that look. I mean, he's *polished* that black look, and it's very, very frightening." Alex kept insisting that he had no power. "I have influence, which is different from power," he would say. The truth was that he exerted a great deal of power over a great many people's lives and careers, but he preferred to do so indirectly, in ways that did not show. One of his great assets as art director was his lack of rigidity, his ability to say, "Well, if you don't like orange, how about blue?" He could almost always get his way through seduction and charm, without making enemies. Most of his colleagues came to believe that his taste and his sense of quality were infallible.

It was not by any means a solo performance that he put on. Alex needed the input and the reactions of the talented people around him; he would walk into the art department, and, with a few casual-sounding questions, elicit from the editor in charge the essential points about every feature or picture spread. His great gift was the sureness of his judgment in putting everything together. He could analyze the problems, zero in on the most exciting images or ideas, and lay out *Vogue*'s editorial pages in an hour or less. The process was like a form of collage; he liked to think of it as "controlled chance." There was a prodigious amount of hard work involved, of course, but it did not show. Alex's was a high-wire act, in the course of which he could often lift his associates up on the wire with him, and a lot of the excitement generated in this process was passed on to the reader.

Alexey Brodovitch was a teacher; Alex was not. He encouraged people, stimulated their thinking, got them to go beyond what they had done before, but he did not try to instill specific ideas or methods, and he was open to any new approach. Alex worked well with established prewar stars like Horst and Cecil Beaton (whose banishment over the anti-Semitic incident in 1938 had been quietly rescinded in 1940), while giving greater and greater prominence to the more daring and innovative work of Erwin Blumenfeld and Irving Penn. Both *Harper's Bazaar* and *Vogue* were assigning more fashion work to women photographers in the 1950s: Louise Dahl-Wolfe, Lillian Bassman, and Toni Frissell at *Bazaar*; Frances McLaughlin, Karen Radkai, and Kay Bell at *Vogue.* Alex wanted fashion shots in which the models had the look of not being observed, and he thought that a woman photographer might be able to do that better than a man. Remembering paintings by Degas and Bonnard, he wanted to show women dressing or undressing, in the intimacy of the bedroom or the bath, but here he ran into problems with Jessica Daves. She vetoed anything that struck her as suggestive—a category that included rear views of girls in bathing suits, and nightgowns modeled in proximity to beds.

Innovations of any sort did not flourish under Miss Daves. Blumenfeld's covers were arresting and sometimes astonishing, nevertheless —his famous image of Jean Patchett, metamorphosed in the darkroom so that all one saw of her was one eye, two lips, and a delectable beauty spot, appeared on the cover of the January 1950 issue—and Penn's work continually surprised both the eye and the mind. Of all the *Vogue* photographers, Penn was the most rewarding and the most demanding. He wanted to discuss each assignment in detail with Alex beforehand, and usually he would not start to work until Alex had made a sketch as a jumping-off point. "I would sketch things that were like dreams of possible images," as Alex explained it, "and then Penn would realize them, going beyond the sketch. He would put in his passion for meticulous detail. For example, I suggested to Penn that he make a picture of glasses falling off a tray, which he did. Of course, I didn't know he would use Baccarat, or that the shot would require him to break five dozen glasses." When the pictures had been taken and the transparencies developed, Penn would insist that Alex decide which one to use. "I valued his choice more than mine," Penn said. "He was always searching for something of mine that I didn't recognize. And I would sometimes fight him about it. He was grateful for the surprises that came out of my lack of knowledge." Their collaboration was so close in those years that Alex began to feel he was being drained by it; eventually he would be forced to withdraw.

* Frissell had switched from *Vogue* to *Bazaar*; Radkai and Bell, from *Bazaar* to *Vogue*.

The static, tightly composed nature of Penn's early photographs gave way in the fifties to a more spontaneous feeling that was actively encouraged by Alex. "I admired his early work because it was so pure and direct," Alex said. "He was able to put reality on paper—and remember, this was a period when artifice was still very prevalent in the work of Beaton, Horst, and others. But I always tried, when I looked at his contacts, to find the break in his facade. Out of a hundred pictures there would be one that moved or that was a little out of focus, and I would pounce on that. It took a lot of persuading. When I picked out a shot from his Moroccan trip, of two little girls running, quite blurred, he swore that if I published that he would never take another photograph for *Vogue*. But it turned out to be one of his key pictures, one that's been reprinted over and over."

Penn's fashion photographs were too strong for some *Vogue* editors. Just two years after his breakthrough work on the 1950 Paris collections, Alex warned him that there had been complaints. "I must tell you that the editors say your pictures 'burned on the page,' " said Alex, who told Penn to soften them a little. "Up to then I had been trying to make a picture," Penn said; afterward, "I began to try to make a commodity. That's what I've been doing in fashion photography ever since." Although the quality of his fashion work did not appear to decline, it was often overshadowed in the fifties by the other work he did for *Vogue*. Penn's portraits defined whole galaxies of prominent people: the Washington, D.C., power structure, the New York cultural establishment, London's literary intellectuals. He much preferred taking portraits to doing fashion work, and he resisted taking cover photographs. (Penn's covers never sold very well.) Alex gave him the idea of doing a series of photographs of working men in the clothes or the uniforms that they wore to work—a counterpart to Eugène Atget's famous turn-of-the-century photographs of the *"petits métiers"* in Paris— and started him on a brilliant series of flower photographs that enriched the Christmas issues of *Vogue* in the sixties. For the annual Christmas issue, Penn would often go off on an open-ended assignment to New Guinea or Cameroon or some other exotic locale. " 'Bring us a treasure for Christmas,' Alex would tell me. 'I don't want to hear about the cost. I'll save you twelve or fourteen pages.' "

Over at *Harper's Bazaar*, Richard Avedon was setting new parameters for fashion photography. He caught his subjects in movement and in outlandish situations that mocked the artifice of studio poses. Avedon's models were shown kissing bicycle champions, leaping puddles, dodging taxicabs, roller-skating through the Place de la Concorde. His famous 1955 photograph of Dovima at the Cirque d'Hiver in Paris, gowned by Dior, gesturing magisterially with one arm while the other rests on the trunk of a restless elephant, was a stunning *coup de théâtre*; his annual coverage of the Paris collections turned those staid events into theatrical happenings of another sort, with a subtext invented by Avedon. The scenarios that he devised for his models to act out explored what Avedon referred to as "the complex nature of what it is to be dressed up, the vulnerability, the anxiety, the isolation of being a beauty." The fact that his photographs also showed the clothes so well made it possible for him to get away with almost anything. Avedon established a close working relationship with his favorite models (it was more than a working relationship with Dorcas Nowell, whom he married), and he did away with the aloof, haughty look that some fashion models still affected then. Technically brilliant and endlessly imaginative, Avedon proved that fashion photography could be as complicated and as strong as any other kind.

Looking for someone who could bring this kind of visual excitement to *Vogue*, Alex's alert eye fell on some photographs by William Klein in the Italian architectural magazine *Domus*. Klein was then a young art student in Paris—"an American from the Bronx," Alex said, "with a brashness and a sort of violence that I admired." Alex brought him to New York and offered him a job as assistant art director, then thought better of it and let him do what he really wanted, which was to spend some time photographing New York City. Klein's harsh, gritty snapshots of city streets and shop windows and people and buildings, many of them taken with a wide-angle or a telephoto lens, did not appear in *Vogue*; they were collected in a book called *New York*, which was published in London and Paris but never in New York. Along with the photographs of Robert Frank, whose first book, *The Americans*, was published in 1958, they helped to usher in the snapshot esthetic, which would characterize the work of Garry Winogrand, Bruce Davidson, Lee Friedlander, and other influential photographers of their generation. Klein and Frank jettisoned print quality, composition, balance, careful lighting, and other photographic standards in their pursuit of the raw, jumbled, accidental, and incongruous look of everyday life, and *Harper's Bazaar*, which published portfolios of prints by Brassaï, Cartier-Bresson, Bill Brandt, Walker Evans, and (later) Diane Arbus, became an important outlet for their work.

Alex, who did not believe in photography as an art form, had no interest in publishing print portfolios; even Penn's nonfashion work was presented in *Vogue* as a superior form of illustration, with no pretensions to art. Alex was committed to banishing "visions of loveliness" from the pages of *Vogue*, though, and in 1956 he thought it would be interesting to let William Klein try his hand at fashion photography. For the next few years, Klein's ironic, witty shots of fashion models, often surrounded by heavy traffic or reflected in windshields, vied with Avedon's in originality. The models he used were seldom conventionally pretty. Klein looked for what he called "hard girls"—independent-looking street kids or sophisticates who smoked cigarettes through their veils and looked the viewer knowingly in the eye. He "loosened up fashion photography," according to the art historian Martin Harrison, and "in doing so he opened the way for others, Helmut Newton and David Bailey, for example, at the beginning of the 1960s."

A little Klein went a long way in *Vogue*, and Alex was careful to surround it with pages and pages of less jarring work by John Rawlings, Frances McLaughlin, Serge Balkin, Constantin Joffé, Clifford Coffin, Karen Radkai, Gordon Parks, Norman Parkinson, and, toward the end of the decade, the brash young English photographer Antony Armstrong-Jones. *Harper's Bazaar* startled its readers in 1962 with Avedon's portrait of Countess Christina Paolozzi, frontally nude and staring right at the camera, an image that had a lot to say about fashion magazines and their changing audience, but *Vogue* in the late 1950s and the early 1960s still retained much of the same flavor and many of the same features as *Vogue* in the 1920s and the 1930s, when it functioned as "the authentic journal of society." Along with its coverage of Paris haute couture and its gradually increasing emphasis on European and American ready-to-wear fashions, the magazine kept right on informing its readers about important society balls and weddings (Francine's marriage to Cleve Gray in 1957 rated a full-page picture of the bride, by Irving Penn), telling them how to decorate their houses, and illustrating the leisure of the very rich. Society was not what it used to be, of course. Old money was rapidly losing its clout, and the *Social Register* no longer dictated whose party could be mentioned in *Vogue*; but some prewar attitudes and authority figures still reigned supreme at the magazine.

Coco Chanel, for example. The French had punished Chanel for her wartime love affair with Dincklage ("Spatz"), the Nazi spy. When she finally reopened her Paris salon in 1954, after a self-imposed period of exile, her first collections were boycotted by all the leading French journalists, including Lucien Vogel, who had returned from New York in 1947 to edit *Jardin des Modes*, and his brother-in-law Michel de Brunhoff, the editor of French *Vogue*. In American *Vogue*, however, it was another story. Fashion editor Bettina Ballard's enthusiastic coverage of Chanel's tweed suits, silk shirts, and signature strings of pearls set in motion the designer's postwar renaissance, which was well established by the 1956 season. Ballard's decision to support Chanel met with no opposition from Alex Liberman. A few years earlier, Chanel had come to New York and made a point of being introduced to Alex and Tatiana (whom she must have heard about from Dincklage). "Her business manager at the time was a Russian named Count Koutouzoff," Alex recalled, "whose daughter was a friend of our friend Elena Schouvaloff. Koutouzoff brought Chanel to our house, and we became great friends. I enjoyed her company enormously. I loved the Proustian aspect of Chanel, the stories and legends, and her involvement with Diaghilev and Picasso and Cocteau and Reverdy. She was a constant lesson in refinement. Tatiana was extremely refined, of course, but it was interesting to see how refinement worked when you had the means to achieve perfection in everything. Tatiana and Chanel got along well on the surface, although I don't think there was ever much warmth between them. Later, Chanel kept wanting to design something for Tatiana, but Tatiana always wriggled out of it. Tatiana liked femininity without frills, she liked seduction and prettiness, and Chanel's clothes were too masculine for her. She preferred Dior, and then Saint Laurent."

Chanel liked Alex so much that she tried to get him to work for her. " 'At last you're here,' she said when I got to Paris that summer, because she took it for granted that I couldn't refuse the offer that was going to be made. The next thing she did was ask me to change the light bulb in the models' dressing room. She said, 'You won't have to have dinner with me every night,' but as we talked, it became clear that she was very lonely, and that she probably would expect just that, and lunch, too, and I thought to myself that this was becoming too complicated. I knew she had had a long affair with the Grand Duke Dmitri, that she liked Russians, and that Count Koutouzoff had recently retired as her business manager; she probably wanted another Russian with good manners, of which I had plenty. But what about Tatiana? Anyway, the next day I went to see Mr. Wertheimer, her financial backer, who offered to pay me whatever I wanted. Would a quarter of a million dollars a year do? I said, 'Mr. Wertheimer, there is nothing you can offer me. I am not interested.' And you know, afterward, Chanel said she admired that very much, and we went on being great friends. Whenever I went to Paris we would have lunch together, or tea at Smith's, the English bookstore, and she would take me driving in her big Delage sedan in the Parc de Saint-Cloud, just the two of us and her chauffeur, whom she always referred to as her '*mecanicien*.' It was very romantic, even though she was in her seventies at the time. I always felt that she somewhat resented Tatiana."

The world of high fashion did not really interest Alex, or so he

At a country restaurant in France. From left, Gitta Sereny, Irving Penn, Francine (standing), Tatiana, Don Honeyman (*Vogue* photographer, Gitta's husband), Tatiana's aunt Sandra.

Henriette at one of her cocktail parties.

Henriette performing in her Paris nightclub act, "The Streets of Paris."
Shown here as "The Prostitute," "The Bum," "The Japanese Magician,"
and "The Baron and His Mistress."

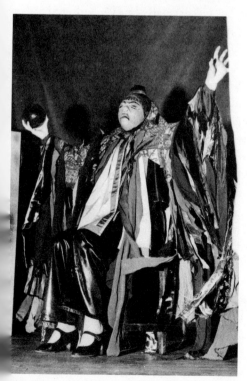

maintained. ("Alex and I like to think we have nothing to do with fashion," said Penn.) In Paris, Alex would go with Tatiana to a few of the leading designers' showrooms; to appear at the spring collections was good for Tatiana's hat business, and Alex enjoyed watching the models perform on the runway. He loved the atmosphere of luxury in the salons of Christian Dior, Balenciaga, and the other *grands couturiers*. The luxury of haute couture, with its basis in feminine seduction, was associated in his mind with the great European artistic tradition of the female image, "from Titian and Velázquez to Matisse." Since *Vogue* paid for his and Tatiana's boat passage to Europe, moreover, Alex had to show some interest in the world of fashion. He had to know what was happening in it, at least, and he knew a good deal more than he let on.

His mother kept telling him that he was wasting his life. In her almost daily letters to him, she returned again and again to a familiar lament: he had become the slave of a superficial and snobbish milieu, and it was preventing him from realizing his true "mission" in life—the mission of an artist. Alex bore the cross of his mother with great fortitude. He supported her financially. (By the 1950s he was also supporting Tatiana's aunt Sandra, the opera singer, who was living in semiretirement in Paris.) He arranged and paid for Henriette's summers in hotels on the Côte d'Azur, because neither he nor Tatiana could stand having her visit them at Va-et-Vient for more than a few days at a time. Occasionally he even suffered through her performances in seedy Paris nightclubs. Henriette had devised a new act for herself, with a set in the form of a giant book whose pages turned to provide backdrops for her masked pantomimes. "She would come out as a *clochard*, in rags, smoking a stub of cigar, and then the page would turn and there would be a lamppost, and another mask, and she would be a prostitute. It was degrading, appalling, and so badly done, so third-rate." Hoping perhaps to redirect her creative energies in a less embarrassing direction, Alex encouraged her to write. She finished her autobiographical novel, *The Errant Heart*.* She dashed off short stories and essays, and complained because Alex would not publish them in his magazines. Lack of energy was never her problem. At one period she gave lessons in etiquette, advertising in the newspaper and receiving pupils in her studio apartment at 6, rue Quentin-Bauchart. "A few people from the provinces came," Alex recalled, "butchers' wives and so forth. She would teach them how to sit

---

* It was privately published, in an English translation, by a New York vanity press in 1950. A later version, in French, called *Mariorca*, written with the help of the French journalist Marcel Haedrich, appeared in Paris in 1973.

down, how to put on lipstick, how to hold a teacup, all done with the most ridiculous flourishes. Those poor women. And, of course, she was constantly picking up men in cafés and going to bed with them. She had six or seven face-lifts, and something like seventeen abortions over the years."

Henriette Pascar walked across Paris every day to keep her remarkably durable body in shape. When Alex was there he would sometimes walk with her in the Bois de Boulogne, having all he could do to keep up while she lectured him about his talent and his mission as an artist. "And, frankly," he said, "I liked hearing it. I would come back after one of those brainwashing walks, and I would be cooler to Tatiana. It made her literally sick. My mother was an enormous poison. She was incredibly jealous of Tatiana, and I think maybe her criticizing my work for Condé Nast was just a way of getting at Tatiana. But I listened to what she said, and it left a sediment."

Painting on weekends was Alex's spiritual anchor. All through the 1950s he kept painting his variations on the circle, more than two hundred of them in all: severe, hard-edge abstractions that nobody seemed to want to show, but that gave another and deeper dimension to his life. Because of his painting, Alex could take his work at Condé Nast more lightly. He could stay detached from the petty frustrations and ambitions of office work, because he felt that his real life, his mission, lay elsewhere. In the fifties, Alex withdrew a lot of his creative energy from Irving Penn. "I'd been giving an enormous part of myself to Penn," he said, "and I felt I should put that into my own work. Penn missed it a lot, I think."

He had moved his studio from the library to the fourth floor of their house, now that Elena Schouvaloff was no longer living there. The space was still too small for the big, mural-size canvases that Alex, impressed by the expanding scale of Abstract Expressionist painting, wanted to work on, but he could not afford a real studio. Although Alex's salary was climbing—it reached $40,000 in 1959—he and Tatiana were continually in debt. They borrowed from the bank and sometimes from Condé Nast to support their extravagant style of life—a style that involved constant acts of generosity toward friends, servants, and casual acquaintances, as well as Francine and Cleve, Henriette, Tatiana's aunt Sandra, and later on her father (who lived with them for several months in New York toward the end of his life), and a host of others. When their finances got desperate, Alex would sell a work of art—unfortunately, not his own. He sold the Pollock *She-Wolf* drawing he had acquired at auction in 1942 (it wound up eventually at the Museum of Modern Art), and another one that he had bought from Betty Parsons some years later. He sold his Picasso drawing, which Picasso had arranged to let him buy after their day together in

Vallauris. On learning that Alex wanted a souvenir, Picasso had picked out one of his recent, "classical" drawings of nymphs and fauns and given it to a friend of his, a Hungarian photographer who badly needed money, and Alex had bought it from the Hungarian for six hundred dollars. Alex sold a number of the intricate box constructions that Joseph Cornell had given to him in the early 1950s, and he would have sold his Légers if anyone had been willing to offer a decent price for them—Tatiana hated Léger's work, which she considered "Communist art." The only painting of his own that he sold was a watercolor of circles, which a Milwaukee collector named Charles Zadok bought for two hundred dollars. (Zadok, who ran the Saks Fifth Avenue store in Milwaukee, had been brought to Alex's studio in 1953 by Adam and Sophie Gimbel, Tatiana's employers.) Two years later, when Alex's financial troubles were especially acute, he asked Zadok for a loan and was turned down. It was the first and last time he approached any of their rich friends for help.

Iva Patcévitch once startled Alex by suggesting, or seeming to suggest, that he should perhaps think about leaving Condé Nast. The conversation took place in the south of France, and it "made me very uncomfortable," as Alex recalled. "I was surprised and upset." He knew he could always find another job. In addition to the offer from Chanel, Hélène Lazareff, the founder of *Elle*, had tried to lure him back to Paris in the late 1940s as its art director, at a salary considerably higher than the one he was making at Condé Nast; and in the fifties he had been approached by Jean Prouvost, the Henry Luce of French publishing, about a high-level job at the illustrated weekly *Paris-Match*. Alex had listened carefully to both offers, but in the end he was not seriously tempted. Both he and Tatiana felt committed to New York—they never wanted to live anywhere else—and besides, in spite of his mother's repeated jeremiads about wasting his life, Alex was proud of the work he did for *Vogue*. The other magazines, *House & Garden* and *Glamour*, mattered much less to him; he chose their covers and laid out each issue with flair and inventiveness, but it was *Vogue*, the flagship, the crown jewel of the Condé Nast empire, that occupied the major share of his attention. *Vogue* had its own mission, which in Alex's mind was to "involve women in the life of the moment."

He was proud of bringing serious art—contemporary art included—to the attention of *Vogue*'s readers. Although he sometimes worried that the magazine was simply paying lip service to the fine arts, the truth was that *Vogue* had become an important catalyst in the American public's postwar love affair with art. The art features in *Vogue* never cheapened or trivialized the subject, and their level of sophistication, thanks to

Alex, was fairly high. Almost every issue carried an essay by an important critic: Harold Rosenberg, Lawrence Alloway, and Clement Greenberg were among the contributors. The critics, however, were getting to be as competitively jealous as the artists. Some years later, when *Vogue* published a Penn portrait of Greenberg in its "People Are Talking About" section, along with an admiring note that called him "the American critic best known around the world," Harold Rosenberg cut Alex dead on the street, wrote him an angry letter, and then broke off all relations between them.

Alex still clung to his own belief in the "nobility" of *Vogue*'s civilizing mission. The word cropped up whenever he was called on to write something for or about *Vogue*—an article on beauty, a preface to a book of fashion photographs. In his mind, the concept of woman at her best was a noble ideal, to which *Vogue* gave far more than lip service. He knew, of course, that there was another side to this coin. The female image was being used more and more blatantly to sell products of all kinds—cars and dishwashers and cigarettes as well as haute couture—and *Vogue* was coming to be looked upon in some circles, along with other fashion journals, as nothing more than a seductive environment for advertising. "Seventh Avenue"—that is, the garment trade—had more power over *Vogue*'s editorial decisions than Alex or anyone else cared to admit. Until the 1980s, however, Alex was still able to find a measure of "nobility" in his work at Condé Nast. "In choosing a *Vogue* cover," he said, "I never used to think, 'Will it sell?' I honestly did not. Our attitude in those days was that if something was right for *Vogue*, the readers would have to like it." Although he always insisted that layout was "not a creative process," he pushed himself and his colleagues in the art department to surpass themselves month after month. "He would come in the art department and rip everything up, but you never felt he was destroying anything," said Tina Fredericks, whom Alex made art director of *Glamour* when she was only twenty-three. "He was always positive. He raised your confidence level. I felt he was my mentor, my father, my favorite man in the whole world, and I think a hundred other women must have felt the same way."

All his trips to the studios of major artists had convinced him that he could not live their sort of life, or endure the solitude that it required. Whenever a photographer talked about doing "serious" work for *Vogue*, Alex would offer the same advice. Treat *Vogue* as a commercial job, he would say, and use the money to do your serious work on the side. His own case, however, was more complicated. Alex's work for *Vogue* was as serious, and in some ways as deeply committed, as the work he did on weekends in his studio. His mother had it wrong: he needed both.

Alex in his studio. Photographed by Cecil Beaton.

Transitions

In the late 1950s, Condé Nast's well-bred family of class publications was suddenly menaced by barbarians at the gate. Lord Camrose, the British financier who came to Nast's rescue in the 1930s, had allowed Nast and then Patcévitch to run the company as they saw fit, without interference; Patcévitch used to keep the absentee owner informed and answer any questions he might have during his annual weekend visit to Camrose's country house outside London. After Camrose died in 1954, the sceptre passed to his son, Michael Berry, who let things continue just the way they always had until 1958, when he sold the family's Amalgamated Press holdings to Cecil King, publisher of the *Daily Mirror* and other sex-and-scandal-oriented British tabloids. Patcévitch went over for a meeting with King, and what he heard must not have been reassuring, for he came back determined to find another buyer for Condé Nast.

There was a clause in the original agreement between Camrose and Nast stating that if Camrose ever sold his press holdings, Condé Nast would be given a six-month option to repurchase its own stock. Having no funds of his own, Iva Patcévitch approached several major publishers, in-

cluding Time-Life and Collier's, but the price he was asking—about twice
what Condé Nast shares were selling for on the New York Stock
Exchange—struck them as too high. Patcévitch and his executive assistant,
Daniel Salem, argued that recent losses by *Vogue Patterns*, the dress-pattern
supplement started in 1921 by Condé Nast, had artificially depressed the
firm's stock. *Vogue, House & Garden,* and the recently acquired *Bride's*
magazine were all operating in the black, and *Glamour,* with a circulation
of 749,025 was generating more income than the three others combined.
Certain well-entrenched but decidedly extravagant management policies
worked to offset the gains, however, and during the last two years, on gross
revenues of $30 million, the company had managed to lose more than
$500,000 a year. Patcévitch was getting desperate. Five of his six months
had gone by without a deal in sight. But then, out of the blue by way of
New Jersey, came Samuel I. Newhouse.

It is tempting to imagine a first encounter between the tall, aristocratic, movie-star-handsome Patcévitch and the short (five-foot, two-
inch), blunt, and totally focused Newhouse. About the only thing they had
in common was their Russian heritage, although even in that they were
poles apart. Meyer Newhouse, Sam's father, had emigrated from the Pale
of Settlement, near the border of eastern Russia, in the 1880s and had
wound up in Bayonne, New Jersey, where he failed dismally at everything
except procreation—he provided his wife with eight children. While Patcévitch was establishing himself on Wall Street, young Sam, the eldest of
Meyer's brood, was clawing his way out of poverty. Sam became acting
head of the family at thirteen, when his father's health broke down. He
dropped out of school and went to work for Hyman Lazarus, a police-court
judge who also maintained an active law practice in Bayonne. Although
Lazarus paid him nothing at all for the first two weeks, the agreed-on trial
period, he was so impressed by the zeal and ingenuity of his diminutive
clerk, who spent his evenings studying law, that he soon began giving him
more and more to do.

In payment for a bad debt, Lazarus had acquired a 51-percent
interest in the Bayonne *Times,* a moribund weekly newspaper whose
offices were in the same building as his own. One day in 1912, having
fired the latest in a series of incompetent editors, Lazarus turned to his
seventeen-year-old clerk and told him to "go down and take care of the
paper until we can get rid of it." Sam's previous working career had included
part-time jobs as a newsboy, lugging stacks of papers over on the ferry to
Manhattan, and he knew a thing or two about how the big-city papers

operated. Within a matter of months, he had canvassed dozens of local stores, helped their managers to plan sales and advertising campaigns, and sold enough ads to get the Bayonne *Times* out of debt. Shrewdly, he also asked for a cut of the future profits in lieu of salary. Four years later, Sam was earning $20,000 a year from the paper and finding jobs on its expanded payroll for his brothers and cousins. The family's days in poverty were over.

It was a mere accident that Sam Newhouse made his fortune in newspapers; he would have made it in anything else, and probably just as quickly. He had no particular interest in newspapering. He didn't care what his papers printed or what editorial positions they took, and he was not in the least concerned with influencing people or altering the course of human events. All he insisted on was that his papers make money. He bought his first paper, the Staten Island *Advance*, in 1922, and from then on (according to his biographer, Richard H. Meeker), "He was so intent upon building an empire that he had no other interests." In time he came to own twenty-nine papers in twenty-two cities, outdistancing his principal rivals, Hearst and Scripps-Howard, in terms of numbers and circulation, and leaving them far behind in the matter of profits. His detractors accused him of slash-and-burn tactics—buying two competing papers in the same town, folding one, and then raising the ad rates. The editors on the papers he bought were grateful for his policy of "local autonomy," though; he never questioned their editorial decisions, and his cost-cutting measures on the business side usually made good sense. "The key to Newhouse's success is that—with very few exceptions—he has acquired highly profitable papers in prosperous, growing communities and has invested heavily to modernize production facilities," *Business Week* concluded in 1976. According to *Time*, which ran a generally admiring cover story on him in 1962, "Monopolist Sam Newhouse has probably done journalism more good than harm."

Newhouse had built his empire without putting on the trappings of an emperor. A self-effacing man who never even maintained an office, he ran the whole show out of his head, traveling constantly from one of the cities where he owned papers to another, making notes on little pieces of yellow paper that he stuffed in his pockets, putting his trust in the local managers, more than a few of whom were his relatives. (Newhouse at one time had sixty-four relatives on the payroll.) Left to himself, he would have put every cent he made back into the business. Luckily for him, though, he had his wife, Mitzi, to think about. Mitzi Newhouse, née Epstein, was the daughter of a moderately successful manufacturer of women's clothing. She had grown up in comfortable surroundings on the Upper West Side of Manhattan, and she was a graduate of the Parsons School of Design. Mitzi loved clothes, dancing, parties, and going to the theater. Even during the years when she was stuck out in Staten Island, raising their two sons while Sam traveled the country buying newspapers, Mitzi would manage to snatch Sam away from work now and then and make him take her tea-dancing at the Pierre Hotel in New York on a Saturday afternoon. They looked like "a couple of kids at their first dancing class," an acquaintance remembered—at four feet, eight inches, Mitzi had the inestimable asset of making Sam feel tall.

Mitzi finally persuaded Sam to move to Manhattan in the early 1940s. They bought a large apartment at 730 Park Avenue, which Mitzi filled with expensive Louis XV and Louis XVI furniture, and they also acquired an eighteenth-century country house near Princeton, New Jersey, with a swimming pool, a tennis court, a riding stable, and a five-car garage. Sam's work habits didn't change, but the Newhouses became regular first-nighters at the theater and the opera—their seats were always in the first row, so they didn't have to look over anyone—and Mitzi started going to the collections and buying her clothes from Givenchy and Dior. Sam adored her and denied her nothing. The one humorous remark anybody remembers him making was that Mitzi had asked him to go downstairs and buy her a fashion magazine, "and so I went out and bought Vogue."

Although Newhouse's purchase of Condé Nast was often described as a thirty-fifth-anniversary present for his wife, it was in reality a shrewd business decision. Newhouse saw right away that the glamorous bevy of magazines was not earning nearly as much as it could, and he knew just what to do about that. Shortly after buying a controlling interest in Condé Nast, he snapped up Street and Smith, the nation's oldest magazine chain, the publishers of Charm, Mademoiselle, and Living for Young Homemakers; using his familiar tactics, he folded Charm into Glamour, and Living for Young Homemakers into House & Garden, cutting costs and boosting profits in the same breath. (Mademoiselle, whose appeal was to the college-educated career girl rather than the lower-income working girls who supposedly bought Glamour, was allowed to continue as before.) More savings resulted from a Newhouse deal to lease Vogue Patterns to the Butterick Company, and from his decision to shut down Condé Nast's engraving studio in Manhattan and its printing press in Greenwich, Connecticut. The Greenwich plant had been Condé Nast's personal pride and joy, a high-quality press that printed not only the Condé Nast magazines but such distin-

Sam and Mitzi Newhouse, photographed by Alex.

guished outsiders as *Scientific American* and *The New Yorker*; by giving the work to more modern and efficient printing plants in the Middle West, Newhouse figured he could save nearly a million dollars a year. Nine months after buying Condé Nast, Newhouse's biographer reports, "its losses of $500,000 in 1957 and 1958 had been transformed into net profits of $1,627,252."

Iva S. V.-Patcévitch, seemingly unperturbed by the changes that were transforming the company, managed to behave as if the new owner did not quite exist. Even after Newhouse had acquired 100 percent of the stock (for approximately $15 million) and turned it into a private corporation, Patcévitch continued to refer to him as the "principal stockholder," rather than the owner. To some extent his attitude reflected a social bias. According to Alex, Patcévitch was something of an anti-Semite, and his tendencies in this direction were reinforced by the lady who eventually became his second wife. Following his painful convalescence from the affair with Marlene Dietrich, Patcévitch had found solace in a close friendship with Charles and Chesborough Amory, an upper-class American couple with limited funds but top-notch connections. The three of them saw each other constantly, traveled together (Alex and Tatiana went with them to Venice and Nassau), and developed into such a compatible ménage à trois that nothing was essentially changed when Chesborough ("Chessy") divorced Amory and married Patcévitch instead. Chessy, a stylish, confident, very beautiful woman with the same pale-blond, greyhound looks as Patcévitch's first wife, Nada, tended toward the sort of prewar, unthinking anti-Semitism that had begun to strike many educated Americans as somewhat crude.

Sam Newhouse, who spoke of his newspapers as "products" and identified them by location (as in "I just bought Syracuse"), was very clearly not right for Vogue, as the late Edna Chase might have phrased it, but the uncomfortable truth was that the company now belonged to him, and Patcévitch, his disdainful attitude notwithstanding, was no fool. He played his cards carefully enough in the early years of the Newhouse regime, and one of his best cards, he realized at the outset, was Alexander Liberman. When Patcévitch took the Newhouses out to dinner for the first time, he invited his highest-ranking Jewish employee to join them. Sam Newhouse liked Alex immediately. After that evening, the Libermans were frequently invited to 730 Park Avenue, where Newhouse would take Alex aside after dinner and ask question after question about Condé Nast while Mitzi chatted happily to Tatiana about clothes and servants and society. Tatiana was on her best behavior on these occasions, of course, and Alex exerted all his virtuoso charm. Both of them felt that their future was on the line. "When Newhouse bought Condé Nast," Alex said, "I had no protection whatsoever. Pat had a stock option, but I had no stock, no contract, nothing. I remember asking Pat to speak to Newhouse about this, and Pat telling me to write him a letter, which I did—a long letter saying that perhaps my salary should be increased and that I should have a contract. But it was never acknowledged. I'm not even sure Newhouse saw the letter, which went through Pat."

The relationship between Alex and Patcévitch had cooled recently, for reasons that Alex never understood. When Patcévitch returned from his crucial meeting with Cecil King in London, Alex, wanting impulsively to show his support, had gone out to the airport to meet him. "What are you doing here?" Patcévitch had said, in obvious irritation. Although they continued to work easily together at the office, the close friendship of nearly twenty years had eroded somewhat, and Alex, the eternal refugee, the survivor, had instinctively set about building new bridges. "I became in a way Newhouse's confidant," he said. "It was a little like what had happened with Condé Nast. I think Newhouse felt more comfortable with me than he ever did with Pat. He really listened to me, and he learned a lot about how the magazines operated as a result. It was a very difficult situation, because I considered Pat a close, intimate friend, and I was working for him. But still, I loved the company and the magazines, and I had to exist."

Opening night of Alex's 1963 show at Betty Parsons:
Alex and Barnett Newman.

Great Mysteries

lexander Liberman was finally gaining recognition as an artist. Ironically, for someone who did not believe that photographs could be art, he gained it first as a photographer, when an exhibition of his pictures of artists and their studios appeared at the Museum of Modern Art in the fall of 1959.

William S. Lieberman, then the curator of prints at the museum, had met the Libermans a year or so earlier, when they came to a screening of two Marlene Dietrich films at MOMA; Lieberman had arranged the screening for his old friend Roland Penrose, the British collector and art historian, who was married to the former *Vogue* model and photographer Lee Miller. Marlene herself was there, and she brought Alex and Tatiana. Bill Lieberman had heard about Alex's photographs of the School of Paris. That evening he asked to see them, and the end result was a small but extremely well received exhibition, which opened at MOMA on November 29, 1959, and ran through the following January. The show had important repercussions for Alex. It led directly to the publication, a year later, of *The Artist in His Studio* by the Viking Press (Albert Skira had long since abandoned the book project, and no one else had been interested until the MOMA show). The book received splendid reviews throughout the country and went through many editions. It also led, indirectly, to Alex's first show, at the Betty Parsons Gallery. Alex had told Lieberman that Betty Parsons was thinking about giving him a show—a slight exaggeration, perhaps; she had been to his studio several times, and Barnett Newman had urged her to show the work. When Lieberman was preparing a press release for the "Artist in His Studio" exhibition, he called Parsons and pressed her to set a date so that he could include it in the release. "He really pinned her down," Alex said gratefully. "He was a wonderful friend."

The show of geometric circle paintings and small three-dimensional cutouts by Alexander Liberman that opened at the Betty Parsons Gallery on April 4, 1960, excited very little attention. The anonymous New York *Herald Tribune* reviewer called it "an abstractionist's dream of austerity and restraint." In the *Times*, Dore Ashton referred to "esthetic problems" being worked out with "considerable ingenuity"—critical clichés masking professional indifference. Allene Talmey published a photograph of one of the circle paintings (*White Dominant*), along with a note on the show, in *Vogue*'s "People Are Talking About" section. For Alex, though, the reviews were almost beside the point. Having his work shown by Betty Parsons, the dealer he respected more than any other, the one who had picked up where Peggy Guggenheim left off in showing Pollock, Rothko, Still, Newman, and other first-generation Abstract Expressionists, seemed like an immense vote of confidence—even though Parsons had appeared somewhat reluctant in agreeing to the show. Alex always felt that she had been nudged into it by Bill Lieberman at MOMA, and also by Barney Newman, who was consistently enthusiastic about Alex's work. Newman, a theoretician and polemicist as well as a painter, had great influence with Betty Parsons. He was her intellectual godfather, advising her about art and artists, writing catalogue essays for her exhibitions, and even helping to hang her shows. Newman hung Alex's first show at her gallery, and he was on hand at the opening, along with Rothko and most of the other gallery artists.

The most important visitor came a few days after the opening. Alfred H. Barr, Jr., the Museum of Modern Art's founding director and still, in spite of having been fired from that post in 1943, its presiding intelligence and esthetic authority, had already paid a visit to the new studio that Alex had found and moved into in 1959; it was on the ground floor of a former funeral parlor, at 132 East Seventieth Street, just a few doors from his house. As usual, the contact had come about through Alex's network of friends, in this case Jane Gunther, the writer John Gunther's wife, "a very intelligent woman of whom I was very fond. The Gunthers had a house on the same lake in Vermont that the Barrs went to every

Right: Alfred Barr and Alex at the opening of Alex's "Artist in His Studio" exhibition at the Museum of Modern Art, 1959.

Below: At the same opening, with Alfred A. Knopf.

summer, and I think Jane must have told Alfred that he should look at my work. In those days, of course, to have Barr visit your studio was like having Zeus come down from Olympus; one shook and trembled with expectancy. He came, and he seemed very interested in the work." Barr was not just being polite. When he came to the show at Betty Parsons, he chose two works for the museum: *Continuous on Red*, a circle painting that was actually a large red circle (tondo) enclosing four smaller circles, two blue and two black; and *Passage*, one of the small Plexiglas sculptures that Ed Kasper had made from Alex's drawings. As it turned out, Fernand and Beatrice Leval bought *Continuous on Red* and gave it to the museum; Barr, whose purchase funds were limited, was adept at finding donors for the things he wanted. There were no other sales, but that hardly mattered. Alex now belonged to that elite group of living artists on whom the gods had smiled.

Neither then nor later did he become an accepted member of the so-called New York School. The downtown art scene, with its rivalries and provocations, its weekly gatherings and discussions at the Club on Eighth Street, and its hard-drinking revels at the Cedar Tavern, remained terra incognita for Alex. His work was recognized and discussed by the downtown crowd, sometimes heatedly—Alex was reviled by a few New York artists as "the guy who doesn't even make his own paintings"—but his job, his marriage, and the social obligations that went with them conspired to keep him on the fringes of the expanding, contentious, and fiercely self-protective New York art world. For some years to come, his only real link to the art community would be Barnett Newman, who was something of an outsider himself.

The close friendship with Newman that sprang up after Alex's first show at Betty Parsons coincided with Newman's own re-emergence as an artist after a long period of self-imposed exile. Newman had achieved his breakthrough in 1948, when he abandoned the semiabstract, mystical subject matter of his earlier work and started to paint single-color canvases divided by one or more narrow bands of another color. These majestic, austere paintings startled his fellow artists almost as much as they distressed the critics. Even Thomas B. Hess, the editor who turned the magazine *Art News* into a fiery supporter of Willem de Kooning, Jackson Pollock, and other first-generation Abstract Expressionists, wrote about Newman as a "genial theoretician" who presented "ideas" rather than paintings. (He changed his mind a few years later.) The reactions by critics and artists alike to Newman's first two one-man shows at Betty Parsons, in 1950 and 1951, were so negative, and so upsetting to Newman, that he did not show again in New York until 1959. His charismatic influence continued to be felt, however, through his activities as Betty Parsons's adviser and confidant, and in the late fifties his work, which had grown larger in scale and richer in color, was coming to be re-evaluated as one of the most important achievements in recent American art—a vital alternative to the "gestural" Abstract Expressionism of Pollock, de Kooning, and Franz Kline.

The New York art world had changed radically since the heroic early years of the postwar period. The spirit of solidarity among the advanced artists, the "stockade mentality" that had prevailed when nobody was buying their work, had given way to feuds, jealousies, and accusations of "selling out." As the fifties advanced and the number of galleries showing contemporary work proliferated, a second generation of Abstract Expressionist artists had emerged; they built on the long-delayed success of Pollock, de Kooning, and the other gestural painters, getting shows while they were still in their twenties or thirties, finding buyers, winning recognition that the older artists tended to think was unearned. Toward the end of the decade, it began to be said that the gestural wing of Abstract Expressionism had lost its momentum. Too many of the younger artists seemed merely to be imitating the drip-and-splatter methods of the late Jackson Pollock (killed in a 1956 automobile crash), without the passionate conviction that had inspired them. Clement Greenberg, Pollock's early champion and the most influential critic of the period, wrote in 1964 that Abstract Expressionism had "turned into a school, then into a manner, and finally into a set of mannerisms." Greenberg's own allegiance had shifted from the gestural artists to the color-field painters of the first generation—Clyfford Still, Mark Rothko, Barnett Newman—and to newcomers such as Morris Louis, Kenneth Noland, and Helen Frankenthaler, whose innovation was to "stain" unprimed canvases with spreading fields of acrylic colors. The true direction of modern art, according to Greenberg, was the path of purity—the tendency of each art form to purge itself of everything except those properties that were unique to itself, which in the case of painting meant line, color, and shape imposed on a flat surface.

At the same time, other challengers were taking art in different and contrary directions. Robert Rauschenberg and Jasper Johns, the two young artists whom Alex Liberman had tried unsuccessfully to use for *Vogue*, introduced commonplace objects and images from commercial art into their Abstract Expressionist–influenced pictures, thereby opening the door to Pop Art, Happenings, and other highly energetic but "impure" developments that tended to break down the barriers between art and life. Frank Stella, whose monumental black-stripe paintings grew out of his rejection of the emotional content of art ("My painting," he said, "is based

Alex's first show at the Betty Parsons Gallery, April 1960:
Betty Parsons and Alex.

With Salvador Dali.

At the Parsons opening: *above,* Franz Kline and Dali; *left,* Alex with Willem de Kooning; *below,* Sam and Mitzi Newhouse.

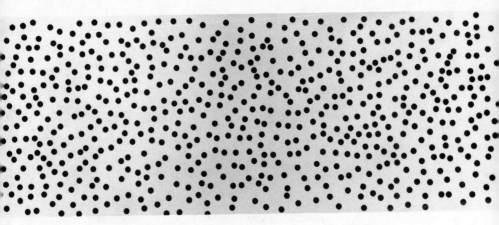

Six Hundred and Thirty-Nine, 1959, acrylic and oil on
canvas, 49 1/4 x 137". "I threw poker chips at random,
and then put tracing paper over them. Eddie Kasper and I
did the tracing. I separated the very few chips that overlapped—that's the only correcting of chance I did. Kasper
executed the painting while I sailed off to France."

Alpha III, 1961, oil on canvas, 80" x 60"—
the circles expand.

A thirteen-year focus on the circle: Alex at work in his funeral-parlor studio, 132 East Seventieth Street.

on the fact that only what can be seen there *is* there"), sounded the note that would soon become the anthem of Minimal Art. The ferment and frivolity of the 1960s were just around the corner. The New York School, until recently a tightly knit band of embattled pariahs, was now the focus of conflicting energies that were felt throughout the international art world.

At least a dozen years before Minimalism arrived on the scene, Alex's circle paintings anticipated that movement's stripped-down, impersonal surfaces and literal stance: Stella's "what you see is what's there." Alex had pursued the implications that later and younger artists would address as though for the first time—exploring repeatability and symmetry, using industrial paints and materials, even questioning the craft side of art by giving instructions over the telephone for paintings to be executed by his assistant. Having received little or no encouragement, he now stood poised to enjoy the acclaim and the attention due a pioneer—someone who had gone his own way and opened new territory that was now proving to be rich in possibilities. Instead, Alex chose this moment to retreat, to take stock, and to change his style.

The change was gradual. In his second exhibition at Betty Parsons, in February 1962, he again showed geometric circle paintings—larger and bolder ones, in primary colors. There was also a group of polished aluminum sculptures that Alex had had fabricated to his designs at the metalwork shop of Treitel Gratz, in Long Island City; suggested by the paintings, they were composed of circles and half-circles, arcs, and rectangular forms welded together in precise conformations. The show was a great success. Every painting sold, and several of the sculptures as well; Alfred Barr bought one for the Museum of Modern Art. Barney Newman was ecstatic, and Clem Greenberg, who had walked through Alex's first show in 1960 with a pad and pencil, grading the pictures according to a system all his own (three of them received the highest grade, a triple plus-sign), came up to Alex a few days after the 1962 opening and said, "Continue with this, Alex, and I will write about you." Greenberg's enthusiasm was thrilling; as an esthetic authority and tastemaker, he wielded almost as much influence as Barr in those days. The trouble was, Alex had grown bored with his own work. He was tired of geometric painting—tired of what had come to seem "the negativism and the severity of it" and of the "moral straitjacket" that he had imposed on himself. For a dozen years, Alex had rigidly excluded emotion and any personal "touch" from his paintings. "I was working against the grain of everything," he told Barbara Rose when she interviewed him for her book-length monograph on his work some years later, "against value. That was the idea. No value. I had theories about paintings being imprinted on the mind. I resented Abstract Expressionism. . . . The self was hateful. The hand of the artist shouldn't be seen." By 1962, however, the self was making a comeback.

Two dramatic changes—one in his personal life, the other at Condé Nast—had helped to raise his own self-esteem. In September 1961, after suffering through another of his periodic bouts with bleeding ulcers, Alex underwent major gastrointestinal surgery that cured him of this problem for the rest of his life. He was out of the office for nearly three months, convalescing at home; Sam Newhouse climbed the stairs to his third-floor bedroom to pay a visit, which was about the most reassuring thing that had ever happened to Alex at Condé Nast. ("I always found him a kind and considerate man," Alex said. "Not generous, but thoughtful.") The other change came late in 1962, when Alex's name was listed just below Patcévitch's on the mastheads of all five Condé Nast magazines with a new title: Editorial Director. The position had been created to take care of a specific problem, as we shall see, but it meant that he now outranked everyone else on the combined staffs, and that he no longer had to worry about his future with the company. His salary went up accordingly, to $45,000, and so did the multiple, often lavish Condé Nast perks (limousines, expense accounts, travel allowances) that made life pleasanter for him and were so very gratifying to Tatiana.

In better health than he could ever remember, and riding high in the job that provided his income, Alex became a more ambitious artist. He wanted to imbue his paintings with spiritual values and universal symbols—the sort of exalted metaphorical content that the Abstract Expressionists had always claimed as the basis of their work. How much of this came out of his friendship with Barnett Newman is an open question. "Barney was for me the essence of the American artist that I was trying to become," he said at one point. Newman set great store by his own search for the "sublime." The titles of his monochromatic paintings, with their now-famous vertical or horizontal dividers (which he called "zips"), often carried mystical and religious overtones—*Onement, The Word, The Gate, Vir Heroicus Sublimis*—and in 1958 he had embarked on his series of fourteen *Stations of the Cross*. If Newman influenced the new direction in Alex's art, though, he did so indirectly, through his paintings, which Alex had seen and been profoundly impressed by at the 1959 Newman semiretrospective organized by Clement Greenberg at the French and Company gallery in New York.

Although Newman's written statements were full of portentous reflections on the function of art, in private conversation he was engagingly colloquial and down-to-earth. A born New Yorker whose parents had both emigrated from Poland, he loved good jokes, baseball, city politics (he had once run, not too seriously, for mayor of New York), and art-world gossip. Alex could never recall having a profound philosophical discussion with him. Newman and his wife, Annalee, who had supported her husband's work for many years with her salary as a public-school teacher, came for dinner several times at the Libermans' house. Tatiana rather dreaded these evenings, because Barney was a slow leaver. He would stand on the stairs or by the front door for forty minutes or more, drawing out the final good-night while he got off one more anecdote; at that point he was neither famous nor successful enough to earn Tatiana's indulgence. Alex cherished the friendship nevertheless, and had long telephone conversations with Barney nearly every day. When Barney and Annalee made their first trip to Europe, in 1964, Alex took them out to JFK airport by limousine—a gesture that evidently meant a great deal to Newman. ("We shall never forget the day and the trouble you went to," he wrote from London. "You made our going away a memorable occasion.")

Barbara Rose cites Alex's reading of certain key books, among them Georgy Kepes's *The Language of Vision* and Wassily Kandinsky's *Concerning the Spiritual in Art*, as the real source of his break with hard-edge geometrical painting. When questioned about this, though, Alex smiled and admitted that he had never really read the books; he had "flipped through" them and "looked at the illustrations." Perhaps his years of experience with magazines enabled him to pick ideas out of the air, so to speak—to assimilate currents of thought that might be useful, without having to slog through oppressive miasmas of theory and dogma. At any rate, he began in 1962 to deal with the circle motif in a new way. Instead of self-contained circles within a rectangular or a circular format, the arcs of much larger circles now appeared in his paintings—sections of great circles that extended far beyond the frame. The colors in these new paintings were darker: muted earth greens and browns, deep reds and purples, subtly modulated grays and blacks. Cleve Gray, Francine's painter-husband, had introduced Alex to Liquitex paint, a fast-drying, water-based pigment that could be applied evenly over large areas. In his funeral-parlor studio, Alex could now work on a much bigger scale than before. Using a giant-sized draftsman's compass made for him by a French cabinetmaker, he could inscribe arcs of circles whose radius was sixty feet. The titles of the new paintings announced his expanding vision; a whole series was called *The Great Mysteries*. He wanted them to convey a sense of cosmic space, an experience beyond the visual. What you saw was only part of what was there.

The transition from a cerebral style to something much warmer and more personal accelerated in 1963. Clean, precise divisions between his color areas broke down; impersonal, uniform surfaces gave way to "painterly" brush strokes; the circular forms, their contours no longer pure or even complete, were invaded by freehand splashes and broad streaks of color. By late 1964 the circle motif had virtually disappeared. Working with his canvases laid flat on the floor, Alex poured and flung paint from buckets, using the technique that Pollock had made famous, opening the way to chance and all its attendant perils and rewards. "Pollock was certainly the guide," he said. "I would take pails of color and throw them, but not just accidentally. I would try to give a sweep, a sort of diagonal gesture. Sometimes I used floor mops in place of brushes. Barney Newman had taught me about cotton duck, which you could buy in long rolls at a sailmaker's loft called Boyle's, downtown. I started using that in larger and larger sizes. And I found that I enormously enjoyed the physical effort of putting myself into it that way. After having fought against Abstract Expressionism, I now felt that they were on the right track."

Betty Parsons thought Alex was out of his mind. Having failed to sell a single painting from his 1963 show, she came to his studio and told him he was making a terrible mistake. Even before this, Alex had received a letter from Betty that he found immensely disheartening. She was losing her gallery space at 15 East Fifty-seventh Street, she said, and her uncertainty about a future space "forces me . . . to suggest that you should perhaps seek new gallery associations." Betty eventually relocated in another Fifty-seventh Street building, where Alex continued to show his painting until 1973; but he never again had the feeling that she believed in his work. Her plea to reconsider the direction he was taking had no effect on him whatsoever. "I did what I had to do," he said. "And I must say, I enormously enjoyed getting out of that straitjacket. Art should be a search, not an achievement. Hard-edge for me was an absolute, but an easy absolute, and I never regretted giving it up."

Diana Vreeland confers with Alex in her office at *Vogue*, which
was a meeting place for the "beautiful people." "Cecil Beaton and
Truman Capote would come in and try on hats there," said Alex.

The Myth of
the Next Reality

W hen Diana Vreeland left *Harper's Bazaar* to join *Vogue* in 1962, it was big news in the fashion world but nowhere else. Vreeland had not yet become a legendary figure in American culture. At *Bazaar*, where she had been top fashion editor since the late 1930s, she was part of a high-powered, marvelously inventive triumverate that included Alexey Brodovitch, the art director, and Carmel Snow, the editor in chief, and her flamboyant style, which was responsible for such beguiling absurdities as the "Why Don't You?" columns in *Bazaar* ("Why don't you rinse your blond child's hair in dead champagne to keep it gold, as they do in France?"), had always been tempered by the perfect editorial pitch of Snow. This remarkable era ended abruptly in 1958, when Brodovitch and Snow both retired. A procession of art directors tried to carry on in Brodovitch's long shadow. The brilliant but temperamental Marvin Israel stayed less than a year and was succeeded by his two assistants (and students), Bea Feitler and Ruth Ansel. Carmel Snow, who had warned the Hearst organization that Diana Vreeland lacked the discipline and the judgment to be editor in chief of *Bazaar*, was succeeded by her niece, Nancy White, a longtime *Good Housekeeping* editor. Vreeland continued to perform with her customary élan as fashion editor for the next four years, but the combination of her unimpressive salary and the floundering editorial direction at *Bazaar* put her in a receptive mood when Alex Liberman came courting. "They offered me a very large salary, an endless expense account . . . and Europe whenever I wanted to go," she wrote in her not entirely dependable memoir, *D.V.* "That's what hooked me."

In less than six months, Vreeland's boundless energy and non-stop inventiveness as the new *Vogue* fashion editor had driven poor Jessica Daves, that devoted guardian of the status quo, into angry retirement. There was friction between them from the outset, and it got worse very quickly. Vreeland's name replaced Daves's at the top of the January 1963 *Vogue* masthead as editor in chief. A month earlier, Alexander Liberman had become editorial director of all the Condé Nast magazines. (Patcévitch and others had wanted to make Alex editor in chief of *Vogue*, but he had refused; he thought a woman should have that title, and besides, he didn't want to be that much involved with fashion.) Naming Alex editorial director was the solution that Patcévitch and Edwin F. Russell, the man whom Sam Newhouse had installed as publisher of *Vogue*, had hit upon to keep the mercurial Vreeland under control. She used her authority to remake fashion journalism in her own image, nevertheless, and in doing so she catapulted *Vogue* into its period of absolute dominance.

Truman Capote once described Diana Vreeland, in a self-congratulatory aside, as "the kind of genius that very few people will ever recognize because you have to be a genius yourself to recognize it. Otherwise you just think she's a rather foolish woman." She had an uncanny ability to set the creative juices flowing in other people. "You really weren't supposed to take what she said literally," according to Richard Avedon, who had worked with her for many years at *Harper's Bazaar*. "She had this way of speaking in code, throwing the ball out and expecting you to bring it back with bells on." Vreeland once told Irving Penn to go to Spain and photograph a Gypsy queen who "bathed in milk and had the most wonderful skin in the world." As Penn told the story later, he "chased Gypsies all over Spain," and "not only was there no queen, but they rarely bathed, let alone in milk. I came back and told Mrs. Vreeland that I hadn't been able to find the Gypsy queen, and she looked at me and said, 'What Gypsy queen?'" *Vogue* published thirteen pages of Penn's photographs of "The Gypsies of Estremadura," nevertheless, and Vreeland continued to send him and other top photographers to far-off places for the exotic images that were her stock-in-trade. She sent them to Turkey and Mexico and North Africa and India, to Monument Valley in Arizona and to the mountains of northern Hokkaido, places where the high-style clothes that she favored could be seen against surroundings every bit as outré as they were. The money to do all this had not been available before, of course; being part of the Newhouse empire made many things possible, including the salary that had lured Vreeland to *Vogue*. But much of the magazine's new extravagance was the result of Vreeland's unfettered high spirits.

Kate Lloyd, the assistant features editor at *Vogue* when Vreeland arrived, tells this story of her first encounter with the new editor in chief. "I had done a sixteen-page spread on Bettina, whom Mrs. Vreeland always called a grand courtesan. She was the mistress of Ali Khan. It had everything—her house in Paris, her trip down the Nile, her exercise program, her clothes, her beauty secrets. It had taken an awful lot of work, and because I could never talk to Bettina, a lot of it had to be made up out of whole cloth. Well, I sent the portfolio, text and pictures, down to Mrs. Vreeland, very pleased with myself, and a while later the phone rang.

" 'Mrs. Lloyd?'

" 'Yes, Mrs. Vreeland.'

" 'I don't think you've quite gotten the feeling for this portfolio.' I was turning red in the face, because I'd been there a hell of a lot longer than Mrs. Vreeland. 'Mrs. Lloyd,' she said, 'I don't think you quite understand what *Vogue* is.'

"The steam started coming out of my ears at that point. I said, 'Tell me, Mrs. Vreeland, what is *Vogue*?'

"She said, '*Vogue* is the myth of the next reality.' And I got it. I absolutely got it. Take the words apart and they don't mean a thing, but I saw exactly what she was driving at, and I never had a moment's difficulty with her again."

The next reality, of course, was the 1960s, whose youth-worshiping, iconoclastic spirit Diana Vreeland did so much to define and spur along. Although she was sixty-three when she came to *Vogue*, Vreeland struck many of her colleagues as being twenty or thirty years younger. She adored the clothes and clothing styles that emanated from the little shops on London's King's Road, and she coined the word "youthquake" to apply to the anarchic attitudes that produced them. "It was a marvelous time to be a fashion journalist," she said when the sixties were over and done with. "I don't think anyone has ever been in a better place at a better time than I was." Although the sixties would also provide generous helpings of violence and social ugliness, Vreeland saw the decade as one when "youth went out to life, instead of waiting for life to come to them, which is the difference between the sixties and any other decade I've lived in."

More than ever before, *Vogue* under Vreeland influenced as well as reported on the latest fashion news. Vreeland was a dictatorial gadfly, telling designers what was wrong with their new lines and what to do about it. She celebrated miniskirts and she welcomed bikinis, which Jessica Daves had refused to show in the magazine, as "the biggest thing since the atom bomb." Her private network of information was worldwide. She spent her mornings in bed, talking on the telephone, and arrived at the office ablaze with fresh ideas and international gossip. "Good morning, ladies," or "Hi, kiddos," she would sing out, loping through the corridors in a knee-length black skirt and beige Givenchy tunic, with a brilliant scarf knotted casually at her throat. She rarely remembered names. (Her friends called her Diane, pronouncing it "Dee-Anne"; to most *Vogue* staffers she was "Mrs. Vreeland.") Even her gait was unique—one of the editors said she walked like a camel. In the corner office that she had had painted Chinese red (her favorite color), she often worked on the floor, flopping down in a great jangle of bracelets to study photographs or fabrics or test shots or layouts. Like Kate Lloyd, most of the editors succumbed to her spell without a struggle. "She was just enormous fun to be around," Lloyd said. Priscilla Peck, Alex's former protégée and art director of *Vogue*, quite literally fell in love with Vreeland. Although never a beauty, Vreeland had a personal style that was as seductive as Alex's, and a great deal more vivid. Truman Capote, who became one of her great pals, said she was like an "extraordinary parrot—a wild thing that's flung itself out of the jungle and talks in some amazing language." She was one of the few women whom Tatiana Liberman genuinely admired. "Tatiana thought she was someone very special," according to Alex, "and so did I, for a long time."

Except for the fact that she preferred to work with male photographers and tended to give less work to Frances McLaughlin and Karen Radkai as a result, Vreeland's attitude toward photography was very much like Alex's. "A good photograph was never what I was looking for," she said in *Allure*, the 1980 picture book that she did with Christopher Hemphill. She loved the paparazzi style that had developed mainly in Europe, the snapshot that caught "that *thing* . . . the revelation of personality," and she thought that "laying out a beautiful picture in a beautiful way is a bloody bore. I think you've got to blow it right across the page and down the side, crop it, cut it in half, combine it with something else . . . *do* something with it." If necessary, doing something might include radical surgery. Vreeland described in *Allure* the shocked reaction of the editors at *Vogue* when she ordered a composite photograph using the legs of one model and the torso and head of another: "I thought they'd fall on the floor . . . so I said, 'Listen, photographers aren't artists, for goodness sake! There's very little art in the world. What there is is splendid, but let's not confuse it with fashion.' At *Harper's Bazaar* we often used composite photos. . . . I was always using Cyd Charisse's legs because I was mad about their *length*. . . . Then, at *Vogue*, I *really* went to town. I put *legs* and *arms* and *heads* and everything *else* together . . . to give the perfect whole. And I was the world's greatest retoucher. . . . I never took out fewer than two ribs."

Her dismissal of photography as art did not seem to bother the photographers, who more than ever looked to *Vogue* to make their reputations. Fashion photographers were becoming culture heroes in much the same way that foreign correspondents were in the 1940s. The popular 1957 film *Funny Face*, starring Audrey Hepburn, costarred Fred Astaire as a fashion photographer whose personality and career were based on Richard Avedon's. (In the role of the magazine editor who ordered her minions to "think pink," Kay Thompson did a great spoof of Diana Vreeland.) The lead character in Michelangelo Antonioni's 1966 *Blow-Up* was suggested by David Bailey, the young British photographer whose irreverent, street-smart pictures of Twiggy and the "swinging London" scene in the 1960s helped to cement the new alliance between fashion and popular culture. Fashion ideas were coming from the streets, as young people raided thrift shops and costume outlets to make up their own styles of dress and behavior. The sexual revolution was in full swing, triggered as much by the baby-boom generation's rejection of adult authority as by the pill, and some of its results could be seen each month in the pages of *Vogue*. Sexual references and more and more bare skin surfaced in the photographs of Bailey, Art Kane, Bob Richardson, Bert Stern, and especially Helmut Newton, who explored the once-unthinkable backwaters of sadomasochistic fantasies and same-sex attraction. Stern's nude photos of Marilyn Monroe, taken shortly before she committed suicide in 1962, were not used by *Vogue*; Jessica Daves was still at the helm then, and Stern was told to go back and reshoot Monroe in a variety of elegant frocks. Eight years later, even the great Irving Penn could be prevailed upon to photograph Marisa Berenson wearing an openwork necklace and nothing else.

Vreeland provided copious and detailed guidance to photographers and fashion models alike, in the form of memos that she wrote out herself on a portable typewriter. "Dear darling Penelope and David," she wrote to Penelope Tree and David Bailey, who had fallen in love with each other and gone off to India on a fashion shoot. "We want the clothes to look as covered up *and* as un-dressed as possible—we don't want Penelope to wear a body stocking but there is very little transparency. . . . Penelope: please look very very happy—*because I know you are*—and please make it radiate through each and every picture. . . . When you think barefoot is best— by all means, bare feet. . . . If you find the houseboats in Kashmir appear a bit shabby, by all means buy some cheap Indian cotton and sari material and drape them and cover the pillows etc. so that everything looks very delicious and like a fairy tale. . . . If there are some dripping trees—*get under them*."

Vreeland's star rose even higher when Richard Avedon left *Harper's Bazaar* in 1965 to work with her at *Vogue*. Alex had tried to hire Avedon way back in 1943, and over the years he had kept a line of communication open to the man who was universally acclaimed, even by Penn, as the best and most influential fashion photographer of his time. ("One of the reasons I wanted Avedon," Alex said, "was that Penn resisted doing fashion work.") Avedon had been invited three or four times to private lunches at Alex's house on Seventieth Street; Alex had talked generally about his working for *Vogue*, but there had been no direct offers or proposals. Late in 1965, however, on instructions from Alex, Vreeland called him and asked whether his contract with Hearst wasn't coming up for renewal. Avedon said it was, and that, after six months of negotiation, he had just that week worked out a new and much more favorable contract. "I want to know something," he recalls her saying to him. "Are you even remotely interested in listening to what Alex Liberman has to say?" Avedon, well aware that *Bazaar's* great days were over, said he might be and immediately went off with his son on a tour of New England boarding schools. When he got back, he says, he found that Alex had left half a dozen telephone messages for him. The next day, a Saturday, he went to the Seventieth Street house to talk with Alex, who had met earlier in the day with Sam

Vogue fashion editor Polly Mellen on location in the Bahamas, October 1968,
with Richard Avedon and Lauren Hutton.

Newhouse and Iva Patcévitch to see how much they were willing to pay
for the world's premier fashion photographer. The financial details of the
unprecedented million-dollar agreement (to be paid in advance) were ironed
out the next day by teams of lawyers.

In his last years at *Bazaar*, Avedon had been given a great deal of
creative freedom. Six pages of each issue had been set aside for his
"Observations"—photographs of the civil rights movement and other nonfashion subjects—and the entire April 1965 issue had been given over to
his "guest editorship." He looked forward to exercising the same sort of
freedom at *Vogue*, but he was in for a shock. When he asked Alex, at their
first lunch together after signing the contract, what particular qualities in
his editorial work they wanted to emphasize at *Vogue*, "Alex said, 'Dear
friend, your Du Pont ads. You and Jean Shrimpton. There is no one who

can make a woman look as beautiful as you can." This was perfectly compatible with Alex's usual advice to photographers—that they give their commercial expertise to *Vogue* and save their esthetic aspirations for their own work—but Avedon was appalled. His complicated feelings about female beauty—that it was more often a misery than a gift—had led him to explore the underside of artifice and fashion in some extremely unsettling photographs for *Bazaar*, and it was immediately evident to him that *Vogue* would have no interest in that sort of work. His disillusionment deepened when *Vogue* sent him off on his first major assignment—to photograph furs in the mountains of northern Japan. Avedon wanted to take Donyale Luna, his discovery, the first black model to crash the lily-white high-fashion barrier; he had used her several times at *Harper's Bazaar*. *Vogue* was dubious about using Luna. According to Avedon, the magazine was afraid of losing advertisers. Avedon kept insisting, and a compromise was reached: he would take two models—Donyale Luna and Veruschka, the blond sensation from Germany. "When I got to Paris, en route to Japan, I was informed that they had canceled Donyale Luna," Avedon said. "It was too late for me to cancel the trip. That's pretty rough pool."

Avedon simmered down soon enough, and over the next five years at *Vogue* he produced the most exciting and original fashion work of that period. Avedon and Vreeland seemed to stimulate and to push each other to the edge of what was possible in those days, demonstrating again and again Jean Cocteau's famous aphorism that genius lay in knowing how far to go too far. Together they discovered and promoted a new image of fashion and a new kind of fashion model—the offbeat, androgynous, barely postadolescent waif. Penelope Tree, the daughter of the socially prominent Marietta Tree, was seventeen when Avedon's first pictures of her appeared in *Vogue*. Twiggy, with her Botticelli-angel's face and a Cockney accent that would have made Eliza Doolittle blush, was a year younger. (They were known as "the Twig" and "the Tree.") Diana Vreeland published their names in the magazine, along with Veruschka's and Jean Shrimpton's and Lauren Hutton's, and as a result they became superstars and began commanding fees to match. In Avedon's photographs—and in the work of the many younger photographers who were influenced by Avedon—these sixties girls danced, leaped through the air, rode bicycles, watched TV, bared their breasts, turned cartwheels, and somehow managed to look perfectly comfortable wearing the absurd metallic and plastic garments that Courrèges and Rudi Gernreich and other sixties designers cooked up for them, if not for the average Bloomingdale's shopper.

Although it might have seemed at times as though Avedon had taken over *Vogue*, this was far from being the case. Irving Penn's indelible images held their own against Avedon's nervous brilliance—the rivalry between these two superb photographers, both appearing every month in the same magazine, created an excitement all its own. Alex Liberman had always insisted on having a wide range of photographic styles in the magazine, and catholicity prevailed throughout the 1960s, with work by such seasoned talents as Horst, Cecil Beaton, and Norman Parkinson appearing alongside the brash, disquieting visions of David Bailey, Bruce Davidson, Helmut Newton, and Jeanloup Sieff. Expert diplomacy was needed to keep all these photographic egos in check. Alex had become a master of subtle flattery, persuasion, and compromise—the ability to compromise, he said, "is perhaps one of the strongest things in me"—but his diplomacy had limits. Francesco Scavullo, a photographer known mainly for his heavily retouched *Cosmopolitan* covers, let temperament outdistance talent when he tore up a copy of *Vogue*'s layout of his work and sent the pieces back in a garbage bag to Alex; although Scavullo later regretted the gesture and wrote plaintive letters, Alex never used him again. On another, more memorable occasion, Alex ordered the British photographer Norman Parkinson out of his office and never used him again, either. "Parkinson was a very good photographer," he said, "before he became such a social dandy. He had a wonderful sense of integrating fashion with landscape. But then he got to be an archsnob and a phony, and I couldn't stand that falseness. I can't even remember why I got so furious at him that day—it was probably a sitting he refused to take. I just said, 'Get out,' and he did."

When Alex called Penn into his office in 1965 and told him that *Vogue* had hired Avedon, Penn felt as though he had been kicked in the gut. Alex quickly added that he was upping Penn's guarantee to two hundred pages a year, but Penn walked the streets all that night, worrying about his future; it was a turning point in his life, he said, because after that he decided to start concentrating more on his own work apart from *Vogue*. Penn had continuing difficulties with Vreeland, whose idea of fashion as theater conflicted with his own more formal, classical sense of composition; but Penn's work was essential to Alex's concept of *Vogue*. There was a "nobility" to Penn's vision and an admiration for women that Alex found missing in Avedon's. "I don't think Avedon really likes 'beautiful' women,"

Alex said once. "He likes women with character and women with allure, and he's interested in discovering fresh visions of beauty, but his women often look as though they don't like men." Avedon has been accused of taking ferociously unflattering portraits of famous people in order to exorcise the guilt he feels over doing fashion work, but this is much too simplistic an explanation. He has always been obsessed by female beauty and its effect on those who have it—"how isolating it is to be a beautiful woman, as isolating as genius or being a hunchback, and all it can do is go away." Avedon claims that until he came to Vogue, he made no distinction between his fashion photographs and his "serious" work. "I was never interested in a woman until I could bring out something that had to do with the complexity of her character," he said, "but that complexity was of no interest to Vogue."

Avedon's Vogue covers tended to exacerbate the prickly relationship between Avedon and Liberman. "Alex Liberman was the art director, the fashion editor, and the mind behind all Vogue covers," Avedon said. "He placed the orders: 'Her eyes are too small.' 'The nose is too big—watch the nostrils, dear friend, raise the camera, lower the chin.' He was the customer and I was the supermarket." Alex saw it quite differently. He felt increasingly excluded from the close and highly charged working relationship between Avedon and Vreeland. For years Alex had chosen virtually every photograph that went into the magazine—Irving Penn brought his contact sheets to the office so that Alex could pick the best shots—but Vreeland and Avedon changed all that. "They worked quite secretly together," according to Alex. "Vreeland liked to pick her own pictures, and Avedon would only send in two or three of his preferences. Vreeland would plan the sittings without involving me. So the whole operation was rather, you might say, confidential." For quite a long time Alex seemed to accept the new situation, but toward the end of the sixties the people who had worked with him the longest could see that he was bothered by it. Besides which, the magazine was losing ground financially. "Vreeland and Avedon were two very strong personalities," he said many years later. "They pushed each other to the limit, and out of that combination came pictures that were often somewhat disturbing. There was a sense of the dominating, overpowering woman, in aggressive poses, legs apart as though she were standing on top of the world. Lion tamers. Vreeland picked the fashion pictures; she would take them home and initial them, and I wouldn't question her. I accepted the fact that Vreeland was a phenomenon, that Avedon was a fantastic photographer. And I must say I liked working with those very strong pictures. But in retrospect, I think maybe it was all a little too daring for the time."

What he did not say was that *Vogue* was becoming less responsive to his own esthetic vision. The problem of controlling Vreeland had turned out to be more difficult than he or anyone else had anticipated.

Alex with Coco Chanel, in her rue Cambon salon. Chanel had just made her
triumphal postwar comeback.

Art vs. Fashion

At the opening of his third one-man show at the Betty Parsons Gallery, in the spring of 1963, Alex saw Diana Vreeland edging her way through the crowd to speak to him. "Oh, Alex," she said, gesturing toward the pictures on the wall, "they'd make such beautiful sweaters!"

Inane but indelible, the remark pinpointed Alex's dilemma. How could he be a serious artist and still devote the major part of his working life to *Vogue* magazine? Once again, Barnett Newman had installed the show, and Newman and several other Parsons artists turned up for the opening, but most of the people there were associated either with Condé Nast or with the social world that was reflected in *Vogue*—the world that *Vogue* had recently started to refer to as "the beautiful people." Alex had his own answer to the art-versus-fashion question. He kept his job at Condé Nast, he said, so that he could be free in his art, unconstrained by the whims of rich collectors or venal critics. But beneath the suave, urbane exterior that was so seductive to his female colleagues at the magazine, Alex was beset by painful doubts. Sometime in 1963, he wrote out in longhand a fifty-one-page manuscript called "The Mistake," which he showed to no one. It took the form of a first-person confession by a fifty-

year-old man (Alex had turned fifty in 1962) who is a painter, but an
unhappy painter, "not a good painter," someone who feels he may have
missed his real vocation. He traces his lifelong "mistake" back to a childhood
incident at boarding school, when he sent home to his mother a quick
sketch of Charlie Chaplin that he passed off as his own, although it was
actually done by one of his classmates. His mother, who had always wanted
him to be a painter, took the drawing as vindication of her faith in his
talent, and from that moment on it was "too late" for him to escape from
her domineering ambition. Ironically, when he becomes an artist, his
mother does not approve of the abstract work of his mature years; she feels
that he has never fulfilled his youthful promise. Years later, he tries to tell
her the truth about the childhood drawing that she had loved so much.
She refuses to believe him. For her, the drawing will always be the proof
of the great artist he might have become.

     We need not wring too much significance from this rather maudlin
confession. The incident of the Chaplin drawing did occur, when Alex was
at school in England, and the lifelong struggle to please his mother and at
the same time to escape from her was all too real. But doubt, after all, is
part of the baggage that few artists can leave behind them. (Willem de
Kooning said once that he "worked out of doubt.") Alex's contact with the
New York art world was confined at that time to his conversations with
Newman and, to a lesser degree, with the critic Lawrence Alloway, who
became a friend for a while in the early 1960s, until he had a row with
Tatiana and was banished. Alloway intensely disliked Tatiana and took
pride in having reduced her to tears once, in an argument at dinner. "She
was a surly old bitch," in his opinion. Newman, Cleve Gray, and Alloway
gave Alex strong support, but the critical notices that his work received
were not encouraging. Now that he had abandoned the radical, hard-edge
geometrical style of his first show, the reviewers tended to find his paintings
intelligent and well made, but not much more than that; the influential
young critic Michael Fried, writing in Art International, described Alex's
1963 show at Parsons as "a refined and competent but wholly unoriginal
body of work." (Only one painting was sold—a big letdown after the successful 1962 show.) For all his doubts and uncertainties, though, and in
spite of the increased responsibilities of his job at Condé Nast, Alex was
in the midst of an intensive period of artistic development—probably the
most intensive of his career.

     His recent change of direction had set him apart from most of the
new forces that were shaping the art of the 1960s. The young American

artists who emerged in the late 1950s, partly in reaction to what they considered the inflated emotional claims and windy rhetoric of the first-generation Abstract Expressionists, had adopted a whole new set of attitudes and goals. The Pop artists, looking out at the world instead of dwelling on their own reactions to it, brought an ironic sensibility to bear upon the billboards, comic strips, newspaper headlines, and blown-up advertising images of the new, media-soaked popular culture. The Minimalist object-makers, who elevated mind over matter in their stripped-down, impersonal, machine-made forms, carried Clement Greenberg's reductionist theories to an extreme that Greenberg himself might not have envisaged. As the 1960s advanced, it became clear that these two seemingly opposed directions were not so far apart after all. Both Pop and Minimal went in for clearly defined forms and large areas of unmodulated color, and both of them more or less ruled out emotional content. A good deal of the art of the sixties, in fact, developed along the same lines that Alex himself had charted for thirteen years in his circle paintings, and it is quite likely that if Alex had continued along those lines, he would have had greater success as an artist. By giving up his circle image, moreover, he relinquished more than the simple motif. The first generation of Abstract Expressionists (Alex's own generation) set great store by their unique "image," meaning the pictorial device by which they had established their mature style—Newman's "zip," Rothko's floating rectangles of color, Adolph Gottlieb's chromatic "bursts"—and one of their achievements was to show what a wide range of esthetic and human emotion they could pack into this rather narrow signature image. Alex gave up his image because it had come to feel too "tidy" and too cerebral and altogether too limiting, but in doing so he sabotaged his reputation and magnified the problems he already faced in being taken seriously as an artist.

For a time in the early 1960s, the visual ideas that had preoccupied him in the circle paintings continued to serve as the basis for the metal sculptures that he designed and had fabricated at Treitel Gratz. A group of these were photographed and published in 1963 by *Architectural Forum*, where they were seen and admired by the architect Philip Johnson. When Johnson commissioned Robert Rauschenberg, Andy Warhol, and eight other contemporary artists to make works for his New York State building at the 1964 World's Fair in Flushing Meadow, Alex Liberman was one of the two sculptors invited; his *Prometheus*, an aluminum relief sculpture with two large circular elements, was installed over the main entrance. (Improperly installed, as it turned out; the heavy central element crashed to the ground during a storm, which luckily occurred at night, when nobody was around. Repaired and reinstalled, the sculpture lasted out the fair and was eventually donated by Alex to the University of Minnesota.)

Alex had been making sculpture since the early 1950s, when he molded some small, cylinderlike forms in plaster. He had included three-dimensional works in Plexiglas or metal in his first three exhibitions of paintings at Parsons, with some success: Alfred Barr had bought one for the Museum of Modern Art, and Ethel Woodward de Croisset, the wealthy New Yorker whose brother, William Woodward, Jr., would gain unwelcome notoriety for being shot dead by his wife, had commissioned an enlarged version of another for her house in Spain. (This was Alex's first commission.) The aluminum sculptures drew mixed reviews—sometimes from the same critic. Barbara Rose, in a 1963 note in *Art International*, found them "intelligent, well-executed, and almost excruciatingly tasteful," but went on to say that "they remain, alas, merely decorative cutouts and not sculpture." A year later, after dismissing Alex's new paintings as "overblown," Rose singled out the two oxidized aluminum sculptures in his show as "very satisfying and original." By then, however, Alex's sculpture was going in the same direction as his painting, toward freer and more personal forms of expression. Having pushed the idea of industrial fabrication to its limit by giving instructions over the telephone for a new piece to be made by Treitel Gratz, he found the result so lifeless and disappointing that he abandoned the practice entirely and started making his sculptures by hand.

He had had a revelation about sculpture several years before, in the south of France. Maria Coppo, the housekeeper at Va-et-Vient, was married to a man who earned his living making and repairing iron balconies in Ste. Maxime. One day in the summer of 1959, Alex asked Coppo to show him how to use a welder's torch. "That was when my sculptural passion really started," he said, "when I first saw the spark from the welding rod, and the molten metal." It was an erotic experience for him, an explosion of light and fire that ignited a corresponding emotional response. From that moment on, Alex was dying to make welded sculpture, but he didn't start to do so for two more years, and it was his son-in-law, Cleve Gray, who made it possible.

Cleve and Francine had settled in Warren, Connecticut, on a 134-acre farm property that Cleve's parents had bought ten years earlier. Alex and Tatiana came to visit them nearly every weekend. Cleve recalls Tatiana walking into their house for the first time, on a warm spring day, pointing peremptorily to the empty fireplace, and saying, "Put logs! Fireplace without logs is like man without erection." In 1961, Cleve turned over one of the barns on the property to Alex to use as a sculpture studio; he also gave him five thousand dollars to renovate and equip it. Bill Harris and Jane Grant, who owned the Connecticut plant nursery called White Flower Farm, and who were close friends of both the Libermans and the Grays (Francine had met Cleve at their house), chipped in by giving Alex an arc welder and face mask, and Alex set to work with his customary élan, cutting up and welding together elements from discarded farm machinery that had been accumulating for years on the Grays' property. Twelve months later he had populated one of Cleve's fields with twenty-five or thirty pieces of sculpture—rough, jagged unpainted pieces, whose proliferation became a problem. Francine, struggling to establish her own emotional independence from two powerful, seductive parents, fed and housed Alex and Tatiana without complaint on weekends (they often brought their own weekend guests), but the field full of sculptures began to seem oppressive to her, and Cleve, who had no objection to them, finally spoke to Alex about it. Alex then moved them or cut them up for reuse. Several of these early welded sculptures were shown in Alex's first one-man sculpture exhibition, at the Jewish Museum in 1966. The Jewish Museum functioned for a few years in the 1960s, under the direction of Alan Solomon, as a showcase for lively and provocative contemporary art, and Alex's appearance there put him in the company of Robert Rauschenberg, Jasper Johns, and other rising young American artists.

A local road builder named William Layman began, in 1963, at Cleve's suggestion, to help Alex make sculpture. Layman was an expert welder and a resourceful man. One weekend he brought over in the back of his pickup an old cast-iron boiler—a rusted hulk that he had picked up for nothing at a junkyard. Alex saw the possibilities right away. Boilers and discarded gas tanks were big, cheap, and readily available; they could be cut up in various ways—horizontally, vertically, or diagonally (the diagonal cut was a way to get very large, elliptical shapes)—and, with Layman's help, the elements could be welded together to make large-scale sculptures. Alex gave Layman seven hundred dollars to buy a used truck with a rigging boom. Layman gradually gave up his other jobs to work full-time for Alex.

Exhilarating as it was to work in three dimensions, though, Alex never felt that sculpture was his true métier. Painting remained the source of his deepest yearnings and ambitions, and in the series of very dark paintings that he began in 1964, he went deeper than he had ever tried to go before. The immense scale of these canvases—the largest measured twelve by seventeen feet—was made possible by his having been able to

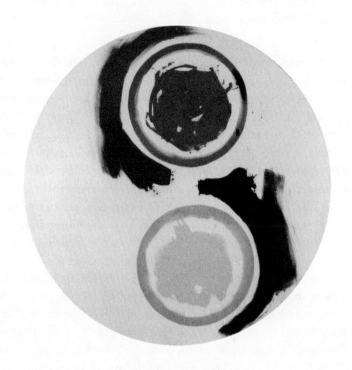

Untitled, 1963, acrylic on unprimed canvas, 65" tondo:
Alex abandons the geometric hard edge.

Robert Motherwell, Alex, and Helen Frankenthaler at Alex's 1964
Bennington College show.

Triad on High, 1967, acrylic and enamel on canvas, 97 1/2" x 73"—one of Alex's black paintings. He aimed to evoke "the deep tradition of the erotic that religion sublimates."

rent the second floor of the former funeral parlor on Seventieth Street, with its high ceilings and excellent light. The somber tonality and brooding, mystical presence of these paintings had more complex origins. Tatiana hated them, of course; she thought they were unpardonably ugly. When Iva Patcévitch saw the black paintings, he worried that Alex must be having a nervous breakdown. Alex himself looked on them, at the time and later, as the most important paintings he had ever done—the ones in which he had come closest to the erotic roots of human experience. The central element in many of them was a massive purplish-black vertical form that seemed to descend into an all-enveloping blackness; in others, two or more horizontal elements pressed in from both sides. The sense of phallic penetration was unmistakable and fully intended. "I think most of my work is really about symbolizing the erotic experience and finding forms that express the deep tradition of the erotic that religion sublimates," he said once. Sexual symbolism had become for Alex a means to invoke the spiritual mysteries that Newman, Rothko, and the other first-generation masters regularly laid claim to in their art.

Barnett Newman thought the black paintings were extraordinary. "He told me I was the only artist making really black paintings," Alex recalled, "and he was very interested in the technique I had worked out for them. I would take unprimed duck canvas and cover a large area with black Liquitex paint—Helen Frankenthaler had told me how to make Liquitex soak into unprimed canvas, by adding a little kitchen detergent to it—and then, before it was dry, I would pour thinned black Duco enamel over the Liquitex and scrape off the excess with a very large squeegee. When the painting dried, it looked as though it was made of black marble dust. Also, the contrast of the oil and the acrylic paints made it seem as though there were two kinds of light in the painting, one reflecting off the surface and the other coming from within."

When Newman said that Alex's were the only really black paintings being done, he may well have been aiming a dig at some of his peers. Clyfford Still had done huge, predominantly black pictures in the 1950s, and so had Mark Rothko. Ad Reinhardt, a former friend who was now Newman's bitter enemy (Newman had sued him in 1953 for defamation of character), was still producing variations of his famous series of canvases, dating back to 1949, that appeared to be totally black until you looked at them for several minutes, after which a subtly luminous cruciform image would emerge. The black paintings of Robert Rauschenberg, with their viscous layers of house paint slathered over crumpled newsprint, had helped to establish him in the mid-fifties as the accredited *enfant terrible* of American art. A decision to abjure color and work exclusively with black and white is one that many artists make at some point in their career, for that matter, and Alex did so out of his own esthetic needs and promptings, but once again his timing worked against him. The exuberant color and high spirits of so much mid-sixties painting set the tone of that period, and critics tended to see Alex's dark meditations on sex and the sublime as *retardataire* at best, and at worst derivative. Nobody bought one.

The black paintings had been preceded by a series of large, richly colored abstractions, a number of which were shown in Alex's one-man exhibition at Bennington College in the spring of 1964. Paul Feeley, the artist who ran Bennington's very lively art department, had made the college's art gallery a significant showcase for advanced work. He had done a Newman show there in 1958, a year before the breakthrough Newman exhibition at French and Company in New York, and his decision to show Liberman gave a big boost to Alex's career.

Alex went up before the opening (Tatiana didn't feel like making the trip to Vermont) and walked around the airy, barnlike rooms of the gallery with two new artist friends, Robert Motherwell and Helen Frankenthaler. Cleve and Francine had introduced him to the Motherwells a few months earlier, at a party in New York, and Tatiana, who tended to accept artists only if they were very famous, had taken a liking to both of them. Helen came from a well-to-do New York family. A former Bennington student herself (and a favorite of Clement Greenberg, who was teaching there at the time), she had established her credentials as an artist very early with abstract paintings in which the paint was allowed to soak directly into unsized canvas, spreading out in thin veils the way ink does on blotting paper; this new technique was immediately authenticated by Greenberg, with whom Helen was then romantically involved, and it was adopted soon afterward by Morris Louis, Kenneth Noland, and other practitioners of the color-field "stain" painting that became a major element in 1960s abstraction. Frankenthaler brought André Emmerich, her dealer, to Connecticut in 1964 to look at Alex's new sculptures, which were too big for Betty Parsons to show. Emmerich, who had established his gallery by showing the work of Frankenthaler, Kenneth Noland, Morris Louis, Jules Olitski, and other color-field painters in the elite group anointed by Greenberg, gave Alex his first sculpture show there three years later and has been his dealer for both paintings and sculpture since 1974.

Robert Motherwell, whom Frankenthaler married in 1958, was the youngest member of the first generation of Abstract Expressionists. Already a recognized master, he was also an intellectual who wrote essays, published

books, and irritated some of his older peers with art-historical statements
that they considered self-serving and inaccurate. Both Frankenthaler and
Motherwell were "uptown" artists, sophisticated and civilized enough to
overcome Tatiana's uneasiness with those outside her own social circle;
Motherwell, whose background was even wealthier than Frankenthaler's,
had the extra advantage of speaking excellent French. At Alex's Bennington
show, Motherwell stood in front of each painting for a fairly long time,
finally nodding and murmuring "masterpiece," and Alex felt thoroughly
elated. "Wonderful," he remembers thinking. "Twelve masterpieces."

Perry Ruston, the recently named vice president of Condé Nast,
was so struck by the more colorful abstract paintings in Alex's Bennington
show that he purchased three of them with company funds and installed
them at strategic points in the office; it was a good way, he said, to supplement Alex's salary. Ruston was not the sort of influential buyer who
could help Alex's career, but Robert C. Scull, the taxi magnate who became
in the 1960s a flamboyant and energetic collector of Pop Art, most certainly
was. Scull and his socially ambitious wife, Ethel, bought one of the more
colorful abstractions from Alex's 1963 show at Parsons. (It was the only
painting that sold.) They hung it in their dining room and gave a dinner
party in Alex's honor. "Of course we went," Alex recalled, "and of course
they had Eugenia Sheppard, who wrote about it in her New York *Herald
Tribune* column, 'Inside Fashion.' I think my painting was taken down the
next day." (An eight-page story titled "The Robert Scull Collection" ran
in *Vogue* a year later.) Although Scull eventually acquired one of Alex's big
tubular sculptures, he never bought another Liberman painting.

The New York art world was just starting to reappraise the hard-
edge, geometric Liberman of the previous decade. *Continuous on Red*, the
big tondo that Alfred Barr had selected from Alex's first show at Parsons,
dominated the entrance gallery of the "Responsive Eye" exhibition at the
Museum of Modern Art in 1965, and William C. Seitz, the show's curator,
borrowed Alex's much earlier *Interchange* for the "Optical" painting section.
Two younger artists were so struck by Alex's two paintings in "The Responsive Eye" that they got in touch with him and suggested exchanging
pictures. One was Frank Stella. The other was Ellsworth Kelly, whose
rigorously simplified hard-edge abstractions, begun in the late 1940s in
Paris and not seen in New York until the mid-1950s, had much in common
with Alex's work during the same period. Alex turned down both requests.
"I had never heard of Stella," he said—a claim that seems surprising in
view of Stella's rapid emergence as one of the most admired and influential
artists of the sixties. Ellsworth Kelly had joined Betty Parsons's stable in

Lunch at the Libermans' in 1963: left to right,
Lawrence Alloway, Beatrice Leval, Barnett
Newman, Alex, Sylvia Sleigh (Alloway's wife),
Robert Motherwell, Annalee Newman.

Fire—Alex's first commissioned sculpture
(for Ethel Woodward de Croisset)—was
executed in painted aluminum in 1963.

1956, so Alex was certainly aware of his work; in fact, Alex sometimes wondered whether Kelly had been responsible for Betty's apparent reluctance to show his own paintings, which were similar in some ways to Kelly's.

Both Stella and Kelly were headed for the kind of international acclaim that has eluded Liberman. Could he have had it if he had stuck to the hard-edge circle motif? Some critics thought so at the time—and accused their confreres of an unspoken bias. Reviewing Alex's 1964 show at Parsons, *The New York Times*'s Stuart Preston wrote that his "lyrical hurricanes of touch and color" had "a soaring, decorative character, compounded of finesse, audacity and sheer accident that identifies Liberman as the Tiepolo of abstract expressionism." But more often the reviewers talked about his "refined taste" and referred to his career at Condé Nast. The British-born critic Lawrence Alloway, who is credited with coining the term "Pop Art" (and who wrote the catalogue interview for Alex's 1964 show at Bennington), put it more succinctly. In the New York art world of the 1960s, he said, "You weren't supposed to have both Condé Nast and Betty Parsons."

"Condé Nast" in this sense meant not only the magazines but the social panoply of international wealth, privilege, and publicity that went with them. And in the fast-moving, jet-set society of the 1960s, Alex and Tatiana Liberman were increasingly prominent participants. Their cocktail parties were irresistible fodder for gossip columnists, since the guest lists included celebrities of all kinds mixed in with millionaires and European titles. They gave parties to honor visiting notables from the worlds of fashion and the arts—parties that socially ambitious New Yorkers who had not been invited read about the next day with envy and awe. Sam and Mitzi Newhouse always seemed to be there.* "Tatiana and Alex Liberman invited dozens of friends into their art-filled (pictures, pictures everywhere) apartment to meet Tatiana's sister and brother-in-law, the Duke and Duchess de Caylus," Suzy reported in the *Daily News* in 1965. (A bit of a giggle, that; Tatiana's younger sister, Lila, had taken as her second husband a man whose only claim to the title was that he had previously been married

---

* Mitzi was so mad about clothes that Nicolas de Gunzburg, a well-connected socialite on the fashion staff at *Vogue*, was delegated to help her shop. For a while he had her wearing rather sophisticated outfits, but Sam Newhouse raised a vigorous protest. "He wanted his old, adorable Mitzi back," according to Babs Simpson, a *Vogue* fashion editor, "and he got her. She went back to dressing in bright colors and lots of frills, sort of like a charming little circus pony."

to a Spanish duchess. The two sisters, who had never liked each other, became increasingly antagonistic after Lila moved to New York.)

Tatiana had long since stopped using her own title, but she was very keen on having titled Europeans come to her parties. Princess Margaret and her husband, Lord Snowdon, whose wedding had been exhaustively documented in *Vogue*, stayed with the Libermans when they came to New York, and, of course, there were parties for them; Snowdon, formerly Antony Armstrong-Jones, owed much of his celebrity as a photographer to Alex's patronage.* "My dear, they were all there at the Libermans' big party" for Régine, the Paris night-life entrepreneur, Suzy gushed, adding that "Princess Margaret and the Earl of Snowdon will be staying there the middle of next month. . . . Faye Dunaway was there looking not a bit bonnie but rather Doctor Zhivago in something black and Cossack. . . . Penelope Tree, the huge-eyed young modeling sensation, was there with her friend, Jonathan Lieberson. . . . Then there was Caterine Milinaire, the Duchess of Bedford's daughter, and the cute young Marquess and Marchioness of Dufferin and Ava . . . Irene Dunne . . . Françoise de Langlade de la Renta . . . the Charles Revsons, Salvador Dali and his ocelot and, well, you get the picture, I'm sure." The Libermans' presence at other people's galas was invariably noted in the columns. Tatiana's striking looks and Yves Saint Laurent gowns—Tatiana and *Vogue* both had transferred their allegiance from Dior to Saint Laurent—seemed to insure the success of any New York gathering. Alex himself made Eugenia Sheppard's list of best-dressed men in 1965, in company with the Duke of Windsor, Fred Astaire, Cary Grant, Carter Burden, and Oleg Cassini, and in 1981 he was installed as a life member of the International Hall of Fame of best-dressed men. That, too, was something of a laugh, since he was never seen in anything but a gray suit at the office and a dark-blue suit in the evening—identical models that he had made for him by Stovel & Mason in London—set off by the pale-blue shirts that he bought by the gross from a shirtmaker named King, across the street from the Grand Hotel in Rome (no pockets; shirt pockets were for accountants), and the narrow, hand-knit navy-blue silk ties from Bowring and Arundel in London. "You have to invent a uniform that suits you and stick to it all your life," he said. A lot of people got the picture of Alex and Tatiana as trendy socialites, though, and judged Alex accordingly.

---

* Snowdon was staying with the Libermans, alone, in 1967, when rumors of the royal couple's separation surfaced. Alex, to his acute discomfort, had to preside over a press conference at which he read a statement by the absent lord.

At the Gritti in Venice: Babe Paley,
"Slim" Keith Hayward, Tatiana, Leland
Hayward, William Paley.

Tatiana with Philippe and Pauline de
Rothschild, in Ischia.

On the beach at Deauville with Henriette.

On the beach at St. Tropez with Tatiana.

Alex with Francine's children,
Thaddeus and Luke.

Francine and Cleve, Tatiana
and Alex, on the Goulandrises'
boat in 1965.

If asked, he would always maintain that the social whirl bored him and that he did it partly for business reasons but mostly for Tatiana. Tatiana retired from Saks in 1965, after twenty-three years, and the powerful current of her liberated energies was redirected mainly into two receptacles: her social life and her grandchildren.* The passionate and highly critical attention that she focused on Thaddeus and Luke Gray (born in 1959 and 1961, respectively) was so overwhelming at times that Cleve asked Alex if he could somehow get her to slack off a bit. Alex tried, but this was not the sort of thing he could talk to Tatiana about in a serious way; instead, he dropped hints here and there. As far as entertaining and going out were concerned, it gave him pleasure to see her enjoying herself, and nobody enjoyed herself more at parties than Tatiana—barking orders at her friends, telling them how awful they looked, making outrageous remarks that were sure to offend somebody. "What kind of orgasm does she have?" Tatiana demanded in a hoarse whisper, after being introduced to the dewy young girl friend of a man she hardly knew. "Vaginal or clitoral?" The people who adored and doted on her may not have outnumbered the people she offended, but who cared about them? Tatiana was *hors concours*, a sacred monster, one of those vivid presences who serve as a necessary counterweight to huge-eyed young modeling sensations.

Like many of their New York friends in those days, Tatiana took a lot of prescription drugs. She took Seconal at night to help her sleep and Dexedrine when she got up in the morning. Since leaving her job at Saks, she had also started to drink a little—vodka and Dubonnet before lunch. She never drank much, but at times, according to people who knew her well, she could seem slightly muddled. Alex in later years fiercely denied this. "Tatiana was absolutely clean and pure!" he said. "She was a glorious, glorious human being, with an extraordinary tenderness and generosity and grandeur. She was for me like a Delphic oracle. I always felt that Tatiana was in touch with the essential truths of existence."

Condé Nast paid for the Libermans' parties. The editorial director still had no real financial security—no savings, no stock in the company. His salary had reached a respectable level by publishing standards, but it did not come close to that of a corporate president, or, for that matter, a top-echelon *Vogue* photographer like Avedon. An expense account that effectively doubled his salary helped Alex and Tatiana to keep right on living like the rich

---

* Alex called Adam Gimbel, at Saks, to ask why Tatiana was not receiving a pension. "Oh, come on," Gimbel replied. "You have a good position, and she's a countess."

without being rich, however, and this was never more apparent than during their summers in Europe. Alex and Tatiana traveled first-class on the *France* or one of the Cunard liners. Although the age of jet travel had dawned, Tatiana resolutely refused to fly; her lifelong claustrophobia had been exacerbated by two experiences in stalled elevators soon after she came to America, and the thought of an enclosed airplane cabin terrified her. They spent the obligatory two weeks in Paris, where Alex, who had been awarded the Legion of Honor in 1951 for his services to French culture and couture, fulfilled his Condé Nast obligations by visiting the *Vogue* offices on the Place Palais-Bourbon and offering suggestions about the French edition of the magazine. He also showed up, with Tatiana, for the spring collections at Yves Saint Laurent, Balenciaga, and Chanel. By the mid-sixties, Diana Vreeland had imposed her own chaotic style on *Vogue*'s coverage of the collections. During that mid-July week, *Vogue* virtually moved from the Place Palais-Bourbon to Vreeland's suite at the Crillon, where she had desks installed and special telephone lines put in and fleets of *cyclistes* rushing back and forth across town with clothes to be photographed. Vreeland's expense account made Alex's look minuscule. He and Tatiana didn't stay at the Crillon. For several years they had put up at a relatively inexpensive Right Bank hotel called the San Régis, but in the sixties, at the insistence of Coco Chanel, they moved to the Ritz, taking a room on the rue Cambon side, where Chanel lived. (Her salon was just down the street.)

    One of Alex's problems in Europe was explaining to his mother why he couldn't get her invited to the collections or to the lavish costume balls put on each year by the Beisteguis or the Patiños or some other South American oligarch, in the vain hope of dazzling the ultrasnob *gratin* of Paris. Henriette, now in her seventies, had taken to dressing like Brigitte Bardot, in very short skirts and see-through blouses. She still walked across Paris every day to keep her figure trim, from her apartment on the rue Quentin-Bauchart to the Etoile and back. Alex would go to see her the minute he arrived, and she insisted that he devote himself to her exclusively (without Tatiana) for at least one weekend in Paris and another one later in the south of France. It struck him, if not Tatiana, as a small price to pay for the fact that she impinged on their life so little during the rest of the year.

    His mother embarrassed him as much as ever. "She still picked up men in cafés," he said ruefully. "The few jewels she had left were given away or stolen from her. At some point during this period she even managed to get herself engaged as a dancer with a traveling nightclub troupe. She went to Spain with them, and, of course, at the frontier she had to produce her passport, which showed that she was born in 1886, and they realized they had hired a seventy-five-year-old dancer. Another time, I took her to the casino in Deauville. Tatiana had always wanted me to take her there, and I never did, so this caused a problem. My mother had forgotten her passport, of course, so she had to fill out a paper, and she put her age down as forty-five. My passport showed that I was fifty-something, and they said, 'But you told us she was your mother.' Whenever I was with her I would keep saying 'Mother' in a loud voice, because she tried to make people think I was her 'friend'—she couldn't stand the idea of this white-haired man being her son. And the makeup! Even her hands were always covered with pancake makeup, so you came away from her smeared with it. There is an amusing word in Russian, *glupaya*, which means rather stupid. I once said to Tatiana that my mother was *glupaya*, and Tatiana said, 'Well, absolutely!' "

After their two weeks in Paris, Alex and Tatiana would spend a full month in the south of France. Henriette came with them for the first few days—Tatiana could martyr herself to that extent—after which she went off (reluctantly) to spend the rest of the summer in a luxury hotel in Cannes, at Alex's expense. Her place was immediately taken by friends—Tatiana's friends for the most part, members of her international brigade of admirers and cronies. Iva Patcévitch was no longer a regular guest; his new wife, Chessy, did not get along with Tatiana anymore. But Françoise Sagan came, and René Clair, and the Gregorys, and Hélène Desoffy (from prewar days), and the couturier Jacques Tiffeau (who was Christian Dior's boy friend), and so on. They came to bask in the bright glow of Tatiana's personality, these worldly groupies. They adored her bullying sense of humor and her sudden flashes of warmth—the unpredictable prodigality of her affection. Tatiana still swam long distances in the tepid waters of the Gulf of St. Tropez. On the crowded beach, she amused young and old with her educated toes—she could undress a man with her toes, untying his necktie and unbuttoning his shirt. It was all part of the mildly salacious humor that went hand in hand with her essentially puritanical nature.

Francine and Cleve and their two young sons came one summer for a one-month visit, which Francine later drew upon for a chapter in *Lovers and Tyrants*, her first novel: "My mother patrols the beach. She is statuesque, jeweled, coffee brown, golden-haired, dressed in barbaric colors. Her rich and deep voice booms over the beach. She laughs with friends, predicts the lines of the next Paris collections, roars lunch orders at the waiters, commands women to oil their children, builds sand castles for her grandsons. My stepfather lies gleaming and placid on his mattress, his eyes half closed with contentment, looking with admiration at his little family."

The Grays' visit was not a success. Cleve and Francine hated what had happened to the Riviera, and by this time even Alex and Tatiana were forced to admit that its original charm was badly tarnished. "There was the traffic problem," Alex said. "The trucks going by on the road made it hard to sleep at night, and getting to the beach at St. Tropez took nearly an hour sometimes, instead of seven minutes. We really loved our little house, which Tatiana had painted white inside and decorated charmingly with low-priced antiques, but things had changed. The Midi had become overbuilt, and there were just too many people. We would often have twelve to fourteen people for lunch or dinner at one of the little restaurants in St. Tropez, and on the beach I would be getting up every two minutes to shake hands with somebody."

For two summers in the mid-sixties, Alex and Tatiana spent part of their vacation in Greece. The shipping magnate Nicolas Goulandris, whose wife, Dolly, had become a great friend of theirs in New York, put his air-conditioned Cadillac and his private yacht at their disposal so that Alex could visit and photograph the ancient shrines and monuments of Greek art. For Alex, this direct contact with the Classical past was a moving experience. Out of it came *Greece, Gods, and Art*, a book of his photographs published by the Viking Press in 1968, with an introduction by Robert Graves and a detailed text by the archaeologist Iris C. Love. Alex, whose somewhat hazy sense of Greek civilization had led him to give many of his earlier paintings titles taken from Greek mythology, wrote a brief introduction to the book in which he said he had attempted to communicate through his photographs "something beyond documentation—the mood of each site and epoch that unexpectedly overwhelms one in the presence of the past, still real as if alive." While many of the photographs are simply reproductions of specific works of art—from Cycladic marble figures to fifth-century statues to Byzantine mosaics, which Alex photographed with his Leica in museums and churches—others show the ruined temples and relics of the antique world in their natural context of sea and sky and islands and distant mountains, bathed in the pellucid light of Greece. The photographs make no claim to art in themselves (some of them are even a mite out of focus), and the book itself is a curious amalgam; the scholarly text by Iris Love seems to belong in some other volume, and Robert Graves's quirky introduction has no apparent connection to either the pictures or the text. It is a handsome and highly original book, nevertheless, but not, like *The Artist in His Studio*, a minor classic.

The summer of 1965 was the last one that Alex and Tatiana would spend at Va-et-Vient. Through Jacques Tiffeau they had discovered Ischia, the volcanic island in the Bay of Naples, where they stayed for a week that summer at the Regina Isabella Hotel and immersed themselves in the healing mudbaths. The baths helped Alex's back, which he had strained lifting a heavy piece of metal from Bill Layman's truck. All at once the idea of a vacation hotel began to seem infinitely preferable to the rigors and responsibilities of a villa in overcrowded Ste. Maxime. Alex sold Va-et-Vient that September—sold it quickly, for considerably less than it was worth—and for the next fifteen years he and Tatiana returned every summer to Ischia, taking the same room (number 243) at the Regina Isabella, where they were surrounded by many of the same people who used to visit them in Ste. Maxime. Alex took the cure, swam, dined regally, entertained royally, tipped overgenerously, and was beloved in the way that free-spending Americans can be in Italy and nowhere else.

No painting got done during these European summers, needless to say. In the early sixties, Alex did some lithographs at the Mourlot atelier in Paris, where Picasso, Miró and other School of Paris masters printed, and in the seventies he printed at an experimental graphics workshop in Rome. But aside from that, his summers were vacations from art making as well as from Condé Nast. Alex did manage to take Tatiana off on one or two intensive art-education trips in Italy, which gave him his first direct contact with the old masters of the early Renaissance. Writing to Francine, he spoke of having "with the Giottos of Assisi . . . one of the greatest art experiences of my life. The frescoes are impossible to describe—mystery, tragedy, elegance, poetry, faith all expressed with a fearlessness and love and visual splendour—unique in human achievement!"

Alex had always been stirred by the spiritual in art. The religious basis of Greek sculpture and architecture was the focus of his book on Greece, and the immense spread wings of the angels in Byzantine churches, which he had photographed in 1965 and featured in *Vogue*'s Christmas issue that year, were among the factors that inspired the new series of paintings that he began in 1967, whose central image was a triangle. For the next seven years, his canvases would be structured around the triangle—vast, clearly defined triangles at first, stretching from one edge of the picture to the other, the apex always pointing down. Barnett Newman, who was experimenting with triangular-shaped canvases about this

time, argued that the image was stronger the other way, with the apex at
the top, like a pyramid; but for Alex the downward-pointing triangle implied
wings, flight, and spiritual ascension—he also thought of the form as "looking upward for the message that comes from above"—and he never painted
it any other way. His triangles floated in fields of rich and vibrant acrylic
color, "Venetian" color, as he thought of it. Like Newman, he also tried
some triangular-shaped canvases. Alex was using brushes to apply the
pigment now, rather than pouring or mopping it, and in the process he
allowed more and more personal expression and "touch" to appear in the
work. As the series advanced, the clear outline of the triangle shape was
invaded and broken by splashes and bursts of increasingly violent, Abstract
Expressionist–type brushwork, scratched or scribbled markings, and other
signs of intense emotion.

His sculpture was also becoming increasingly expressionistic, and
more widely known. In addition to annual or biennial shows at the
André Emmerich Gallery, Liberman sculptures had also appeared in group
shows at the Los Angeles County Museum of Art and the Museum of
Modern Art, in addition to his one-man exhibition at the Jewish Museum.
Alex and Bill Layman had moved out of Cleve's barn and set up a sculpture
studio at Layman's place, a couple of miles away, where the big truck garage
and the surrounding fields gradually filled up with boilers, gas tanks, and
welded sculptures in various stages of completion. In 1968, Alex and Tatiana bought a house on the land adjoining Cleve and Francine's property
in Warren, Connecticut, and Alex transferred all his studio operations to
the country. Before buying the house, Alex asked whether the Grays had
any objection to their doing so, and suggested that they think about it
overnight. Francine and Cleve, who had alerted them to the house's avail-
ability, and who were all in favor of their having a place of their own rather
than continuing as more or less permanent weekend guests, offended Alex
by agreeing to his think-about-it-overnight suggestion—he had expected
them to say they didn't have to do that. According to Cleve and Francine,
they *did* say they didn't need to think about it, but Alex insisted—a typical
family misunderstanding in this extremely complicated family.

A few years earlier, Robert Motherwell and Helen Frankenthaler
had taken Alex to meet David Smith, the most admired sculptor of the first
Abstract Expressionist generation, at his studio in Bolton Landing, in upstate New York. "Come and live with me, Alex, and I'll teach you all I
know," Smith had said, echoing Picasso's invitation a decade earlier. Two
weeks after that he was dead, killed in an accident when his truck turned
over. Alex admired the strength and authority of Smith's beautifully con-

trolled forms, but in his own recent work in three dimensions he had opted for improvisation and chance rather than composition and control. What he did take from their single encounter was a memory of the ruggedly built sculptor sitting in the seat of his farm tractor and saying that he wanted to make really monumental works. "I've got to go much bigger," he said. "The future is in really large scale." A younger American artist, Mark di Suvero, had already started to work with cranes, I-beams, and other industrial elements to make huge sculptures; although Alex had seen them only in photographs, he has said that it was di Suvero who really liberated his own sculptural imagination.

Alex's sculpture evolved rapidly in the late sixties, from welded scrap-metal pieces to bigger, "linear" assemblages made out of twisted and bent automobile exhaust pipes, and then to a series of powerful and somewhat menacing-looking objects in which heavy industrial pipes enclosed or pierced flat metal plates. In *Tropic* (1969), the central element is a thirty-foot-high bent tube that forms a triangular arch or gate—an image that would recur in many subsequent works. By this time, Alex and Bill Layman were finding all sorts of new methods to bend, twist, cut, and shape metal. They crushed tanks by running over them with a bulldozer. They even tried putting a stick of dynamite inside a boiler—too small a charge the first time, but on the second attempt metal fragments flew in all directions, and the fire department sent a truck to investigate. One of the crumpled metal forms left over from this experiment became the model for the much larger central element in *Eve*, a forty-four-foot-long assemblage of thrusting diagonal tubes and hulking shapes painted cadmium red, the color that he now applied to all his metal sculptures; Tatiana preferred that to the black he had been using before. (Red, the Russian word for which, *krasnoe*, is the same as the word for "beautiful," carried visual echoes of the Russian Constructivist posters that he had seen as a child.) *Eve* and its even larger companion piece, *Adam*, announced a new chapter in Alex's work: they were truly monumental works, made to be seen in public places. Layman had acquired a big crane, with which he could hoist enormous metal pieces and move them around. He and Alex were able to work with much bigger gas storage tanks as a result.

Alex would exploit his mastery of large scale to great effect during the next two decades, becoming in the process one of the most successful public artists of his time—a paradoxical triumph from which he received no great financial rewards and very little art-world acclaim, and one that brought him no closer to the recognition as a painter that he longed for most of all.

The Editorial Director of Condé Nast, photographed
by Helmut Newton in 1974.

Dismissals

To celebrate its one-hundredth birthday in 1970, the Metropolitan Museum of Art in New York raised $4 million and spent most of it on a year-long party. Among the special events were five major centennial exhibitions, the first of which, called "New York Painting and Sculpture: 1940–1970," was also a celebration of New York's proud claim to be the world capital of contemporary art. It was a huge show, the largest exhibition of modern American painting and sculpture ever assembled— 408 works of art by 43 artists, spread over 35 galleries whose combined area exceeded the entire exhibition space of the Whitney Museum. It was also hugely controversial. Henry Geldzahler, the show's young curator, came under attack from a ferocious artillery of critics, dealers, and artists, most of whom were enraged not so much by the people he had chosen to show as by those he had left out. Although it was well known that Geldzahler and Geldzahler alone had made the selections for what everyone called "Henry's show," the fact that it was taking place at the Met implied that his inclusions and omissions would have some influence on future art historians, and also, more to the point, on the rapidly expanding art market; to be left out of a show that celebrated the glories of postwar American art, from the heroic early days of Abstract Expressionism to the flowering of neo-Dada, Pop, Minimal, and color-field abstraction, could be seen (and was seen) as a serious setback to an artist's career. Among those left out, along with such established names as Louise Nevelson, Larry Rivers, Jim Dine, and Cy Twombly, was Alexander Liberman.

Up to this point, Alex had been able to think of himself as an artist of some significance—an innovator who had gone his own way, refusing to bend to prevailing winds or critical currents. His work had appeared regularly in two of the best Fifty-seventh Street galleries; his career had seemed to follow a rising curve. Not being included in the Metropolitan show, he admitted, was "one of the greatest disappointments of my life." The hurt was alleviated, though, by his having been offered a retrospective exhibition that same year at the Corcoran Gallery of Art in Washington, D.C.

The Corcoran's original charter went back to 1869, making it one year older than the Metropolitan. Chronically underendowed, and weighed down by an overlarge and unwieldy board of trustees, the gallery had recently hired as its director an energetic but short-tempered young man named James Harithas, who was trying to breathe life into the place by putting on shows of new and challenging contemporary work. The Liberman retrospective was his idea. Harithas made the initial arrangements with Betty Parsons and Alex, set the organizational gears in motion, but then proceeded to get into such a violent dispute about another matter with the chairman of his board of trustees that he resigned on the spot. Fortunately, the person who succeeded him as director, Walter Hopps, knew and admired Liberman's work; unfortunately, Hopps soon found himself caught in a crossfire between employees who were attempting to unionize the Corcoran's work force and trustees who were determined to block them—a dispute that eventually resulted in Hopps's being fired. Hopps and James Pilgrim, his chief curator, managed nevertheless to assemble and install seventy-three of Alex's paintings and forty of his sculptures in time for the opening in the spring of 1970, and Alex, who had reached the age of fifty-seven without achieving recognition as a major artist, could not help entertaining thoughts of a career breakthrough.

To Hopps's dismay, the trustees had scheduled the opening to coincide with the annual Corcoran Ball, a Washington social event attended by a great many people who never set foot in the museum at any other time. Also in attendance this year were quite a few socially prominent New Yorkers, who had come down on the Metroliner to honor their very own Alex; the following day's society columns listed Diana Vreeland, Mitzi and Sam Newhouse, São Schlumberger, and Chessy Patcévitch, along with such exotics as "TV's David Frost and artist Barnett Newman." Under the circumstances, the paintings may have been harder to see than they usually are at black-tie openings.

There was only one important review of the exhibition, by the Washington *Post* critic Paul Richard, who saw little to admire. To Richard, Liberman was an artist whose "formidable imagination has bowed to Good Design . . . even his hairiest paint-splashed canvases, even his heaviest steel sculptures, have about them something that recalls the sleek and stunning pages of the magazine he works for." This devastating indictment might have been less painful if it had been balanced by even one or two contrasting views, but there were none. Not a single New York magazine or newspaper reviewed the show, and the art press mostly ignored it. The beautiful people were there for Alex, but the art world turned its back on him.

After the show closed at the Corcoran it went on to the Houston Museum of Fine Arts. Alex's self-esteem was abysmally low by this time; he told several friends that he thought the only reason Houston had taken the show was that Philippe de Montebello, the director, was related to Ethel de Croisset, Alex's great friend, who had given him his first sculpture commission. (De Montebello had little interest in contemporary art at that time; he became more receptive to it after he was named director of the Metropolitan Museum in 1978.)

There was a farcical coda to the whole enterprise. At Walter Hopps's request, Alex had left *Adam*, his thirty-foot-high, orange-red sculpture, on long-term loan to the Corcoran after the exhibition closed. Hopps installed it outside the museum, on a grassy plot at the corner of New York Avenue and Seventeenth Street, where it was visible from the White House. One day in 1972, the White House ordered it removed. Amused newspaper accounts attributed the order to President Richard Nixon, who was said to be "no fan of modern art," but Hopps's inside sources told him that the person who really hated *Adam* was H. R. Haldeman, the president's widely unloved chief of staff. The National Parks Service carted the seven-ton sculpture to a marshy site at Haines Point, near the Tidal Basin, where it languished for several months. Then, by a happy turn of fate, it was bought by the Storm King Art Center in Mountainville, New York, a beautifully landscaped natural site devoted entirely to large works of contemporary sculpture. The piece was seen and admired there a few years later by I. M. Pei, the architect, and J. Carter Brown, the director of the National Gallery in Washington, D.C., who arranged to borrow it for the inauguration of Pei's East Building addition to the National Gallery—whether they remembered its earlier banishment is unclear. At any rate, *Adam* had its moment of triumph in 1978, installed at the entrance to the East Building, officially vindicated ("Adam's Revenge" was the headline in one paper), before returning to the Storm King Art Center, where it rests today on a green hillside, along with two other, even larger Liberman sculptures: *Adonai*, which was purchased in 1974, and *Iliad*, which was acquired after the artist's 1977 exhibition there.

If the Corcoran retrospective was the high-water mark in Alex's career as an artist, its failure to establish his reputation must count as an even greater disappointment than being left out of "Henry's show." "I thought I'd be able to leave Condé Nast and finally become an artist," he said years later. "That never happened. There were no other museum offers. But then things got a lot busier at Condé Nast."

Condé Nast was going through its own time of troubles in the late 1960s. One of the main problems was Iva Patcévitch. Sam Newhouse, whose policy of "local autonomy" applied only to editorial matters, thought that *Vogue* and the other Condé Nast magazines were not being run as profitably as they could be. According to Alex, Patcévitch ignored all of Newhouse's suggestions. He continued to treat the owner with lordly disdain, refusing to acknowledge that he was anything more than a "principal stockholder" and referring to him irritably, in private, as a "kibitzer." Patcévitch rarely got to his office before ten-thirty in the morning. Since his marriage to Chessy Amory he had become involved with a rather stuffy crowd of rich people who divided their time between Palm Beach in the winter and Southampton, Long Island, in the summer, and it seemed clear to Alex and others that his social life took precedence over the company he had been running since 1942. ("Thank God I didn't marry him," Marlene Dietrich commented at the time. "Can you see me, the grande dame in Palm Beach, with nothing better to do than play canasta all day?") Patcévitch had changed from a Russian aristocrat to a rather uptight American WASP, and like most members of that tribe, he had become more and more impervious to the notion of change.

Ever since the incident at Kennedy airport, when Alex had gone to meet Patcévitch after his crucial discussion with Cecil King in London, and Patcévitch had brushed him aside with a curt "What are you doing here?," their friendship had been in decline. Chessy Patcévitch clearly disliked Tatiana; Alex thought she resented Tatiana's continuing friendship with Marlene Dietrich, for one thing. After two vacation trips together as a foursome—one to Venice, the other to Nassau—Alex declined an invitation to join the Patcévitches on a Caribbean cruise, because Patcévitch

Adam's revenge—Alex's red steel sculpture returns to the nation's capital in triumph for the opening of the East Building of the National Gallery.

Above: Chessy and Iva Patcévitch.

Left: Young Si Newhouse and his mentor in Venice, 1967.

Below: On holiday in Ischia, Grace Mirabella and Alex.

had asked him not to bring Tatiana. The days when Patcévitch had poured out his despair to Alex over losing Marlene and Alex had painted with him on weekends to ease the pain, the years when "Uncle Pat" had been part of the family and godfather to Cleve and Francine's first child, the summers that Alex and Pat had spent together, as easy and relaxed as two brothers—all that seemed very long ago, even though they still saw each other every day at the office and conferred about stories, budgets, personnel problems, and a hundred other questions. Patcévitch depended very heavily on Alex's judgment and Alex's editorial control and Alex's indefinable sense of what was right for the magazines, and this put Alex in an increasingly uncomfortable position, because over the last few years he had also become the confidant of Sam Newhouse.

"Sam would invite me to his apartment for dinner, and afterward he would always want to talk about the magazines. 'How are things?' he would say. It was a little like what had happened to me with Condé Nast: I had become Nast's confidant, and then Pat's, and now Newhouse's. He trusted me, and I respected him—I agreed with his ideas about building the company and reducing certain areas of expenditures—and frankly, I felt that Pat was damaging the company by the way he treated Newhouse. It was becoming a kind of open warfare between them, and I thought it was rude and grotesque on Pat's part. I was in a terribly difficult position, because I still felt I owed everything to Pat. Ben Sonnenberg, the publicist, who worked for Sam Newhouse—I imagine he was the one who alerted Sam to the possibility of buying Condé Nast in the first place—Sonnenberg took an interest in me at one point. He invited me to lunch and told me that if I played my cards right I could have Patcévitch's job, but I said, 'Forget it.' I didn't want Pat's job. I'm not a money man; I've never been interested in the financial aspect—I'm a journalist and an artist. But I owe my life to Condé Nast. Condé Nast stands for something that I respect and admire—a certain dignity, a certain decency, a sense of quality, a chance for people to be creative—and I resented enormously Pat's attitude toward Newhouse. I felt in this case that Newhouse was right and Pat was wrong. And so, when Newhouse asked me, after dinner at his apartment, whether Patcévitch was doing a good job or not, I simply could not lie."

Alex had nothing to do, however, with the incident that precipitated Patcévitch's downfall. He and Tatiana did not go to the week-long series of festivities orchestrated by the Antenor Patiños (and who else but a Bolivian tin tycoon could orchestrate them on such a scale?) at the Portuguese resort of Estoril in the late summer of 1968, when much of Europe and large parts of the United States were being torn apart by a generation's rage against the established order. "A glorious splurge . . . a Portuguese week of balls and bulls and *festas* and fireworks," was the way *Vogue* led off its breathless, twelve-page report on the Patiño extravaganza. "The Antenor Patiños picked the date for their ball a year in advance, checking the almanac for a night of full moon . . . and then made sure the full moon shone on Quinta Patiño by having a plane seed the air with dry ice to forestall mist." Every European with a title, real or bogus, seemed to have wangled an invitation, along with Greek shipowners, American trophy wives, and reconstructed German arms merchants. "It was really the last great jet-set happening," said Alexis Gregory, the son of Alex and Tatiana's great friends. "There have been parties since, but nothing quite like that."

Samuel and Mitzi Newhouse were there, of course, staying at the Palacio Hotel with most of the other guests. They went to both the all-night balls—the Patiños' full-moon "spectacular" and the one given two nights earlier by São Schlumberger—and to most of the satellite lunches and cocktail parties and breakfasts that made it so necessary for prescient ladies to have brought along their personal hairdressers, and in some cases their dress designers. The Newhouses were not invited, however, to a cocktail party that was given at the Palacio Hotel by Iva and Chessy Patcévitch. Mitzi learned about the Patcévitches' party from her hairdresser. Iva Patcévitch, dispensing his silver-haired charm in the soft evening air of Estoril, would very soon find out who really owned Condé Nast.

The denouement was blurred in the usual corporate niceties. Patcévitch became "chairman" of the company soon after the Estoril incident, and ceased to have any real duties. Perry Ruston, who had risen to the level of vice president after forty-one years with Condé Nast, was named president and took over Patcévitch's old corner office. The real crunch came when Sam Newhouse informed Patcévitch that he would have to move out of his house on East Seventieth Street—the house that Alex had found for him, on the same block where Alex and Tatiana lived. The house belonged to Condé Nast, which had paid for it originally. Patcévitch seems to have assumed that he could continue living there indefinitely, and Chessy apparently thought it belonged to them; they both were stunned when Sam informed Patcévitch that the premises were required for *Vogue*'s recently named publishing director, who just happened to be Sam's elder son, Samuel I. Newhouse, Jr. The Patcévitches retreated in helpless fury to their big house in Southampton and their slightly smaller house in Palm Beach, where they kept right on living the life they were accustomed to; Patcévitch himself was a wealthy man by then, thanks to Newhouse's purchase of his stock in Condé Nast. In the midst of all this, Alex's conflicted loyalties persuaded him to go to Patcévitch's office and offer his own resignation, as an expression of support. To his credit, Patcévitch said, "No, Alex, this has nothing to do with you." They parted on good terms, but it was the end of their friendship. They didn't see each other again for many years.

"Alex always knew which side his bread was buttered on," one of his more cynical friends observed. "He courted the Newhouses, and it paid off." But in truth, the Newhouses courted Alex more than he courted them. Sam had gone to visit Alex after his stomach operation, and for years he had solicited Alex's advice about the magazines. When Sam and Mitzi redecorated their Park Avenue apartment, jettisoning the French antiques for a gold-and-beige environment designed for them by Valerian Rybar and Mario Buatta, they bought one of Alex's largest triangle paintings to hang prominently in the dining room. By this time their elder son had adopted Alex as his guide to modern art.

Samuel I. Newhouse, Jr., known as Si, had languished for more years than he liked to count in the shadow of his parents' disapproval. He had been an unruly child, "a rambunctious, crazy kid," one friend of the family told Sam Newhouse's biographer, Richard Meeker. Obviously bright, but undisciplined, he had been an indifferent student at the Horace Mann school and at Syracuse University, where he was expelled from the journalism department for poor grades. He dropped out of college in his junior year, served two years in the U.S. Army (1950–51), and then bounced around in a succession of jobs within the Newhouse media empire—selling ads for a radio station in Portland, Oregon, writing for the Long Island *Daily Press* (his stories never got printed), reporting for the Advance News Services in Washington, D.C., where his comic ineptitude led his colleagues to refer to him privately as "Jerry Lewis." Donald Newhouse, Si's younger brother, had taken to the newspaper business like a duck to water; in fact, everything Donald did seemed to gratify his parents' hopes. Si kept on being the ugly duckling until 1961, when he went to work in the promotion department at *Glamour* and began to show a serious interest in magazine publishing.

At this point in his career, Si Newhouse was thirty-three and unmarried; his recent divorce, after ten years of marriage and three children, had greatly upset Mitzi, who adored her grandchildren and was very fond of their mother. He had moved into a six-room penthouse on Manhattan's Upper East Side, where it occurred to him that he should have some pictures to hang on the walls. How do you go about buying pictures? he asked Miki Denhof, the very savvy art director of *Glamour*. Denhof

Alex

advised him to talk with Alex Liberman. She even took him to Alex's studio in the former funeral parlor, and before Si left that day he had bought his first two pictures—a hard-edge circle painting from the 1950s and a more recent, purple-and-green tondo showing a loosely brushed, painterly circle. It was the beginning of Newhouse's career as an art collector. It was also the beginning of an odd, impersonal, and yet extremely close friendship that has been of great importance to both men—and to Condé Nast.

Much nonsense has been written and voiced about this relationship. It was never really a father-son sort of bond (although, as Newhouse said in his eightieth-birthday note to Alex, there were elements of that), and its parameters included only two areas of common interest: Condé Nast and contemporary art. Contrary to rumor, Alex did not have to teach Si how to use a knife and fork properly. Very little instruction of any kind was involved, for that matter. "I don't think Alex tried to teach me or indoctrinate me in any way about art," Newhouse has said. "I went up there to his studio and I looked at his paintings and I reacted, and that was it. Whatever education I got later came from reading about art, or from discussing it with Barney Newman and with Alex. Alex introduced me to Newman on June 4, 1966, and that opened up the whole field for me. I started to absorb the culture of painting through Barney. But I have always wanted Alex to see work I'm interested in—if possible, before I buy it."

Newhouse started buying contemporary art in a serious way in 1966, after he had left *Glamour* and become the publisher of *Vogue*. Si and Alex would visit art galleries during their lunch hour—sometimes to see work by an artist Alex felt Si should look at, sometimes the other way around. "Si was very tense in those days," Alex recalled. "He'd run into my office with a catalogue to a current show and say, 'What do you think?' He was always in a hurry. He walked fast, he ate fast. In a restaurant, he'd tie a napkin around his neck and he'd ask questions about the magazines, and I'd have to try to answer while eating very quickly to keep up with him. We'd get through all the problems of every Condé Nast magazine in forty-five minutes. This hasn't changed. Everything Si does develops very quickly—snap judgments; quick, instinctive decisions." Barnett Newman, who was reluctant to sell his paintings to people he did not know and trust, let Newhouse purchase several of his most important late works. Si was "so passionate about my painting, I can't refuse him anything," Newman wrote in a letter to Alex. "He is pure spirit—total passion." Later on, Newhouse showed a similar enthusiasm for selling his treasures. He sold

Newman's magisterial *Chartres*, one of three rare triangular-shaped canvases, for a reported $3 million in 1990.

Si Newhouse bought several more Liberman paintings during the next few years. He also paid a visit to Henry Geldzahler at the Metropolitan in 1969 and tried to persuade him to include Liberman in his "New York Painting and Sculpture" show. Geldzahler listened politely but said that he found Liberman's work too close to Ellsworth Kelly's, which he considered stronger and more original. (Alex didn't know this until twenty years later.) In time, Newhouse's collecting passion narrowed to a focus on major works by Jasper Johns, Frank Stella, Willem de Kooning, and other giants of postwar American art, and he stopped buying Liberman. This had no apparent effect on their relationship. He continued to ask Alex's opinion about works of art, and Alex was always happy to give it. "Often I have not bought something that I thought I liked, or did like, because I got a cool response from him," Newhouse has said. "And I think his own work has been consistently interesting. But I kind of decided not to deal with it, not to collect it, because my being so close to him makes it too complicated."

Although Sam Newhouse showed no signs of relinquishing control, the future division of his empire became clear in the late 1960s: Donald would look after the newspapers and the radio and television outlets, Si would handle the magazines. Unlike their father, though, Si wanted to be involved in every aspect of the magazine business, including the editorial side.* Because of the symbiotic nature of his working relationship with Alex, Si was able to do this without setting off the sort of business-versus-editorial conflicts that alienate editors and destroy magazines. He was involved, therefore, with the other crisis that had been building up at *Vogue* since the mid-1960s—a crisis over what to do about the incomparable but no longer controllable Diana Vreeland.

"It was like trying to catch up with a wild horse," Alex said ruefully in trying to describe the Vreeland dilemma. "Everything was extravagance and luxury and excess. She was given too much power; she took too much power. I was the editorial director. I would be presented with a layout that she had done with Priscilla Peck, and I would say, 'We can't give sixteen

---

* Alex remembers only one instance of Sam Newhouse making an editorial request: soon after the unpleasant incident in Estoril, Sam called Alex and told him to make sure there was a photograph of Mitzi in *Vogue*'s coverage of the Patiño ball. Alex ran a picture of both of them.

pages to this, it's too much,' but she had her court of admirers who would say, 'No, Alex, it's wonderful, you're wrong,' and I would be sort of impotent. The business side was very upset. Circulation was dropping, there were complaints from the stores, we were losing advertising—the whole thing just got out of control."

Vreeland's admirers on the staff blamed Alex for what happened. "He chose to take things the wrong way," said one *Vogue* editor. "He had no sense of humor about her. He felt she was belittling him, and he chose to be insulted by things that weren't meant that way. I remember Mr. Liberman throwing down her layouts and walking out of the room. It was an obvious campaign against Mrs. Vreeland, a wish to cut her down."

Priscilla Peck, the art director, Alex's former protégée and early confidante, turned venomously against him over Vreeland. Peck had fallen in love with Diana Vreeland the day she came to work at *Vogue*. According to fashion editor Babs Simpson, Peck became "obsessed with hatred for Alex, like a love affair in reverse. She was like a black spider at her desk, exuding hatred, never losing an opportunity to say something nasty about him." Babs Simpson herself admired Vreeland but sided with Alex. "Dee-Anne almost wrecked the magazine," she said. "She was there for ten years, and the first four or five were absolutely glorious, wonderful. She was the greatest fashion editor who ever lived. But what brought us down was that she persisted in doing flower children and blue faces and orange hair long after all that was over. She would take a beautiful evening dress by Norman Norell and put boots with it. She'd try to disguise clothes she thought were dowdy. The Seventh Avenue designers were up in arms—Adele Simpson said she didn't want her name on our pages. In Paris, Dee-Anne only went to the collections that amused her, Balenciaga and Givenchy and Saint Laurent, and this, of course, infuriated all the others. Periodically she would say, 'I've been called upstairs by the men again; they say we're losing business,' but she would just dismiss that. 'The men don't know what they're talking about,' she'd say."

In fact, the circulation and advertising losses at *Vogue* were no larger than those at *Harper's Bazaar* at the time. A business recession affected most magazines in the early 1970s, but none so dramatically as the two leading fashion journals: advertising pages at *Vogue* declined by 26.3 percent from 1970 to 1971; at *Bazaar*, by 26.6 percent. By contrast, *Glamour's* figures did not decline at all, and this made Perry Ruston and his associates on the business side think that a more broadly based, less elitist, high-style editorial approach might be in order for *Vogue*. Vreeland had no patience with that sort of talk; her mind was on other things entirely. "Why is it that boys and girls are beginning to dress alike?" she once asked Carol Phillips, the managing editor. "What do you think it means?" Vreeland wanted to pinpoint social changes before anyone else and to show them happening. She wanted Richard Avedon's pictures of Rudolf Nureyev in the nude and of Jean Shrimpton dressed to look like an eighteenth-century portrait by George Romney. She wanted the Patiño ball and the Duchess of Windsor and fourteen pages of Penelope Tree in Gypsy raiment on the moors of Cornwall: "Penelope Tree, who acts out every minute of her life with a lively combination of wit, spirit, and style," as the hard-pressed *Vogue* caption writer put it. "Performance is all I cared about as a child," said Vreeland, "and it's all I care about now."

Her theatrical style, which drove some editors to distraction— Allene Talmey is said to have quit *Vogue* because she couldn't work with Vreeland—mesmerized the members of her inner circle. Two secretaries vied to prepare her daily lunch in the office; it consisted of a peanut-butter-and-marmalade sandwich, a tumbler of whiskey, and a dish of semimelted vanilla ice cream that had to be taken out of the icebox at just the right moment to achieve the proper consistency. Carrie Donovan, who came to *Vogue* the same year Vreeland did (she went on to become the fashion editor of *The New York Times Magazine*), remembers with awe the sight of Vreeland receiving her vitamin shot in the office. "She just kept right on with whatever she was doing. The nurse comes in, Dee-Anne pulls up her skirt, nurse steps behind her, kr-r-r-rk, thank you very much, no interruption in the conversation. Alex or anybody could be there."

Alex warned her again and again about the extravagance and the expenses and the dropping ad revenues, but he, too, was somewhat in awe of Vreeland. Her husband's death in 1966, after a long battle with cancer, made the situation even more delicate. Having enjoyed a full and happy married life and raised two sons before she ever thought of working, Vreeland was deeply affected by the loss. "Reed Vreeland ran the household and was the discipline in her life," according to Alex, and everyone knew that she worshiped and adored him. She soldiered on at the magazine with hardly a break, but some people, Alex included, thought she began drinking too much. "After she had her tumbler of whiskey at lunch," Alex said, "frankly, the afternoon decisions were very confused and difficult." She seemed to change her mind more capriciously, with more disruptive results. Once she failed to show up for a fashion meeting that she had scheduled for a Friday afternoon in July; clothes had been brought in from a number of top designers, and everyone else had delayed their weekend getaways for it. To her admirers, though, her drinking was never an issue. "Diana drank like a gentleman," according to Carol Phillips; the tumbler never held more than "a thimbleful" of whiskey. (This was the era, remember, of the gentlemen's two-martini lunch.) Phillips also disagreed with Alex about Vreeland's having too much power. "I don't think power was on her mind, ever," she said firmly. "She didn't think that way. She thought about doing something exciting, about being turned on. And with a woman like that, you can't really tell whether she's drunk or not."

One afternoon in the spring of 1971, Vreeland came back from a visit to "the men" upstairs and announced that she had been fired. "The men" in this case meant Perry Ruston, the president of Condé Nast, who still found it difficult twenty years later to talk about that day. So did Alex. Although Vreeland later told people that Alex had been in Ruston's office when he fired her, her memory was faulty; he was in his own office, waiting tensely for Ruston to call and say he had done it. A few minutes later, Alex called on Vreeland in her office. She was quite calm, he said— "stunned, maybe. She didn't expect it at all, at all. I said to her, 'Diana, I'm sorry, but I warned you.' She didn't react."

Vreeland insisted on hearing the news directly from Si Newhouse. "We just sat there for what seemed to me like about ten minutes," Newhouse recalled, "each waiting for the other to say something. Finally I said that it wasn't working out, and that we were going to ask her to retire. She just watched me deal with her, perhaps in amusement, perhaps in shock. She was very cool. That night I had a very bad dream about it, a wild nightmare."

Diana Vreeland was not really "fired," of course. Ruston and Alex had been discussing the eventuality and how they would handle it for a year or more. Ruston's formal announcement said that she would "maintain her close association with Vogue as Consulting Editor," and she stayed on the payroll for another seven months, the amount of time necessary to complete the ten-year employment period that qualified her for full retirement benefits. (It was Alex who insisted on that point; he arranged subsequently for her benefits to be increased.) They gave her another office and painted it her particular shade of Chinese red. Unfortunately, it was Margaret Case's office, which had been vacant for some time because Case, the society editor, was over eighty then and ill with cancer; when Case went out the window of her fourteenth-floor apartment not long afterward, some of her friends, including Vreeland, blamed it on Vogue for taking away her office and asking her to work at home. Vreeland didn't do much consulting, at any rate. She went to Europe for four months, on "the first holiday I'd really ever had." Eventually, through the efforts of various friends and admirers, she was offered a job at the Metropolitan Museum as chairman of its Costume Institute, a fairly moribund department that she soon transformed into one of the most exciting places in the museum, putting on a series of dazzling exhibitions that revitalized the whole concept of couture and placed a fitting capstone on her remarkable career. By then, she could tell an interviewer that being fired from *Vogue* "wasn't a tragedy" and "wasn't the end of anything," but at the time it happened she was very bitter. And there was no question in her mind as to who was responsible.

"I have known White Russians; I have known Red Russians," she said in an aside that was picked up and printed by the columnist Liz Smith. "I have never before known a yellow Russian."

Alex with *Adonai*, his first monumental tank sculpture.
It is 35 feet high, 50 feet wide, and 75 feet long.

The Balancing Act

Grace Mirabella was as surprised as everyone else by Vreeland's downfall. A quietly efficient, hard-working staffer who had started out in the merchandising department at *Vogue* in 1951, checking picture captions for store credits, Mirabella had relinquished her job as sportswear editor to become Vreeland's principal assistant and deputy. "I had no idea what was going on," she recalls, "and neither did she. I was in California on a fashion shoot, and I got a telegram telling me to come back to New York. Vreeland called me as I was packing, to ask about something, and I said, 'Well, listen, I'll be back tomorrow and we can talk about it then,' and she said, 'You will?,' which struck me as peculiar." In his May 17, 1971, memo announcing Vreeland's new "advisory" role, Perry Ruston informed the staff that Grace Mirabella would take over editorial responsibilities at *Vogue*, "under the over-all guidance of Mr. Liberman, Editorial Director of Condé Nast."

When asked some years later why she thought the job had been offered to her, Mirabella said, "I suppose Alex looked around and said to himself, 'Who is likely to think the way I do?' And there I was. We rarely disagree on anything." The only child of a wine importer named Anthony

Mirabella and his Italian-born wife, Grace had grown up in Maplewood, New Jersey, and she had graduated from Skidmore College with a degree in economics. She and Alex got along wonderfully from the beginning. Their relaxed, lightly flirtatious working relationship stimulated Alex's creative energies, and Mirabella, who was not awarded the title of editor in chief until 1973, apparently welcomed the guidance that Alex was determined to impose. (She even let him supervise the redecoration of her office, which went from Vreeland red and black,. with zebra rugs, to soothingly neutral, allover beige.) Grace Mirabella, moreover, turned out to be almost perfectly attuned to the changing attitudes of American women in the 1970s. Newsstand sales of *Vogue* and *Harper's Bazaar* had been plummeting because so many of these women came to feel that the fashion magazines had nothing to do with their lives. Waiflike models in exotic settings, wearing clothes so outrageous that very few stores even stocked them, could only irritate the ambitious working woman—and it seemed that even women who didn't have to work now wanted to. Having refused, by and large, to wear the midiskirts that *Vogue* had decreed to be the hot new style in 1970, American women were "in revolt," as the fashion writers liked to say, against high-style artifice and fashion dictation, and in the mood for naturalness, comfort, and good sense—exactly the qualities that Mirabella believed in and wanted to promote. In the July 1971 issue—the first that was exclusively her own—she informed her readers that "the teeth-and-feathers thing is behind us; we are out of costume." From now on, the magazine would concern itself with "real-life fashion."

A new crop of real-life fashion models took over the pages of *Vogue*. They were big, confident, healthy-looking girls, for the most part —no more anorexic bodies or Pre-Raphaelite hair—and often they appeared to be preening, prancing, and going about their narcissistic lives without the least awareness of being photographed. "These girls have the looks that are changing the whole meaning of beauty today," *Vogue* announced. "The glorious charge of health and vitality and fitness each of them has. The clear clean skin. The thick shiny hair. The strong wonderful bodies. The extraordinary sense of well-being. The 'high' of health. It's what American good looks are all about." Lisa Taylor, Rene Russo, Beverly Johnson, Roseanne Vela, and the other new models were also, and not incidentally, much sexier than their predecessors. There was nothing aloof or fey about these young Amazons, and in the work of Richard Avedon, Helmut Newton, Guy Bourdin, and several other photographers, they pro-

jected a frank sexuality that some readers found unsettling. Newton's shot
of Lisa Taylor sitting with her legs apart, twirling a strand of hair while
she directs a coolly appraising look at a man walking past her wearing tight
white pants and no shirt, invoked irate letters and canceled subscriptions.
Avedon's cinematic scenario in the Fort Worth Water Gardens, which ends
with the male model apparently slapping Rene Russo in the face, brought
more angry mail,* and so did Newton's "The Story of Ohhh . . .," shot in
St. Tropez, where one man and two women play out a series of highly
ambivalent erotic encounters. The most disturbing single image, though,
was Deborah Turbeville's photograph of five girls in bathing suits in a
public bathhouse; their isolation from one another, the strange, harsh
lighting, and the fact that the girl in the foreground is apparently mastur-
bating distressed a great many people, some of whom said it reminded them
of Auschwitz. "At a time when health and energy were being stressed,"
Alex explained, photographers such as Turbeville and Newton "brought a
mysterious reminder that everything in life is not health and happiness."
Alex liked the work of Newton and Turbeville, and he was very much
behind the new, sexier approach to fashion. An interested scanner of *Playboy*
and *Penthouse*, whose "pioneering approach" to female beauty he preferred
to the "beatnik seduction" of Twiggy or Penelope Tree, he went so far as
to hire *Penthouse* photographer Stan Malinowski to work for *Vogue*. What
some critics saw as "porno chic" Alex saw as naturalness, and "naturalness,"
he said, "is a kind of nobility."

Every photograph, every layout, every idea and story and personality, every caption and cover line that went into the magazine now required
Alex's approval. For all his denials that he had or wanted to have any real
power—"the only power at Condé Nast is Si," he insisted—Alex was clearly
pleased with the new chain of command. Since Mirabella's vision of a more
down-to-earth, journalistic *Vogue* coincided so well with his own, he could
exercise complete control without appearing to do so—an ideal situation
for someone who was never comfortable acting like a boss. Priscilla Peck
had been let go after nearly thirty years at *Vogue*; still furious with Alex
over Vreeland, she had become impossible to work with any longer. Alex
hired Rochelle Udell to replace her as art director, but, of course, he himself
was in full control of layouts and covers. He brought Leo Lerman over from
Mademoiselle in 1972 to be in charge of all the nonfashion features in

* The deadpan photo caption informs us that Ms. Russo is wearing a jumpsuit by
John Anthony.

Vogue—under Alex's supervision, of course. Lerman's interests encompassed a wide cultural range, and as a result, coverage of theater, movies, music, literature, and dance in *Vogue* became much livelier. Alex brought in the critic Barbara Rose to write on the visual arts, which continued to get a lot of space in the magazine. Politics and world affairs were largely absent; the civil rights struggle, Vietnam, and the more militant aspects of the feminist movement rated barely a mention, although it could be argued that Mirabella's "real-life" fashion sense and the fashion photographers' depiction of women as strong, independent, sexually aware creatures, whose agendas were not confined to attracting males, reflected feminist goals.

Grace Mirabella never felt diminished by Alex's behind-the-scenes guidance. "He was very good at giving confidence," she said. "I could talk freely to him, and he always listened, and I knew he'd turn it around in his head and come up with a way to make things happen. He understood that I was trying to get out of the rather arch fashion sensibility and into something easier, something more journalistic. He was an incredibly modern person, with constant curiosity about everything and not a shred of nostalgia. I hated it when he went away in the summer. I didn't trust anyone else's eye. Probably I fell a little bit too much into depending on him. I didn't think I did at the time, but I have a feeling I did."

Si Newhouse was dependent on Alex in other ways. In addition to making him responsible for the look of all his magazines, Newhouse wanted Alex's opinions on personnel and hiring and corporate policy as well as on works of art, and he also wanted Alex to act as his intermediary with the top editors of all five Condé Nast magazines. Although Newhouse was by no means a shy man, as some people thought, he was socially inept. He was absolutely incapable of small talk, for one thing. His very lack of pretensions—a trait he shared with his father and his brother—tended to make him feel awkward when dealing with the highly talented and sophisticated men and women who worked for him, and for many years he counted on Alex to relieve him of that burden. (Si's marriage in 1973 to the former Victoria Benedict had relieved him of the burden of being New York's most eligible bachelor; his second wife, like Tatiana, had previously been married to a French count.) One of the older editors at *Vogue* says that in the early years of Newhouse's reign as publisher, he was eager to accept new advertising accounts that would have cheapened the image of the magazine, and that Alex consistently talked him out of doing so. "Alex saved us from vulgarity over and over again," this editor affirms. If so, he was never willing to discuss the point; according to Alex, he and Newhouse usually agreed on important questions, and there was never a moment's friction between them. "The one time I annoyed him," Newhouse said, "was when I brought my coffee into his office. He looked at me in horror and told me about people who had upset coffee over layouts."

They were certainly in agreement on the decision to change *Vogue* from a bimonthly to a monthly in 1973. Newhouse had noticed that the issue that came out on the fifteenth of the month almost always sold fewer copies than the one that came out on the first. By eliminating the weaker issue, the magazine's circulation instantly went up by about 50,000 copies a month. And it went right on climbing—from just over 400,000 in 1973 to more than a million by the end of the decade.* The growth was almost too fast. Fearing that advertising revenues could not keep pace with the costs of production and circulation—the fate of mass-market dinosaurs such as *Life*, *Look*, and the *Saturday Evening Post* in the 1970s—Newhouse kept raising the cover price of *Vogue*. But circulation kept growing, and so did ad revenues. *Vogue's* gross revenues rose from $9.1 million in 1973 to $26.9 million in 1979 (during the same period, *Harper's Bazaar's* increased from $3.5 million to $8.3 million). The Mirabella-Liberman team was obviously doing a lot of things right. Their *Vogue* was packed with useful information—about beauty, health, and fitness as well as fashion. Its pages were increasingly crowded, its layouts liberated forever from "visions of loveliness." *Vogue* no longer looked like a luxury magazine, even though it still covered European haute couture; instead of breathless reports on the costume balls of the superrich, it gave readers Monty Python's Flying Circus, in the nude, photographed by Richard Avedon, and Irving Penn's magisterial studies of squashed cigarette butts. In the new era of highly specialized publications that followed the demise of the mass-market giants, *Vogue* appeared to have hit the jackpot—it had wooed and won the middle-class woman without losing the socialite.

Si Newhouse took over as chairman of Condé Nast in 1975, two years before his father suffered a stroke that left him largely incapacitated. (Sam Newhouse died in July 1979.) Having served a lengthy apprenticeship under Sam's gimlet-eyed supervision, both Newhouse brothers were well prepared to manage their allotted sectors of the Newhouse media empire. Their management styles differed from their father's in some respects. At Condé Nast, which had recently moved from the Graybar building to more elegant quarters at 350 Madison Avenue, two changes were quickly ap-

---

* In 1977, *Vogue* went to a slightly smaller page size to reduce its printing and mailing costs—a move that had Alex's enthusiastic approval.

parent: Si Newhouse wanted to be directly involved in running the magazines, and more money was now available for editorial salaries and special projects.

Alex's own financial position became a great deal more luxurious after Si took charge. His salary went up to $500,000 a year. In a written agreement drawn up for Alex with the help of a prominent theatrical lawyer, Newhouse agreed that if he stayed with the company for another five years, his salary would continue at its then-current level in the event of his retirement or permanent disability; if Alex died, Tatiana would receive the same amount annually, until her death. Naturally, he continued to spend every cent of his increased salary and subsidiary benefits. (Alex never balanced his personal checkbooks; he just signed checks and depended on his secretary to tell him when there was no money left in the account.) More and more money flowed out in gifts and loans and other outlets for his and Tatiana's improvident generosity, and a great deal of it went into his painting and sculpture. Ever since the real-estate developer Harry Macklowe had borrowed six big welded-metal Libermans in 1971 for a temporary installation on the outdoor terrace of Dag Hammarskjöld Plaza, an office building at the corner of Second Avenue and Forty-eighth Street, the demand for Alex's sculpture had been on the rise. The Museum of Modern Art bought *Above*, one of the Hammarskjöld Plaza pieces, and installed it in the garden; Nelson Rockefeller liked it so much that he asked Alex to make another one just like it, only bigger, for his family estate at Pocantico Hills. That same year, the State of Hawaii commissioned Alex to make a monumental work for the campus of the University of Hawaii. It was the first of many public commissions that would come his way. New federal and state percent-for-art programs in the late 1960s had stimulated a nationwide boom for art in public places, and as the 1970s advanced, more and more huge, cadmium-red Libermans went up in parks and plazas and outside corporate office buildings throughout the country.

Like a number of other artists working in the public area, however, Alex found that the costs of fabrication often equaled or exceeded the agreed-on fee. Bill Layman and two of Layman's sons were working for him full-time; since Alex's work habits invoked chance as a basic principle, and therefore required continual revision and reconstruction, the labor costs kept going up. Alex did all his painting and sculpture in the country now, on weekends. He had given up his last Manhattan studio, a gloomy industrial space at 418 East Seventy-fifth Street, and renovated the room over the garage of his Connecticut house to paint in. Two years later, he had it rebuilt twice as large, with a floor-to-ceiling opening at one end to accommodate extra-large canvases, just like the one he had seen years before in Cézanne's studio in Aix. His paintings got wilder and more violent each year. Loose, slashing brushwork, poured paint, thick impasto gouged by jagged linear markings—a kind of frenzied drawing in paint—came close to obliterating the residual triangle motif. Reviewing his 1973 show at André Emmerich, the *Newsweek* critic called them "horrific paintings . . . bordering as much on ugliness as on beauty." A lot of barely controlled anger seemed to emanate from these paintings, which nobody bought. "More and more I rebel," he told Barbara Rose, "maybe even because I ·work in a magazine that surrounds itself with civilized behavior, taste, and so forth."

Somehow, in addition to running *Vogue*, overseeing the other magazines, fulfilling sculptural commissions, and painting, he continued to devote limitless time and energy to his marriage. Tatiana and Tatiana's happiness came first in his priorities, no doubt about that, and as she grew older, her dependence on him increased. They were never apart for more than a few hours at a time. Alex called her several times a day from the office, and his longtime secretary, Gladys Pohl, was invariably struck by the tenderness in his voice when he talked with her. To many of their acquaints the marriage seemed truly remarkable. Aside from the mild flirtation with Brigitte Tichenor, there had never been a single hint or rumor of infidelity on either side. Alex was aware, of course, that any straying on his part would be as disastrous to the marriage as Bertrand du Plessix's dalliance with Katia Krassin had been; Tatiana would not have forgiven him. He was surrounded every day at Condé Nast by chic and glamorous women, with whom he flirted as a matter of course. Alex, moreover, got better and better looking as he aged. His white hair, grown longer and not slicked down as it used to be, gave his head a distinguished and rather noble (Alex's favorite adjective) handsomeness; people who used to say that he looked like the actor David Niven were now inclined to compare him to Walter Cronkite. "Every woman who's ever worked for Alex has had a crush on him," according to Rochelle Udell. "We would sit around and talk about what it would be like to go out with Alex, to sleep with Alex. He's the sexiest guy around." And yet, at a time when divorce and extramarital liaisons seemed obligatory in their set, Alex's devotion to Tatiana (whom everyone knew to be "difficult") never faltered.

Tatiana was famously difficult. She browbeat everyone, pouncing on flaws in her friends' attire or their conversation, looking them up and down with nearsighted rigor and then telling them in her hoarse, peremptory voice how awful they looked or how wrong they were. She scolded Helen Frankenthaler furiously one day for bringing an armful of roses to a lunch party in Connecticut. It was frightfully rude to bring cut flowers, Tatiana said, because then the hostess had to take time out to get a vase with water and arrange them; one should send them earlier in the day, or the next day, or, preferably, bring a potted plant. "Take off that sweater, it's disgusting," she commanded Frederic Tuten, a young writer who often visited them in the country—and then she dragged him off to the local general store and insisted on buying him another one, in a slightly darker shade of brown. Tuten adored her. "Tatiana *chose* people," he said. "We'd be sitting in the living room, reading, and she'd get up and come over and say 'I luff you,' for no reason. You didn't know what her magic was, but you certainly wanted her to like you."

Another of her younger admirers, *Time*'s art critic Robert Hughes, saw Tatiana as the kind of displaced Russian who was determined to reconstitute Russia wherever she went. "She's absurdly generous and deeply irrational," Hughes said. "Rides on instinct. Has an amazing bullshit detector, and is tremendously unfair and categorical and imperious in her likes and dislikes. Alex can live without the strain of making harsh discriminations, because she does that for him. And at the same time she's very vulnerable and highly superstitious—a real Russian. She is kind of a female version of the starets, the holy men who had such a powerful effect on people in the late czarist court. Tatiana is the portable essence of Mother Russia, whom he has carried with him, and that's why she's been so tremendously important to his imaginative life."

She was quite capable of making melodramatic scenes. At a dinner party given in 1973 by the publisher Roger Straus to celebrate the publication of Hilton Kramer's book *The Age of the Avant-Garde*, Tatiana locked horns with the guest of honor. She had been talking about Joseph Brodsky, the Russian poet in exile, who was a great friend of hers. (At their first meeting, Tatiana had announced categorically that he would win the Nobel Prize, which he did in 1987.) Kramer, the *New York Times* art critic, who was sitting across the table from Tatiana, mentioned that when he visited the Soviet Union in 1967, he had met a young writer who had been incarcerated in the same insane asylum with Brodsky. Tatiana immediately wanted to know his name. Kramer explained that the people who introduced him to this writer had made him promise not to write about him or reveal his name, because to do so might put him in danger. "She became very agitated at that point," according to Kramer.

"She said that she was a great advocate of the Russian dissidents, that she had supported them here, and I said I knew she had done wonderful things but that I had given my word, and I wasn't going to break it now. Well, she began really making an issue of it. Roger Straus kept trying to change the subject, but she kept hammering away, and saying 'I can help this person.' Finally I got a bit fed up—it was my party, after all—and I said, 'I'm terribly sorry, Mrs. Liberman, but I'm not going to tell you this man's name. After all, you could be working for the KGB yourself.' Well, that sent her up in smoke. She stood up and yelled, 'Aleex, we are leaving.' Alex got right up. Dorothea Straus came over, but nothing could calm her. 'This man called me a spy. I have never been so insulted!' Her coat had to be brought up from downstairs, which took a few minutes. As she and Alex were leaving I sort of approached her to say good night, and she turned to me and said, 'You're absolutely right, nobody is to be trusted'—and walked out."

Her public behavior never seemed to embarrass or upset Alex. "I'd been taught in my life to be polite, to conform," he said, "and I always found it wonderfully refreshing that she could say whatever she thought. She could be as violent about the taste of a soup or the shape of a dress as she was about human shortcomings." At the large cocktail parties that they continued to give at least once a month in New York, Tatiana scolded old friends and perfect strangers with equal vigor. The old friends rather adored her for it; the new ones were often dazzled by her lightninglike insights. Barbara Rose used to bring her boy friends out to the Libermans' country house on weekends, to get Tatiana's reaction to them. "She's really supernatural," Rose decided. "I was once going with a very famous artist, and I was thinking of marrying him. [This was some years after her marriage to Frank Stella.] We went out to the Libermans', and afterward I said, 'All right, Tatiana, what is it?' And she said, 'Very lovely American gentleman.' I said, 'Yes?' Then she said, 'Darling, is killer. In two weeks he is killing you.' And I thought about it, and I got out of it. She was right."

The house in Connecticut had been Tatiana's idea. Alex would have preferred the seashore, but Tatiana wanted to be near Francine, now that the old tensions between them had abated somewhat. Tatiana was fiercely proud of her daughter and her daughter's family. Cleve was the best son-in-law imaginable, Luke and Thaddeus the best possible grandsons. (Thaddeus, the older boy, would become an investment banker; Luke was on his way toward becoming an artist.) Cleve found Alex and Tatiana fascinating. He enjoyed their company and would often go over to their house for lunch on Saturdays; this rather annoyed Francine, who never wanted to spend that much time there—she might drop by for a cup of tea after lunch. The mother-daughter tensions might have abated, but they certainly had not disappeared.

Francine and Cleve lived a disciplined, somewhat reclusive life in the country, writing and painting, associating mainly with fellow intellectuals, supporting progressive causes. They joined sit-ins and vigils against the war in Vietnam—a subject they could not discuss with Alex and Tatiana. Alex's refugee mentality made it impossible for him to oppose an official policy of the United States government; to Tatiana, left-wing sentiments were pro-Communist, and therefore dangerous. ("You are selling yourself to the Vietcong," she told Francine.) Tatiana took great pride, nonetheless, in the favorable response to Francine's *New Yorker* articles on Daniel and Philip Berrigan, the left-wing Catholic activists, and when Francine's first novel, *Lovers and Tyrants*, was published in 1976, to generally admiring reviews, Tatiana was ecstatic. Alex deeply resented what he considered the unflattering and rather cruel portrait of Tatiana in the book, but he never spoke to Francine about it; according to Alex, Tatiana never really read the book. (She had great trouble reading English.) The important thing to Tatiana was that Francine, her brilliant daughter, had become a literary success.

The Connecticut house itself was a reflection of Tatiana's taste. Dark and gloomy when they bought it, with wood-paneled walls and small windows, and trees blocking out the views, it became an all-white space filled with natural light. The wood paneling came out, the walls were painted white, new windows appeared, the hardwood floor disappeared under a layer of white vinyl tiles. Since the house came furnished, Tatiana spray-painted a few usable pieces white (she also spray-painted the TV), threw out the rest, and bought some chairs and sofas upholstered in white plastic at Bon Marché in New York. The total bill for furnishings was less than a thousand dollars. She filled the house with oversized flowering plants and kept the temperature below sixty-five degrees, winter and summer, to make them grow better. Tatiana had a famously green thumb. "Pinch, pinch," she would say, when asked how she did it.

Tatiana also had several big trees on the property cut down, to let in more light and improve the view. "Tatiana always wants to cut things," Alex observed. "Trees, limbs, flowers—even paintings. She cut out the background of a painting that René Bouché had done of Tatiana and me at the opera. She cut away everything but the face in my portrait drawing of Francine as a young girl. 'Isn't it better that way?' she asked me. 'Don't

The sitting room at Hillside, the Libermans' Connecticut house:
white plastic furniture, vinyl tile, and lots of plants. The painting
over the fireplace is from Alex's triangle series.

Russian friends in the country: Joseph Brodsky and
Mikhail Baryshnikov.

you think so?' And, of course, I had to say yes." He was not unaware of the Freudian interpretation of her mania for excision. "She even tries to cut me down to size," he said. "I must say, I find her castration complex a very stimulating challenge."

Francine, leading a life that was in almost every respect different from her mother's, felt great admiration for Alex's perennial "balancing act." "It's what makes him tick," she said, "the thrill of keeping this wild beast tame, and at the same time walking the tightrope of power and winning respect as a serious artist. The challenge and triumph of his life has been to keep her from destroying him. My mother is so Russian—an enormously powerful personality who at the same time wants to be totally protected. Alex has always done everything in that household, from planning meals to calling the plumber. He resolves all problems, so that she can live like a queen. I remember one night in 1978, I was staying over with them in New York. I'd broken my leg in a fall on an icy road the previous year, it had been badly set, and that night I broke it again. When I came in about eleven-thirty I knew I was in trouble, couldn't sleep all night because of the pain. A little before seven, the telephone rang, and I answered because mine was the only telephone in the house that was turned on. It was Dominique Nabokov, our great friend, weeping; her husband, Nicolas, had died suddenly during the night. Just then I saw the light go on in the bathroom. It was Alex, who always got up early. I crawled across the hall, knocked on the door, and told him that Nicolas Nabokov had died, that Dominique was in bad shape, and that unfortunately I'd broken my leg again and I needed some advice about who to go to. 'Don't worry, I'll take care of it all,' he said. Within an hour he had called Dominique, gotten somebody over there to take care of her, made preliminary arrangements with the funeral parlor, called Dr. Rosenfeld, his physician, who referred him to the best bone man, who happened to be right around the corner, taken me there, arranged for his chauffeur to pick me up, and then gone to his office at Condé Nast. And my mother was still sleeping."

It would not have been easy to wake her up. Tatiana placed great importance on getting a minimum of eight hours of sleep every night. She took sleeping pills when she went to bed, and she wore earplugs and a mask to keep out the light. Her bed was across the room from Alex's. When Tatiana woke up during the night, she usually wanted Alex to wake up, too; if calling out to him failed, she would throw a magazine at his bed. She left notes in Russian on his bedside table, saying things like "Every hour I love you more," with a drawing of two hearts inside a clock, and "I

so regret that I am not Akhmatova, so I could tell you how I love you."
Alex felt that she found extraordinary words to express her most tender
feelings—always in Russian, of course. "Russian was our basic language
for anything that was meaningful. I've always felt that people who shared
the same childhood language have the best chance of happiness together."
Tatiana had had a slight heart attack in 1976, an atrial fibrillation that
kept her in the hospital for ten anxious days before it stabilized. She was
aging visibly, and he adored her as much as ever. Tatiana was the fulcrum
of his existence.

They went to the same places in Europe each summer—Paris,
Rome, Venice, Ischia: Alex called it "the milk run." Alex performed his
"Superman" tricks, handing out huge tips to smooth their way through
customs and to secure the best rooms and the best tables and the most
agreeable chauffeurs. (Overtipping was like a jolt of adrenaline to his
nervous system.) In Rome, where they stopped off en route to Ischia to
attend the summer fashion shows, Alex got interested in photographing
the Campidoglio square, with its equestrian statue of Marcus Aurelius.
(The statue, by Michelangelo, had helped to push Alex in the direction of
public sculpture.) He photographed it at different times of the day and
from every conceivable point of view—a project that continued to occupy
him for several years. He also began making aquatints and etchings at
2RC, an experimental print workshop owned by Walter and Eleanor Rossi,
and run by a young American named Danny Berger. Printmaking seemed
to release a linear energy that he had not tapped before in his work—a
nervous, broken, impetuous line, which soon became a dominant element
in his paintings. At the Regina Isabella in Ischia, Alex was somehow
able to blend work and play into a seamless continuum. Rossi and Berger
would bring zinc plates for him to etch, and he would do that for several
hours in the morning, then spend the rest of the day relaxing. He had
always avoided any sort of strenuous exercise. Unlike Tatiana, who used
to swim across the Gulf of St. Tropez, and who still did laps in the Regina
Isabella's pool, Alex was content to float lazily on a rubber mattress in
some secluded cove, admiring the strange volcanic formations of the rocky
coastline. In the evenings he presided over a little court of international
socialites (Ethel de Croisset, São Schlumberger, Oscar and Françoise de
la Renta, Philippe and Pauline de Rothschild) in one of the good local
restaurants. Francine and Cleve visited them in Ischia once and hated the
place. "There wasn't even a beach," according to Francine. "Just one gray
rock, and everybody crammed together on it like sardines, and names,
names, names." Both Alex and Tatiana took the mud baths and claimed

to feel rejuvenated. They also spent a lot of time alone together. "We could always withdraw into our *solitude à deux*," Alex said. "That was one of our secrets."

Sometimes they rented a car and driver and went sightseeing. "The car would be crammed with things for Tatiana's comfort—candies, music tapes, fur wraps for her legs because of the air conditioning," according to the writer Gregor von Rezzori, a close friend who, with his wife, Beatrice Monti della Corte, an art dealer who showed Alex's work in her Milan gallery, accompanied them on several of these excursions. "Alex, the connoisseur, took us from one beautiful church to another, while Tatiana and I giggled together. Alex is not an intellectual—he is too intelligent to be an intellectual—but he and Beatrice were more serious than Tatiana and I were about imbibing culture. I've never seen anyone more understanding with his own wife. When Tatiana dismissed something or someone in her epic Russian way, he would smile and shrug and say, 'Boubous, you're eccentric.' And every now and then you would see that they were holding hands. When you were chosen by them, you had the feeling of never having had better friends. You felt you really belonged to them."

Alex's mother, Tatiana's only rival, no longer cast her jealous shadow over their European summers. She had died in 1974, of cancer, in a private clinic in Paris. During the last year of her life, Alex had cut himself off from her to some degree. He paid her bills, as always, and he talked to her on the telephone, but he did not go to see her when she was dying. Simone Eyrard, an employee of French *Vogue* whom Alex had known since his days at *Vu*, had become Henriette's faithful companion, and she kept him informed about his mother's declining condition. At the end, Simone was to call him in New York if his mother emerged from the coma into which she had lapsed, but she died without regaining consciousness. Alex was in his office at Condé Nast when he got the news. Rochelle Udell came in to ask a question and saw right away that something was wrong. "He just sort of sat there, looking as though he didn't know what to do," she recalled. "I asked what had happened, and he said his mother had died. I said, 'Alex, go home.' He looked up and said, 'I'm going.' "

Henriette Pascar's last will and testament, handwritten in her still-firm and flamboyant script, took the form of a four-page letter to Alex, to whom she left her meager residue of worldly possessions. "Adieu, my great love," the document concluded. "We were often cruel to one another, let God forgive us." She had given Simone Eyrard precise instructions for her burial. She wanted to be dressed in her most stylish outfit, with her newest wig and full makeup, prior to being cremated. Then, at six o'clock on a beautiful evening, when the light was just right, she wanted her ashes taken to the bridge at the Place de la Concorde and thrown into the Seine. Alex denied her that last piece of theater. (He says he never knew about it.) His mother's ashes were flown to Kennedy airport, where there was a mixup; they were not on the plane they were supposed to be on, and it took several hours to trace them. He buried them at the Woodlawn Cemetery in Ardsley, next to his father's. Once again he managed to set aside his unresolved feelings toward the first all-encompassing female presence in his life. The only emotion he remembered feeling at the cemetery was a vague and weary sense of relief.

Si Newhouse, Jr., in his working clothes—an Armani sweatshirt.
The stripped-down, spartan office is Alex's, and so is the painting.

"I'm Afraid It's True"

For a man who was so finely attuned to the complexities and contradictions of twentieth-century urban culture, Alex Liberman led a remarkably unexamined life. The idea of consulting a psychiatrist never crossed his mind. He believed that people in general (and Francine and Cleve in particular) were too inclined to verbalize their problems, to talk things to death—something that he and Tatiana successfully avoided for more than fifty years. And it was not only with Tatiana that he found ways to bypass troublesome issues and encounters. Alex glided on the surface of his life with the agility and grace of a water spider, never allowing himself to be maneuvered into a position from which there was no available exit, never confronting problems head-on. The lightness of his manner, the ironic courtliness that became a sort of game between himself and others, was one aspect of his extraordinary charm. In any gathering, Alex could seem like the youngest person in the room.

According to Si Newhouse, Alex's refusal to lock himself into any specific point of view was one of the things that made him so indispensable at Condé Nast. "He is not predisposed to like or not like things," Newhouse said admiringly. "He deals with magazines as live, practical problems that change and have to change over the years. Anything is possible with him;

the only real issue is how well it can be done." Alex did not hold on to things—that was the key. Was it the Gypsy strain on his mother's side that made him an intellectual nomad? "He loves to move from one subject to another very quickly, without connections," Newhouse said. "He does that in conversation, in his work, and in his life." Alex could change his mind about a person or a story or an idea in the twinkling of an eye—could even take up the opposite point of view without the least embarrassment. His intelligence was not superficial, but neither was it noticeably deep; it was, in fact, the perfect instrument for dealing with the daily requirements of magazine journalism. Alex's was the quintessential magazine intelligence, swift-moving and allusive, buoyantly unsentimental, alert to every nuance and shift in the culture at large, a resource whose rarity and value Si Newhouse was able to appreciate in full measure.

Alex's lack of rigidity and his ability to turn work into play stemmed in part, of course, from his having two careers. Although he gave the lion's share of his time and energy to Condé Nast, sometimes going so far as to say that Condé Nast "is my life, after all," he could always tell himself that his real work lay elsewhere, in what he did as an artist. Being an artist made it easier for him to take chances at the office, to experiment with layouts and features, to change the look of a magazine's cover or to redesign its entire format. *Glamour* had achieved a hard-won independence under Ruth Whitney; when she became editor in chief in 1967, it was with the explicit understanding that Alex Liberman would no longer be involved with the magazine in any way. Alex took this in good grace. "I had built the damn magazine, and I had hired Whitney," he said, "but I backed off." He did not hesitate to take Whitney to lunch at one point, however, and tell her he thought her magazine had begun to look badly designed and "cheap." She was very upset at the time, but she fired the art director and got a new one. *Glamour*, the magazine for the working girl, was Condé Nast's most successful product; its two-million-plus circulation made it the biggest-selling fashion-and-beauty publication in the world. Alex, who had been instrumental in shaping its mass-market appeal, was willing to step back so long as Ruth Whitney maintained the standards he had set for it. Like all the other Condé Nast titles, though, *Glamour* "was still my responsibility in the end."

Under Si Newhouse, the Condé Nast magazine empire was starting a process of expansion that would vastly increase its power and its profitability. *Self*, the first new publication launched by Condé Nast in forty years, appeared on the newsstands early in 1979; one of a number of magazines generated in response to the feminist movement, its special focus was health and fitness. Newhouse bought into the growing interest in men's clothing styles that fall when he acquired *Gentlemen's Quarterly* from *Esquire*; renamed *GQ*, it was pitched to a younger, post–Brooks Brothers audience. Two years later, Newhouse and Alex decided to turn *House & Garden* into a different magazine for a different audience. A stagnant and rather dowdy monthly that offered household hints to middle-income readers, *House & Garden* was "repositioned" to compete directly with *Architectural Digest*, the highly successful luxury magazine for affluent homeowners. Its price went from $1.50 to $4.00 a copy; circulation was cut in half; ad rates went up sharply; text and photographs were edited for wealthier and more sophisticated readers.

By far the most significant new Condé Nast venture, however, was the revival of *Vanity Fair*. For years, Alex's generation of editors had talked nostalgically about Frank Crowninshield and his legendary magazine, whose demise in 1936 had seemed to mark the close of an enchanted era in New York. For S. I. Newhouse, Jr., who was too young to have read the magazine when it was alive, the dream of a reborn *Vanity Fair* became something of an obsession. Although he had been a very active and involved chairman of the company since 1975, Newhouse still had not put his personal stamp on Condé Nast or established himself as a recognized presence in New York cultural circles. The new *Vanity Fair*, whose birth pangs would cost him more than $10 million, was his personal declaration of independence.

Alex's editorial eye and Alex's editorial judgment were as important as ever in Newhouse's major decisions, and Newhouse counted on Alex to help make the new *Vanity Fair* a stunning success. They had agreed that it would be a "cultural and literary magazine on a very high level," more contemporary in feeling (and less long-winded) than *The New Yorker*, with the sort of breezy, iconoclastic slant that had distinguished the Crowninshield original. After considering a host of potential editors, Alex settled on Richard Locke, the deputy editor of *The New York Times Book Review*. Locke had been recommended by Francine and Cleve Gray, among others. He was relatively young (forty), intellectual, and enthusiastic; in the course of several lunches at The Four Seasons, Alex had found him extremely agreeable and open to suggestions. Locke's appointment was announced in August 1981. Over the next eighteen months, he hired a staff of well-known writers and critics, bought literary manuscripts from several even better known authors, and paid as little attention as possible to the massive publicity buildup that was preparing readers for a very different magazine from the one he had in mind.

"Locke," Alex said with a sigh, "was dreaming of a literary-cultural magazine for the very few. He had great difficulty in dealing with his staff—he was suspicious of everything, questioned everything. None of this had come out in my lunches with him. Also, he resented any sense of modernity in the graphics. He wouldn't let me do the layouts I wanted to do. But you know, in spite of everything, those early issues of his, if you look at them today, are actually quite good. I think the real problem was that the magazine had been overpromoted and overpublicized. There were big ads on all the buses—'the greatest magazine,' 'the most exciting.' People expected some sort of Second Coming. And then the press pounced on the first issue with a vengeance that was perhaps more anti-Newhouse than anything else. I have never seen a magazine attacked so savagely."

The chorus of derision that greeted Locke's first issue in March 1983 does seem in retrospect to have been somewhat excessive, considering a table of contents that included articles by John Leonard, Clement Greenberg, Nora Ephron, and Stephen Jay Gould; a portfolio of photographs by Richard Avedon ("In the American West"); and a complete novella by Gabriel García Márquez. Even more embarrassing, however, were the flood of canceled subscriptions and the defection of advertisers. Newhouse's reaction was swift and brutal; before the third issue appeared, he had fired Richard Locke. Locke's only public comment, before he retreated into a dignified and permanent silence on the subject, indirectly blamed Alex Liberman for the debacle. From the beginning, he said, there had been "a conflict between a magazine that I believe I was asked to create, a magazine of writing and ideas, or a magazine of jazzy layout and bits and pieces. And jazzy layout won."

The editor chosen to replace Locke was Leo Lerman, whose tenure turned out to be only slightly less brief. In his many years at Condé Nast—most of them spent as the "cultural heart" of *Mademoiselle*, the last eleven as features editor of *Vogue*—Lerman had often said that one of his greatest ambitions in life was to edit a revived *Vanity Fair*. Denied the opportunity when it first arose, he now embraced it with ardor, announcing that he planned to retain the magazine's literary bias while adding "wit, irony and a look at life with humanity and richness." At Alex's suggestion, Lerman assigned Irving Penn to take a series of eye-catching black-and-white portraits for the magazine's covers. (One of them was of Francine Gray, whose award-winning report on the Nazi war criminal Klaus Barbie ran in that issue.) Under heavy pressure from Newhouse, who continued to pour money into the operation, Alex kept urging Lerman to make it less literary and more appealing to middlebrow readers. Although the layouts got jazzier, the journalistic mix of high and popular culture that Lerman was trying for never quite seemed to jell. Looking back on that disastrous year, Alex felt that he and Lerman were trying too hard to duplicate the original *Vanity Fair*, which had appealed, after all, to a distinctly limited audience of sophisticated people. Circulation, ad revenues, and staff morale continued to sink with each issue. Lerman, who was sixty-nine when he became the editor, simply did not have the physical stamina to turn the situation around. It was at this desperate juncture that Alex, giving way to his gambler's instinct, persuaded Newhouse to bump Lerman (who had joined Condé Nast only a few months after Alex had, and who had been a close friend of Alex's mother and father) and give his job to a thirty-year-old Englishwoman named Tina Brown.

Alex had met Tina Brown in the spring of 1983, when she came to New York on a visit. He already knew a little about her. As the editor of England's 270-year-old *Tatler*, she had tripled that venerable journal's minuscule circulation by printing amusing and somewhat racy (but not too racy) articles about upper-class London society. A blond, blue-eyed charmer whose looks reminded many people of Princess Diana's, Brown, the daughter of a successful British movie producer, had made a name for herself as an Oxford undergraduate by writing witty, somewhat caustic pieces for *Isis*, the university magazine. She was soon selling free-lance articles to *Punch, The New Statesman*, and *The Sunday Times*, whose editor, Harold Evans, was so dazzled by their author that he would eventually divorce his wife to marry her. Brown had been named England's "Young Journalist of the Year" in 1979, the same year she took over the editorship of the *Tatler*. (She was twenty-six at the time.) She resigned from the *Tatler* in 1983, because, she said, she wanted to go back to writing, and it was at this point that she was summoned to a lunch in New York with Si Newhouse and Alex Liberman.

Very bright, very ambitious, and brimming with ideas, Tina Brown impressed Alex and Newhouse as someone who might inject badly needed youthful vitality into the failing magazine, and Alex arranged for her to be put on the staff of *Vanity Fair* that summer as a "consultant." "I remember several meetings in Leo Lerman's office with Tina," Alex said. "Tina would come up with ideas, and Leo wouldn't agree to any of them. So she went back to London. Then she wrote me a letter, saying, among other things, that she really felt she was ready to take over *Vanity Fair* and to do something wonderful with it. I spoke to Si, and we decided that perhaps this was the answer." Lerman was given the title of "editorial advisor" to all the Condé Nast magazines and asked to lend his expertise to *Gourmet*, the food journal that Newhouse had bought in 1983. Tina Brown started work as *Vanity*

Fair's new editor in chief (the third in a year) on New Year's Day 1984, and set in motion one of the great success stories in American publishing.

The turnaround did not come right away. *Vanity Fair* kept on losing huge amounts of money, and in the spring of 1985 Brown learned that Newhouse was preparing to abandon ship. "I didn't realize it," she told an interviewer, "but everyone on the staff had sort of tentative reassignments to other magazines, and they were going to break the news on Memorial Day." Brown went directly to Newhouse with an eloquent plea for more time—but before that, she went to Alex Liberman. She had been very careful to keep Alex involved in all phases of the editing process at *Vanity Fair*, feeling, rightly, that "he was responsible for my being hired." Tina Brown had a great advantage over Richard Locke and Leo Lerman in that she could play the role of a gifted student who was grateful to receive lessons from the established master—perhaps this was how she truly saw herself. "It's a wonderful thing to be able to call on Alex and have him bring that extra something," she once said. "It's like being an art student who's got Picasso upstairs. Alex has the gift of making you more than you are." This attitude did her no harm in dealing with an editorial director whose tolerance for flattery, always fairly high, was increasing with his years. At any rate, when Brown went to Newhouse and told him about all the exciting articles and features she had in the works, Newhouse agreed to give her another year on the job.

The magic editorial touch with which Tina Brown turned *Vanity Fair* into the hot magazine of the 1980s had very little to do with literary culture and a lot to do with celebrity—which, as Andy Warhol had predicted, was rapidly becoming the nirvana of the masses. Although Brown's magazine developed a reputation for insider gossip, the profiles of Sylvester Stallone, Madonna, Cher, and other Hollywood celebrities were generally admiring, and tough, in-depth stories, such as Dominick Dunne's long piece about the trial of Claus von Bülow (photographed for the article by Helmut Newton with his then mistress Andrea Reynolds in sinister black leather outfits), were relatively rare. The magazine's most striking features were often visual, in particular the strangely intimate, frequently disturbing photographs that Annie Leibovitz took of well-known people. Leibovitz became *Vanity Fair*'s in-house photographer under Tina Brown, and her work played a key role in the magazine's widening appeal.

Brown's unprecedentedly high word-rates attracted more and more talented writers to the magazine, though, and a combination of good editing and lavish tokens of appreciation (bottles of champagne delivered to the writer's door, limousines and first-class airline tickets and invitations to parties at Tina and Harry's Upper East Side apartment) tended to keep them there. The high-low "mix" that Leo Lerman had sought in vain began to coalesce near the low end of the cultural scale of values, and circulation woke up. For a while, *Vanity Fair* seemed to become the house organ of the yuppie generation, whose free-spending, self-promoting heroes and heroines (from Donald Trump to Pamela Harriman) were prominently featured in its pages. "Then they started doing something that seems to me kind of interesting," said Calvin Trillin, the *New Yorker* writer, who had contributed an article to one of Locke's early issues, "which was to have one serious piece per month, typically about something horrible happening in Central Africa. . . . This was the piece you were supposed to say you were reading if someone saw you with the magazine and said, 'Why are you just reading gossip?' "

Tina Brown's magazine had its share of detractors. They cited the abundance of flattering articles on major advertisers such as Calvin Klein, Ralph Lauren, Bill Blass, Karl Lagerfeld, and Ronald Lauder (whose family owned the Estée Lauder cosmetics firm), and they derided the personality-centered approach, which titillated readers while giving them nothing more (the critics said) than a verbose version of *People* magazine. *Vanity Fair* was carrying more and more ambitious, well-researched pieces on politics, environmental issues, and other grownup subject matter, though, and more and more people were finding that they couldn't do without it. In the affluent American society of the 1980s, Tina Brown's formula worked. Circulation climbed slowly at first, then took off, reaching almost 1.2 million in 1992. Advertising revenues soared; the number of ad pages rose from 335 in 1984, her first year, to 1,440 in 1991. Whether the magazine was actually making money was harder to judge. Sam Newhouse had turned Condé Nast into a private corporation, which did not reveal its profit or loss figures; some media analysts thought *Vanity Fair*'s high costs might offset its rising income. But nobody could deny that the magazine was a huge popular success.

Tina Brown had brought off her miracle, moreover, with very little help from Alex Liberman. She managed quite skillfully to make him feel that his contribution was essential—calling him down to look at layouts, asking his advice on covers—while she went about inventing a magazine that bore little resemblance to the one that Alex himself had once envisaged. "I still thought that a distinguished cultural magazine could be done," Alex said in 1990. "Tina's magazine is not my dream of subject matter, but I admire her for doing it. It's brilliantly edited and enormously successful."

Another bright, attractive, and ambitious young Englishwoman caught Alex Liberman's eye in 1983—the same year that Tina Brown came to *Vanity Fair*. Her name was Anna Wintour, and she was actually half-American; her father, Charles Wintour, the greatly respected former editor and managing director of the London *Evening Standard*, had married the daughter of a Harvard law professor. Anna, the second of four children, skipped college for an early start in her father's profession. After a stint with the British edition of *Harper's Bazaar* in London, she came to New York in 1976 to work briefly for American *Bazaar*. She was fired after three months and told that she would never understand the American market. Undismayed, she worked briefly for Bob Guccione's *Viva* magazine, and then landed a job at *New York* magazine, where she soon rose to the position of senior editor in charge of fashion, interior design, and home entertaining. Wintour's twice-yearly special fashion issues at *New York* dazzled the industry. She had an eye for photographers and layouts as well as for clothes—the American market, after all, was just her dish—and it wasn't long before she started getting calls from other magazines. Neither Wintour nor Alex remembers just how it came about—whether he sought her out or she initiated the contact—but sometime in the spring of 1983 she had a brief interview with Alex at Condé Nast. When he asked her what she wanted to do with her life, she said that she would like to be the editor in chief of *Vogue*.

Their next meeting was at Alex and Tatiana's house in Connecticut. Anna's husband, David Shaffer, a South African–born doctor who was the head of pediatric psychiatry at Columbia-Presbyterian Medical Center, picked her up at her office on a weekday morning and they drove out together, stopping at a motel so that Anna could change her clothes. "She looked marvelous," said Alex, who always noticed such things. "She wore a wonderfully simple gray tunic, and I was absolutely enchanted with her." (Tatiana was less enchanted; Wintour's very brief miniskirt aroused her derision, and she had brought cut flowers instead of a plant—and not even roses, but zinnias.) Alex made up his mind that this slim beauty with cropped brown hair, stylish legs, and a whiplash intelligence belonged at *Vogue*.

Just where she could fit in at the magazine, though, was a problem. Both Alex and Si Newhouse felt that the fashion coverage at *Vogue* could use some fresh ideas, but Wintour refused, quite shrewdly, to have anything to do with fashion sittings. There was tension between Wintour and Grace Mirabella, the editor in chief, from their first meeting—a mutual dislike that reflected personal differences as well as professional rivalry. Wintour was aware that Mirabella kept a tight grip on the magazine's fashion coverage, in part because she had been tacitly relieved of responsibility for all

Tina Brown in her office at *Vanity Fair*.

Alex and *Vogue* editor in chief Anna Wintour.

other areas of *Vogue*. Alex, who did not feel that Grace Mirabella's grasp
of cultural affairs was sufficiently wide or deep, had taken over the editing
of *Vogue*'s nonfashion features, at first in collaboration with Leo Lerman
and then, after Lerman made his ill-fated move to *Vanity Fair*, with a young
protégée named Amy Gross, whom Alex had brought over from *Mademoiselle*. The solution that Alex came up with for Anna Wintour was to make
her the "creative director" of *Vogue*, a completely new job that was described, in a masterfully vague announcement to the staff that August, as
"working to enrich the looks of the pages and bringing to the pages other
aspects of a woman's interests."

The experiment was not a success. After having been responsible
for twelve pages a week at *New York*, plus special issues and other features,
Wintour felt underused and out of place at *Vogue*. She had taken the job,
she said, because of Alex: "It was totally to do with him that I decided to
go. I just realized that if you wanted to learn about magazines, and fashion
magazines in particular, there was simply nowhere else to be." She did
work with him on illustrating certain features, and she had the frequent
opportunity to observe him in his most impressive role—laying out the
pages of what was supposedly Grace Mirabella's magazine. "Alex would do
every layout," she recalled, "unless he was away on his annual holiday. He
would do it with everybody else standing around and watching. I used to
stand around. Grace used to stand around. Roger Schoening [*Vogue*'s art
director] would stand around, and the other people from the art department
would stand around, watching the maestro. He would do it all, and very
quickly." Wintour made a mental note that when she became the editor
of *Vogue* (as she fully intended to do), these matters would proceed somewhat differently.

After two years of increasing frustration, Wintour went back to
London to take over British *Vogue*. Beatrix Miller, its editor for twenty-
two years, was retiring, and Bernard H. Leser, the managing director of
Condé Nast's London office, had asked for Wintour to replace her. "Anna
is the twenty-first century," Leser said. Alex was very reluctant to let her
go. In his usual way, he had managed to overlook the tension between
Wintour and Mirabella, and he continued to hope that the two of them
could work together somehow.

Wintour's crisp and impatient managerial style went over rather
badly at first in London, where it was viewed as being altogether too
American. British *Vogue*, which had been a quirky and sometimes whimsical fashion magazine under Miller, became under Wintour ("Nuclear
Wintour," they called her) a much closer relation to American *Vogue*,

with emphasis on the kind of "real-life" fashions that Grace Mirabella favored. Like Tina Brown, Wintour took pains to keep her relationship with Alex in good repair. "Anna would send me the dummies of her layouts from London," Alex recalled. "She would call me on the phone to ask if I liked the cover. When she had problems with the front of the book, she came to New York and we redesigned it for her." She flew to New York as often as she could that year, bringing along her one-year-old son, Charlie, so they could both spend a few days with his father; David Shaffer could rarely get away from his job at Presbyterian Medical Center. Pregnant with her second child, Anna was unhappy in London. Si Newhouse was aware of this. Determined not to lose her, Si flew over to London for a breakfast meeting with Wintour in 1987. She hoped he was going to offer her American *Vogue*. Instead, he offered to make her editor in chief of *House & Garden*. "I was totally stunned," said Wintour. "I went right back to the office and called Alex, and he said, 'Absolutely, you have to come.' It was apparently Alex who pushed for me to go to *House & Garden*."

There was much speculation in the press at the time that *House & Garden* would be merely a temporary stop on Anna Wintour's route to the top job at *Vogue*. Newhouse denied the rumor, and so did Alex. "We were having problems at *House & Garden* at the time," said Newhouse. "So I suggested she come back and take it over." The problems at *House & Garden* came as news to the magazine's staff. Since its reorientation in 1983 as a showcase for expensive living, it had received a lot of favorable attention—for good writing as much as for its luxurious photo layouts. What publishers call "the numbers" were less favorable, however; while *House & Garden* had virtually caught up with *Architectural Digest* in circulation, it was still behind in advertising revenue, and there had been no growth in either area for some time. Newhouse believed in taking action before serious troubles set in. The action in this case, though, was so sudden that Louis Oliver Gropp, the editor in chief, only learned he had been replaced by Anna Wintour three days after the fact; he was on vacation at the time, in the summer of 1987, and could not be reached.

The changes that Wintour brought to *House & Garden* were a great deal more drastic than anything she had done at British *Vogue*, and the fallout was infinitely more spectacular. In her first week on the job, she reportedly threw out $2 million worth of contracted articles and photographs ("She destroyed *House & Garden* in two days," snarled one infuriated editor, who had also been jettisoned). She truncated the magazine's title to *HG*, brought in her own art director to redesign the format, and broke with the tradition of showing beautiful rooms in empty houses by presenting beautiful rooms with people in them—preferably beautiful young people. Her most radical (and controversial) change, however, was to introduce fashion coverage into a magazine that was supposedly about houses and gardens. The cover of the first issue for which she was wholly responsible (March 1988) featured a garden scene in which the garden was upstaged by a fashion model in a $2,300 cotton frock by Karl Lagerfeld, and designer clothes were so prominent in subsequent issues that wags began referring to the magazine as "House and Garment." Wintour, whose interest in home furnishings was minimal at best, had boldly conceived her mandate as an attempt to focus on style as a way of life. She built entire issues around a central theme: the "Gauguin" number, which coincided with a Gauguin retrospective at the National Gallery in Washington, D.C., evoked the spirit of Polynesian escape with thatched villas, thatched chairs, and Azzedine Alaïa's fringed skirts. (It also evoked the wrath of John Richardson, the art historian and *House & Garden* contributor, who deplored the use of great art to promote commercial design.) Newhouse and Liberman went along with Wintour's brash concept, although Newhouse was the more enthusiastic of the two. "I saw every layout," Alex said. "Anna wanted my approval. I personally questioned the introduction of fashion, but she was so innovative and daring about it, and Si loved what she was doing. We were both stimulated and excited by the idea of a total magazine of style."

The new *HG* excited a lot of people, but it also alienated subscribers and advertisers in record numbers. Condé Nast had to set up a special 800 number to handle the volume of complaints and canceled subscriptions. How long Newhouse would have continued to go along with Wintour's concept, if other problems had not become more pressing, is an open question. Since the Newhouse brothers' combined holdings provided them with assets that were estimated then at more than $12 billion, they could well afford to lose money on interesting ventures; Si, in fact, had recently bought *The New Yorker*, which had fallen on financial hard times after more than half a century as the nation's most admired magazine, and he seemed to be willing to keep it running indefinitely. Newhouse, however, had become seriously concerned about *Vogue*, the flagship of the Condé Nast empire. In spite of Alex's having redesigned *Vogue*'s editorial pages in 1988, both Newhouse and Liberman thought it was time for a major shakeup and reorientation of the magazine, but they had not yet found a means of conveying this message to Grace Mirabella.

By all the accepted indicators, *Vogue* was doing splendidly. Circulation had climbed from 400,000 in 1971, Mirabella's first year as editor,

HOUSE & GARDEN
MARCH 1988 $4.00

HG

**DECORATIVE BETTE MIDLER
THE MODERN ROTHSCHILDS
HOCKNEY AT HOME**

romance!

Anna Wintour's first *House & Garden* cover:
too much style for the home crowd.

to 1,245,000 in 1987, and ad revenues had hit a record $79.5 million. *Harper's Bazaar*, with a 1987 circulation of 700,000 and revenues totaling $32.5 million, was not even in contention anymore. The circulation of *Vogue* dropped slightly in 1987, though, and it was down again for the first six months of 1988. The fashion industry, moreover, had been watching with interest the swift advance of *Elle*, whose American edition had already surpassed the circulation and ad figures of *Harper's Bazaar*. *Elle* had suddenly become a "hot book," with its brightly colored layouts, youthful, sexy fashions, and minimum reliance on written text. "I'm not sure *Elle* took many readers from *Vogue*," Alex said, "but its success certainly impressed us. There was no feature content—just bright colors, page after page of flash. It made *Vogue*'s earnestness and nobility, its respect for art and for women's intelligence, look a bit quaint."

Vogue, moreover, had a weight problem. "We were overstaffed," according to Alex. "It was partly my fault, because I could never fire anybody. I'm often accused of hiring two people for the same job and letting them compete for it. I certainly have done that, but very often they both stay, and so the organization just grows and grows. I simply cannot fire, which I suppose is cowardly of me. Si does the firing."

Alex also seemed to be unable to warn Mirabella that major changes were needed. He tried several times, but he did so in "words I didn't quite understand," as Mirabella tactfully put it a few years later. What made the situation especially painful for Alex was that he and Grace were genuinely fond of each other and that the *Vogue* which now needed shaking up was so much their joint creation. "In the early years with Grace," he remembered, "it was like a young adventure. We'd play hookey sometimes and have long lunches at The Four Seasons or at Chateaubriand. I liked Grace's mind. She was very sensitive to a sort of modernity in the American woman, to a no-frills attractiveness that I also admired. Vreeland had been much more involved with European culture, whereas Grace was completely American. She was one of the first to appreciate Halston. For a while, Grace would be the only woman wearing pants at an evening party. Tatiana was shocked, but I loved it. Her interests were all in the working woman and in the whole feminist gain of strength in those years."

Grace Mirabella had asked Alex to be a witness at her wedding, in 1974, to the prominent cancer surgeon William A. Cahan. She felt that she could talk to Alex about anything and that he would always listen. Toward the end, though, she had the feeling that he listened less and less. "I thought that *Elle* should not be the definer of what we did at *Vogue*," she said. "I thought we should be finding and redefining what we were doing and moving in a different direction." She was unable to do that, she said, "because Alex wouldn't let me." According to Alex, Grace had told him several times that she was tired of editing *Vogue*—had even asked him once about the possibility of her leaving *Vogue* to edit *Self*. Mirabella was not worried, though, about the persistent rumor that she was about to be replaced as editor in chief by Anna Wintour. Both Alex and Si Newhouse had flatly denied it, and she believed them.

A little after five o'clock on the afternoon of June 28, 1988, Dr. William Cahan was watching the television news in his Upper East Side apartment when a friend telephoned and said that Liz Smith was talking about his wife on Channel 4. Cahan switched channels in time to catch the gossip columnist's announcement that Anna Wintour would be taking over as editor in chief of *Vogue* on August 1. Cahan immediately called his wife, who was still at the office. She went straight to Alex's office and confronted him. According to Alex, "she said, 'Bill has just called. Is this true?' I couldn't lie to her. I said, 'Yes, I'm afraid it's true.' "

The decision had actually been made more than a month earlier, at a meeting in Alex's office. Newhouse, Alex, and Bernard Leser (recently promoted from the London office to the presidency of Condé Nast) had agreed to rededicate *HG* to houses and gardens, and to give Anna Wintour the job she had always wanted at *Vogue*. In spite of their denials before and after the fact, this had been the plan right along; the only uncertainty had involved its timing. Alex kept trying to put it off. Newhouse, however, had a specific reason for wanting to go ahead. "If Alex had been forty-two," he said afterward, "it could have waited. But we definitely saw the need to develop a *Vogue* that was appropriate for the changing tastes and interests and life styles of our readers, and it was very important that the new editor come on board while Alex was around to be part of the transition."

Alex was not fading out of the picture—far from it. He had had a serious scare the year before—prostate cancer, which went into remission after daily radiation treatments over several months—but nobody at the office even knew about that. Alex was working harder than ever, going back and forth to the offices of the new magazines that required his advice and attention several times a day. One of the reasons Newhouse thought *Vogue* needed a new editor in chief was that Alex, who had held that responsibility without the title for seventeen years, now had less time to give to it. Grace Mirabella seemed to depend on him more and more, even asking him to sit in on fashion and beauty meetings, but it was not Alex who wanted her replaced. "Frankly," he said later, "I couldn't face the replacement of Grace. Newhouse wanted the change. I didn't push for Anna Wintour. She was a demand of Si's."

At the meeting in Alex's office, the three men agreed that the changeover would take place at the end of the summer. Newhouse and Leser were all for doing it right away (Leser was afraid the news would get out), but Alex had argued for more time. Tormented by sadness at the thought of losing Grace—and also by his own ambivalent feelings over losing control of *Vogue*—he kept hoping that some other solution might turn up.

Anna Wintour was informed of the decision and told to start thinking about successors for her job at *HG*. "There were endless meetings with Si and Alex," she recalled, "at which we talked mostly about dates and timing, because Alex was so undecided. Sometimes it was going to be September, and sometimes the following January. The whole thing was unfair to Grace, who had not been told, and unfair to me, because I had to come back from the meetings and try to do a magazine that I knew I wasn't going to be at for very long, and lie to all my people. It was awful, really awful."

Nobody ever found out who leaked the news to Liz Smith, but things got a good deal more awful after that. In the avalanche of news stories on the firing of Grace Mirabella, Newhouse, already the recipient of widespread criticism for his recent summary dismissals of Lou Gropp of *House & Garden* and William Shawn, the legendary editor of *The New Yorker*, was often presented as a sort of troglodyte who enjoyed humbling his top talent. When Anna Wintour took over at *Vogue* in August, she was immediately hit with another Liz Smith exclusive, this one linking her romantically with Si Newhouse. The rumor, which surfaced in Smith's *Daily News* column, stayed afloat for more than a month, fueled by the sort of apocryphal firsthand knowledge that some New Yorkers can always produce for any occasion, and not exactly put to rest by Newhouse's "genial" comment, to Liz Smith herself, that he was enormously flattered by the rumor but "very much in love with my wife and my wife's dog." There was no truth to the tale, as Newhouse said, but it put a severe strain on Wintour's marriage nevertheless and gave her and David Shaffer a miserable summer.

Alex Liberman, safely removed to his house in Connecticut for the summer, drew relatively little criticism for his part in the debacle, mainly because Grace Mirabella had nothing really bad to say about him or anyone else. (She had received, in what was already becoming a Newhouse tradition, an extremely generous financial settlement from Condé Nast.) Confining herself to a mild comment or two about a classy organization behaving in an unclassy way, she kept her dignity and her sense of humor, and emerged from the affair with the editorship of a brand-new magazine of her own, created for her and financed by the Australian press lord Rupert Murdoch. Edited for the audience of mature and intelligent women that she had wanted *Vogue* to address in new ways, *Mirabella*, as the new magazine was called, soon found its niche as a modestly successful monthly that would never pose a serious threat to Anna Wintour's *Vogue*.

Alex, photographed by Irving Penn, 1977.

Art vs. Life

Anna Wintour had brought several of her top people over from *HG*, and one of her first priorities was to weed out the overgrown *Vogue* staff. Within six weeks, thirty people had resigned or been fired. Richard Avedon, who had been doing *Vogue* covers since 1965, discovered that he was not going to do any more of them. Wintour announced her arrival with an outdoor cover, shot by the photographer Peter Lindbergh, of a long-haired model wearing blue jeans below and a $10,000 jewel-encrusted jacket by Christian Lacroix above, with a generous slice of bare belly in between. The new *Vogue*, like so many new *Vogue*s in the past, was against artifice and for its own particular brand of naturalness—in this case, for youthful informality and sexy iconoclasm. "I wanted the covers to show gorgeous real girls looking the way they looked out on the street," Wintour said, "rather than the plastic kind of retouched look that had been the *Vogue* face for such a long time. I wanted to bring in new photographers and just liven the whole thing up a bit."

The first three months of livening up were rough on everybody, including Alex. Although it was widely rumored that Anna Wintour (like Ruth Whitney at *Glamour*) had exacted a promise from Newhouse that Alex would no longer have anything to do with *Vogue*, she has said that this was "rubbish"—that she very much wanted him involved. Newhouse did tell Alex, however, that Wintour should have "total control" of the magazine, including the features, and for a time, until Newhouse spoke to Anna about it, Alex felt excluded. "I guess I was trying too hard to prove that I was not going to be like Grace Mirabella," Wintour conceded later. "I kept him involved, but probably I forgot how much he had been involved before. We'd had a couple of funny lunches early on, where he kept saying, 'What will it be like?' and 'How will we get along?' I was probably too pushy, and all the people who had been with me at *HG* were used to reporting to me. But Alex and I talked about it, and gradually things got worked out."

Alex let go, but Anna kept him involved—that was the compromise they arrived at. Letting go of *Vogue* was more difficult than he had anticipated, but after a while he came to like what Anna was doing with the magazine. She made a point of showing him layouts and asking his advice, and in some ways it was a great relief not to be in charge there anymore. Anna Wintour reminded him at times of Diana Vreeland when she had first come to *Vogue*. In some ways she seemed even more daring than Vreeland. "Vreeland's was artificial daring," he said. "It was all based on flamboyance, on accessories, on gesture. Anna's is closer to pure femininity; her great genius is feminine seduction. Maybe this is what it takes to make *Vogue* exciting—a Vreeland, a Wintour. I may have made *Vogue* handsome, noble, or interesting, but I don't think I made its fashion pages exciting."

The other magazines kept him busy enough. He spent a lot of time helping Harry Evans develop *Condé Nast Traveler*, a new travel magazine whose first issue appeared in September 1987. Harry Evans was married to Tina Brown. When they met, in the early 1980s, Evans had been the editor of *The Sunday Times* in London and one of England's most influential journalists. A run-in with Rupert Murdoch, the paper's autocratic owner, had ended his career there, and he had done a number of other things before coming to Condé Nast. He had been the director of a film and television company in London; he had written a best-selling memoir called *Good Times, Bad Times*; and then, after moving to New York, he had served for two years as the editor of *U.S. News and World Report*. Through Tina he had also become a great admirer of Alex Liberman. Evans tried to get Weidenfeld and Nicolson, the British book publishers, with whom he was associated for a while, to republish *The Artist in His Studio*. Alex was flattered, but he felt he should let the Newhouse-owned firm of Random House publish it, which they did in 1988. When Evans came to Condé

Nast in 1986, he made sure that Alex was closely involved in planning *Condé Nast Traveler.* Their aim was to make it better written, better designed, and also more truthful than the other two magazines in the field (*Travel & Leisure* and *European Travel & Life*), in that it would report objectively, and at times critically, on the resorts and services it chose to feature. The magazine was an immediate success.

Alex also oversaw the reconversion of *HG*, whose new editor, Nancy Novogrod, had spent most of her pre–Condé Nast career in book publishing. The magazine kept its abbreviated title but jettisoned fashion coverage and most of Anna Wintour's other innovations, and Novogrod gradually built circulation and coaxed back some of the outraged advertisers who had left when Wintour took over.* Alex kept his eye on the layouts and the covers and the editorial features in *HG, Self, Vanity Fair, Gourmet,* and *Mademoiselle,* as well as *Vogue.* (*Bride's* required little attention, since the editorial content changed so little from issue to issue.) He discussed the problems of each magazine with Si Newhouse every day, often more than once a day; he saw the figures on circulation, newsstand sales, and advertising revenues; he kept a sharp eye out for new photographers and continued to work closely with veterans such as Irving Penn (who still expected Alex to provide him with sketches for visual ideas); and although he turned seventy-five in 1987—and had a number of medical problems— the idea of his retiring never came up. Alex needed Condé Nast as much as Condé Nast needed him. He needed the bustle and excitement of the office, where he made his thousand daily decisions in the company of attractive women who admired and quite often adored him. And the great thing was that on the weekends, far from feeling drained or exhausted, he could lose himself in what he thought of as his real work.

Ever since his 1977 show at the Storm King Art Center in upstate New York, people had come to think of Alex more as a sculptor than a painter. His huge red sculptures had dominated the rolling green hillsides at Storm King—there had been room to hang only a small selection of his paintings in the indoor gallery—and reviews of the show had referred mainly to the giant pieces such as *Adonai,* which was thirty-five feet high and seventy-five feet long. John Russell, the *New York Times* art critic (and a frequent *Vogue* contributor), caught the erotic overtones in these works, the thrust and penetration of monumental forms shaped from old boilers

---

* The recovery was too sluggish for Newhouse. He closed the ninety-two-year-old magazine for good in 1993, the year he bought out its more lucrative rival, *Architectural Digest.*

and gas storage tanks, by describing them as "phallic artillery"; *Iliad*, he wrote, "looks as if whole sections were about to leave for a scheduled destination two million miles away." Alex's old friend Tom Hess, writing about the show in *New York* magazine, saw "the drama of a breakthrough" and suggested that Liberman had been underrated all these years by the New York art world because "he's done too many things too well."

The New York art world continued to give short shrift to Alex's paintings, which he showed nearly every year at the André Emmerich Gallery, but throughout the late 1970s and the 1980s his sculptures were impossible to ignore. They appeared in city after city—in public parks and in front of office buildings, on college campuses, and in the middle of vast shopping malls. More than forty commissioned sculptures in those years made him the most prolific public artist of his time and kept Bill Layman and his sons working six or seven days a week. The yard in back of Layman's truck garage had become a fantastic junkyard, with dozens of huge gas tanks and discarded sections of metal lying around and spilling over into the scrubby woods beyond. Alex was spending $30,000 a month just to keep his sculpture operation going, and the commissions, for fees as high as $350,000, never quite equaled the costs. "I don't think I like my sculpture," he decided at one point. "I'm sort of condemned to do it, because it pays for the studio and the assistants, but I just don't have the same passion for sculpture that I have for painting. It's too limited, in color and in shape —I don't really control the shapes. And people always want a repeat. Most of the commissions come because somebody has seen something of mine and says, 'I want one like the thing you did in Dallas, or Cleveland, or St. Louis.' "

In the early 1960s he had modeled a few small clay sculptures that he then had cast in bronze, which he thought of as the "noblest" sculptural medium. Working in bronze was too expensive then, even for Alex, but in 1973 Cleve Gray introduced him to an old man in Torrington, Connecticut, who made aluminum waffle irons by the ancient method of sand casting, and Cleve and Alex persuaded him to adapt this relatively inexpensive technique to bronze sculptures. Alex brought him sections of industrial I-beams and other metal fragments, and had him cast them in bronze. He liked the rough texture that was the result of granules of sand fusing with the molten metal. The sculptures that he constructed from these bronze elements, which he welded together and polished himself, were different from his other works in three dimensions. The *Sacred Precinct* series suggested primitive shrines or temples; some of the large cast bronzes—ten-foot-high assemblages of industrial forms—had a concentrated power that

From the most prolific public sculptor of his day: *To*, 1973, 30' x 36' x 30',
one of the huge steel sculptures that art critic John Russell described as
"phallic artillery."

Argo, 1973–74, 15' x 31' x 36'.

Aria, 1979–90, 42' x 43' x 33'.

Olympic Iliad, 1983–84, 45' x 62' x 70'.

Abracadabra, 1981–92, 27' x 39' x 18'.

he had never tapped before, either in painting or sculpture. "I think I could have done something quite interesting there," Alex said nearly three decades later. "But it takes a different sort of life. To do that kind of work, you have to spend days and days in a foundry, watching over the casting process. I never had the time."

His weekend grapplings with discarded boilers and gas tanks and cold rolled steel were more spontaneous, and they led to bigger and bigger sculptures. Some of them ascended to heights of fifty feet or more. The colossal scale of these works amazed people who knew Alex only socially or through his work at Condé Nast. Where, they wondered, was the huge ego necessary to produce such megaworks? Alex himself was at a loss to explain it. "One of the excitements of America," he once said, "is the possibility of scale. Somehow I feel that without scale, something is missing, even in great art. I have a horror of the appreciation of small pleasures— what the French call *jouissance*. I think the Abstract Expressionists were right to go for large scale in their striving for the sublime, and this is why I adored Cézanne, who did a painting so big he had to break through the wall of his studio to get it out."

David Smith had told Alex that the future of sculpture was in large scale, but few people could have predicted that Alex would come to work on a larger scale than almost any of his contemporaries. (Michael Heizer, Robert Smithson, and some of the other earth artists, who used the living landscape as raw material, were the only people who worked bigger.) Alex, moreover, had nothing but scorn for the whole notion of "site-specific" sculpture, which had become the operational term for many American artists working in the public area. To provide an object that was designed with reference to the contours and particularities of a specific place struck him as reducing art to functional ends, and he wanted no part of that. "My involvement is with the heroic," he said, "and with the search for art beyond limits." He was immensely pleased when Countess Marian Dönhoff, the owner and publisher of *Die Zeit*, a vastly respected woman who was related to one of the German army officers hanged after their unsuccessful attempt to assassinate Hitler in 1944, came to him and asked to buy one of his sculptures, to use as a memorial to the plotters. He refused to accept money for the work, which was installed in a private ceremony in 1986 on a site near Hamburg.

His public sculptures provided their own context. For years he had tried to build into them, in addition to the erotic drama, a sense of elevation that was spiritual as well as physical. He hoped to make the spectator feel the same kind of exaltation that worshipers had always felt in cathedrals and in mosques, with their soaring towers and minarets, and it is true that some of his biggest sculptures have a buoyant quality that belies their tremendous mass and weight. (He even made some that were to be suspended by cables.) In their gravity-defying look of ascension they are about as far removed as possible from the monolithic steel slabs and tilted arcs of Richard Serra, the period's most admired (and most reviled) site-specific sculptor. *The Way*, the largest Liberman of all—one hundred feet long by fifty feet wide by fifty feet high—actually has a kind of elephantine playfulness about it, a lighthearted counterpoint in the diagonal thrust of its huge steel cylinders; although Alex had no specific site in mind when he was working on it, the piece seems entirely appropriate to its eventual setting in leafy Laumeier Park in St. Louis, where it was dedicated, with great fanfare and considerable public approval, in the spring of 1980.

Working on sculpture, directing a heavy-duty crane as its operator raised a piece of cut steel forty feet in the air and maneuvered it into different positions in relation to the other forms in a four-story-high abstract structure, Alex Liberman looked to be a man in his element—poised, confident, brimming with controlled energy. He looked that way, at any rate, in *A Lifetime Burning*, the documentary film that was made about his work, which had its premiere at the Guggenheim Museum in 1981. In the film, he spoke eloquently about his theory of "educated chance . . . the slow ripening from right to wrong to right again," and about the lofty spiritual dimensions of his work. Monumental sculpture is also a declaration of power—the larger the scale, the louder the declaration. Henry Kissinger, who became a friend of Alex's and Tatiana's in the 1980s, used to take people to the sculpture field behind the Laymans' garage and say, with the conviction of a connoisseur, "Now, that's power." Working on such a giant scale may have helped Alex to compensate for a lifetime of compromises and deferred confrontations, but it also seems to have left him feeling vaguely uneasy and dissatisfied. Although he went about making sculpture with vast confidence—relying neither on drawings nor on small-scale maquettes but rather on the chancy process of trial-and-error to reach his decisions about placement, scale, and structure—when talking about his sculpture in private he sometimes sounded self-critical and unsure.

"Seeing that blinding flash of the welder's torch for the first time—that was when my sculpture passion started," he said once. "But it's turned into something much too slick. I loved the early sculptures I did with a torch, with rough, found metals—there was something elemental and very meaningful to me there. But I feel that much of this so-called monumental sculpture is just playing with forms. I'm not even sure it should be called sculpture. What do you call something that your hand hasn't touched, or chiseled, or molded? I sometimes think artists are remnants of a different civilization and that people like me are dreamers—or maybe actors. We act out our impulses and try to materialize them. I find sculpture easy. There's nothing revolutionary about my sculpture. It's big, and people like to be impressed, to be awed. Sometimes I think I missed the boat on sculpture. But, you know, you know, I'd sacrifice my life with joy for a great painting."

He never did, of course. He never could have given up his life at Condé Nast. Cleve Gray, whose whole life was devoted to painting, could not understand why Alex didn't leave Condé Nast and paint all the time. "Over and over, I've said, 'Alex, for God's sake, why can't you retire, or maybe just go in to the office once every few weeks?' He had a financial settlement and a guarantee that would have made that possible, and painting was clearly the joy of his life. I'm sure he sensed that he could do more profound work if that was all he did. He would say, 'Well, I can't. There's Tatiana, there's this, there's that . . .' But it must have been something else. I guess he just had a deep emotional need for Condé Nast."

The paintings that he did in the 1980s had a wild, extravagant vitality. The jagged scribbling that began with his experiments in the Rossis' print studio in Rome had become an integral element in most of them. He would draw in wet acrylic paint with a palette knife or a charcoal crayon, pushing the crayon so hard that it shattered into fragments, which became part of the painting. The triangle motif had disappeared entirely. A series of paintings begun in 1983 evoked the rectangular "gate" theme that preoccupied him in his monumental sculptures (he called them the *Vrata* paintings, using an archaic Russian word for gate), but gradually he abandoned any sort of structuring device and tried to let his hand break free of conscious control. Chance, he had come to think, was the key to everything. "Chance disconnects the will from creation. I think the will is the enemy of creation. The will is necessary as an urge to create, to get you going, but then you have to float, to disconnect, to reach a state of something like unconsciousness. I think the act of painting is very close to the act of gambling."

Now and then a critic had something good to say about his paintings, but more often his shows at Emmerich were not even reviewed. This, however, was preferable to the periodic hostility of Hilton Kramer, who wrote in 1978 that Liberman's new paintings were "gruesomely akin to icing whipped up in a pastry shop" and referred to Alex six years later as "a third-rate modernist pasticheur." There was no question that the Libermans' social prominence worked against Alex's painting career. Robert

Hughes, the *Time* art critic, told Alex that he had gone into the Time-Life library and removed from the Liberman file everything that had to do with Alex and Tatiana's social life. Hughes thought Alex's big sculptures were his most important works. "Some of those big welded-steel pieces are of real importance in recent American sculpture," he said. Hughes had become a friend of the Libermans' through Barbara Rose; he and Barbara used to visit them in Connecticut in the mid-1970s, when Barbara was writing her monograph on Alex.

Since Barney Newman's death in 1970, Alex had felt increasingly cut off from the art world. Tom Hess, the editor and critic who became the leading champion of the first-generation Abstract Expressionists, took Newman's place for several years as Alex's closest friend and confidant, but Hess died in 1978, cut down by a heart attack six months after he was named curator of twentieth-century art at the Metropolitan Museum. Except for his son-in-law, Cleve Gray, Alex had no artist friends. He and Cleve had a complicated relationship. Not far apart in age (Cleve was only six years younger), they were very different in temperament, as well as in their attitudes toward art. "Art, to me, is a vehicle for contemplation," Cleve said once. "Alex always tells me that's old-fashioned, a lot of baloney, no one's going to pay any attention to that subtle stuff. But then, a week later, he'll visit my studio and talk about the spiritual subtleties in my work."

Cleve had helped Alex to get started in sculpture—had given him $5,000 and a barn to work in and found Bill Layman to be his assistant. Sometimes he felt that the relationship was a little one-sided. Not once in thirty-five years had there been an article about Cleve's work in any of the Condé Nast magazines—something that could hardly be said about Alex, whose paintings and sculptures had been featured in *Vogue* more than once, and whose house in Connecticut had been featured on the cover of *House & Garden* in 1970, with one of his new triangle paintings prominently displayed over the fireplace. Alex has always maintained, rather indignantly, that he never initiated such features, but Condé Nast editors may have reasoned that it would do them no harm to take the initiative themselves. On the other hand, Cleve welcomed Alex's infrequent visits to his painting studio. "He will look at a picture that's giving me a certain amount of trouble and he'll say, 'Look, Cleve, it's a lovely painting. People will like it. But it's not good enough for you. Get mad at it, the way you can.' Then he'll say, 'I have spoken,' and walk out. I could murder him when he says, 'I have spoken.' God, how I hate that remark. But I'll go back and sit in my chair, and I'll get mad first at Alex and then, inevitably, at the picture. And, of course, that's when very good things happen—either you destroy the painting or you make it into something worthwhile. And so that kind of criticism is very, very helpful." Cleve also visited Alex's studio and sometimes offered critiques, but "I'm much more careful with him than he is with me," he said, "because I think he's much more easily wounded."

One of the few artists Tatiana had ever liked was Helen Frankenthaler, but they saw her less often after her breakup with Robert Motherwell. In her later years, Tatiana's favorite artist was Andy Warhol. The white-haired impresario of Pop Art showed up regularly at their cocktail parties, and for several years he came around to deliver a personal Russian Easter gift—one of the small paintings he reserved for special friends. (This was a habit left over from Warhol's years as a commercial artist, when he would give handmade Christmas reminders to art directors and others who might be in the market for his work.) Alex himself detested Pop Art—"an art for primitive appetites that have grown up on the comics"—but he rather liked the little abstract "shadow painting" that Warhol gave Tatiana one year, and it pleased him that Warhol was so obviously captivated by Tatiana. During the 1970s, when Warhol was doing his portraits of society people and celebrities, Tatiana yearned to have him do one of Alex—it would have been the sort of badge of success that she valued so highly—but they couldn't afford the fee, and Andy didn't volunteer his services.

Barbara Rose's book on Alex came out in 1981, in a lavishly illus-trated, large-format edition published by Harry Abrams. It helped to solidify his reputation, but the spare-no-expense publication and the fact that its author was the *Vogue* art critic* also tended to give ammunition to those who questioned his credentials as a serious artist. It was the same old dilemma. When he published essays by influential critics in *Vogue*, some people would always say he was bringing pressure on them to write favorably about his own work, although, in fact, it often had the opposite effect. Neither Clement Greenberg nor Harold Rosenberg ever wrote about Alex; Rosenberg once mentioned him along with several other artists in a *New Yorker* article and then offended Alex no end by saying, when they next met, "Did you see that I mentioned you?"

It seemed quite clear that nothing Alex did at Condé Nast was

---

* One of this book's authors writes for *Vogue* and has also written for *House & Garden*. The Empire never sleeps, but its guardians are not as censorious (she hopes) as one might think.

ever going to help his career in art, but this did not prevent Condé Nast editors from trying to feature his art, his photographs, and his living arrangements in their pages. Allene Talmey at *Vogue* had done it first, in 1960, when she ran a photograph of his circle painting *White Dominant* in the "People Are Talking About" section. *Vogue* had carried other photos of his paintings and sculptures over the years, and both *Vogue* and *House & Garden* had featured his houses (the country house in *House & Garden*, the town house in *Vogue*), and when the new edition of *The Artist in His Studio* came out in 1988, *Vanity Fair* devoted twenty-four pages to the event, while *HG* weighed in with an eight-page report by Rosamond Bernier. Bernier's article was a last-minute substitution for an interview with Alex by his old (and apparently former) friend Tony Snowdon, who completely ignored *The Artist in His Studio* and asked such loaded and far-from-friendly questions as why was Alex's byline always in bigger type than any other photographer's in *Vogue*, and wasn't Barbara Rose's monograph the biggest art book ever published? In the twilight of his long and illustrious career, Alex was not going to be subjected to that sort of thing; he had the Snowdon piece quashed.

The odor of sanctity that surrounded Alex at Condé Nast, however, could not make up for the art world's having turned its back on him. The unwritten consensus that decides which living artists are important, significant, or "major" had decided years earlier not just to consign Alexander Liberman to a lesser rank but to ignore him altogether. That consensus did not necessarily coincide with the judgment of art history. Hans Hofmann, an artist whose career suffered for years because he was thought of primarily as a teacher, is now enshrined in the pantheon of Abstract Expressionism. Barnett Newman ascended to those heights only toward the end of his life, when a younger generation of artists looked at his work with fresh eyes. The worldly success that has been such an obstacle to Alex Liberman's reputation may not seem so to future art historians, and his paintings may look quite different as a result. But it is hard not to wonder whether the mercurial quickness and lightness and versatility that served him so well in his career at Condé Nast, the refusal to hold on to things or to take fixed positions, might not have kept him, after all, from attaining his deepest aspirations in art. "Go deeper!" Alexandre Iacovleff had said to him in Paris, when twelve-year-old Alex showed the artist his drawings, but Alex had never really been willing to do that. His essential commitment—a very deep one, paradoxically—was to the complex and ever-changing surface of life. "Alex had and has enormous talent," William Rubin, the Museum of Modern Art's former director of painting and sculpture, once said. "But talent is a funny thing. It can be worked against by genius, and that produces something great, or it can be skated on, and that produces something that is very impressive but not necessarily great."

Two other obstacles exist in Alex's case. One is the fact that there has been no unique, "signature" Liberman style in painting—no combination of image and facture that sets his work apart from the work of all other artists. In this century, Picasso is the only visual artist who has been able to change his style at will and get away with it—and a Picasso in any style is always instantly recognizable as a Picasso.

The other obstacle lies within the mind of Alex Liberman. The doubt that every artist wrestles with at certain moments has rarely been absent from his mind. "I have constant doubt about my talent," he said one day. "I don't ever, ever get free of it, and maybe that's why I create so much—to find out who I am and what I am. I'm always being surprised. Did I do this? Is this really me? I'm very sensitive to all criticism, because I find all criticism probably true. And I sometimes wonder, was I programmed to be an artist? Am I just trying to fulfill a preplanned function? Maybe a real artist is more self-destructive. Maybe I didn't have the angry, absolute faith, the ruthlessness to be a great artist. Great art is a toxic poison, and my physical nature couldn't take it. I am very insecure, and I have to live with that doubt."

A pervasive sense of doubt lay at the core of his personality, affecting him in many different ways. It ruled out arrogance and self-importance, for example, inducing him to gain his ends by seduction and compromise rather than confrontation. It made him the ideal *éminence grise*, the confidant to powerful men, over whom he exerted a subtly controlling influence. Doubt underlay his lack of rigidity, and doubt caused him to suspect that his sculpture, hugely ambitious though it might be, was no more than a playing with forms. The deep, ingrown doubt of the refugee, of one who constantly felt that his life and his world might be overturned at any moment, had been refined over many years into an instrument of rare sensitivity—had become so much a part of him that it struck others as charm, elegance, a sort of Old World civility, which never failed to impress. Although in his case doubt did not lead to introspection, it had become his form of self-knowledge.

Doubt also lay at the heart of his marriage. This enduring marriage that seemed so unbelievably romantic to so many people was based on the willing submission of one soul to another. ("Somehow, since childhood," he once said, "I've been interested in the experience of subjugation.") Alex put Tatiana and Tatiana's needs and Tatiana's happiness ahead of everything else in his life. The shock of seeing how the great artists of the School of Paris treated their wives had finally discouraged any thoughts he himself might have had of becoming an artist full-time. Living well, indulging oneself with the luxuries of a refined and civilized taste was important to Alex, but it was absolutely essential to his conception of how Tatiana should be treated, and he devoted himself to this goal with the zeal and passion that might otherwise have gone into his painting. He did so because, in the end, he never quite believed that he could succeed in pleasing her. She kept him in a state of perpetual, but by no means unhappy, anxiety—a state of balance that lasted throughout their entire life together.

Soon after Alex started making sculpture, he placed three large welded-metal pieces on the upper level of the driveway leading down to their house in Connecticut. They were painted black, as were nearly all his early sculptures. Tatiana, who hated black, insisted that he repaint them red. He did it, of course. "Sure," he said. "Why not? I've always felt that life comes ahead of art. I think art has to survive somehow with this attitude and be as good as it can be. Tatiana's happiness comes first—because it made my happiness, and made my life possible. The anchor of my art is in the emotional peace—the erotic peace, if there is such a thing—that a life in common has given me. Everything is made possible by this extraordinary relationship."

Alex and Tatiana in the field outside their Connecticut house.

Tatiana

Old age claimed her quite suddenly, one spring morning in 1981. She doubled over as she was getting up and screamed with pain. Dr. Isadore Rosenfeld, the doctor who had treated both Alex and Tatiana for years, came over at once. He suspected a recurrence of heart trouble—Tatiana had been hospitalized five years earlier for atrial fibrillation—but a cardiogram showed nothing amiss, and the pains stopped. Tatiana and Alex went off to Europe for the summer, as usual (they took the Concorde: their first transatlantic flight, after sixty-five crossings by boat), but in Ischia the chest pains started again, and when they got back to New York more tests showed a gallstone lodged in the pancreatic duct, requiring an emergency operation. Tatiana was in such pain afterward that she was allowed rather large doses of Demerol, which continued after she came home from the hospital.

Alex gave her an injection every morning. Usually that would keep her comfortable until four o'clock, when Melinda Pechangco, the nurse who had taken care of her in the hospital, came in to administer the next shot. Melinda had been assigned to Tatiana in the hospital after eleven other trained nurses had been put to rout by her gruff and stubborn refusal to do anything they said. Simply by showing that she could not be cowed, Melinda had charmed the Russian dragon into being reasonably cooperative. Now she had become part of the Liberman household—an increasingly important presence there. She tried her best to limit the Demerol, but that was already a lost cause. Sometimes Tatiana called Alex at the office, and he had to hurry back to give her an extra injection. He gave her one at eight o'clock every evening, before they went out, and a final one at midnight.

Alex and Tatiana never went back to Europe after that summer. Alex had a swimming pool put in behind their house in Connecticut, filled with heated salt water to make it as much like Ischia as possible—Tatiana had always loved the thermal baths there. He asked her what temperature she wanted the water to be, and she said ninety-two degrees, so it was kept permanently at ninety-two, waiting for the moment when Tatiana might decide to go in—a moment that never arrived. The unused pool cost a small fortune to heat, but that meant nothing to Alex, whose Russian soul doted on waste and extravagance. Both their houses had central air conditioning, which remained in use all winter because Tatiana liked a cool bedroom (they kept it at sixty-five degrees) but disliked open windows. She also insisted on keeping the lights in the house turned on at all hours, day and night. More and more as they grew older, every wish or desire of Tatiana's became a challenge that Alex felt he had to fulfill.

Their garden in Connecticut was subject to sudden and drastic alterations. Alex had elected to have a rose garden on one side of the house and an informal "English garden" of assorted perennials on the other. Each spring he ordered two hundred new rosebushes from the Rosedale nurseries in Westchester, to insure a generous display of Tatiana's favorite flower. The English garden was his idea, and it gave him no end of trouble. "I had the top man from the Rosedale nurseries come and plant it," he said, "and I thought it turned out superbly. But then one day, Tatiana walks through it and says, 'There's too much yellow,' and, a little further on, 'I hate things that stick up.' The man had planted three or four big groups of delphinium sticking up in a mass of yellow daisies and other things. So the next spring, I have the whole double border pulled out, because my wife doesn't like yellow and doesn't like flowers that stick up. Then I ask Howard Mastroberti, who works for me in Connecticut, to go and see the manager and director of White Flower Farm and have him draw up a plan for a real English garden.* The manager draws up a plan, and Howard

---

* Why didn't he go to Russell Page, the era's most illustrious garden designer? Because, said Alex, when Russell Page had designed the sculpture garden for Pepsico in Purchase, New York, he had used his influence to keep the corporate client from buying a sculpture by Alexander Liberman.

plants it, just one flower in each little area he designed, one, one, one. If you live for thirty years it would probably grow into a marvelous garden, but we, dying Russians, need immediate results. Potemkin is in our souls. Summer comes, my garden is pathetic. I say to Howard, 'Look at this awful garden. Go and get me bunches of color.' So Howard goes off and brings back bunches of pink, bunches of red, bunches of orange. It's rather vulgar and not at all English, but it's substantial—the American idea of a lush garden. I take Tatiana around it, and she says, '*C'est un jardin de concierge.*' Of course, that demolished me, because in France every concierge has this little backyard patch of bloom.

"What do I do next? There is a lady who wrote a big book on gardening, and I call her in desperation. She comes. Howard is frightfully upset. She pulls out half of what he planted and puts in dainty, tiny little flowers—are they pansies?—that will never grow higher than this. I know nothing about flowers, but I want splendor and fun—immediate splendor. I tell Howard to fix it, and Howard, full of reproach, pulls out her measly little things and puts in some clumps of other things. But I'm at the end of patience. I say to Tatiana, 'Look, let's forget about this garden that has already cost me a fortune. Let's just have grass right to the house.' And she says, 'No, no, no. Keep the garden. I *like* this garden.'"

In New York their social life had slowed down. They still went out to dinner once or twice a week and entertained friends and visiting notables at their infrequent and now rather intimate cocktail parties, but they turned down many invitations, and they went home earlier than they used to. For the first three years after Tatiana's operation, they took a winter vacation in Palm Beach. They stayed at the Breakers and played canasta in their cabana with the Gregorys and other old friends. Alex also lost regularly at backgammon with Charles Amory, a crack player whose ex-wife was married to Iva Patcévitch; they played for high stakes, and Alex, who much preferred to play recklessly and lose than to play carefully and win, dropped anywhere from three to four hundred dollars a day. They made no effort to see the Patcévitches, who were also in Palm Beach. The local society columns noted the Libermans' visit, just as the New York columns continued to report on their parties. In the publicity-mad social circus of the 1980s, though, Alex and Tatiana were a diminishing presence.

The house in Warren, which was now their summer home as well as their weekend place, was becoming more and more like a Russian dacha. The friends who came to visit, the food, and the conversation were all likely to be Russian. This return to their roots was traceable in part to the arrival of Gennady Smakov, the young Russian émigré who came into their lives in 1976. Although he had been born in 1940 and brought up in the Soviet Union, Smakov was like a deeply cultured intellectual of the old order. He spoke eight languages fluently and could read Latin and Greek. In Leningrad he had written a book about the French actor Gérard Philipe. He knew everyone of importance in the fields of Russian literature, music, and ballet; when he met the Libermans he was at work on a biography of Mikhail Baryshnikov. A homosexual, Gennady had managed to get out of the USSR through an arranged, temporary marriage to an American woman, who complicated matters by falling in love with him. Tatiana adored him from the moment they met, at a party at Lydia Gregory's apartment in New York. He knew by heart the works of all her favorite Russian poets. "Genna was like someone from the Russia that she had lost a long time ago, but he was also young and today," according to Ludmila Shtern, an émigré writer who had been a friend of his in Leningrad. "And he absolutely fell in love with Tatiana."

Gennady Smakov soon began spending every weekend at the house in Warren. His skill at cooking traditional Russian dishes consoled them for the death of their great friend Nicolas Nabokov, the composer, who had often done the cooking there in years past. (Mabel Moses, who still worked for the Libermans in New York, did not come to Warren, and Alex and Tatiana always made a point of inviting weekend guests who knew how to cook. Although Alex could make what he called "porridge"—it was actually Quaker oats—and had taught himself to whip up a tunafish mousse in the blender, Tatiana couldn't boil an egg.) From 1980 on, Genna spent the whole summer in Connecticut, too, as one of the family, and the Warren house became a magnet for the Russian artists and intellectuals whose paths he had somehow managed to cross. Baryshnikov came there many times, and Elena Tchernichova, the ballet mistress of American Ballet Theater, and assorted Russian dancers and musicians, and Luda and Victor Shtern, and, of course, Joseph Brodsky, whose 1987 Nobel Prize Tatiana had accurately predicted.

When there were no visitors, Tatiana and Genna would sit together by the hour, reading and reciting Russian poetry. She knew far more of it by heart than he did—she could recite a thousand lines of Akhmatova, Mandelstam, Essenin, Blok, or Pushkin without a pause—and she corrected Genna fiercely if he missed a word or got something wrong. Alex and Genna sometimes rubbed each other the wrong way. They argued continually, and Genna, whose sense of humor disappeared in an argument, would often go into a sulk and not speak to Alex for hours. But there was no jealousy involved. Genna's friendship with Tatiana took some of the pressure off Alex in that department, and allowed him to spend more time in his studio than he might have been able to do otherwise. Alex's studio, according to one of their friends, took the place of a mistress in his life— it was where he went to escape from Tatiana. (Alex furiously denied this: "I never, *ever*, wanted to escape from Tatiana.") He shut himself in and played Wagner tapes on the stereo (Tatiana hated opera); in later years it was rock music, with an extended concentration on Madonna. On weekends he spent the morning in his painting studio, over the garage, and most of the afternoon working on sculpture, and he still managed to be the perfect host to their weekend guests. Marti Stevens, one of Tatiana's favorites, said she had never known anyone who made better use of his time than Alex.

His deepest concern was that he might die before Tatiana. Who would take care of her the way he did? Although his stomach operation in 1961 had cured him of ulcers, Alex could never be accused of enjoying robust health. He had a serious heart condition, he had prostate cancer (in remission), and he was diabetic—the insulin injections he gave himself every day made him more adept at giving Tatiana her Demerol. Tatiana, moreover, was older than people thought. When pressed, she would say that she was two years older than Alex, but the date of birth on her passport was 1906, making her six years older, and she might well have been born before that; she had come out of Russia with no papers except an exit permit. The physical effects of her aging and of the Demerol addiction, the gradual attrition of that magnificent, tall figure, only served to increase his love for her. "I know she's thinking I must love her less because she's old and ugly," he said at the time. "The other day I told her how nice she looked, and she said, 'Don't say that. That really hurts. I know I don't look nice.' But I don't feel pity. I feel sorrow. Sorrow for both of us. I'm watching the end of a life—her life, my life—but the emotional bond between us is just as intense as ever."

She could still be peremptory and outrageous. Her mania for cutting things down fixed at a certain point on a glorious oak tree that was "sticking up" (another detestable vertical!) at the far end of the swimming pool. For once Alex refused to indulge her; the oak was spared. But he "cringed," as he put it, whenever she spoke out at a dinner party, simultaneously fearing and savoring what she might say. They often went to dinner at the Oscar de la Rentas' and the Henry Kissingers', who were among the high-profile newcomers to their part of northwestern Connecticut in the 1980s. Sharon, Kent, Salisbury, and the other picture-perfect towns in that area were attracting wealthy buyers in flight from the social frenzy and over-crowding of the Hamptons; Francine and Cleve Gray rather resented this fashionable intrusion on the quiet literary retreat they had shared for many years with Arthur Miller, Philip Roth, William Styron, and a few others. (The de la Rentas had discovered the area during a weekend at Alex and Tatiana's, and they, in turn, had brought the Kissingers.) Both Oscar de la Renta and Henry Kissinger represented the sort of worldly success that Tatiana admired, and both of them found her irresistible. "I got a huge kick out of Tatiana," said Kissinger, who often was seated next to her at dinner parties. "She was totally herself, and there wasn't a malicious bone in her body." At Kissinger's house one evening, Alex remembered, Victor Gotbaum, the labor arbitrator, had been going on and on about the horrors of life in South Africa, and Tatiana, who had been quiet up until then, broke up the table by announcing her distaste for "café au lait society." On another evening, at the de la Rentas', Gennady Smakov was telling everyone about his plans for a vacation trip to France that summer. When he mentioned going to Chartres, Tatiana said, "*Pas mal, Chartres.*" Oscar de la Renta took her up on this. "Not bad?" he said. "Chartres? The greatest cathedral in the world, with the most beautiful stained-glass windows?" "No, no," Tatiana insisted (in French), "all those awful colors, those are just for the populace. When the kings of France used to go there to be married, you know, they would take those windows out and put in clear glass." (Annette Reed, de la Renta's second wife, told this story one day to John Pope-Hennessy, the English art historian, who astonished her by saying that it was absolutely true.) At another dinner, she set people straight about the literary standing of Fyodor Dostoyevsky. "Dostoyevsky—*journaliste,*" she said with dismissive finality.

"One of the wonders of our life together is that Tatiana is still an unknown to me," Alex liked to boast. Nothing she did or said ever seemed to upset him. Her "atrocious" impatience—which caused her, for example, to begin eating as soon as she was served, whether or not anyone else at the table had food on their plate—caused him no embarrassment. In spite of her long, close friendships with Marlene Dietrich, Hélène Desoffy, Irene Wiley, Lydia Gregory, and one or two others, and her pride in Francine's writing career, Tatiana had little or no respect for women. Their brains, she said, were smaller than men's. (Dietrich believed this, too.) She had nothing but contempt for the feminist movement, which Alex and Grace Mirabella had welcomed and supported at *Vogue,* and she continued throughout her life to be interested only in men who had achieved some form of worldly success. "One doesn't argue with winners," as she often said. It did not even seem to bother Alex that Tatiana never understood or accepted abstract art. Although she grudgingly allowed one of his paintings to hang in their Connecticut house, Alex suspected that she did not like his work—liked it less, in fact, than she did the equally nonfigurative paintings of her son-in-law, Cleve Gray. She never showed any interest in visiting his studio. Two years before she died, though, their friend Elena Tchernichova made a videotape of Alex in the studio, painting. Tatiana and Alex watched it together, sitting on the white sofa in their Connecticut living room, holding hands. At the end, Elena was surprised to see that Tatiana had tears in her eyes. "Thank you," she said, taking Elena's hand. "I never saw that before."

She never went to his office at Condé Nast, either, and her only interest in his work there was the ritual question that she asked every night: "Did you see Si today?" Like Alex, she must have felt at some deep level the permanent anxiety of the refugee. The written agreement guaranteeing that Alex would continue to receive his full salary if he left the company (a salary that was just under a million dollars a year in 1978), and that Tatiana would receive that same amount if Alex died, did not rule out anxiety for either one of them. What would happen, for example, to the multiple perks available to Condé Nast's editorial director—the limousines and first-class accommodations and lavish expense accounts for entertaining? Alex, whose need for Condé Nast was more emotional than financial, had no urge to retire in any case. He did see Si every day, except when one or the other of them happened to be out of town. Newhouse never made an important decision without consulting Alex. The hirings and firings of editors and art directors and photographers, the effectiveness of cover lines on newsstand sales, the ups and downs of every Condé Nast magazine—and the advisability of acquiring or starting new ones—were always prefaced by extended discussions between Alex and Si. As Newhouse became more secure in his control of the magazine empire, his dependence on Alex did not diminish. Alex was his genie in the bottle, an unfailing source of creative guidance.

Newhouse's corporate ambitions led him to keep adding more magazines to the Condé Nast empire. Having bought *GQ* and *Gourmet*, revived *Vanity Fair*, and started up *Self* and *Condé Nast Traveler*, he surprised everyone by acquiring *Details* and *Woman* in 1988. *Details*, a relentlessly hip chronicle of New York's downtown, vanguard culture, replete with cross-dressing fashions and raunchy sex, was transformed into a men's magazine, a sort of youth-oriented version of *GQ*. The *Woman* experiment was a misguided attempt to create a magazine for "blue-collar" women, a segment of the population whose existence Condé Nast had never before acknowledged; it failed dismally, and Newhouse shut it down after nineteen issues. Alex stayed clear of the *Woman* fiasco. He had a great deal more to do with *Details*, which floundered after Newhouse bought it; Alex persuaded both Newhouse and James Truman, the new editor, that the magazine was much too "sinister and dark," visually speaking, to be successful.

He also played a leading role in the creation of *Allure*, the new beauty magazine that he and Newhouse started in 1991. Alex had come up with the idea of a whole magazine devoted to beauty—a subject that seemed to hold more interest for female readers than could be satisfied by the four or five pages that *Vogue, Glamour,* and *Mademoiselle* devoted to it each month. He had convinced Newhouse that their approach should be journalistic, providing up-to-the-minute information on cosmetics, fitness routines, skin care, and other techniques and strategies, and evaluating their relative effectiveness, or lack of it. But a beauty magazine would have to go beyond techniques and strategies, he suggested; it should also consider the psychological, the social, and maybe even the philosophical dimensions of its subject.

Linda Wells, the *New York Times* beauty editor (and former *Vogue* staffer) who was Alex's choice to be the new project's editor in chief, remembers vividly how the magazine got its name. Nobody really liked the working title, which was *Beauty Now*. Alex felt that the word "beauty" when used in a title was too limiting, and Wells—thirty-one and slim, with blue eyes and the glossy, straight blond hair that signaled perfect manners and the right schools—said that it always suggested to her some sort of unattainable perfection. "And then," as she recalled, "all of a sudden Alex said, 'Allure.' I can remember Si nodding and smiling, and for me it was like, *yes.*"

The Condé Nast lawyers did some research and found out that no other magazine had the word "allure" in its title. Diana Vreeland had called her 1980 book *Allure*, of course, but that was not a problem; the embarrassment over Vreeland's being fired was long past, and the association with her name could only be helpful. Wells also learned that in France the word was applied to thoroughbred horses. She brought this up in her next talk with Alex. "The French sometimes say that a horse has *grande allure*," she said. "What does that mean to you?"

"It means motion, energy," he replied.

"Alex gave off some other thoughts," according to Wells, "and then later that afternoon, when I was sitting in my office working on my first editor's letter, the telephone rang and it was Alex, calling from his car. 'Dash, vitality,' he said, and hung up. He called again a few minutes later and said, 'Style, verve.' Then another call: 'Confidence, grace.' And that's what working with him turned out to be like—he had this unending ability to add something new. I'd had no idea he would be so entirely involved with the magazine or have such a passion for it."

Alex worked closely with Linda Wells and with Lucy Sisman, the art director whom he brought in to replace an overly meticulous first incumbent, Rip Georges. It was Alex, in fact, who pulled the plug on the prototype issue that Wells and Georges had spent five months working up. Newhouse had already approved it, but Alex, who could never get Georges to work with him on a collaborative basis, pronounced it a "disaster"— visually flabby and "antediluvian"—and Newhouse then agreed that they should throw it out and start over. The thoroughly revised *Allure*, the fastest-growing magazine in the Condé Nast empire, was another tribute to the fact that Alex, nearing eighty, still had not lost his touch.

He also became thoroughly involved in the renovation of *Self*, a magazine that kept changing its focus. When that magazine's original health-and-fitness orientation began to seem inadequate, Alex and Si had replaced Valerie Weaver, its second editor, with Anthea Disney, a young British woman whom they hired away from *US*, and who tried to tap into Tina Brown's magic formula by featuring Kim Basinger and other Hollywood stars on the covers.* Disney, however, made the fatal error of ignoring or overriding Alex Liberman's tactfully framed "suggestions." Ironically enough, Alex had only recently complained to Newhouse that, what with all the new magazines, and his continuing responsibilities at *Vogue*, and his own and Tatiana's declining health, he had too much to do. Newhouse had responded by hiring back Rochelle Udell, a former *Vogue* art director who had left to work in advertising, and giving her the title of assistant editorial director. Udell, who for a while was rumored to be in line for Alex's job, took over Alex's supervisory functions with some of the magazines—including *Self*. Anthea Disney apparently read this shift too

---

* The "British mafia" among Condé Nast editors—which included Tina Brown, Anna Wintour, Lucy Sisman, James Truman, Gabé Doppelt, and Harry Evans, as well as Anthea Disney—brought echoes of the "Russian mafia" of the 1940s: Patcévitch, Agha, Liberman, Constantin Joffé, Serge Balkin, not to mention Alexey Brodovitch at *Bazaar*. Couldn't Americans play this game? The Canadian-born Graydon Carter, who replaced Tina Brown as editor of *Vanity Fair* when Brown moved to *The New Yorker* in 1992, thinks it may have to do with the small circulations and low budgets of many British magazines, which make it possible for their editors to be innovative and daring in ways that American magazine editors can rarely afford to be.

literally; she reported to Udell and left Alex out of the loop. Disney was fired abruptly in 1989. (This was becoming a Newhouse tradition.) The new editor, Alexandra Penney, was identified in press reports as the author of *How to Make Love to a Man, Great Sex*, and other best-selling books of earthy instruction, but before that she had spent five years at *Glamour* and had been a roving editor at *Vogue*, and she was not going to make Anthea Disney's mistake. At Penney's insistence, her contract stated that she would report only to Alex Liberman. She sang hymns of praise to Alex at every opportunity and allowed no one to touch or alter his layouts, several of which she had framed and hung in her office. Alex, who was aware that his paintings were sometimes dismissed as "layouts" by hostile observers, could appreciate the irony of seeing his layouts treated as works of art.

Alex became so involved with *Self* that for a period of six months it was his principal interest. The covers, which he designed himself, broke new ground with their large blocks of primary color and bold type. For the first time in his life, Alex was willing to concede that "there is not much difference in the psychological process between a composition on canvas and arranging material like this on the page." Some outside observers saw elements of Russian Constructivism, Bauhaus design, and Mondrian in Alex's *Self* covers. Penney gave him carte blanche, and there was no one else whose creative ego needed soothing. "If ever I've done what I'd call my own layouts, it's now at *Self*," Alex said at the time. Unfortunately, the readers' response was dispiriting. Newsstand sales and advertising pages dropped significantly, and they did not start to pick up again until Alex pulled back and let Penney and her art director tone down the covers.

During the period of his intense involvement with *Self*, Alex had what seemed to him a major breakthrough in his painting. A burst of furious activity in the studio produced, first, a series of charcoal drawings in which his hectic, forcefully executed line covered the entire surface in a vigorous, allover pattern. "The lines dart and zip at maximum speed in and out of one another's space, but they never collide or tangle," John Russell wrote in the *Times* when the show opened at André Emmerich in November 1990. "This is an exhibition that one would like to see around for a long time, complete, and preferably in a museum." The Metropolitan Museum did buy one of the drawings—it was Alex's first sale to a museum in many years—and the Art Institute of Chicago bought another. (So did Alexandra Penney, who hung it in her office at *Self*, alongside Alex's framed layouts.) There was less interest in the series of black-and-white acrylic paintings that came out of the drawings, but Alex was immensely excited by his new direction nevertheless. "It's my last fling," he said. "I don't have too much

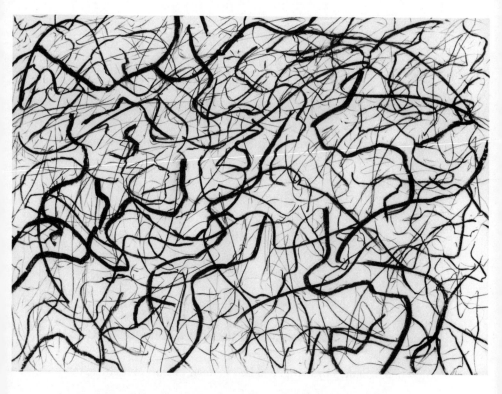

Altyal I, 1989, charcoal on paper, 60" x 80". One of the drawings in this series
was bought by the Metropolitan Museum, another by
the Art Institute of Chicago.

André Emmerich, Alex's art dealer.

Alex, photographed by Lartigue in Leo Lerman's *Vanity Fair* office, 1983.

One of Alex's "random collage layouts" for *Self* in 1989. "The whole idea was that type was an ornamental illustration in itself on a page," Alex said, "and did not necessarily need drawings or photographs to go with it."

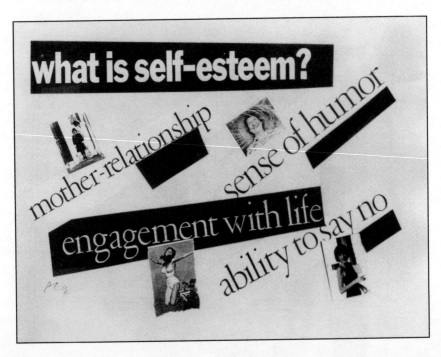

time left, but I'm finally getting to that loss of control I've hoped for. Control is the great, great enemy of creative freedom. In old age one has less control; there's a looseness—maybe hand tremors help, maybe weakened eyesight helps. One is grateful for any help."

Over his work in the studio and his work at Condé Nast, though, lay the shadow of Tatiana's deteriorating health. In 1987 she broke her hip, in the way that older people often do—a fall in the bedroom. Her need for Demerol increased after that, and she began to lose weight. Gennady Smakov's death in 1988, of AIDS, was a catastrophe for her. For Tatiana, it was like losing a son who was also her best friend. She went into a deep depression. Getting her to eat became a major challenge. Thirty-four cooks tried and failed to meet Tatiana's increasingly impossible standards during the next two years. Mabel Moses, the black woman who had run their New York household since the early 1940s, had finally relinquished that role, about the same time that Genna died; unable to fire her, Alex paid Mabel a weekly salary not to come, and advanced her other sums as the need arose, which was fairly often. For years Mabel had been asking Alex to buy her a Mercedes. Tatiana suspected him of giving her the BMW she drove around in, but he denied it.

In his unceasing efforts to please Tatiana, or at least to make her comfortable, Alex kept adding to their domestic staff. Melinda was there all the time now, one of three registered nurses working in round-the-clock shifts. Counting gardeners, cleaning women, nurses, Josef the butler, Howard the major-domo, and assorted others, Alex employed fourteen people in all—seven in the city and seven in the country. (Bill Layman and his three sons were not included in the count.) The thirty-four cooks who came and went were all asked to make vichyssoise, as a test of their ability. "Just a simple vichyssoise," as Alex explained it. "Without any lumps, not too watery, not too thick, not too bland, not too potato-ish." The ones who passed were hired, but sooner or later they proved to be inadequate in some other area.

Occasionally Alex had a *mousse au chocolat* sent over from La Grenouille, which he and Tatiana considered the best French restaurant in New York. (Alex had helped to establish its reputation by featuring it in *Vogue*, and he was treated like royalty by everyone there.) Alex even learned to make the dessert himself, by following Julia Child's recipe. He used the best dark Belgian chocolate, which Tatiana had loved ever since her long convalescence in Antwerp after her automobile accident, and he succeeded, just once, in getting her to approve it; but afterward he could never duplicate his success. He would immediately order anything she expressed the slightest wish for—oysters on the half shell from La Grenouille; chocolate truffles from Fauchon in Paris; the little almond cakes called Calissons d'Aix; Menshikoff chocolates, which could be found only in Chartres (Susan Train, in Vogue's Paris office, would arrange to have these items flown over on short notice). His challenge was to provide her with a moment of remembered pleasure. She would take a small bite of chocolate and be unable to swallow it. "Why so few?" she demanded when presented with a dozen freshly opened oysters, but then she could eat only one of them.

Iuri Tiourin arrived from Russia in 1989 and assumed Genna's place in the Liberman household. Like Genna, Iuri was a man of many parts. During his forty-five years in the Soviet Union he had been a pediatrician, a dentist, a ballet dancer, a critic of music and dance, a journalist, and a television host. He had never been a cook, but he knew about Russian food, and he soon became expert at preparing it—even better than Genna, Tatiana said. Although Iuri lacked Genna's depth of culture, he loved Tatiana and would sit and talk and read poetry to her by the hour, in Russian. Iuri cooked for them in Connecticut, served as Tatiana's companion and confidant, and helped out in all sorts of other respects, very much the way less fortunate relatives used to do in large nineteenth-century Russian households. He found a video store near Brighton Beach, Brooklyn's Russian enclave, where he could rent Russian-language videotapes. They were all terrible, according to Alex, but Tatiana liked to watch them. Night after night, in New York or in Connecticut, Alex and Tatiana would sit together watching television or home videos. "Will you sit with me?" she would ask him, as soon as they finished dinner; if he got up for a moment to close the door or go to the bathroom, she would ask anxiously where he was going. They watched "Dallas," "The Golden Girls," and "The Cosby Show," and after ten-thirty in the evening Tatiana would often want to watch one of the hard-core pornography channels. "Turn on the girls!" she would say with an echo of her old mischief. "They put me to sleep."

"Even if I didn't particularly like what we were watching, it felt so cozy to participate in her pleasure," Alex said. "We would always hold hands. Dominating everything, even then, was this extraordinary physical bond. Passion had existed between us for fifty years, and it still existed, because we still liked to touch each other's skin. Sometimes I felt that Tatiana and I were opposites glued together, and the glue was that erotic contact."

Alex never said any of this to Tatiana, of course, and she would not have listened to him if he had. No one knows what she thought about their marriage. "Alex is Superman," she would say, and leave it at that—

Alex and Tatiana greet Babe Paley at the reopening
of the Museum of Modern Art in 1984.

no intimate discussions, no "Jewish conversations" for her. She did ask
Melinda Pechangco once whether she thought Alex was homosexual, and
in her earlier years she told several of her friends that she had "saved" him
from that fate—a puzzling statement, and quite possibly another example
of Tatiana's never-ending urge to startle and provoke people. What appeared
to be indisputable about Alex and Tatiana's marriage was her dependence
on him and his devotion to her. It was a perfect fit. As Henry Kissinger
said once, you could look around a dinner table and think that any woman
there could be married to any man, but with Alex and Tatiana this was
not the case: "You couldn't imagine either of them with somebody else."

For the last four years of Tatiana's life, they stopped going out.
Tatiana was too frail, and Alex wouldn't go without her. She still went
once a week to have her hair done at Kenneth's when they were in New
York, and she still dressed carefully every evening in a Saint Laurent tunic
and pants, either brown or black satin. Alex had lifts installed in the city
and the country after her hip surgery, so she could get up and down the
stairs. (Tatiana refused to ride in enclosed elevators; this highly inconven-

ient form of her claustrophobia obliged Alex to seek out doctors whose offices were on the ground floor.) She spent the mornings in bed, until eleven or later, in a drugged sleep. When they were in New York, he came home at lunchtime to make her "porridge," because she wouldn't eat it otherwise. She dozed and read in the afternoon, finishing a book a day. Her bed was piled high with magazines and books—Russian poetry, the latest literary-prize novels in French, rarely anything in English except *Women's Wear Daily* and *W*. ("English tires her," Alex said.) Tatiana devoured literature in a way that Alex never did. Alex scanned a great variety of books and publications—French newspapers and magazines, the *Times Literary Supplement, The New York Review of Books, The New Yorker*, the *Daily News* and the *Post, Consumer Reports, The New Criterion*; he could absorb information on the wing, and he knew the essential facts about a lot of books he would never read, but reading, for him, was not the alternative life it had always been for Tatiana.

Almost every Wednesday she still managed to play cards with her regular canasta group. At night, she arranged ten pillows of various shapes and sizes into a ritual nest on her bed, a procedure that always amused Alex. Then she looked at magazines or watched TV, staying up much later than he did. Alex wore an eyeshade and earplugs so he could get to sleep. One night she lay in bed for a long time reading a magazine article about Condé Nast. "It's very complimentary about you," she kept saying in a surprised voice to Alex, who was reading in his own bed across the room. "And then, when she'd finished, she got up and came over to my bedside," Alex said. "This crippled, diminished human being who could hardly walk came to my bed and made a little curtsy—because they'd called me a czar or something in that article—and it just broke my heart. It was so enchanting and so funny. I kissed her hand, and then she kissed my hand. This was the side of Tatiana that nobody else ever saw. There was always a sweet little girlish quality at the bottom of this big strong woman, a childish playfulness that I think only I saw. She was for me a constant amusement and a delight." Her love for him was also a constant reassurance, which, condemned to constant doubt as he was, he never stopped needing. Each night, lying in his own bed across the room from hers, just before he put on his eyeshade and inserted his earplugs, he would call out softly to her, "*Tu m'aimes?*" and she would call back, in her hoarse croak, "*Je t'adore.*"

Early in 1991 Alex frightened both of them by having a heart attack, which was followed by another, less severe one. He was hospitalized each time for more than a week, but few people were aware of it, because Alex didn't want anyone to know. Crosby Coughlin, his young assistant at Condé Nast, brought magazine covers and layouts to his room for him to okay, and Alex kept in close touch with Newhouse, who came to visit him in the hospital. Tatiana was panicky and miserable without him, though, and her own condition grew markedly worse. The night he came home, she demanded that he go out to the store at 1:00 a.m. and buy her some vanilla ice cream. For once he refused. "I'm sick, Boubous," he said. "I can't go out." "But I'm sicker than you are," she groaned, "and you can do anything." She refused to admit that he had had a heart attack; she insisted it was just his diabetes. The doctors made him move to another bedroom, because she kept him awake at night. She had virtually stopped eating.

When Tatiana had to be taken to the hospital later that spring, Alex was on hand to call the ambulance and to make all the arrangements, but then he found himself being admitted as well, for a third heart attack. They were put to bed on separate floors—Tatiana on seventeen, Alex on three—with similar ailments: anemia and heart trouble. Alex was sicker than she was at this point; the doctors were afraid he might have a major heart attack at any moment. They both came back from the hospital in April, and Alex divided his time between the office and Tatiana's endless needs at home.

Two weeks later, on a Friday afternoon, Tatiana was rushed back to New York Hospital. The diagnosis this time was ischemic bowel; she was severely dehydrated from diarrhea, and she weighed less than ninety pounds. Heavy sedation was needed to ease the pain of a huge, spreading bedsore on her back. That evening, Dr. Rosenfeld asked Alex whether he wanted her to be put on artificial life support if her breathing failed. Without hesitation, he said no. Tatiana wanted to die before he did. "Be a gentleman," she had joked after his first heart attack. "Ladies first."

Alex literally could not bear to watch her suffer. She was in great pain, and her screams tore him apart. Dr. Rosenfeld kept telling him to go home, saying he would die himself if he stayed in her hospital room any longer. Her last words to him were in Russian, as he leaned over to kiss her. "Go home," she murmured, "but take me with you."

He did not go to see her the next day. As long as he lived, he would feel that he had been a coward for staying away. That night, she slipped into a coma, and she died without waking.

Alex and Melinda, photographed by Irving Penn, 1993.

Melinda

More than two hundred people came to the funeral service for Tatiana, at the Russian Orthodox Church on East Ninety-third Street. They stood for one hour, each person holding a candle, breathing in the scent of a great profusion of white flowers while the *episkop* read and chanted Russian prayers that only four or five persons present could follow. Alex, seated in front, looked ashen. (In the Orthodox funeral rite, only the oldest members of the immediate family are permitted to sit down.) His right hand shook so badly that Cleve, sitting in the next chair, was afraid the candle wax would spill and burn him. He had a racking, cardiac cough that he tried to alleviate with sips from a blue plastic bottle of cough syrup. Francine, now a frail sixty, sat in back of him, next to Tatiana's sister Lila. Thaddeus and Luke, the grownup grandsons, stood behind them.

After the service, greeting friends and Condé Nast colleagues who had come to pay tribute to him as well as to Tatiana, Alex seemed in complete control of his emotions, and he was shaky but calm at the burial the next day, in a hillside cemetery not far from their house in Connecticut. Francine and Cleve had made all the arrangements. Luke had picked up the urn with Tatiana's ashes at the Frank Campbell Funeral Chapel in

Manhattan and brought it to the cemetery. About twenty mourners had gathered there in the pouring rain—family and one or two close friends, people who had worked for Alex and Tatiana for years, Melinda Pechangco and Iuri Tiourin. Alex had not wanted any words at the burial. Francine asked them all to stand in a circle, holding hands, for a moment of recollection. As she took Alex's hand she noticed that his whole face was trembling, but he didn't break down.

Alex had planned to spend a week in Warren, with Melinda and Iuri, but the house was too full of Tatiana's spirit. The four thousand tulips he had planted for her the previous fall were in full bloom; to enjoy them without her seemed unbearable to him, so after a few days he fled back to town.

His reviving energy in the weeks that followed amazed those who had feared he might not survive his loss. He started going in to his office for several hours a day. Then, three weeks after Tatiana's death, he decided to sell the house on Seventieth Street. He found a buyer right away, although the New York real estate market had been moribund for three years. He also sold his Léger drawings and *Grande Parade* gouache for a million dollars (the "Communist" drawings that Tatiana had never liked), through the New York art dealer Larry Gagosian, and he thought about but decided against selling the rest of the art works he had acquired over the years. With the money he cleared on the house and the drawings—it was the first time in his life he had had a substantial bank balance—he bought an apartment on the twenty-seventh floor of United Nations Plaza, directly under the one that Si and Victoria Newhouse had moved into not long before, with spectacular views up and down the East River. (Even though U.N. Plaza had many Jewish residents, including Newhouse, Alex worried that the co-op board might refuse to accept him.)

Alex put Howard Mastroberti in charge of renovating the new apartment to his exacting specifications—there would be a bedroom for Melinda next to his own, and another bedroom, for Francine and Cleve to use whenever they came to town for the evening. His life became quite hectic, with the Seventieth Street house being dismantled and the new apartment still under construction, and Melinda, who kept a close watch on his still-fragile condition, was concerned about that. In August he was rushed to the hospital by ambulance from Warren, because he was having trouble breathing. He stayed there for two weeks, undergoing a long series of tests. He slept on his own sheets and down pillows, and dined impressively on gourmet dishes cooked and brought in twice a day by Iuri Tiourin; hospital life for Alex was never spartan. Anna Wintour came to visit him, bringing fresh flowers and *Vogue* layouts. She was the only Condé Nast editor to break through the cordon sanitaire around him, and her determined concern made a deep impression. On the day he came home—home was still the Seventieth Street house—he had a massive heart attack that very nearly killed him.

It was clear that he was not going to live much longer in his present condition. Most of the doctors on the case were convinced, however, that he was not strong enough to survive major heart surgery. He almost died of renal failure after an angioplasty procedure in mid-September. Against all odds—the medical evidence suggested that his chances of survival were about one in six—Dr. Rosenfeld decided to go ahead with a triple-bypass heart operation. Alex himself was all for it; he seemed almost euphoric about the prospect of a high-risk gamble. The operation, which took place on November 4 and lasted four hours, was an unqualified success. Alex went home from the hospital to his spectacular new apartment one week later, with his prospects for survival miraculously enhanced.

"I never felt that Tatiana dominated me, but I enjoyed leading her life," Alex had said soon after the funeral. Now, for the first time in more than fifty years, he had to think about leading his own life. He hired a new cook, an Argentinian named Silvia Berenstein, who turned out to be wonderful, and he found a witty and efficient young butler named Lance Houston, who had polished his skills while working for Mrs. John Hay Whitney. Alex began inviting people to the apartment for dinner and going out to restaurants, movies, and the Metropolitan Opera—things he had not been able to do for years because Tatiana was too sick. (Tatiana had never wanted to go to the opera; the memory of her aunt Sandra practicing scales in the house in Paris had given her a lifelong distaste for it.) Leon Azoulay, known as "Frenchie," the Moroccan-born chauffeur who had been driving him for years, retired from the limousine service he worked for and became Alex's personal driver; the secret of the good life, Alex had always known, was to have more than enough people working for you. In February he took Melinda, Iuri, Silvia, and Lance to Palm Beach, where Si Newhouse had put his beach house at Alex's disposal for three weeks. Tatiana's sister Lila, the Duchess, now a rich widow, came for lunch one day; she was staying at the Breakers. "But Alex," she said, looking around reproachfully, "you live like a billionaire!"

Back in New York, he went to the office every day, looked at layouts and covers, conferred with editors and art directors, met with Si. Now and then he confided to his biographers (whom he talked to at least once and often several times a day) that he had very little to do there anymore and said he was thinking of pulling out entirely, but it was obvious that he had no intention of doing so. Si relied on him as much as ever. Alex and Si's regular Thursday lunches now took place at Alex's U.N. Plaza apartment, where the food, thanks to Silvia, was better than at The Four Seasons.

Alex's relationship with Anna Wintour was developing into a real friendship. She kept him involved at *Vogue*, asking his advice on feature ideas, bringing him layouts for approval, soliciting his help in lining up new photographers or keeping old ones from defecting to *Harper's Bazaar*. History was repeating itself in the 1990s, as *Bazaar*, after thirty years of slow decline, suited up for a competitive run at *Vogue*. Fueled by a massive new infusion of Hearst money, *Bazaar* had hired Elizabeth Tilberis, Wintour's replacement as editor of British *Vogue*, to be its new editor in chief, and Tilberis had managed to lure away some of Wintour's most valued assets, including the photographers Patrick Demarchelier and Peter Lindbergh. The renewed rivalry made things more exciting, and besides, Alex still loved going to the office. He might have less to do there, but he took great pleasure in his status as the legendary gray eminence, "the Silver Fox" (an occasional journalistic title he shared with First Lady Barbara Bush, of all people), the vastly respected figure with whom every young woman in the Condé Nast building tended to flirt as a matter of course. "When I walk down the corridors at *Vogue*," he told Anna Wintour, "especially in the summer, with all those ravishing young creatures in their summer nothings, I feel like Matisse with his odalisques."

Wintour's *Vogue*—more youthful-looking than the Liberman-Mirabella version, splashier and sexier and more innovative in its fashion coverage and its features—had beaten back the *Elle* challenge. In 1991 it carried three times as many ad pages as *Elle* or *Bazaar*. Alex liked and admired Anna Wintour, and approved of what she was doing with the magazine. He had reservations about some things, of course, such as her decision to put Ivana Trump on the cover while she and her husband, Donald, were waging an unusually vulgar divorce battle, but nostalgia for his own concept of a more "noble" fashion magazine did not sour his appreciation of Anna's talent. Nostalgia, as Grace Mirabella had said, was never one of Alex's traits. He had observed with interest the progressive blurring of the line between advertising and editorial pages in the magazine, a change that had begun well before Anna Wintour took over. "There's a joke," he said, "that when an issue is fat with advertising, it's a well-edited issue. Fat issues sell more copies. And advertising has become so good that it's harder and harder to tell it from editorial. Advertisers use the same photographers we do, they use the same models, they even copy the typography. It's hard to compete with Bruce Weber's photographic layouts for Calvin Klein, or Ellen von Unwerth's for Guess? And, of course, Penn does those remarkable still-life ads for Clinique. But listen—who cares? I think rock music has taken over as the new empire of the imagination. Magazines are a rear-guard action."

Alex had discarded his illusions about magazine publishing, he said, when *Vogue* began printing the little bar code on its cover in the 1970s, for easy checkout at the supermarkets. "That's when I realized that basically this is a business," he said. "I used to think we were communicating civilization, communicating culture, treating women in a serious way by offering them intelligent features. I even thought that by publishing all those essays and photographs on art and artists—not frivolous artists like Erté or Vertès, either, but the major School of Paris masters, and Rauschenberg and Johns, and Richard Serra, and de Kooning and Newman and Rothko—that we were performing a real service, because one of the magical things about exposing people to art is that art allows you to dare, and maybe, maybe, maybe some of that remains and the reader is subliminally altered. But it was Vreeland who said to me, 'Alex, after all, this is just entertainment.' And, of course, she was right. Producing a fashion magazine is theater. It's a show, a monthly show—bimonthly in the old days. You have to have variety, surprise, contrast, pace, and not attach enormous importance to any of it, because it's fleeting. You make a decision, it's printed, it's gone."

Sculpture was theater, too, he felt—a series of playful gestures in space. Although Bill Layman and his sons stayed busy in Connecticut working on new Liberman commissions, Alex, who never went to Warren anymore (his house there was on the market), had more or less stopped thinking about his sculpture operation. Somehow he had come to feel that he had "missed the boat" with sculpture, and in this case—in this case only—he blamed his double career. His experiments with bronze casting in the late 1970s had given him an idea of what he might have accomplished in that medium if he had had the opportunity to work for weeks at a time in a well-equipped and staffed foundry; but, of course, that had never been possible for him. He had always preferred to work "desperately and quickly" on weekends, as he put it, and, in the end, he felt that this had been the right way for him to work. "This eternal thing of people asking me wouldn't I like to paint all the time, wouldn't I like to do sculpture all the time— it's nonsense," he said. "It's not me. Has Condé Nast prevented me from doing good work? I don't think so. Maybe if I'd given up Condé Nast my work would have been worse. I don't think it would be better. And as I learned a long time ago, the life of the artist is quite horrible. There is no success in art. I always felt that life was more important, and that if I had to make the choice I would drop art to save Tatiana, any day. I have absolutely no regrets of any kind."

He did start to paint again. Si Newhouse had arranged for him to use a former *Vogue* photo studio on East Forty-fifth Street, only a few blocks from U.N. Plaza—five thousand square feet of space, with excellent light—and he began working there again in the spring of 1992, trying out a new technique that involved melting down oilstick pigment and pouring it on canvas, where it hardened into thick, shiny pools and rivers. Melinda Pechangco came with him to the studio, to make sure he did not overexert himself. Melinda was his constant companion, his guardian, and his link to Tatiana. She had stayed with Tatiana through all her agonies, an unfailing source of comfort and reassurance, and she had done the same for Alex, getting him to the hospital when any delay would have been fatal, calling Dr. Rosenfeld in the middle of the night, seeing to it that he got the correct medications and treatments, lifting his spirits time after time with her quiet, levelheaded optimism.

Melinda had been raised in a small town in the Philippines. Her Chinese father was the sanitary inspector for that region; her mother came from a middle-class Spanish family. The next-to-youngest of eleven children, she had studied nursing in Manila and had practiced in hospitals in Chicago, Phoenix, and Los Angeles before coming to New York in 1974. Although she still called him "Mr. Liberman," their affection for each other was increasingly apparent, and when they were seen together in evening dress at *Vogue's* hundredth-birthday celebration in April, the New York rumor mill began to buzz with reports that Alex Liberman was going to marry his nurse. The potentially embarrassing aspects of such a union (not exactly unprecedented among elderly gentlemen whose wives have died) seemed to cause him no distress. His conscience was as clear as his mind, which had lost none of its ironic edge. He knew perfectly well that some people would disapprove of the ripening friendship, and the thought of their disapproval made him secretly defiant—just as his parents' opposition, all those years ago, had made him more determined to marry Hilda Sturm. He was also aware that comparisons between Melinda and Tatiana could hardly be avoided: Melinda, at fifty-five, was neither tall nor slim; she lacked the "aureole of blondness" that he had always looked for in women (and, of course, she did not speak Russian), but she was certainly attractive, with her own natural grace and warmth and a refreshing sense of humor, and

Victoria and Si Newhouse with Alex at the
hundredth-birthday celebration for *Vogue*.

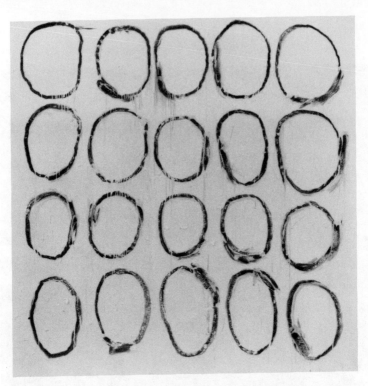

Full Circle, 1993, oil and oil stick on canvas, 90" x 90".
One of Alex's most recent paintings.

Augury, 1993, 106" x 77" x 120".

she made Alex feel loved and cared for and content in ways that he had never known before—made him realize, as he said, that he "liked being helpless." Never in his life had there been someone whose primary concern was taking care of him. But Melinda gave him something far more important than professional care—she gave him her even-tempered and unsentimental affection. "The bond with Tatiana will continue as long as I live," he said. "Nobody can ever penetrate my heart the way Tatiana did." On the other hand, he had never believed in holding on to things. Having come so close to death, he felt at times as though he had been dealt a whole new hand that he could play any way he liked. He told Francine and Cleve that he was thinking of marrying Melinda "in a year or so"—a time period that might well be subject to downward revision. "She's saved my life so many times," he said, "and I cannot live without a strong female presence."

Marlene Dietrich died in May 1992, just a year after Tatiana. First Anna Wintour and then Tina Brown asked Alex if she could publish some of the photographs that he had taken of Marlene, in the years when she and Tatiana were such close friends, and Alex gave his assent to both of them. Harry Evans, Tina's husband, who had left *Traveler* to become editor in chief of Random House, came up with a project to publish a large selection of Alex's Dietrich photographs in a book, with a personal reminiscence by Alex. At first Alex demurred. He could never agree, he said, to make money out of a friendship. Two days later, he asked Evans what sort of advance he could get for such a book, and Evans suggested fifty thousand dollars —the same advance he had received for the new Random House edition of *The Artist in His Studio*. Alex managed to imply that this was not enough. The figure went up a bit, and while Alex's literary agent bargained for more, Alex turned in a fully executed layout of seventy photographs, along with a six-page introduction, thereby leaving his agent out on a limb. *Marlene Dietrich: An Intimate Photographic Memoir* came out in the fall, along with a compact disc of Marlene singing. Alex started to think about resurrecting his project for a photographic book on the Campidoglio in Rome; his friend Joseph Brodsky offered to write a preface to it. Although Alex had never altered his belief that photography was documentation, not art, he sometimes thought that it might be his ironic fate to be remembered mainly as a photographer. Plans also developed with Harry Evans for a paperback edition of *The Artist in His Studio*, for a new edition of *Greece, Gods, and Art*, and for two more books of his photographic portraits.

Life went on. He bought a larger apartment at U.N. Plaza, so that Melinda could have a more comfortable bedroom. He rented a beach house for the summer in Quogue, Long Island, and announced that he wanted to spend the rest of his life there—he himself would always have preferred to live by the sea, he said; it was Tatiana who had insisted on the house in Connecticut, so that she could be near Francine and her family. He bought some new clothes at Comme des Garçons and an antique crystal chandelier for the new apartment. "But Grandpa, that's not your style," said Thaddeus Gray, forgetting that the Liberman style was protean and renewable. He discovered a long-buried passion for gambling and won a thousand dollars on a Thanksgiving Day's outing to Atlantic City. He bought a penthouse apartment in Miami, the new mecca for trend-setting New Yorkers—Melinda, who already had an apartment there, was very fond of Miami. By this time, Alex had lost all interest in Quogue. He supervised the renovation of a faltering *Mademoiselle*, alternately charming and terrorizing its new young editor in chief, Gabé Doppelt. He was eighty years old and full of ideas.

Tina Brown got him involved in redesigning *The New Yorker*. Brown left *Vanity Fair* in June 1992, to take over the editorship of the country's most admired magazine, which was still losing money after five years under Robert Gottlieb. Newhouse, with Alex's concurrence, had decided that Tina Brown's perfect journalistic pitch might be the solution, and the transition, on the surface, at least, was carried out smoothly and with few recriminations. The news, which stunned the New York media world, came as something of a relief to Anna Wintour, who had been worried by the rumors that Brown was about to take over Alex's job as editorial director of all Condé Nast magazines. Anna Wintour and Tina Brown, rival stars in the Newhouse firmament, were sometimes perceived as vying for Alex's favor and Alex's attention, if not for his job. It was by no means unpleasant for Alex to be aware of this, and to know that his power at Condé Nast—the power he had always denied having—remained so cheeringly intact. Tina Brown, asked by a reporter about taking over Alex's job, had gratified Alex greatly by replying, "I don't think Alex Liberman's job is a job; it's Alex Liberman."

He was even more gratified when the high-flying art dealer Larry Gagosian offered to mount a show, in the fall of 1993, of Alex's geometric circle paintings of the 1950s. André Emmerich had recently sold one of these for $125,000, the highest price ever paid for a Liberman painting, but they had not been exhibited for almost twenty years. Emmerich himself was planning a show of Alex's most recent paintings, a new series based once again on the circle. Alex discovered, moreover, that he had not given up sculpture after all. Commissions kept coming in for his huge welded sculptures, and he also started to make smaller pieces in a completely new way at the Forty-fifth Street studio—by cutting up waxed-cardboard industrial tubes into free-form shapes, covering them with more wax, and having them cast in bronze. There was talk of a vast Liberman retrospective in Rome—paintings, sculptures, and photographs exhibited simultaneously in three separate locations. Perhaps the long-awaited Liberman revival was at hand.

Soviet Communism disintegrated. Alex, who had witnessed its birth seventy-five years earlier, was not particularly moved to have outlived it. He had never once felt the slightest urge to revisit the land of his birth. "I feel absolutely no links with Russia," he said. "None at all." Unlike Tatiana, he had become an American, which is to say, in one of many possible definitions, an optimist who believes that you can let go of the past and start again.

On December 7, 1992, in room 402 of the U.S. Courthouse on Centre Street in lower Manhattan, Alexander Liberman married Melinda Pechangco. The civil ceremony was performed by Judge Pierre Leval, whose parents, Beatrice and Fernand Leval, had witnessed Alex's marriage to Tatiana du Plessix fifty years before. Si and Victoria Newhouse invited the wedding party (family and a few close friends) to a lunch afterward at Da Silvano, the art world's favorite downtown restaurant, and it turned out to be one of those occasions when affection and high spirits seem to become the universal laws of life. Cleve Gray, sitting across the long, narrow table from his new mother-in-law, said at one point that never before in his experience had he seen Alex looking so happy.

Alex in Miami, 1993.

Envoi

I s that all?" Alex said, after he had read the last chapter of the book in typescript. We were in the sitting room of his U.N. Plaza apartment, and he was hopping mad.

"You don't like it?"

"Why should I like it? It's not a successful life. I think I come out as a total failure at everything."

"Alex, that's absurd."

"Where's the essence? What is it that I have contributed in my life? I'm not sure you talk about the actual doing. My eyes have seen millions of photographs. There's hard work involved. There's a deeper side that is not touched on."

"Which is?"

"Which is—to be part of a certain cultural eternity. And maybe even to attain, through art, through the creative process, some inkling of what our existence is all about."

"Do you think you've attained that?"

"I think that throughout my life I've had a deeper dream. It seems silly. How can you be involved with *Vogue* and have these philosophical yearnings? Well, that was my case."

Index

Note: Page numbers in *italics* refer to illustrations of Liberman's works

Photographic Credits

A Note About the Authors

DODIE KAZANJIAN *has written for* Vogue *since 1988. This is her first book.* CALVIN TOMKINS *is a staff writer for* The New Yorker *and the author of* The Bride and the Bachelors, Merchants and Masterpieces: The Story of the Metropolitan Museum of Art, *and* Living Well Is the Best Revenge. *He is currently working on a biography of Marcel Duchamp. They are married and live in New York.*

A Note on the Type

The text of this book was set in a digitized version of Fairfield, a typeface designed by the distinguished American artist and engraver Rudolph Ruzicka (1883–1978). Fairfield displays the sober and sane qualities of a master craftsman whose talent has long been dedicated to clarity.

Rudolph Ruzicka was born in Bohemia and came to America in 1894. He designed and illustrated many books and was the creator of a considerable list of individual prints in a variety of techniques.

*Composed by PennSet,
Bloomsburg, Pennsylvania*

*Printed and bound by
Arcata Graphics/Martinsburg,
Martinsburg, West Virginia*

Designed by Iris Weinstein